Discovering Infinity Volume 1A:

The Disintegration of the World's Financial System

A science discovery series
by Rolf A. F. Witzsche

(c) Copyright, 2003, Rolf A. F. Witzsche

all rights reserved

Published by Cygni Communications Ltd.
North Vancouver, BC, Canada
(http://books.rolf-witzsche.com)

cover image: developed by Lyndon H. LaRouche Jr.
presented in many LaRouche publications

When the 'giant' becomes an empty shell the inevitable happens.

Research by Rolf Witzsche, exploring the fallacies in modern economics. Yes the 'giant' has become an empty shell; the world's financial system has been in a state of gradual disintegration for decades towards the inevitable catastrophe that now many fear, few dare to acknowledge, and fewer still might survive the consequences of that are already looming on the horizon. We are rushing towards a New Dark Age of which unemployment, homelessness, slavery, and war are but a few early tell-tale 'ripples.' While the world-financial system cannot be saved in its present form, mankind can still be saved if the deeply fundamental mistakes are reversed in time in its financial foundation that supports the world's economies, some of which are failures by intent.

The book presented here, *The Disintegration of the World's Financial System*, is Volume 1A of the research series, *Discovering Infinity*. The book is based on works by Lyndon H. LaRouche Jr.. and others.

The research series, *Discovering Infinity*, was originally created over the span of two decades, beginning in the late 1980s, and was updated periodically. The series is structured as two sets of three volumes, with each set corresponding to the three-step sequence of *Hell*, *Purgatory*, and *Paradise* that we find in the poetic trilogy the *Divine Comedy* by Dante Alighierie created in the early 1300s. The first set of three volumes of the series *Discovering Infinity* represents the view of Dante's "pilgrim," while the second set represents the view of his "guide." In some cases a volume of this series is made up of several distinct books. For more details, see the appendix: *About the research series, Discovering Infinity.*

In parallel with the research series *Discovering Infinity* a series of twelve novels with the summary title, *The lodging for the Rose,* was created. The platform of the novel was deemed necessary for this different venue of exploration since the real dimension of love tends to become lost on any kind of theoretical platform, rather than be born out as a light to uplift civilization from the grassroots level up. The individual titles of the series of novels are shown in the appendix: More works by the author. The series *The Lodging for the Rose* has two individual novels leading into it as a kind of preface that is gently opening the portal to the Principle of Universal Love, which is the main theme of the series of twelve novels. The Principle of Universal Love is the thread that ties both series together.

Contents

Prolog: Introduction

Before we look into the details of why the present world-financial system is collapsing, let's take a wider look at ourselves and our world. From a physical standpoint we live in an incredibly rich world with a near ideal climate for agriculture that gives us the potential to create food resources for several times the present world population. From a technological standpoint we also have the potential to far supercede the potential that the natural environment offers. Some day in the not so distant future we will have to rely on our technological potential when the next Ice Age cycle disables the world's natural agricultural resources. Thus, the question arises, "why isn't mankind living in a self-made paradise with all these vast potentials at hand?" Such type of question has probably been asked many times already in trying to solve the great paradox of our world, as to why in the background of our vast unrealized potential several tens of thousands of human beings are forced to perish each single day, mostly children, from poverty related causes and easily preventable diseases.

. The obvious answer is that the realization of mankind's potential is being prevented. One is tempted here to point to conspiracies as a cause, of which no doubt there are many, but mostly it appears that society should look at the tip of its finger and see where it is pointed, as it is pointing to itself! No external force from outside our planet is manipulating mankind. The tragedies we create and suffer, and those that we have prepared for ourselves, are all caused by us, exclusively. For example, no one from outside the Earth is forcing mankind to build and maintain the tens of thousands of atomic bombs that we have provided for ourselves, which exist for only one purpose, to massively annihilate human beings. Something is obviously wrong in the human equation since the current insanity of bomb building is evident around the world. Many of the world's great nations have the bomb, such as the USA, Russia, China, Britain, France, India, Pakistan, Israel, and probably some others. The reason why we have those monster bombs 'polluting' our 'backyard' as a human society is probably the same as the reason why our vast economic potential isn't realized so that tens of thousands of human beings, especially our children, are forced to death each single day.

In order to avoid getting lost in the political traps of actual conspiracies, which are probably far too well hidden anyway, let's consider a fictional one that illustrates some of the human failures that we have trapped ourselves in and appear to be unable to get out of. A brief fictional scenario has been included in the Prolog for this purpose. It opens the Prolog and is an expert from the story "Perfidious Albion," from my novel, "Winning without Victory." The fictional story is a dialog between an imperial recruiter and a protagonist, his reluctant victim. The story makes up the first part of the Prolog. The phrase, Perfidious Albion, was not coined by this author. It was a phrase used by a high-ranking imperial official talking to journalists in Germany at the time of the East Timor crisis in Indonesia.

The second part of the Prolog is a non-fictional element that puts the story into perspective with a high-level overview of the real principle of economics, and of mankind's failure in acknowledging this principle. This part was originally created in the late 1990s as a standalone presentation. It is also offered by itself in the form of a small-volume research book. The research book presented here was originally written in the early 1990s, but without the two-part Prolog attached. Many if the financial figures in the book are from this period. They are valid still in that they illustrate a trend rather than today's situation, which is dramatically worse.

It is my hope that this rather unique opening with the double-prolog for this rather extensive research book on economics that is presented here, sets the kind of stage that is needed for an exploration of the hidden processes and failures in principle that stand behind the presently ongoing collapse of the world-financial system. Hopefully, by understanding the processes behind it, the collapse will be brought to a halt before the entire system disintegrates. As incredible as it may seem, mankind is facing a great crisis with the ongoing collapse of one of its chief physical support systems, its financial system. The entire physical economy of the world is hinging on a financial system that has become an empty shell, like a soap bubble that shimmers in the sunlight, but never survives for long. When a rift develops somewhere along its shiny skin, the entire soap bubble disintegrates. Then the fine spray of mist that remains bears no resemblance to what the bubble has been. The result is similar to the pile of rubble that remained of the World Trade Center in New York after 911, which bore little resemblance with what had stood there before. Obviously, the rubble that remained could never be put back together again. That's the warning that one hears about the present financial system of the world that everyone depends on to a large degree.

A graphic illustration of the now ongoing trend towards the total collapse of our present world-financial system has been made the enter image of the cover of this book. The illustration has been authored by the

American economist Lyndon H. LaRouche Jr., a man who after 35 years of warnings about the present danger, now in his early eighties, has become known for his work around the world, especially in many high-level spheres of governments and institutions and also within the empires where his name is held in contempt and his warnings are regarded with fear.

In part, the background of this book is rooted in Lyndon LaRouche's work on economics, on his discovery of universal principles, and on in his fight for these principles. Another part of the background is rooted in Mary Baker Eddy's work, specifically her scientific focus on the Principle of Universal Love. Mary Baker Eddy (1821-1910) is the discoverer and founder of Christian Science - America's pioneer of the "divine Principle of scientific mental healing." The book combines both backgrounds. It has been designed to discover and to help society explore, failures in concepts related to economics. It is hoped that when the destructive processes are understood, the failures can be corrected. And so they should be corrected. Mankind is too precious for great calamities to be embraced that tear its civilization apart. Mankind is also too resourceful as an intelligent being for it to allow this to happen. The book is designed to inspire a processes of healing.

Since this book is a part of the research series, Discovering Infinity, the healing I expect goes deeper than an exploration of merely technical issues of economic policies, but requires also a healing of our perception of the nature of the human being, and thereby a healing of the perception of ourselves.

For example, in the modern world an imperial agent of the early stages of the private British Empire, a man named Adam Smith, is worshiped highly, nearly as a god, as the inventor of modern economics. He is telling society that the raw greed of a man in the pursuit of his lust is the foundation for the public good in that it drives the economic processes required to fulfill his lust. In scientific terms this is a counterproductive process, and it was meant to be that.

Adam Smith was commissioned by Lord Shelburne of the East India Company that had become a world-empire, to explore processes that could be used to destroy the American republic should its independence drive succeed. This happened before the USA was formed as a nation-state republic. Adam Smith was commissioned to study the free-trade process as a weapon, and to study the causes for the collapse of Roman Empire. The free-trade process was later inserted by Lord Shelburne into the Paris Peace Treaty after America won its War of Independence. Lord Shelburne became Prime Minister for one year to assure that this would happen. Indeed, the free-trade process worked well. Within a short time America was bankrupted. The American republic was saved, however, from this chaos of its bankruptcy by Alexander Hamilton's policies of federalism on the basis of the General Welfare Principle. The principle was implemented through federal banking for national industrial development and through tariff protection of the national industries. On this platform of the nation's self-development by its own resources the USA became the richest country on earth and the envy and the model for mankind. Unfortunately Hamilton was killed before Adam Smith's second weapon of greed-based fascism, misnamed an economic principle, was gaining popularity. Now the economic and financial system of the world has been driven to the brink of collapse by the sword of the weapon of greed.

Contrary to Adam Smith's historic propaganda the human being is not a creature of greed by nature, but is a creature of love and respect for one-another as human beings. The greed element has been artificially cultured and promoted to justify the existence of empires that have no natural universal principle for their existence and purport. The fact that greed is not native to the human being is well illustrated by the following anecdote centered on a question of economics during the time of so-called Asian financial crisis when many a nation in Asia was raked over the coals by powerful and ruthless financial speculators. During a meeting in exploring the tragedy that had became a near catastrophe for some nations, one person defended the speculators. He said that the strong players in the market that have spent years developing their financial might have every right to be successful in exploiting weakness that offer opportunities to profit them. At this point another man asked the person a simple question. He asked that if a man had the resources at hand to go to a hardware store and buy himself a sledgehammer, who thereby would have the might to smash down his neighbor's door and steal all of his belongings while his neighbor was away at work, would he have the right to do that? This simple question changed the tone of the discussion. The first person conceded that no one has the right to steal by any means. In fact, he suggested that he personally would be more inclined to actively protect his neighbors home from would-be thieves, as would be anyone else. It would be certainly far from his mind to break down his neighbor's door and steal.

This small incidence proves to some degree that the fascism of greed is not an element of human nature, but has been artificially induced, and been taught and nurtured in order to justify certain objectives. Since these objectives are contrary to the natural principles of economics, just as stealing is contrary to the principles of civilization, we find that these unprincipled objectives have wrecked the economic processes around the world and are now threatening to collapse civilization. The healing therefore has to reach down to the underlying strata in society's self-perception as human beings. Fortunately, since the fascism of greed is an artificially created phenomenon, it can be healed by reverting back to the principles of our humanity such as the Principle of Universal Love.

The Disintegration of the World's Financial System

*1

- Focus on Truth -

There was a time when death by lightening was a justified concern. In recent decades this type of concern has become lost into the background of a vast array of much larger threats to life. The irony is, that people feel more secure in this highly insecure world, even as they are actively involved in increasing the danger to themselves at a staggering rate. When people feared death by lightening, as irrational as this may seem now, mankind was ruled by a much greater sanity than is prevailing today. It is a sign of insanity that mankind stands in the shadow of immensely great dangers, with hardly anyone recognizing them. We have an amazing paradox, here, even a frightening one that would make a mockery of the truth by denying it.

Suppose a group of highly intelligent extraterrestrial beings would find their way to this planet to observe its people. What would their reaction be? What would they see? Surely, they would be utterly horrified. They would see what humanity denies itself to see. They would see an intelligent species at the threshold of an immensely bright future, standing at the edge of a cliff, determined to commit suicide.

Intelligent visitors would shy away from this planet, inhabited by such paradoxical people. They would turn their space ship and leave in search of more rational worlds to explore. It is an irony that virtually all people of humanity, at this advanced scientific age, do fail to recognize the greatest paradox in human history which so deeply effects the very foundation of their existence, that their existence is thereby put at risk.

Are the above statements justified?

Evidence indicates that they are. Judge for yourself. The economies of the western world have collapsed over the last two decades. The western economies are no longer able to maintain themselves, much less support the advanced development of society. The world is drowning in debt, while human civilization is collapsing into poverty, slavery, barbarism, and genocide. A regression has begun. The regression is evident by strong increases in child labor coupled with ever growing unemployment in the western world. This dual trend has idled 30% of the western work force and brought with it a corresponding increase in homelessness and death by starvation and other underdevelopment related causes, especially among children. The entire western society is caught up in this regression. Even the U.S.A., the 'richest' nation on the planet, is drowning in debt. The total outstanding debt in the U.S.A., in 2003, has exceeded 45 trillion dollars. If one were to pile up thousand-dollar bills, as high as the World Trade Center stood in New York, one would require ten-thousand such piles to pay off the 45 trillion dollar debt. The bottom line is, this debt in unpayable. Instead of creating wealth, the nation is dying under its load. The more business close and people become unemployed, the less likely it is that even the debt-service interest can be paid, much of which is rolled over into new debt. The simple reality is that the present system is fundamentally flawed, since it is unsustainable on the platform on which it has been founded. The system is gone. It needs to be scrapped in a bankruptcy reorganization, and be replaced with an economic system that supports the needs of society.

How did we get into this mess?

We got into it by design. In order to understand this design we need to go back into history, to the mid 1700s when the British Empire's North American colonies began to talk about claiming their independence. Even before it came to that, Lord William Petty, the second earl Shelburne and a major shareholder of the British East India company, was trying to come up with a way of dealing with the breakdown of the colonial system that the American independence movement threatened. During a carriage ride from Edinburgh to London, Lord Shelburne, hastily commissioned one of his advisors, Adam Smith, to produce two studies for possibles processes that could be used to save the empire. One of these studies was an apologea for free trade, and the other a study of the causes of the fall of Rome.

When the U.S.A. declared its independence in 1776, when it soon thereafter became evident that the American colonies would not be recaptured by force, Adam Smith's free trade platform was chosen as a process for bankrupting the new American nation. In order to do this, Lord Shelburne became Prime Minister for one year, during which he personally negotiated the 1873 Paris Peace Treaty with America, into which he incorporated Adam Smith's free trade platform.

Indeed, his efforts bore fruit. The process worked so well, that within a few years America became bankrupted. At this point Alexander Hamilton recognized what had been done, and reversed the process. The British free trade was scrapped, and was replaced with a strong tariff protection for America's industries, which were further supported by low cost financial credits extended to the nation by a national bank. This became an exceedingly productive platform for the nation, in comparison with the high interest borrowing schemes from private lenders. Eventually Hamilton's process became known as the world-renowned American System of economy.

As it was, the British Empire didn't give up that easily. When the Civil War was instigated by the empire through the land-owner circles in the South, the break up the Union almost succeeded, and perhaps even a complete recolonialization. Thanks to Abraham Lincoln this renewed imperial assault was repulsed. Lincoln was fully aware what the nation and humanity would loose, if he lost that war. Thus the victory was won, but at a horrendous sacrifice.

Nevertheless the empire was in no mood to give up. It resorted once again to Adam Smith's creations. This time it brought out his famous system of greed based economics. Smith evidently had recognized that greed based economics had caused the Roman empire to collapse. He proposed this as a platform for America. With that in mind, Adam Smith was brought to America and hailed as a genius, and everyone cheered. Thus, the general welfare principle of the country's constitution became displaced with greed based economics.

The first major defeat for America was suffered in 1875 with an act of Congress, called the Specie Resumption Act. This act took a way the nation's currency as a credit vehicle for industrial development and replaced with a gold and silver currency that turned money into an estate that could be utilized as a value pond for private lending institution. From this point on a shift in focus was unfolding, away from industrialization and production, to making money by simply manipulating money. In this manner, profits were drawn from processes in which nothing was produced of tangible value for society. In a sense, the profits were stolen. Greed became the governing factor.

This greed factor became evermore pronounced as time went on, by which the theft profiteering increased. Then in 1913, the entire central banking operation and nation's monetary policies were taken away from the nation and put into private hands in an act of Congress that had created the now infamous Federal Reserve system. The Federal Reserve is not a federal institution. The name is a fraud. The Federal Reserve is a shareholder owned, profit oriented, private banking empire. The general welfare principle has been sold out to the shareholder value system. With the stroke of a pen, the nation lost the chief keystone of it's sovereignty. In the same year, as it were to feed the profiteering system, the 1913 "Underwood Tariff Act" initiated the income tax system that still exists to the present day, that all citizens became bound to from that time onward.

The American nation has never recovered from these ever widening theft for profit looting impositions. Only during the Franklin Roosevelt years were the worst features of this system temporarily set aside (until his death in 1945). Today, greed runs absolutely everything. The entire economy has become focused on theft-based profit. Even the nations' currencies have become gambling chips in a vast speculative privatization of the population for private profiteering.

Adam Smith insists that the individual person's greed enriches society by acting as an engine for progress. Of course, as he had recognized correctly by studying the fall of the Roman empire, in real terms, the opposite is true, as greed destroys everything that society has created. I am certain Adam Smith's advise to Shelburne has been well proven, as it has accomplished precisely what Shelburne had intended.

Unfortunately, the process of greed based economics that has destroyed America is not so easily overturned. It has been hailed for decades by every 'financial expert.' By this treacherous glorification the system's real face has been kept hidden from society. Surprisingly it continues to remain hidden, even from those whose livelihood became destroyed in the progress. In today's age over 80% of the national income goes to a wealthy minority, while the remaining 20% gets spread across the rest of the population. The exact opposite used to be the case not so long ago.

In the 1960s, or instance a single worker's wage in industrial employment would support a spouse and a family with up to three or four children. Now, three members of such a family need to work in order to make ends meet. And even if they were lucky enough to find those jobs, they would still not be living as well as they would have lived in the 1960s on a single worker's salary. That's the hidden face of the visible collapse of the system. Nothing within the greed centered system can repair its self-deeding collapse.

The system has become dysfunctional. It is gone. It cannot be brought back to life. We are not in a cyclic slump today. We are in a systemic breakdown crisis, and what is more amazing still, is that this crisis is unfolding as it had been intended to unfold.

So what are we going to do, if we are wise? We scrap the system. We ace as serious a situation today as Lincoln did during the civil war. We must act accordingly. Just like Alexander Hamilton scrapped the British free-trade system in the early years of the U.S.A. as a nation, so the present greed-based system needs to be scrapped and put through a bankruptcy reorganization in order to save whatever is left of society's pensions and employment, and of the nation's productive industries on which its welfare depends.

The only useful indicator of the functioning of an economy lies outside stock indexes and corporate profit reports. It is found in the state of the general welfare of society. After all, isn't that what an economy exists to promote in a civilized society? It is in the measurement of the general welfare, that is of the market basket that an average worker's income provides for a family, where we find the most revealing statistic of a society's economic performance.

This market basket measurement was pioneered in the late 1990s by the American economist and statesman Lyndon H. LaRouche Jr.. The measurement of the market basket includes the food that can be purchased by a wage earner, and also clothing, housing, education, transportation, and recreation, and so on. In the U.S.A. that market basket has shrunk by 50% since 1967. And even as it had shrunk, only a portion of that smaller basket of goods comes from the national economy. The rest is imported. Free-trade imports make up an ever greater portion of the shrinking market basket of the once industrialized nations.

The collapse of the western economies is further evident in the monumental amounts of debt that are choking both the private and public sectors. Public debt results from deindustrialization and free trade, both of which collapse the revenue base of a nation and add an enormous increase in social service demands. This increase comes at the time of a shrinking tax base and escalating debt service requirements. It is plain to see that this kind of progression leads to the disintegration of the whole system. Nothing can be done about it without reversing the whole system. It is impossible to cut social support outlays beyond a certain point, within the sphere of a collapsing economy, without killing the population. The real choice comes down to this: shut down what is causing the economic collapse, or the default will shut down humanity.

Nothing else apart from this choice will be able to save humanity and civilization. Social payments must ultimately be considered a waste, since this 'investment' doesn't improve the productive capacity of society and the state of civilization. It merely slows the collapse a bit, but it won't stop it. The debt choked financial system tends to collapse whatever infrastructures may still exist by which a society maintains itself and its economy. Hospitals are being shut down for lack of funds, research centers are eliminated, even agriculture begins to collapse. Even the more fundamental physical infrastructures, such a water supply systems, bridges, railroads, power grids, and airlines, can no longer be maintained as needed, in a debt ridden, collapsing economy. In some areas the decay is already catastrophic.

The driver for the economic collapse is actually another paradox. The paradox is this: It is universally believed by today's supposedly intelligent society, that a society can profit from stealing. You may not agree, but this is the fact. It is certainly possible for the small minority of a royal society to profit from stealing whatever they need, from the lives of humanity. But for humanity, itself, this option is closed. A society cannot profit from stealing from itself. Imagine a neighborhood in which each one was out to rob their neighbor. The financial elite would tell you: that's Ok, its a zero sum game; there are as many winners as there are losers. That's a deception. The whole neighborhood would loose. Nothing productive would be going on. The game would consume all the attention, energy, and resources of the entire community. No one would have any time for productive activities.

Unfortunately, this is exactly what is happening on a global scale. The game is played in the financial arena. The elite tells the world the entirety of the financial arena operates as a zero-sum game. When aggregates are traded on the financial markets there are as many losers as there are winners. That's not true. The global society looses. There are no real winners. A society cannot profit from stealing as the royals do. It would be stealing from itself.

Trading financial aggregates, in speculative markets, may increase the perceived value of them as the trading fever raises hopes beyond reason. But the process of trading, itself, produces nothing in terms of physical wealth being created that benefits society. When a trader sells a share of stock to his neighbor for twice than what he bought it for, he is stealing by trickery, because the true value has not changed. This is how financial speculation has created a black hole that sucks up all available investment funds, while it generates nothing accept the glorious illusion that everyone loves, namely, that hyperinflated financial values represent reality. Thus the world is deprived of the funding that should create the infrastructures for living, such as farming, housing, transportation, science, art, industries, technologies, medicine, whatever supports human living.

Today, humanity finds itself trapped into a gargantuan game of theft with which it tears itself to pieces, and it loves it so much that it can't stop. That's the paradox.

The developing paradox

The irony is, that while there is no money available for the society to maintain its infrastructures and economies, huge sums are poured into financial speculation. This trend began in August 1971 when the U.S. dollar was taken off the gold standard by President Richard Nixon. Since that day, speculation has become spectacular, and has grown into a $100 trillion dollar monster that has looted and destabilized the entire world-financial system to the point of its impending disintegration. It has already begun taking down national currencies, national banks, and entire economies.

There have been numerous currency devaluations around the world since the speculation binge began. At first they were small. Now, devaluations in the order of 30% have become almost common place, adding further to the instability in the financial world. The Thailand currency crisis in the summer of 1997 is an example in point. It began with a $30 billion loss in real estate related loans, most of which were financed by Japanese banks. The Japanese banks hold altogether more than a trillion dollars in worthless paper from loans that went "non-performing" (on which no payments are being made). The volatility of the Japanese banking system is such, that, apparently, it couldn't tolerate the relatively tiny additional losses incurred in Thailand, which were probably no greater than 2% of Japan's already existing portfolio of bad loans. The danger that this small increase might blow the whole Japanese banking system out of the water was so great that $16 billion in additional loans were quickly arranged to gloss over a large portion of the otherwise defaulting loans. By this action Thailand, Japan, and the world were saved, so it seems, for another day. For this the IMF declared itself a hero.

Today, the bankruptcy of the financial system has been spread throughout much of Asia, while the need for bail-out funds almost doubles by the week. By mid December the needs far exceeded what the banks and governments can supply, which can barely hold their own. Nor do such rescue operations save anything. Mexico, which was saved with a $50 billion infusion, is virtually bankrupt again. The reality is, that nothing has been saved pouring in the moneys.

In Thailand, the collapse was far greater than Mexico's was. Of its 91 financial firms, 51 were shut down, the currency was floated and allowed to drop in a free fall fashion, new taxes were imposed, together with drastic spending cuts, including the lay-off of 40,000 people. While all this was in progress the need for rescue funding grew from $20 billion to $100 billion in a matter of weeks.

And still, nothing has fundamentally been saved, because another tens of billion in debt-paper matures in less than a year, in number of countries, for which no resources exist in the world to cover the shortfall. The IMF has congratulated itself in public for having come up with a $16 billion bail-out package, which by all accounts was not easy to assemble, while Thailand's real need stood at $70 billion at this point. Also, this scenario covers only one country of the Asian Tigers, which no longer roar. The reality is, that the IMF simply doesn't have the resources to prop up the rapidly collapsing world-financial system, not now, and certainly not in the future. Even the biggest banking system in the world, the Japanese banks, can no longer tolerate any more losses, even small ones, though it appears Japan will be forced to absorb vastly more defaults as the economies around the world continue to be looted by financial speculation, to the point that entire system disintegrates.

One must realize, of course, that before the Japanese banking system dies, the U.S. banking system will become wiped out as well, because the Japanese will naturally try to save themselves. Japan owns such a huge mountain of U.S. treasury bills, which it will need to dump much of it onto the market if it gets deeper into trouble. Such dumping will wipe out the U.S. bond market. Should this become necessary, no institution in the world will be big enough to prevent a global financial disintegration.

The world has come very close in recent years to this actually happening. The most dangerous crisis was prevented only a few years ago, with a $500 billion line of credit that was set up for Japan by the U.S. Federal Reserve. But even this enormously gigantic loan didn't fix anything. It didn't even overcome the volatility of the Japanese banking sector, which is now much greater that it had been before. The new credit merely inflated the speculative bubble some more and increased its volatility. Of course, it also added a huge chunk of debt to Japan's already immense problem.

As of mid 1997 Japan's loan losses are still rising. Nor can this increase in loan losses be avoided in a generally collapsing economy that is being looted by uncontrolled speculation. It should be noted that the "Asian Tigers," which suddenly died, were not so long ago hailed as the miracle economies of the world.

What we see here, however, is nothing fundamentally new. There have been numerous financial earthquakes in the past. But all of these were isolated events. Now, the once isolated events have become a continuous, unbroken stream. The death of the Asian Tigers, which were killed, one by one in rapid succession, reflect a corresponding increase in financial speculation. The impending disintegration of the system, because of its bankruptcy, is creating a confidence crisis among the 'in' circles, which invariably leads to intensified speculation.

These intensified processes are presently looting the physical economy of virtually all its development resources. Japan bears the brunt of the consequences, for the moment, of the dying "tigers." Japan's losses, as small as they were in the global context, were nevertheless sufficiently frightening on the local level, to have caused panic in the streets, setting off runs on the banks in Japan.

As the crisis worsens, in its struggle to survive, Japan may at length be forced to liquidate its vast holdings of U.S. Treasury bills. Such an act, invariably, destroys all established financial values, forcing deep discounts in bonds. A collapse on such a scale also spills over into the stock markets and the U.S. banking system, both of which are tied into the bond market, and bankrupt them also.

The U.S. banking system is also in trouble over consumer debt that has become a multi-trillion dollar monster. Right now, 1.2 million personal bankruptcies are declared each year. An additional 40 million accounts are considered to be in trouble, some with balances reaching upwards to $50,000. This are barely being maintained, usually by refinancing the debt service cost through additional loans. An upset that wipes out personal earnings, naturally, has enormous repercussions in this sphere. It can overwhelm the banking system all by itself.

In addition, the global financial system faces a crisis from the stock-markets themselves. These markets have become bloated by an enormous increase in speculation. In many nations, up to 90% of the society's savings, and in addition, huge piles of money borrowed against homes and businesses, are riding the dice, now, in a game of astronomically leveraged stock trading at pricing that have lost all relationship to reality.

With a yield of 2% in dividends paid across the U.S. stock markets, and taxes having to be paid on that yield, investors would have to wait close to 100 years, at current stock prices, to earn their money back, not to mention profits. In order words, a person would have to be insane to buy stocks under such circumstances.

The reality is, stocks are not bought for this reason. Stocks are bought for the potential profits from trading. Financial gains can be realized from trading a certain stock certificate back and forth at successively higher prices. In some cases huge profits are realized for a few clever traders. They may be as high as 50-100%, and more. The problem is, that the process of trading paper from one hand to another doesn't produce anything of substance. It doesn't create any real profit for society. In fact, the needs of society become neglected, thereby. Instead of putting money into infrastructures and industries that produce the necessary items for living, like food, clothing, housing, transportation, education, etc., society throws its money into the financial gambling pits and lets its physical economy decay.

In a very real way, society is celebrating its own demise by celebrating the rapidly increasing values in the stock-markets. In real terms, these celebrated stock-value increases are a measure of the intensity of the society's looting of its physical economy by which it lives. The famous Dow Jones index, "the Dow," should therefore be regarded as an insanity index which indicates how much has been looted out of the sphere of human living and has been poured into the financial gambling arena.

What this index is telling us, is actually quite frightening. The index indicates a hyperbolic rate of growth. The growth was very slight at first, but soon became more rapid. Now it rises very steeply. This is what has been happening to the stock-value index when seen in the long term perspective. Now one must realize that this steeply rising index represents a destructive process.

The damage that society has inflicted on itself, which is indirectly measured by this index, is, of course, increasing as sharply as the index increases, and this increase follows the nature of a hyperbolic curve. It becomes plain from this that the presently far advanced self-amplifying destructive process cannot be maintained much longer. It is a terminal process nearing its end.

Someone, jokingly, compared the present society to a dog that carries a thousand-pound-flea. The flea is the speculative financial system. In this symbiosis both the flea and the dog are doomed. As the flea is sucking the dog dry it kills the very resource that it is feeding on, and dies also. This type of symbiosis is a terminal process.

The drain on the world-economy, caused by speculation, goes far. It is literally killing people. Some put the death toll resulting from world-wide economic underdevelopment as high as 100 million persons per year, of which 10 million, or 33,000 a day, are the deaths of children below the age of five.

In the beginning, this death toll was mostly concentrated in the poor countries. Now the circle is widening as the economies of the so-called rich nations are collapsing towards the earlier third-world status. Eventually the point will be reached when the constantly increasing demands for gambling funds can no longer be met. Then, the flea (the inflated financial bubble) dies. But the dog dies first.

The Dow Jones should be called an insanity index, because the so-called profits gained from financial trading, though they exact a tall price from society, aren't profits at all. If there were real profits generated in the stock trading market, society would benefit and develop by the process. Instead, it collapses. The collapse proves that there are no profits generated by the con game in which investors steal from each other as they sell their wares to one another at ever higher prices and rob the physical economy in order to be able to so. The inevitable end result will be the disintegration of the entire financial and economic system.

The world-financial system is in trouble over the society's massive financial speculating, especially its financial derivatives gambling. This type of gambling is made up of various types of side-bets placed on the performance of stocks or other elements of the financial markets. A whopping $100 trillion in these side-bets contracts are typically outstanding at any one time, globally. This sum is so huge that a single upset could overwhelm the entire world-financial system several times over, like a financial atom bomb. When it blows, every bank, financial institution, investment house, etc., could be bankrupted over night, especially the banks. The U.S. banks presently carry an "off-balance-sheet" exposure that exceeds $22 trillion. This exposure, which doesn't even appear on the banks' balance sheets, is nearly five times greater than all the bank's assets combined ($4.5 trillion), and is 73 times greater than all the banks' equity. When this happens, one really can't talk about a "banking" system anymore. The traditional banking institution, the monument of stability, no longer exists. The banks have become gambling casinos, and the public's deposits are on the table while the wheel spins. Today's bankers are so deep into the game, they are literally betting the bank and their depositor's money. Will thy be winning the next round?

The upper echelons of the world-financial empire are well aware of the systemic volatility that the global gambling orgy has created throughout the entire world-financial system. This realization was reflected in a strange phenomenon in the financial press, where, in August 1997, one suddenly reads, all over the world, that investors are advised to sell their stock; that a major crash is about to happen. Most writers predict a market melt-down in the order of 20-50%. "Sell your stock now!" they urge their readers. In real terms, this warning in not for their readers' benefit, though the readers would be well advised to heed the warning.

This story is evidently floated to hide the real weakness in the system, the systemic volatility that becomes ever more difficult to hide. Thus, a tiny bit is admitted in order to keep the focus off the big stuff, the derivatives exposures. In this manner, 'investors' are becoming desensitized towards sizable losses that normally cause panic. Thus, when the tremors hit, investors have been 'educated' to see it as merely "a correction," while in reality a global catastrophe is unfolding in which even the biggest banks, funds, and financial enterprises may be wiped off the map; in which entire currencies can become non-negotiable.

Does this sound unbelievable? It should! Unfortunately, this is where the reality lies. The fact is, that a $.03 trillion in additional write-offs nearly wiped out the Japanese banking system, the biggest in the world, that carries over seven trillion dollars in assets. If this tiny amount causes earthquakes, it takes no genius to extrapolate the effects that a major upset in a $100 trillion market can produce, which itself, is anchored in the most volatile 'waters' on the planet.

Speculation and self-interest, as seen in the larger context.

Speculation is related to self-interest. There are four types of self-interest by which persons aim to gain a stronger position in the world.

.1. A person can participate in the universal development of society and find a richer life through the advance of civilization. This is reflected in the principle of the nation-state.

.2. A person can also gain a stronger relative position by stealing from others and by destroying their prospects. This is reflected in all feudalist structures.

.3. A person can push forward independently to gain advantage over others by exploiting their needs and general reactions, without any concern for their impact on society. This is reflected in speculation.

.4. A person can also do nothing, and imagine himself to be drifting in the right direction while regression erodes all standards that define the quality of life.

Each of the four processes relate to a different type of self-interest. The feudalist process (see item 2), for instance, developed out of the interests of the rich, influential, and powerful - the oligarchy. The oligarchic interest is focused on creating short-cut processes to wealth that bypass creative productivity in favor of various forms of stealing or looting. Historically, this involved colonialization and slavery. The modern means for colonialization are found in the cartelization of resources through mining cartels, oil cartels, food cartels, etc.. The modern means for slavery are provided by free trade between unequal-wage-cost economies, and the creation of debt bound economies (some call this usury or interest rate slavery).

As economic theft through colonialization and slavery is strongly antisocial, the oligarchy has found it necessary throughout the ages to artificially create an environment that protects its position of power. This involved two platforms: The creation of poverty and the creation of impotence, not for itself, but for the general society.

In historic times, feudalism created sufficient poverty on its own, to satisfy the oligarchy. Except, this is no longer deemed to be enough as in modern times poverty has been eroded through technological and industrial progress. In modern times, therefore, the stark poverty of bygone ages is being recreated by means of deindustrialization (the post-industrial society dogma); by means of a general devolution of education and housing; and by the glorification of mysticism and the deculturalization of society through drugs, focus on sex, degradation of music, art, and literature.

In historic times, feudalism also created a general impotence among society. The peasant presented not a threat to the status of the lord. A highly developed and population rich society, however, poses a great threat to feudal oligarchism. The creation of impotence, therefore, became important to the oligarchy in the modern times, which it aims to achieve through depopulation.

Depopulation has long been an oligarchic objective, involving large scale operations of genocide, such as the Irish genocide during the Potato Famine; or the creation of wars, such as World War I and II. Gang to gang warfare, terrorism, fascist genocide, are all widely employed methods. In modern times the prevention of economic development has been added to the list, because poverty is a potent killer. Even mankind's gentle, environmental conscience has been abused for murderous goals.

The motivation of individuals under oligarchism is a complex subject, because every facet of it is unnatural, artificial, and is well disguised behind a shiny facade. While the focus of feudalism, in modern times, has been shifted away from land-estate types of feudalism, the underlying process hasn't changed. Land-based feudalism is inherently limited by the available land. Therefore, a shift occurred in the oligarchic system that created the "money-estate" feudalism of today, that has none of the inherent limits of "land-estate" feudalism. Under the new feudalism the 'peasant' pays a hefty rent for his use of the lord's property, called "royalty", "interest", or "debt service charges." In earlier times this "money-estate" feudalist system was called "usury" and was banned by the church. Now, it has become the global system. It is no longer resisted, and consequently it is now looting nearly the entire global society.

A still more advanced form of the ancient types of feudalism is the phenomenon of free trade between unequal-wage-cost economies. This goes back to the time of colonialism. It, too, has become a global phenomenon. Under this system the strength of the world's poor, defenseless, nations is being exploited like one may exploit a natural resource. Furthermore, while this strength is being looted, at the same time, is used to undermine the strength of richer nations, whereby both nations fall.

In this context one can recognize two types of oligarchy. One type might be called the "establishment" oligarchy. Is is that which operates within the sphere of a nation. To some degree, this type of oligarch aids a nation's development, even as it operates as a paradise.

The other type of oligarchy is that which operates the free-trade process of international looting. For this broader involvement, this oligarchy might therefore be recognized as a "transworld" oligarchy as its focus is no longer concerned with national issues, except for destroying them wherever they stand in the way of the objectives. In real terms, the "establishment" oligarchy of previous times, has restructured itself and become the "transworld" oligarchy of today. Its globalized operations are presently looting society on a world-wide scale.

Historically, the transworld oligarchy may have had its beginning in the early centuries of the second millennium AD. At this time certain Byzantine assets took refuge on some tiny islands off the coast of Italy before the Lambard invasion, and established from this sanctuary a trading and financial empire. This empire had ruled much of the European region, economically, and parts of Asia.

Without an economy of its own that it could loot, the Venetian oligarchy had no option to become a "transworld" type oligarchy in nature. For all practical purposes it was the "transworld" oligarchy of the time. In later centuries this oligarchy expanded itself northward and took over the Netherlands and Britain, by assimilation, from where it extended itself across all of the world, especially into North America where it found a rich and fertile economy to loot.

When one speaks of the "British Empire," therefore, one speaks of the "transworld" oligarchy of to-today which may well be more predominant in the United States than anywhere else on the planet. Its operational and ideological center, however, remains in Britain, undeniably, irrefutably, for which the British monarchy serves as the structural base, as the ideological driver, and as the legal platform for its power. It embraces all aspects that pertain to feudal oligarchism.

Technically speaking, the British Empire no longer exists. Its colonial possessions have all gained their independence, nominally, though they remain under the organizational umbrella of the British Commonwealth of Nations whose sovereign is the Queen of England, the monarch of the United Kingdom, the Queen of British Empire. At this center all "transworld" oligarchic structures merge into one. The "transworld"/British Empire presently rules the planet. Its avenues for total, global control are many, and include the direct domination of much of the world through its near global ownership of the media, research institutions, and environmental institutions. Its avenues also include a strong 'bought' dominance in national governments, and the near direct control of such global institutions as the U.N., the I.M.F., the World Bank, etc., by which its process of looting the world becomes protected and legalized.

In a fundamental sense, the arch enemy of the oligarchic system is the nation-state which promotes the processes which elevate, strengthen, develop, and enrich a society. All, these, the oligarchy aims to destroy in order to maintain its power. Indeed, the oligarchy is fully aware that it must destroy the institution of the nation-state, or else the days of its own institution are numbered. The power of the nation-state was frighteningly demonstrated to the oligarchy by the F. D. Roosevelt administration of the U.S.A. during World War II, which had demanded, and almost brought about, an end to the British Empire, the center of feudalism and slavery.

The society (1), however, does not have the option to steal or to loot in order to advance itself, as the oligarchy pursues. Its goal for self-advancement can only be reached through progressive self-development by investing its energies into productive infrastructures, education, culture, technologies, and industries by which its physical, social, and spiritual existence becomes enriched. A nation cannot steal from itself. It can only develop itself.

The most advanced institution that has been created for the self-development of a society, which has not been superseded to the present day, is the sovereign nation-state, which is able to provide a platform for an infinitely developing economy. No other platform can achieve this end. The oligarchic platform, at its very best, represents a terminal economic system that creates huge bubbles of shiny financial estates which time and time again implode into nothing, creating depression and social chaos. Right now, the world faces the biggest of such bubbles ever created, and the most chaotic implosion of all times as the inflated system once again pops, and terminates.

The rescue apparatus that has brought the nations out of the most recent historic implosions of the oligarchic financial system, has always been the nation-state. Unfortunately, this institution is extensively weakened, today, through numerous oligarchic assaults, world-wide, from without and from within. The society's survival during the presently impending financial implosion crisis, the potentially greatest crisis in all of human history, requires an unprecedented re-dedication by society to the principle that underlies the institution of the nation-state.

The motivation of the spectator (3), in contrast, lies between the two above mentioned poles. Originally, the idea of a stockmarket was not to facilitate speculation, but to provide a platform on which the public could join hands in setting up large companies that are jointly owned with the profits being shared. By this process large, efficient structures can be created that can never be created on an individual basis. Apart from this characteristic, a public company is no different than any other enterprise. The invested capital is never repaid, but is applied to create the business. The value of a person's share in such an enterprise, therefore, reflects the profits generated and shared.

Now, a person may speculate that the profits will increase in the future. Therefore, in order to get hold of these shares, to be able to cash in on those future profits, a higher price will be offered than what the shares are actually worth at the time. Thus, a profit is generated for the original owner out of the process of speculative trading. As the trading process continues, evermore cash, of course, will have to be put up. Unfortunately, for society, none of that extra cash produces anything as it doesn't flow into the business enterprise to enhance its activities. To th contrary, this cash is drained out of the physical economy which is thereby deprived of potential investment resources. In other words, once financial speculation sets in, the society's money no longer flows into the productive processes that enrich its lives, but is siphoned off into a speculative treadmill. The speculator, unfortunately, doesn't care about this. His range of perception doesn't reach that far. He lives in a competitive world were one must outsmart one another, where nothing solid is build, where all profits are actually illusions as no backing exists for them in physical wealth or wealth creating capacity.

When one 'investor' finds a good angle, frequently half the world jumps on the band-wagon. Then, huge bubbles are created in which the financial values are hyperinflated in relationship to what they represent in terms of the physical economy. In the 1980s a huge real estate bubble was created on this basis, that eventually popped, and took large chunks of the banking system down, that had financed the bubble.

Compared to the present stock-market and derivatives bubble, the real estate bubble was actually rather minuscule. But one factor combines the two modern bubbles. In each case, the motivation of the 'investor' falls short of considering the consequences to society of the process that is enacted. Nor does the investor consider the unreality of the profits that all his efforts are focused on. For this reason all financial bubbles should be understood as structures built on mental blindness.

The mental sphere of today's general public (4), however, tends to be even more limited than the speculator's mental horizon. The public has developed the strange capacity of staring an unfolding tragedy in the face with a smile, ignoring its mortal danger, at times even closing its eyes to it lest it might see and be stirred to take some meaningful actions, individually as well as collectively. The poison that narrows the public's mental outlook is none other than a carefully cultured devotion to elitism. Subjection to elitism breeds a dense mental blindness, in which humanity behaves like sheep guided to their slaughter.

Four (types of) financial and economic systems.

The four types of self-interest, naturally involve four distinctly different financial and economic systems.

The first type involves an economic system centered on infinite development. Under this system the nation (1) owns its own money and credit creation capability (which are presently in private hands). Thus, the nation receives the profits from the economic process, which, then, can be recycled into advancing its civilization and self-development by strengthening its cultural, scientific, technological, and industrial processes. This self-amplifying process is an infinite process, because nothing is looted out of the society. In other words, the energy within the system is not dissipated through looting, but increases. This is the natural result of enhancing the productive and creative processes by which a society lives and creates its civilization. Such a system is endlessly self-amplifying, creating ever more and richer resources for living out of the creative capacity of the human genius.

This self-development process is typified by the American system of economy that was established shortly after the American independence was won. It had turned the U.S.A. into the richest nation on the planet, until this system was destroyed.

The second type or economic system, the feudal system of economy (2), is a terminal system. Its focus on looting invariably destroys its host. Every empire in history that has been built, and has been lost on this platform. Right now, the feudal system of economy is the global financial/economic system. Under its yoke many of the world's once prosperous nations are literally dying, being choked to death by U.N./I.M.F. austerity demands, deindustrialization demands, and draconian environmental demands - even depopulation demands.

The third type of economic system, the speculative financial system (3), is also a terminal system. It is a negative growth system in which financial aggregates, such as stocks, bonds, derivatives, etc., become insanely inflated far beyond their supposed relationship to the productive economy, which alone creates all wealth and by which all financial claims must be satisfied. The speculative process that is stripping the society's financial resources from its physical self-development, to be used for feeding the financial inflation, creating bubbles upon bubbles, causes both the human and the financial system to disintegrate in a crash proportionate to the size of the inflated financial values.

This type of system is definitely a terminal system, because nothing within the speculative sphere can stop the self-advancing collapse that is fundamental to its nature.

The fourth type of economic system may be called the 'sucker system.' Apathy is a default state that takes over when intelligent self-government stops. In the vacuum of intelligent awareness, the awareness of the general society (4) is 'guided' into its acceptance of imposed processes that benefit not itself, but the purposes of the criminals who seek to rob and destroy it. The world-wide sweep of the privatization process of national industries, resources, and infrastructures, consolidates all the life-supporting structures of the world into a few private hands, who thereby aim to control humanity and its destiny (read depopulation). This consolidation is very far advanced in today's world, both in gold and mineral resources, and in the ownership of the world's food production and industrial capability. And all this is totally accepted by society, who readily gives up its wealth, its basis for living, even its life, to the asking, without as much as a single objection.

Each of the four financial-economic systems is distinct. Of the four, three are terminal systems (which are in operation today), and one is useful as it opens a path to infinity, rather than termination. This one is prohibited as it would obsolete all the terminal systems that the world seems to cherish today in an environment of growing insanity.

Four types of social and political structures.

The four types of self-motivation which are reflected in the four types of economy are also reflected in four distinct types of social and political structures. Three of these structures have become dominant, and again, one is being suppressed. The most dominant of these, in today's world, is the fascist system. It is a feature of the oligarchic background (2).

The fascist system incorporates all types of slavery, and if the situation warrants, genocide as a means for achieving the feudalist objective. The entire free-trade globalism that opens the door to free trade between unequal-wage-cost economies is a balanced system of fascist slavery on one side, and fascist social destruction on the other as the result of the destruction of industries and the creation of a debt economy. Fascism, of course, has countless faces, but they all reflect the nature of the motivation that is anchored in oligarchism and feudal economy.

Another dominant system is the mythological system (3). There are three major mythologies embraced by mankind that are presently reshaping the course of society. One of these is centered on the myth that financial profits can be generated through non-productive processes. This is the domain of speculation.

In the speculation environment, the profits that a few people reap are 'stolen' out of the pockets of others, since speculation doesn't produce anything. A whole 'industry' has been created that drives this thieving speculation binge. Like speculation, itself, this 'industry,' too, drains immense sums (in the form of brokerage fees) out of the productive economy. The commission structure in the brokerage business is intrinsically rich for the 'successful' broker, which becomes a powerful motivating force for increasing the speculation binge, for manipulating the public into feeding the bubble that will eventually kill it.

The mythological system also has other

components. One is centered on environmental myths that are put forward to shape the response of the public contrary to its real self-interest. One of these is the Global Warming myth that is promoted by the oligarchy for targeting the world's energy production capability for its destruction. The reason is, that without large scale energy production a modern society cannot operate. Without it, most people cannot survive. Which means, present world population cannot be maintained. In other words, the intended goal is murder on a vast scale. It provides the kind of social devastation that the oligarchy requires to maintain its relative position of power. By locking up the world's energy fuels, the fossil fuels which the world is totally depended on at the present time, while at the same time shutting down nuclear energy development, billions of people can be starved out of existence under the present ecological agenda.

This type murderous regression is one of the oligarchy's elements for self-protection. In a highly developed society feudalist structures can have no place. Therefore, so the oligarchy concludes, human development must be shut down at all cost. It requires primitive cultures, and tries to promote or create them wherever possible, creating poverty wherever possible.

The depopulation process is based on a myth that the oligarchy has promoted for hundreds of years, already, namely the myth that the earth is to full. It is being said today that depopulation is required in order to save the earth. Under this myth (please note, the earth was deemed to full already in the mid 1800s) the English Poor Laws were set up that had murdered countless people, especially the economically destitute. This century old myth has not been defeated to the present day. Rather, it is given more credibility in order to speed the murdering into large scale genocide.

The ecological mythologies includes many such environmental oriented murdering myths, some of which, by their impact, murder vast numbers of people.

The destructive binge based on environmental myths, like the speculation binge, is promoted by a fee structure. In this case the incentive isn't in the form of commissions, but is paid in the form of 'donations.' Many of the world's environmental organizations have been 'bought' on this basis. Even many of the most respected scientists and scientific institutions have been 'bought' through research grants, publishing rights, and tenure. The people who operate within these mythological systems, however, must be considered as being too limited in their vision to recognize the destructive impact of their demands. This is generally true for all victims of mysticism, whether they were drawn into financial speculation to misguided environmentalism, including eugenics theories and Malthusian ideals.

The third dominant political and social structure is one that is centered on apathy. Apathy is the platform of the 'sucker' economy (4). One of its outstanding feature is a type of 'democracy' that provides a path to power for such men like Adolf Hitler, or whoever the rich and influential oligarchy chooses to promote in the eyes of the public's fancy. This type of democracy is one of their games by which they maintain their political power. In order for the game to operate smoothly the oligarchy has bought itself, to a near total extend, the public's information media, and with it the public's conscience. The society, thereby, has become a prisoner in a concentration camp without fences.

The fourth type of political and social structure is, as mentioned before, currently suppressed. Its platform (1) involves an intelligent responsibility for freedom, and actions that enable the self-development of society's potential. It is a platform for development: economically, financially, morally, and culturally. It is the renaissance platform that has brought a golden age to humanity whenever it was established.

This book is designed to explore the deeper aspects of all four types of systems in the context to financial and economic issues. As these four types of systems tend to overlap, it becomes important for one to be aware of their fundamental nature by which they are set apart in their motivation, structure, and operation.

Since these four systems have a tremendous impact on everyone's living, for which they are obscured by those who control humanity, this book has been designed to explore an area of reality that has been kept hidden from society, which, in fact, most people don't want to hear anything about. The book is designed to explore the fundamental principles that need to be understood, as a platform for dealing with the world's financial and social crisis. The book is also designed for taking a closer look at the three terminal systems have been moving society evermore towards an impending global crisis which promises to have unimaginable consequences, but which can be averted intelligently.

It is certainly possible for all the interlocked processes that have brought about the impending crisis, to be replaced with a process that enables economic development and allows the nation's prosperity to be recreated, or to be created were it never existed before. The infinite system of economy has been powerfully effective whenever it has been implemented throughout history. In other words: there isn't just some faint hope on the horizon. There exists a scientific foundation for hope, with historically demonstrated proof.

Infinite Development or Impending Crisis?

Infinite development! Horrors! - you may say. You may interject and ask: Have we not all been told for the last several decades, by the most prominent of the elite, that large scale development is bad, that industrialization stinks, that mankind has to "lower" its impact on the planet in order to make life on the planet sustainable? We have been told that we need the opposite to industrial development, that we have begun the post-industrial era of environmentalism combined with a service economy and information oriented societies. The presently aimed for utopia is anything but an era of infinite development!

Indeed, mankind has been told all this, and it has lived by the degree of post-industrialism, but it has been a murderous degree. The consequences are still being suffered. They are nothing less than genocidal. Nor has the degree, and its enactment, saved the planet. The opposite is true. Poverty oriented (primitive) economies are highly destructive to the land. If there had been no technological progress and large scale industrialization during the last 150 years, there would not be a single tree standing on the face of the planet. It would all have been hacked down for firewood and building materials. The creation of numerous, high-tech, industrially produced materials has taken the pressure of the forests as a resource. In fact, most modern buildings cannot possibly be constructed out of wood. Likewise, the industrialization of electric energy and natural gas has turned the stinking fog bound cities of the past into clean places to live. Everything that society now regards as essential for its quality of life has been the result of extensive industrialization and development.

Nor do industries pollute, as the opponents to development insist. Poverty pollutes. Industrial pollution is the mark of what might be called investment starved development, which is focused on looting, where everything is done on the cheap in order to maximize profits rather than to do advance the civilization of society. Free-trade competition between nations of unequal wage-cost production, and unequal pollution control standards, causes the destruction of high-standard industries in developed countries and the creation of stinking industrial hell-holes in poor countries; thus creating an economic shift that creates more pollution, rather than solving pollution. Pollution is the mark of neglect. Advanced industrialization improves the quality of life and the environment of living. The problem is, that this goal is not on the agenda, today.

Modern technological advances and industrialization also have had a progressive impact on agriculture to the degree to which it has been pursued. High-yield plant types, together with efficient fertilizers and pesticides have increased production more than ten fold, in some cases, over primitive types of agriculture. The entire planet would likely have to be covered with fields (which is impossible anyway) in order to feed the present world population, were it not for these improvement. And there is lots of room for improvement, yet.

Some say that high tech industrialization takes jobs away. This myth is based on a grave deception. Nothing apart from this could be further from the truth. It is the shutdown of industrialization that has created the debt economy, and unemployment, which are now killing people with increasing poverty. Many of the world's most advanced industries have become rust-buckets, or have been converted into amusement parks, all under the dictates of free-trade and financial austerity policies that are strangely accepted by society.

People are told that industrialization is not needed, but this amounts to an admission of mental blindness or outright lying. The world is presently grossly underdeveloped. Its infrastructures, where some exist at all, are inadequate and decaying. The water systems of nearly every major city in the West are leaking like a sieve. Some systems are over 120 years old and are far past their design life. Bridges and other civil engineering structures are suffering the same fate. Some have become actually dangerous to use. Traffic, in most cities, is chaotic, and is a hindrance to economic activity rather than a supporter of it. The bulk transport systems that are presently employed are probably the worst possible. The still ongoing regression in efficient high speed rail transport service has forced much of the nations' cargo onto trucks, which now clog up its highways. And this is happening in what we call the industrialized world. The people in rest of the world are much worse off. They don't even have a transportation system, electric energy grids, a railway system that is worth mentioning, or large scale water supply systems, highways, and bridges.

For the lack of an effective transportation system some nations exist in near total isolation, without any rational means for transporting goods and food, except by dirt trail truck transports that are cost prohibitive for any large scale use. There remains an immense amount of work that needs urgently to be done just to eradicate the worst poverty in the world. To say that we don't need industrialization to create the needed infrastructures, is a scam. It is a scam designed to enhance poverty and depopulation.

Efficient transportation infrastructures are urgently needed on a global basis as a backbone to support secondary economic development. The validity of this statement is evident in the historic development of societies which first established themselves alongside of rivers that offered easy transport capability. Much of Russia grew up alongside the Volga river, so it seems. In today's world, the initial role of the river based transport system needs to be recreated, and this on a larger scale, by a world-wide high speed rail network that connects Africa, China, Asia, Europe, and the Americas into one single network. To a small degree, this is already happening. Two such projects are under active development, today.

One of these, which is nearly completed, is a rail and road link that will connect Norway and Sweden across Denmark to the transportation grid of central Europe. The project is made up of two parts. One part connects the Danish islands of Zealand and Fuenen across the 13 Km wide narrows of the Storebaelt. This crossing includes an 8 Km long railway tunnel and the longest off-shore suspension bridge in the world with a span of over 1,600 meters. The second part connects the Danish Capital of Copenhagen to the Swedish city of Malmoe across a 16 Km bridge tunnel combination which links the two cities into the largest integrated urban center in Scandinavia with a population of over 3 million people.

The second major infrastructure project that is also under active development and is partly completed, is the so-called Eurasian Land-Bridge development project. It consists of a rail link infrastructure that, since 1992, connects China with western Europe across central Asia. It gives many of the central Asian countries an economic access to the world which they never had before. Presently, the railway technologies involved are in large parts still primitive, but they are being upgraded. Two more of these Eurasian land links are presently in the planning stage: One on these is to stretch across the north of Asia and Russia, and another through the south across Indonesia, India, Pakistan, and Iran, connecting into Africa and Europe.

Another major rail connection is under consideration that would link China with North America. It is presently on the long term drawing board. A 85 Km railway tunnel would be dug under the waters of Bering Strait.*2

Through the construction of both the Eurasian and the Bering Strait links, a development corridor would become established that no only provides fast long-distance transport, but more importantly, enables the economic development of the surrounding regions. It becomes the driver for world-wide industrialization and development.

This is what will happen, because it has to happen for the development of the world. This is not a choice. Only the timing is left as a choice.

At the hub of this development network, which is going to be built sooner or later, sits China. China is therefore of tremendous importance to the whole world.

China happens to be not only the most populous nation on earth, it is also in the midst of the most ambitious internal development effort ever undertaken by any nation on the planet earth. As a modern-nation state, China has over 10,000 major infrastructure projects in progress and planned. They include the creation of 200 brand new cities over the next 20 to 30 years. In the short term, till about 2010, China plans to build 45,000 Km of new railway (doubling its present length to 90,000 Km). It has plans to provide 14 cities with a subway system in this time-frame; to create 11,000 Km of new highways; to build 100 new airports and equally as many new sea and river ports. In 2010 China will also complete its Three Gorges Dam project as the first phase of the largest water development project ever undertaken, anywhere. When completed, the project will irrigate the dry north of the country and enable new agricultural development in an area that is equal in size to all of Germany. Of course, the Three Gorges Dam also provides flood control. The latest flood of the Yangtze river had devastated 33 million hectares of farmland, destroyed 800,000 houses, damaged an additional 2.8 million homes, and killed a thousand people. The nation will be safe from this type of danger after 2010. The Three Gorges project will also make the Yangtze river navigable for an additional 700 Km and provide electric power equal to that of 13 large nuclear power plants.

As huge as this project is, and it is gargantuan by any standard, another development project is under way that is over three times as costly as the giant dam project. This monumental project adds additional capacity to the industrial complexes along the Yangtze river in the region near Shanghai. Further to the north, along the Bohai Coast 3,600 infrastructure projects are planned for the next 15 years, which include a 57 Km bridge across the narrows of Bohai Strait, cutting across 2,000 Km of coastline.

If this type of momentous development already occurs at the hub of the potential east-west development network, the fallout of it, once the east/west transportation network has been created, has the potential to uplift the whole world. Actually China already does this to some extend.

Another Asian tunnel project is under study that will connect Japan to the southern tip of Korea, with a second tunnel cutting across the waters to Japan's northern island, and from there a third tunnel would be connecting the rail-link to Russia's Sakhalin Island with a fourth tunnel to be built between it and the Asian mainland, creating a circular link around the entire Sea of Japan.

"It can't be done!" some say. "It can't be financed!"

Indeed, some economists insist that this is impossible. The reality is that this type of development is already under way in China right now. And it is being financed. Except it is financed on a platform that incorporates some of the features of the model for infinite development.

In real terms, the infinite model has never been fully implemented. The closest implementation occurred during the F. D. Roosevelt Presidency in the U.S., who, from his inaugural address onward, had declared war on the speculative economic system of the "transworld" oligarchy of the British Empire, which is strongly represented on Wall Street. His inaugural speech gave the nation the needed confidence that this war could be won. Consequently the nation supported his actions. The outcome was amazing.

On a platform of national self-development and tall moral objectives, such as Roosevelt's four freedoms that should be guaranteed for all humanity, he created the kind of policies that pulled the nation of the deepest depression that the looting speculative system had created in modern history and developed its potential by which it became the greatest economic, moral, and military force on the planet.

All this was done in a few short years and under conditions that took millions of the nation's finest men onto the fields of war, and required enormous resources to be poured into supplying the engines of war. Imagine what could have been accomplished if all these resources had been plowed into the economic self-development of the nation and the world!

Can anyone imagine what the real potential for a nation's economic self-development is if it is allowed to operate free of parasitism in an environment of global cooperation for the advancement of humanity?

Economic development must be seen as primarily a moral platform, with moral objectives, to which the economic agenda, then, becomes added and becomes tailored to. In the case of China, the objective is to bring the nation out of the poverty ridden chaos of Mao's failed cultural revolution to the 20th century standard where decent food, housing, education, and employment should be guaranteed for all citizens. This goal echoes the moral commitment of Roosevelt's four freedoms that were foundational to his development policies: the freedom of speech, the freedom of religion, the freedom from want, and the freedom from fear - anywhere in the world.

It cannot be said, of course, that the moral commitment that stood behind F. D. Roosevelt's policies, or that which is currently driving the economic development of China, represents a revolutionary commitment. The principle was developed at the end of the Greek Classical Period, or at least it was put on the map at this time as part of the pioneering concepts introduced by Christ Jesus. One of the fundamental principles that Christ Jesus spoke of, was: Love thy neighbor as thy thyself. Out of this background the parable of the (good) Samaritan was created. Both were statements of a fundamental principle that underlies the platform of economy.

Let's explore where the western society stands on this issue, which, unlike China, is presently committed to a death spiral of economic disintegration in an orgy of gargantuan financial speculation. What happened to the principle of: Love thy neighbor in this world? It has been retranslated, to read: Take advantage of thy neighbor; steal from thy neighbor, loot they neighbor; rule over thy neighbor; and murder thy neighbor if there is a buck to be made by it. It is not being said, however: enrich the world of thy neighbor. This, though, is what F. D. Roosevelt had said.

It is actually a self-evident requirement to enrich the world of our neighbor, because the world of our neighbor is the world that we, too, share. The ancient peoples from ages long before Christ Jesus understood this principle. They understood it as a sound economic platform. Reference to this is found in the early section of the Bible*3. One finds even traces of it in the moral code of the Mosaic law. It is remarkable, indeed, that such fundamental truths, which have been self-evident in the primitive world of ancient cultures can no longer be understood in our scientific age. This is so in spite of monumental evidence being demonstrated in support of the ancient truths.

Contrary to this evidence, the opposite 'theology' is being preached from every economic pulpit in the West. And the consequences are horrid. The once thriving industrial economies of the western nations have become rust-heaps, and the nations a social 'basket' case riddled with crime, unemployment, and poverty that are altogether killing people on a very large scale. In Russia this regression is so far advanced that the nation is loosing over a million people per year, in spite of new births. And this is just the beginning of a fast accelerating trend. The world as a whole is in a deep crisis as its global financial and economic system has been so thoroughly looted that it is near the point of a global systemic disintegration, yet the looting continues to grow in intensity as it must, in order to keep the bubble alive by keeping it growing.

Even the so-called "Asian Tigers," the much tooted "miracle economies" of the 1990s lie wounded by speculation, and in ruin, because of it. The weakened tigers had been feasted on by the hyenas of the Empire, the mega-speculators, called "fund-managers." Of these, Gorge Soros (Qantum Fund) was denounced as the undisputed leader of the pack, by Prime Minister Mahathir Mohamad of Malaysia whose nation was hit with a 12% loss of its currency value during a recent speculative attack by George Soros on the Indonesian economies. Mahathir Mohamad pointed out that in this single attack on his nation the economic progress that the Malaysian people had worked for over the last ten years were wiped out in a day. It appears that the tigers were purposely 'cultured' to become food for the hyenas. Nor was Malaysia the only target. All the tigers suffered this fate, most of all Thailand.

It should be noted that the so-called miracle economies that were destroyed during the recent predatory attack can be faulted for only one thing, namely that they had followed the IMF's directives for them to the letter.

Defining the impending crisis.

Most people do not believe that the world is facing a crisis. This is sad, because any intelligent person should be able to realize that it is impossible to squeeze 40% in profits out of a productive industry that produces at the very most a 2% yield. Yet 20-40% is what modern 'investors' expect from the stock and financial markets. On the stock trader's floor such vast profits are indeed realized. Except these profits don't mean anything. The inflow of a few billion dollars into the market, strategically directed, can act as a catalyst to uplift all values across the entire market, which frequently raises the combined market value by hundreds of billions. The resulting increase in perceived value, then, is regarded as profit that people borrow against. In reality, not a single penny of extra wealth has been produced by the industries that the market represents, which means that the assumed value is totally fictitious. The assumed 'value' of stocks is merely the price that an investor is willing to pay. It has nothing to do with any real value based on actual profit being generated by the companies that issued the shares being traded. The assumed value can be sky high today, and a fat zero tomorrow.

Since the currently assumed financial values are infinitely inflated over what they represent, this means, that the assumed value can never be cashed out by society. Right now the assumed value exceeds the generated profits of the physical economy that it should represent, by a large margin. Frequently this financial inflation is an infinite amount, when a company's profits become a negative value due to debt service costs.

What this means in reality, is that all inflated financial values tend to vaporize once the vast disparity between fiction and reality becomes recognized. Every financial bubble that has ever been created throughout history has popped, leaving various types of devastation in its wake, like the Great Depression of the 1930s.

In the 1920s vast sums were borrowed against inflated stock values, which the "most knowledgeable experts" had predicted would remain high forever. The values were said to have attained a "permanent high plateau." However, at the point when the recognition of reality set in, a few months later, the fictitious values became deflated to a level that was more at par with reality. Most values dropped to near zero in the chaos of the transition. The "permanent high plateau" was gone. The entire pyramid scheme disintegrated. Many of the banks that were tied into the scheme disintegrated with it.

It should be noted that in those days the sums involved were tiny in comparison to today's standard. Also the stock purchases were leveraged to much lower levels in the 1920s. In addition, the international financial scene was clam in those days, and the U.S. economy was strong and virtually debt-free. Nor was consumer debt a huge problem in 1929, and the derivatives gambling that is presently as $100 trillion dollar phenomenon, was totally unknown, in which a single bad trade can cause billions in losses and take the strongest institutions down. But in spite of all this relative stability the market crashed and a deep depression resulted in the wake of the crash.

Today's exposures are immensely larger. The economies of the West are in shambles and are drowning in debt. Unemployment, social poverty, crime, and violence have grown to near catastrophic levels, and this even before the financial crash has even occurred. The dynamics of the presently impending crash in the global financial system, that is unfolding against the background of a weakened world, are such that something much worse than merely a depression results, or a few banks won't reopen. The disintegration of the total global financial system will hit simultaneously the entire world, with the possible exception of China, which operates on a higher platform than monetary feudalism and intense speculation. The impending world-wide disintegration has the potential to be so far-reaching as to cause the destruction of civilization, itself, throughout much of the world.

This is what mankind is facing today. Luckily, the game can also be called off before all this happens. This won't be easily accomplished, however. At the moment, nobody is interested in changing anything. The illusions of unearned wealth and easy money are too pleasant for society to concern itself with reality.

History tells us, however, that this disinterest can become the opposite overnight. Today, the population as a whole is much more deeply at risk than it ever has been throughout history. Some say that as much as 90% of the public's life saving is riding the dice in the market. This means that people who have purchased mutual funds for their retirement stand to loose over 90% of their equity when the stock market's crumble. It also means that those who have taken out loans against their homes or businesses to invest into 'income' funds, will loose that equity. Even those who have put their money into bank deposits, will loose it. Deposit insurance has no meaning when the whole banking system dies which carries exposure in derivatives gambling, which, all by themselves, are several times greater than the combined total of all the depositors' assets.

The so-called hedged funds, therefore, are a fraud. There is no such thing as hedging one's stockmarket exposure against a sudden downturn in the market. This works on a small scale, perhaps, with the purchase of compensating options on the derivatives market. But it won't work when a major exposure hits the market. That is why derivatives exposures are not shown on the banks' balance sheets? (The FDI in the U.S. acknowledges the existence of $22 trillion in off-balance-sheet exposures for the U.S. banking system.) The simple fact is, derivatives exposures have to be counted that way, because there exists no backing for them in real equity within the banks' own resources, or for that matter, anywhere in the world, that would cover the exposure. In other words, when the derivatives bets go sour, the bank simply goes under, and so does the whole banking system as all banks play the same game. What liquidity, than, will compensate for any stockmarket losses that the mutual fund industry tells its investors are "hedged"?

In an act of bravery the Financial Standards Accounting Board in the U.S. proposed in 1997 that all derivatives holdings should be reported on the balance sheets, which are largely exposures. This caused such a wave of protest, mainly from the banks and bank-owned politicians, that the Fed-chairman intervened and said in effect: "No way!"

What would have happened had the proposed rule been imposed, J. P. Morgan, for instance, the so-called conservative bank, would have to report that its gambling portfolio in financial derivatives is 473 times greater than the bank's equity. The bank evidently feels that its stockholders have no right to know that their investment is riding the dice at such a tall margin. J. P. Morgan would further have to report that the public's assets that it manages in various types of deposits, some $225 billion all told, represent but a minuscule backing for the bank's gambling portfolio of $5.3 trillion, which is 23 times larger than all the money the public has handed over to the bank to do with as it pleases, for a minuscule return in interest. Evidently, the banks feel that the public has no right to know how extremely vulnerable its money is, when entrusted to the banks. It would recognize, for instance, that in the wake of a sudden upset in the world-financial system, their assets would evaporate into thin air, and even than, only a tiny portion of the derivatives claims against the banks could be satisfied. In other words, the public would loose everything while the bank's obligations would still remain unfulfilled. Full backing for derivatives exposures simply does not exist, anywhere, nor is it possible to amass the $100 trillion in backing for the game, considering that not even the few billion can be found that are desperately needed to save the lives of millions in the most severely looted nations.

Large scale hedging, therefore, is impossible in practice, and is technically a fraud by those who sell the promise. It is also technically a fraud for the banks to accept exposures (for substantial fees) that can never be covered in practice. Unfortunately, this is the face of the deregulated banking system where everything goes that can squeeze a buck out of the public, no matter the cost to society. Deregulation means the surrender of moral ethics; it means legalized theft; it means there exists no lawful protection for the public.

Deregulation was, and still is, hailed as the great Saviour. Indeed it saves the banks and other institutions that deal in derivatives from the imperatives of ethical conduct. Now, everything goes. With the once 'regulated' moral standards gone, the banks are free to commit themselves to obligations (for enormous profits) that they have no intention, nor the resources, ever to fulfill. That is why the the derivatives exposure is not accountable on the balance sheets, which thereby become meaningless.

Deposit insurance is equally meaningless in a systemic disintegration of the financial system. It is designed to handle tiny exposures, not global exposures. When today's great financial bubble pops, it cannot be resurrected by deposit insurance, not even in part, in order to save the public from its folly. It is an indication of insanity for a person to believe that deposits can be insured on a global scale, and that mutual funds are able to hedge their exposures in the stock-market bets with compensating derivatives bets. The entire speculative system is based on a carefully cultured insanity that binds the public's eye to reality, without which the speculative system simply could not exist. This insanity, however, can no shield society from the unfolding consequences.

By its gambling mania, and its submission to the underlying forces that support this mania, the society is literally shooting itself in the foot, both financially and in terms of its physical economics. Still, in spite of the near certain catastrophe that unfolds out of this background, it is possible for society to reverse its direction and save its civilization. This reversal is most likely to happen when a gradual crash occurs that causes universal pain of such intensity that society demands a fundamental change. Then, things may begin to move. Except, can one expect sane responses to emerge in an environment of unfolding anarchy? Can insanity become cured with in the sphere of anarchy?

In order to save society and its civilization, fundamental changes will ideally have to be made before the system blows up. Please note, the current world-financial system cannot be saved. It is doomed by its own processes. A terminal system cannot be cured, it can only be replaced with a healthy system, that is an infinite system, and it must be replaced in its entirety if a world wide financial and social catastrophe is to be avoided. Except, this involves changes of such a magnitude that hardly anyone is willing to even consider them.

The required changes are actually not difficult to make, from a technical standpoint. The U.S. President has the power to make these changes, and it wouldn't take half a day to accomplish the task if there was a willingness to save the nation. Perhaps, when the nation is crying in the streets, demanding action, actions may follow. The modern U.S. President looks to the crowd for his cue, like the Roman rulers did in deciding the fate of gladiators, but we should have moved away from this by now.

What irony we have here! The very person who occupies one of the most powerful offices in the world refuses to be a leader. He drifts with popular opinion, responding to the whim of a society that is largely controlled by mythologies created for its self-destruction. It is an irony that the leader of one of the most powerful offices on the planet shys away from his responsibility and becomes a whimp at the very time when the survival of his nation and civilization are at risk. There is a possibility, however small, that with the proper guidance and demand from the public, the President may yet act in time and act correctly.

Right now the U.S. President doesn't have the courage to do anything to save the nation and its civilization. Evidently, he also lacks the wisdom to properly protect himself in order that he might do what is needed. Thus, the task of saving the nation falls upon the public. Except, the public has no interest in any such matters that are centered on reality, having been mythologically guided to look away from reality. Therefore, the public cannot see the crisis ahead. This, altogether, creates a dangerous situation.

The current lack of awareness is not surprising if one considers that it was carefully cultivated in small, successive steps. Even the financial gambling mania had started small, in the late 1970's, which is now frightfully huge. Having grown quietly in the background, it has become an accepted feature that no one gives any thought to anymore, even though its increase has become evermore phenomenal. The rate of increase has been hyperbolic.

In the early 1980's the global financial derivatives amounted to only a few billion dollars in notional value. By 1993 this small figure had grown to $15 trillion. Now, note this! The same amount that took all these 13 years to build up, tripled during next single year to nearly $45 trillion. That's a sharp increase. Today, this figure is at the $100 trillion mark with an annual turnover in financial instruments in the one quadrillion dollar range in notional value.*4 This adds up to a five trillion dollar 'trade' in gambling instruments (globally) at every single business day. The gambling mania has become so huge that the present exposure in financial derivatives is many times larger than the gross domestic product of the entire world.

The paradox is, that while the gambling orgy is expanding towards the $1,000 trillion dollar mark in annual financial turnover, the desperately needed funds for sustaining human life, which are relatively small, can no longer be found. Some governments have been so hopelessly caught up in the web of the gambling economy that the necessary funds can no longer be raised to keep hospitals operating, or to finance the production of food for people to eat, or to create the needed housing, or to maintain the essential infrastructures that a modern civilization depends on, such as water supply systems, bridges, railways, transportation networks, a healthy farming sector, a healthy energy supply sector, advanced medical research, basic scientific research, advanced research into new physical principles for advanced energy and materials production.

Society has grown into such a deeply perverted mythological sense of security that it feels secure, even as the gap between the assumed reality, and the physical reality, is constantly increasing. This gap is real. It is found in many important areas, not just in the financial world. Many of the world's presently producing oil fields, for instance, will become dry holes in a decade or two, while virtually nothing is done to advance the development of replacement resources. Ironically, the opposite is happening. The only viable option for replacing oil and coal as an energy source that provides the same or greater energy density with a near infinite potential - which is nuclear energy - is presently being sabotaged by every available means. The resource for nuclear energy is not only infinitely abundant, its application is also cheaper, cleaner, and saver, than any other form of large scale energy production on the planet, based on technologies that already exist.

The reality that one sees is rather sad. One sees that a gross self-denial has gripped the global society on this issue which has been carefully nurtured over the last three decades by the public information media of the oligarchic empire that has set the world on a course of devolution towards poverty and impotence for the greater security of its feudal structures. Instead of emphasizing the development of nuclear power on which mankind's future depends, many of the once started research projects towards this end, have been shut down, and those that were planned have been canceled for the lack of funding. The physical fact, however, cannot be bypassed that the world's oil resources are being used up, and that without large scale energy production, which is presently supplied by oil, a modern society cannot exist. Mankind is literally throwing its future away for the sake of saving money that has no intrinsic value anyway, by its refusal to develop the vital nuclear energy option. Moreover, even if the world's petroleum resources were infinite, nuclear power would still be a vital necessity to meet the growing energy requirements of the future of a normally advancing civilization, as such needs are increasing.

The public's present effort to prevent this development is a gross act of self-denial. The resulting poverty will invariably collapse the world-financial and economic systems, and with it civilization as well. Submission to this type of poverty is one of the greatest evils that a society can perpetrate against itself.

Instead of building and rebuilding the infrastructures for living, the present society has so withdrawn itself from the reality that supports its existence and become addicted to dreaming that this evil is presently enforced with great intensity. The evidence is everywhere. The financial system of the world is no longer engaged in supporting the physical economy that sustains life, but robs it intensively. The banks have become gambling centers, and the society's deposits in the banks have been put on the gambling tables while the roulette wheel spins. It doesn't seem to bother anyone that the average commercial bank's exposure in derivatives gambling is many times greater than all its depositors' assets combined. Usually the banks win in this game, often handsomely, because the banking sector controls the odds on the financial scene when everything goes normally. But when the game turns awry, the bank's huge profits become immensely huge losses that will help to disintegrate the whole interlocked world-financial system.

In its awful greed, society actually cheers when the stock market's value rises, as it does on a near exponential scale. Society doesn't recognize that stock indexes indicate the intensity of financial looting that is being perpetrated against it. Nor does society care that ever greater amounts of cash-inflow must be squeezed out of the real economy in order to maintain the necessary increase in value that keeps the bubble afloat - that keeps the 'investors' locked into this pyramid scheme that the stock-related markets have become. According to all evidence nobody cares about the cost of this game to the physical economy, that is draining the society's life-blood into the gambling market, and what will happen when the huge inflow into the market ends, when the illusion evaporates that enables the investors to command ever higher prices for their financial papers, when these papers will resume their real value which is in many cases the pulp value of the paper on which the notes are printed.

At the present time the world is in a true crisis situation as its strongly interlocked financial house, built to insane heights, is shaking at its foundation. During the last years many tremors have been felt throughout the system. In every case, emergency measures have been hastily enacted to repair the system. Many of these measures have come at a great cost in human terms as ever greater portions of the population have been driven into poverty, deprivation, even death, while the patch-up measures become more and more bizarre, showing an increase in insanity. Just think, can anything be fundamentally corrected by introducing evermore imaginative pyramid schemes into the system in an effort to hide the physical and social collapse that these schemes have created? Today, the entire world-financial system hangs on the thin thread of maintaining illusions that are self-evidently false.

What a wonderful foundation for civilization the West has created for itself with the 'tool' of speculation! The global society should be alarmed, because patch-up measures work only to a point, the point at which the house of cards collapses. The fundamental reality is, that the current system cannot be saved. By its underlying nature, the type of system that is currently running the world, is self-destructive. It is a terminal system, and it is functioning according to its design. No repair can be made to this system to prevent its natural self-destruction. It cannot be saved by any means. It is similar to a terminal patient. Death is a certainty, the only question is: when?

Mankind has but two options.

One is to reject the present system. For this, mankind must restructure itself onto a renaissance defined basis of infinite economy. The other option is to do nothing. This is the default option. It includes patching the system up until it disintegrates - which, in real terms amounts to doing nothing.

The first option involves saving the nations and civilization from a potential chaos which promises to be worse than the worst in history. The anarchy that erupted in Albania when a government promoted pyramid investment scheme was recognized for what it was, does not present a good yardstick with which to judge the chaos associated with the disintegration of the entire world-financial system. In Albania, currencies still had value. When the global system disintegrates, this may not be the case. In a statement by the central bank of Switzerland, it was said that the bank is retaining its gold reserve as a possible payment medium when currencies are no longer accepted.

The first option, however, that of mankind saving itself, is not a painless one. It involves taking the dying world-financial system through a bankruptcy reorganization in order to erase all fictitious values while keeping the essential services intact that support the functioning of society, such as business operations, wages, pensions, etc.. The pain in such a bankruptcy reorganization comes from equalizing the huge gap between the super-inflated mythological values of the leveraged-up financial aggregates. The pain occurs when the inflated values are brought into the context of the physical reality of an economy that has been so thoroughly looted that it can no longer maintain itself and fulfill its purpose.

The gap between the imagined and the real is presently immensely large. The pain will be felt most by those who presently believe themselves to be super-wealthy, but have to realize that there is no substance behind the facade. Thus, they will scream. But, they will live. Of course, the same reality will unfold when the presently bloated up financial bubble pops. They will 'scream' in pain when this happens, but they may not survive the onslaught of anarchy that results in such a catastrophe, and die with the death of civilization.

For the rest of humanity, the workers, the pensioners, the business people, etc., the global bankruptcy restructuring would bring a renewal of living, like the tender rain upon a parched field. It would bring life to the dying economy and hope to those who are presently at the edge of despair. If this happens, few of society will even recognize that their life was in danger, whose life will be spared the near certain death that unfolds in every major situation of anarchy. They may even join the chorus of complainers.

It is unlikely, however, that the needed restructuring can be achieved, because, as stated before, no politician or legislator has the courage to call an end to the illusion that there is value to be found, where no value exists. Any president or national-leader who would attempt such a thing would likely be assassinated in short order.

Actually, only two leaders are required to enact such a restructuring. There exist three major power-blocks in the world today. The most formidable is the British Empire, the organizational platform of the transworld oligarchy. The other two are the nation-state of the U.S.A., and China. There exist, therefore, at this moment, only two institutions in the world whose officers can effect a global financial reorganization. These are the President of the United States of America, and the leader of China. Against the cooperation of the two largest economies on the planet, the British Empire may not prevail.

Without a U.S./China cooperation, which is necessary also for China's self-defense against the Empire, China, is doomed, and so is the U.S.A.. But once this decision is made to cooperate, and to place the world-financial system once again on a foundation of national credit creation for the nation's self-development (rather than private credit creation by the banks), the rest of the world, which is presently collapsing under IMF/Maastricht austerity impositions, will likely join this union.

The second option is the default one. It results from doing nothing. It occurs when the actions outlined above, are not taken. What the world will be like when the entire world-financial system disintegrates on its own, and the value of many a national currency is put in doubt so that it is no longer accepted, can hardly be imagined. Since presently all social and economic structures depend on some acknowledged value in currencies, and on a functioning payments interchange system, the collapse of these could be catastrophic. Without the flow of money no food is delivered, no transportation fuel can be offered for sale, and no law-enforcement can be provided, to name just a few areas which are essential for a society to live.

Some rescue effort may perhaps be attempted, in the last minutes, while the disintegration happens. Unfortunately, these efforts will most certainly be focused on saving the dying financial system, rather than to save the lives of society; nor will such efforts solve anything. History tells us that Rome could not be saved with Roman policies, no matter how strongly the rulers imposed them, so that the very attempt to affect a rescue on this platform brought the disintegration closer. The same will always hold true.

In a sense, the ruling financial oligarchy has put its cards on the table in April 1997, when it hastily initiated a conference, called: "Reinventing Bretton Woods Committee." This event appears to have been set up as an organizing committee, controlled from London, for creating a totally private IMF that is designed to control all the money in the world. This may sound like a joke, but it isn't. The proposed structure is designed to eliminate all governmental influence in monetary affairs, except when the banks run into trouble and need government funds to be rescued. By the proposed process the institution of the sovereign nation-state becomes effectively eliminated from the planet. The new private world-monetary structure would be modeled after the old colonial system in which British gun boats were sent out to enforce debt-collection from delinquent subject colonies or nations.

While such a system may indeed be enacted some day, as virtually no one cares to oppose the trend, it doesn't present a real option for avoiding the world-financial disintegration. The proposed course would repeat the tragedy in which Rome tried to reverse its economic collapse by employing an intensified version of the same policies that led to the collapse in the first place. It seems the world-society has not yet learned that Rome could not be saved by Roman policies, and that the attempt to do so resulted in a vastly greater loss of life than would have occurred had the Roman system been scrapped at an earlier stage.

The same principle that destroyed Rome applies also to today's imperial oligarchy and its policy structures of feudal monetarism. The longer the system rules the greater will be the loss of human life before the system disintegrates, and much more so afterwards.

The bases are loaded!

This, then, is the situation in which humanity finds itself in the present age. Standing on the opposite field, against the oligarchic trend, a movement is afoot that lobbies for recreating a world-wide system of sovereign nation-states that own their own currencies and credit for direct investment into infrastructures and the nations' self-development. International financial stability would be guaranteed by some sort of gold-related fixed exchange rate system. The oligarchic team, acting in vehement opposition, aims to turn the world-financial system into a vastly more devastating gambling casino than it already is, but it has no chance of succeeded as the time is running out for this type of system.

Which team will have a home run will likely determine the course of mankind for the next 500 years to come. If the feudal system prevails throughout the calamity of the financial disintegration, mankind may suffer the same tragedy that Greece had suffered, which had lost 87% of its population under Roman rule. If, on the other hand, the infinite system of economy becomes accepted, which is self-amplifying by means of interest free direct investment into infrastructural and industrial development, than the whole world will achieve the kind of phenomenal economic development that China has begun, where vast new resources for living are created.

Never before in history has so much hung in the balance for mankind, than today. Nor has ever before in history existed a greater opportunity for breaking the murderous yoke of oligarchic rule than exists today, now that the feudal world-financial system crumbles and is near its disintegration. To use Richard Wagner's language, the "Twilight of the Gods" has begun. Wallhalla is in flames. The waters may soon become a flood when the Rhine maidens will take back the gold that was stolen from them at the beginning of Wagner's Ring cycle.

It is sad and ironic that most people have closed their eyes to the unfolding of immense movements that will determine their destiny. It is as though much of humanity has been artificially put to sleep, especially in the West, by its controlling manipulators who aim for the disintegration of the physical support system that maintains the life of humanity. This blindness has been created as a cloak under which it intends to reduce the world-population to the level of the feudal ages. Of course, once the regression process is fully under way, even if mankind awakes from its slumber, it becomes infinitely more difficult for it to rescue itself.

Humanity must realize that its strength lies in its intellect, which has presently been put to sleep with mythologies and irrational expectations. In a very real way, mankind is led like sheep to the slaughter. It is here where the fundamental turnaround needs to be effected, where mankind needs to find its always-open door to infinity. No physical limits exist that tie humanity to a terminal system. Still, the footsteps for a reverse in its present course will not unfold automatically. These footsteps must be taken consciously, courageously, and intelligently.

The development of the spiritual dimension of mankind, the human intellect manifesting itself in scientific and cultural thought, has been the great underlying factor for every period of progress throughout human history. During such times the tide of feudalism had been turned back. This essential element in mental development has been fundamental to every renaissance that ever occurred, especially the spiritual renaissance in which Christ Jesus played a leading role. Out of this renaissance Christianity emerged that put a nobler face on humanity than can be found beneath the crowns of all the royalty and princes that ever asserted themselves above their fellow being.

Periods of mental development.

All true development has a mental beginning and a mental driver. Christ Jesus would most likely not have emerged on the world-scene without the background that was created by the cultural and scientific revolution during the Greek Classical Period that immediately preceded the unfolding of the Christ era. Nor is it likely that the Golden Renaissance would have unfolded without the mental foundation that both these historic eras provided. Without the Renaissance, in turn, the institution of the nation-state, which became the foundation for today's advanced civilization, may not have come about. In other words, everything that is reflected in our present civilization and supports human life today is the result of a vast chain of the development of thought. Human freedom is not possible without it.

Few people recognize the vast contribution to human living which mankind's various periods of renaissance have provided. Without them 'man' may never have stood on the moon or developed a physical economy that enables 5.5 billion people to exist on this planet. The fruits of development that mankind enjoys today, in spite of all problems, has been the result of advancing discoveries and scientific breakthroughs that elevated the societies' physical existence. By raising the physical platform, society, in turn, has set itself a stage for the advancement of creativity, enquiry, and learning, that amplifies the mental development of a person by which the physical platform becomes raised again. This results from the advances in science and technologies, which in turn open up evermore abundant new resources, such as do not exist on the natural plane, which are created exclusively by human endeavors. By such a process the development of civilization becomes self-amplifying.

Today, humanity maintains a high state of development, but the support is lacking to advance it further, to increase the development, to match the dynamics of the expansion of life, and to go beyond it. The consequences of this interruption in scientific and technological progress are mounting up.

Worse, still, are the political consequences of the retarded mental development of society. They effect the infrastructures for human living and depress the creative and productive capacity of society. These 'deficits' are already felt in more than just trivial ways. The entire world-financial and economic system is caught up in the depressive effect of the consequences of restarted mental development which are becoming evermore critical with each stage of devolution, portending a collapse of the entire economic system on a global scale.

The fact is, that constant mental development is essential to human existence. It is a certainty that without mental development the human society would still be quite small in numbers and exist at a very primitive stage. From the first moment, however, when our prehistoric ancestors created a tool out of a stone, a chain of self-amplifying mental development was set in motion that has continued, though periodically interrupted, throughout all succeeding ages.

During the stone age, the early societies discovered ways that enabled them it to raise the physical plane of their existence with primitive technologies that gave them access to food resources that had been inaccessible before. As the ages passed, continuing development allowed humanity to create more advanced technologies that opened up vast resources for living of a type that had never existed before on the face of the planet. This development has taken humanity to the present stage at which, 5,500 times the number of people are now able to support themselves on the same planet that once supported but a few people (app. one million people) for several hundred-thousand years who subsisted on the meager offerings of "Mother Nature" in a non-technical type of society.

Without humanity's mental development, which has been largely a path of discovery, the physical scene of society would have remained at the primordial low level, limited by the poverty that corresponds with a sparse environment that offers few resources. If humanity were still bound to this primitive platform, the harshness of life would continue to limit the human life-span to an average of less than twenty years, as had been the norm for hundreds of thousands of years prior to the beginning of mankind's mental development.*5

The difference between such a life, and that which is the norm today, is as vast as the difference between night and day. Humanity stands tall, today, with near infinite resources at its feet and a life-span reaching upwards to a hundred years and beyond. This difference, which is immensely great, has been furnished exclusively by the development of thought. Ironically, it is this very development of thought that is put on hold, today. It is being overpowered by the imposition of modern mythologies, abuse of the sciences, the termination of basic research, and the shutdown of true humanist education. The deculturalization is even manifest in the decay of art, music, and literature. In this arena, politics, philosophy, science, and physical living merge into one, in which a single element affects the whole.

Humanity's scientific and technological development, that began quietly during the stone age. Its has raised the physical platform throughout the ages to the present level which is far above what the primitive earth had provided during the pre-stone age times. But what do we make of it?

Well, there exist still ideologies that define 'man' as a glorified animal, such as a higher ape. In fact, some very highly placed, powerful, and influential people hold this perception about man. But in its mental development, which really defines the nature of man, humanity stands tall and alone. The human species is the only species on the planet that has developed a metaphysical capability by which advancing thought has enabled the species to create its own resources for living as it had uplifted the physical scene that supports its existence. In contrast to this demonstrated capacity for self-development, all the animal species, without exception, remain bound to the meager resources of the primitive world that man has left behind millennia ago. Animal life, in the wild, continues to be a struggle for survival, a merry-go-round of eat and be eaten, exposed to drought, cold, heat, hunger, disease, and predation.

The questions that come to mind, in this context, are imperative ones: Does humanity, or do we individually, still utilize the grand capability of the human intellect to the fullest? Do we continue to lift ourselves above the primitive plain? Do we use our capacities wisely? We have developed great cultures with enormous capacities to produce food, energy, housing, art, finance, transportation infrastructures, and industrial economies, but have we reached an impasse?

We should thoroughly realize that what we take for granted today does not exists on the natural plane. All has been created, and must continue to be created, daily. Except, now, we face a breakdown in the structures of creativity. Has our mental development halted? Is regression a natural component of life?

The answer must be, no. The answer must be, that whenever the development of thought is halted, scientific and technological progress stops and the physical scene falls into regression and disintegration. In other words, we, as the 'tallest' species of life on the planet, have by no means reached a terminal stage, we merely suffer the consequences of a serious self-neglect.

Most of the Empire's economists argue to the contrary. They insist that mankind has reached a physical impasse and development must stop. They insist that industrialization must stop and be reversed. Under the guise of "fighting inflation", the economists who actually believe in an unfolding impasse urge the nations to cut back on their investment into self-development, and invest in the financial markets, instead. Except, by following this advise mankind shoots itself in the foot, as it were, since its entire existence rests on created physical resources that result from scientific, technological, and infrastructural development. Without these created resources humanity simply cannot exist. Without its continuous self-development, out of which new resources are created, humanity has no future.

But, what about inflation? The feudal economist insists that inflation is linked to advanced industrialization and development. Does such a link exist, and is our future limited by it?

Yes, there is a link between economic development and inflation, but this link shows the opposite effect to what is believed by the feudal economist. Let us explore it..

Take a certain product with a volume of X and relate this to the available money supply Y. From this relationship a certain product to price ratio results. If the money supply is increased and nothing more is done, a price inflation occurs as more money is now available for purchasing the same physical volume. If, however, the money supply is expanded for the specific purpose of increasing the produced volume of the same product (through the creation of scientific and technological infrastructures and education, all of which increase the productive capacity of society), than the volume of goods that are available tends to rise dramatically faster than the money supply has been increased to achieve the new productivity. The result is that prosperity increases, rather than inflation. This interrelationship, then, sets the stage for an infinite economy with ever increasing development and prosperity.

If, on the other hand, the money supply is increased, and the increase is immediately absorbed by the financial markets in order to increase speculation, financial inflation occurs. The price for physical goods may remain unaffected, but the financial values will rise. In this case more money is available for trading a fixed volume of financial aggregates, by which the prices of the financial aggregates are driven up. The volume of the financial aggregates that are available for trading does not expand through the process of trading. As more money is poured into a market of fixed size, only two things can happen: either the price of the aggregates becomes inflated, or the money decreases in value. One or the other happens, because the actual value of the market, which is physically determined, remains the same.

The process of creating financial inflation, because it has no direct effect on the physical economy, is deemed desirable as the financial inflation is mistakenly regarded as "profit." Indirectly, however, financial inflation does draw monetary resources out of the physical economy. It deprives it of its vital flow of investment funds as these become absorbed by speculation. By this effect, the financial inflation increases even more. Now, having been robed of its life-blood, the size of the physical economy shrinks. This means that financial inflation becomes still larger, since the financial markets theoretically represent the physical economy.

The end result of this spiral of financial inflation is horrendous. The physical economy moves rapidly towards a terminal state and the physical world fails to function, while financial inflation has created a huge bubble of hot hair that is stressed to the breaking point. This is where the world stands now.

If one adds to the declining economy the accumulative debt, and debt service costs, we will find that, currently, the physical economy represents in general a liability to an investor, rather than an asset. When this occurs the effective financial inflation is infinite so that the entire value system becomes meaningless. Near this point the entire financial system tends to disintegrate.

In this sense only, can it be said that the society has reached an impasse. Its infinitely inflated financial values cannot be saved. Nor can the system be saved that created them. Financial inflation cannot be repaired because the values within such a system are not real. The entire financial system is doomed to disintegrate for this reason, unless it is taken down in a bankruptcy process where the objective is to salvage whatever is still functioning productively.

Only once in modern history have highly inflated investments actually been salvaged. This occurred in the early years of the United States of America, when the nation's subjection to British free-trade had bankrupted it. At this point the U.S. government committed itself to the principle for infinite economy, as presented earlier. Within the dynamics of the momentous economic development that was taking place in response to this policy shift, earlier investments that had become relatively worthless in real terms, actually became valuable again.

Right now the Western world is in a state of inflationary impasse. The impasse, however, can be overcome by restarting the economic process on the foundation of the principle for infinite economy. For as long as the infinite principle is rejected, financial inflation will continue until the system disintegrates. There is no alternative to this, other than shutting the system down.

Right now, in most cases financial inflation has become infinite, which means that the system is near the point at which it becomes 'unglued.' Most of the mountains of debt that have been generated under the influence of financial inflation have lost their relationship to reality and simply cannot be repaid. Thereby, the assumed value of debt-instruments is likewise infinitely inflated. In many countries the situation is so bad that not even the interest can be paid, which is frequently rolled over into new debt to create the illusion that the system still functions.

Now, when a person's income, or that of a government, out of which debt is to be repaid, shrinks to zero, or becomes a negative total as obligations are factored in. Then, the available liquidity for debt repayment diminishes to zero. At such a point it no longer matters to the borrower how large a debt is being carried. Once there is no income, the entire debt becomes unrepayable, so that it makes no difference in this case, whether the debt owed is $1 or $1 billion. Much of the world's presently accumulated debt falls into this category, or is very close to it.

Infinite financial inflation invariably causes the financial system to collapse. We are in the middle of it, right now. The Western world is in an accelerating regression which is shutting ever larger segments of the population out of the productive economy, as this is deemed unnecessary for creating wealth. The result is unemployment. Whether the system will collapse totally depends on how prudent society is. Will it follow the Roman model and staunchly insist on intensifying the course that caused the problem in the first place, or will it adopt the infinite model of economy that China has presently adopted, by which it has achieved the fastest rate of economic growth experienced by any industrialized nation on the planet in the last half a century, if not the whole century? According to Doug Casey's financial newsletter, China's 10% rate of economic growth has also been achieved with virtually no income tax imposed upon society.*6

Many periods of regression have occurred throughout history, but none were as deadly as the current one threatens to be that is unfolding in the western world. Now doubt, some historic crashes had devastating consequences, but they must be judged as mild. It is interesting to note, here, that the time in which these crashes occurred were also the terminal periods of the reigning empires which had caused them. At such junctures a window of opportunity opens up for a radical departure from the defective policy foundation, and the adoption of a totally different one. We are presently at this point. If the West is wise, it will choose the infinite model that China has already chosen, and align itself with China in the creation of a new world-financial system that can serve as a foundation for the economic development of the whole world. If the West is foolish, it will allow the imperial policy to continue which will take it to ever deeper levels of regression and reduce the world population to the level of the 14th century. This radical goal for population reduction is indeed on the agenda and is being pursued from high places.

The contrast between the deadly population reduction goals of the Empire's rulers, and the brightness that is presently achievable through infinite development, which is in our grasp, should cause corresponding actions. One hopes, therefore, that the enormity of the difference will awake humanity from its slumber and cause it to choose life, rather than the default option which leads to the destruction of billions of human lives.

Periods of mental collapse and awakening.

During the period of the Roman Empire the progress of the Greek Classical Period ground to a halt. No major new scientific breakthrough was made throughout the whole of the Roman Period. The Roman economy, operating under a feudal imperial system, actually regressed throughout the entire Roman Period while inhumanity became rampant and human life became cheap. As a consequence of this dual trend the population levels collapsed, and the economies literally ground to a halt. The devastation became so extensive at the end that the Empire could no longer maintain its existence. So it was that one of the mightiest empires in history fell, not in a great battle, but was overrun by a relatively small invading force that put an end to it all.

The world economic collapse that grew out of Roman policies actually lasted long after the Empire, itself, had vanished. It culminated into a period of dark ages in which new empires emerged that carried forwards the cycle of Roman insanity, such as the Byzantine Empire, the Mongol Empire, the Venetian financial Empire, the Ottoman Empire, and not least of all, the British Empire which still rules the world to the present day on the same policy platform that had spelled disaster for Rome and every other empire that succeeded it and had imposed death upon countless millions of human beings.

Every empire, to the present one, has had a devastating influence on the self-development of humanity and hindered the realization of its vast potential. Instead of scientific and technological progress, the imperial axioms promote feudal monetarism, economic and scientific depression, and a rise in poverty. The principles of imperialism have always had a negative impact on population growth and environmental quality, promoting Malthusian ideologies, Eugenics policies, primitive living and tribal mentalities. The imperial platform of feudalism was traditionally based on wealth-extraction from the land by the sweat of human labor. The focus has never been on uplifting society as a whole, through development of new resources and advanced technologies which increase the productivity of human labor in large measures. To the contrary, the policies of imperialism have always been associated with population reduction and the creation of poverty.

The promotion of mental and physical devolution of society is the natural outcome of the imperial platform. The imperial system maintains itself by looting. It loots the land and the populations that live thereon. Speculative and other types of financial looting is merely the modern extension of the age-old looting process of the imperial system. It still is a terminal system. The modern Empire's feudal financial system has never been associated with the platform of development that uplifts civilization. It develops nothing. Its focus is on stealing and on maintaining an environment that is ideal for stealing.

The imperial system, and the infinite development system, are total opposites by their very nature. It can be said, therefore, that there are two distinct economic systems operating in the world today, that have totally opposite effects on society. One system is founded on metaphysical principles by which the power of the human intellect is utilized to uplift the physical platform that supports the lives of society. In this system the resources for human living are created by scientific discoveries and technological development. The opposing system, on the other hand, is not founded on metaphysical principles but is purely physical in nature. It creates nothing. It develops nothing. It merely confiscates what has been created. It operates as a parasite. This is the system of empires. Its principle is feudalism. Its operators are the oligarchs and aristocrats that feed off the labor of humanity and reward it with oppression. They are the rich and influential, who, today, dictate to society the shape of its civilization and the intensity of its poverty. We find their face in the transworld oligarchy that profits from the destruction of nations through postindustrialism, free-trade globalism across unequal-wage-cost economies, child slavery, and debt-bound financial austerity.

In proportion to the intensity of the parasitical looting, the feudal imperial system (that is now the global system) undermines and negates most of the moral and metaphysical process by which civilization is created and advanced. Under the yoke of imperial parasitic oppression and slavery, all forms of scientific progress and technological development, invariably fall by the wayside. The drudgery of toilsome servitude inhibits the creative mental processes and advanced scientific discoveries that develop the resources of the mind. In such an environment the foundation for the creation of physical wealth decays, and with it decays the potential of society to establish itself on a platform of infinite resources. This is were we stand today. This is the type of regression that the western world has gone through and is still experiencing. It is the protective setup behind which the global feudal Empire maintains its power.

That the imperial system is utterly destructive to society has been demonstrated for centuries. It has also been demonstrated that its parasitic devastation, nevertheless, provides for a tiny minority a sufficient platform for an opulent life-style. The parasitic relationship, therefore, tends to be maintained by the oligarchy at all cost and by every means. Thus, the parasitic relationship continues to be maintained until the parasite destroys its host. Society, however, cannot operate on this basis. It cannot exist by stealing from itself. The Mosaic commandment: Thou shalt not steal, is more than just a religious demand. It is a demand of Principle that is fundamental to mankind's survival and civilization.

In other words, society cannot survive on a foundation of feudalism, including feudal monetarism. It needs to be motivated by totally different axioms than those that drive the imperial system. There exists no external resource for mankind, beside itself, that it could loot. Humanity must maintain itself by using the resources it carries within itself, the human intellect by which its physical resources are created. This process of national self-development had been intensively implemented during every period of renaissance.

We have both these processes in operation, today. We have advanced human development in progress in China, and looting oriented axioms destroying society operating through the transworld British Empire. The systems that these two processes represent are contrary to each other. The British system is committed to shut down the Chinese and Asian economic development, and the optimism that unfolds from it that threatens to ignite the dormant spirit of humanity and spark a global development that would spells the end of the British transworld, imperial system. These two systems are, therefore, locked into combat with each other.

It is important to note, also, the difference in the type of development that characterizes each system. The parasitic feudal system develops into evermore intense forms of looting, whereby it becomes a self-terminating or negative development system. The infinite development system, on the other hand, is self-amplifying. It leads to evermore expansive development by its very nature.

The historic significance of the present time is, that the feudal system is near the point of it natural disintegration, while the infinite development system has been firmly established and is making rapid progress. This means that a window of opportunity has opened up for eliminating feudalism from the face of the planet. Historically, these opportunities are rare. World Wars I and II were set up under a policy that was deliberately designed to prevent the economic development of humanity that had been attempted in those days. In those days, however, the imperial structure was strong and had made significant gains through its earlier takeover of America. In contrast, the world-development process had barely moved beyond its infancy stage. Thus, the contest was lost for humanity from the outset and the British imperial system became stronger.

Another such opportunity had occurred at the end of World War II. At this time the contest was more even. The global development policy of Franklin D. Roosevelt had been grounded on a solid demonstrated achievement that had saved the world from Nazi fascism, while the feudal system had been dependent on this development system for its very survival. Had Roosevelt lived, the British Empire would have been finished. However, the Empire wasn't at the point of self-disintegration at that time. The moment that its dependence on America had ended, when the war was won in Europe, Franklin D. Roosevelt was put into a coffin and the imperial system reestablished itself.

Today, the economic development system is strong once again, its achievement is impressive, and it is well protected by an intelligent leadership. The feudal system, in contrast, has destroyed every other nation of the planet, economically, through deindustrialization, austerity, and debt. It steals the nation's resources with ever greater audacity in a move towards total cartelization, aided by terrorism, austerity, modern opium wars, and even large scale genocide. Thus, it is ripe to disintegrate. Here lies the opportunity.

Of course, it is also possible that humanity lets the present opportunity go by and allows the feudal system to reestablish itself after its financial foundation disintegrates. When this occurs, woe be to humanity. The imperial plans for humanity include the most massive depopulation that has ever occurred on the planet.

The axioms of imperialism, which have ancient roots, have changed little over the ages. They still promote primitivism and slave-labor exploitation, as well as free-trade related looting. Wherever such policies become the dominant force, they create the mental and physical environments that lead to economic genocide through poverty and prevented technological advances.

The Empire's population reduction demands are, therefore, not based on the supposed need for securing the stability of civilization, but are designed to take down the state of civilization to a level that is less threatening to the Empire. The feudal platform cannot exist on a progressive basis, the basis on which mankind is able to create for itself the needed support systems that a growing population requires; that has no tolerance for feudalism and imperialism which breed poverty and impotence, such as are conducive for looting.

What is new, in this modern age, is the vast scope of the population reduction demands that the present imperial policies place on mankind. Under the present imperial setup, the world is to be subjected to the greatest depopulation process in history that involves the elimination of 40% to 90% of all people on the planet. This may be hard to believe. Still, one hears such dreadful demands uttered in royal houses, and in institutions that are supported, controlled, or owned by the transworld oligarchy of the British Empire. Its stated demand for global population reduction is in the range between two and five billion people, which according to the Empire's elite must be eliminated to "save the earth."

This intended murdering is on an unbelievably large scale, and the selected time-frame is short. Most of the "depopulation planners" talk about a time-frame in the order of two generations. This involves the murdering of 100 million people per year plus the equivalent of all new births, sustained over 40 years.

This is monstrous, and unattainable, you may tell yourself. Indeed, the goal is brutal, but as brutal as it may seem, it is actually proportionate to the brutality of the Empire's historic geopolitical operations by which ten million people were murdered for such minor reasons as to prevent the construction of a rail link, designed to stretch from central Europe to Japan, for which World War I was launched. This destructive process was actually unleashed twice for essentially the same fundamental cause. World War II was launched for much of the same reasons, in which another fifty million people were sacrificed in order to prevent economic optimism from erupting again, and with it the physical development of the world. For this goal, alone, Adolf Hitler was financed into power by the Empire.

The magnitude of today's depopulation demand shows the same vast overkill and disregard for human life that has become traditional with imperial demands and its operations to fulfill them. Nor are today's horrendously brutal demands by any means out of the range of the achievable. The Empire literally owns the public's consciousness, which it controls. It owns it by means of its ownership of much of the world's media, such as newspapers and television. It also owns the leading environmental and ideological organizations of the world; organization that have a strong influence on public thinking and emotions. By means of this communications monopoly, the Empire has acquired the capability to only shaped public thought to its wishes and created a willingness throughout the public to accept the most horrendous sacrifices, but it has also achieved a subversive influence in the financial realm. Through these channels, the imperial apparatus has promoted myths upon myths which obscure the immense volatility that had developed in the world's financial and economic system, in order to keep the system alive, by which its exists, by sheer force of will. These two subversive processes run largely in parallel and are deeply intertwined. It may well be, that when the Empire's financial system disintegrates, it murderous ideology will continue on its own, like the Roman ideology has after the fall of Rome. It is, here, where society must rebuild itself, where it must reclaim its identity, morality, and dominion. For this it must shut down the imperial operations that mold its thoughts and its conscience.

The centuries of dark ages that unfolded out of the imperial policies of Rome, which be repeated, foreshadow immensely dark ages on today's horizon. Today's prevailing policies are actually worse than those of Rome, so that the Rome generated dark ages may be light by comparison. In this sense, Roman history presents an awesome foreboding. The devastation and regression that the Roman Empire had unleashed in its time, that had turned the lights out for mankind for centuries, from which mankind may not have truly recovered, may yet pail into insignificance in comparison to the current potential for a death spiral that the Empire's global financial and economic disintegration may unleash.

The nature of the disintegration.

The presently impending financial disintegration, apparently, is not intended by the Empire. The looting world-financial system is its 'main sail.' It is its power. It supports its existence. Nevertheless, it is doomed, and the transworld Empire knows this.

Since 1994 the Empire has been in a mode of restructuring its base of wealth from paper into physical equity, such as hoarding rare metals, strategic minerals, food, etc.. Then it went on a global binge of buying up all the essential industries around the world by forcing their privatization. Right now it is engaged in buying up the world's prime mineral deposits and energy resources. It has also achieved near total control over the world's food distribution through its cartel system. Hardly a scrap of food moves on the planet that the Empire's cartels have not a hand in transporting. And most importantly, it has created the political and legal structures by which the looting of humanity is being protected.

The transformation of the Empire out of financial assets into 'hard' assets appears to be nearly complete. Nor is there much left in the world that the Empire considers worth buying. In the mean time its financial and economic system is being kept alive by all means possible, though it is hopelessly bankrupt as it has bankrupted the world. It will likely be kept alive until the Empire's restructuring of its wealth is complete. Then, it will most certainly be allowed to disintegrate, since it, too, has been looted to the bone at this point. The world is very close to this stage right now.

When, finally, the world-financial system disintegrates in a chain of irrepairable failures, the event, however, opens up an opportunity for mankind for some corrective reactions. One of these reaction may be to restructure the world onto a platform that reflects the model for infinite economy. The Empire's goal, of course, will be to revamp the old feudal platform of parasitic monetarism, into some new form which continues to destroy humanity that the Empire feeds on. This has traditionally happened throughout history.

One way or another, unless mankind grasps the present opportunity to reverse course, the implementation of the Empire's coveted population reduction will occur. The implementation won't take a great deal of effort. Numerous environmental organizations, with well established terrorist factions, stand ready and eager to help fulfill this goal. This terrible goal has been fully adapted, in principle, by most environmental organizations, who see it as their own goal. The murderous environmental myths, that have been carefully implanted in the minds of the global society, centered on the notion that the planet is vastly overpopulated, will aid the murdering. What all this means, is, that when the big environmental movements are drawn into the terrible game of active population reduction, the public will likely stand idly by and support the process.

The strength of the public's own antipopulation commitment is well demonstrated by its support for the global ban of DDT and CFC, which had once elevated and protected human life. These creations of the human genius have been banned without any real evidence that they have caused the slightest harm to the environment, or people. All this has already been admitted. In other words, these substances have been banned for their dramatic effect in saving human lives. This, too, has been admitted by some of the more honest members of the scientific community.

That one might see a dramatic increase in antipopulation activity in times of a major crisis, especially by activists of the environmental movements, cannot be ruled out. In fact, this escalation is almost certain in an environment of anarchy when long-established axioms, rather than sanity, become the motivating force. If the world-financial disintegration is not prevented by replacing the defective global system with a new one modeled after the infinite development system, anarchy and its effects cannot be prevented.

The needed restructuring could possibly be achieved in the early stages of disintegration. The world-financial system can be restructured in hours if the infinite system of economy is chosen, under which a nation provides credit to itself without having to borrow credits from the looting feudal institutions. On this platform all the essential functions of the physical economy can be preserved when the feudal system disintegrates. Wages can be paid, pensions can be secured, essential obligations can be honored, and credits can be created for the much needed redevelopment of the economy, even the world-economy, which includes the reindustrialization of the once rich nations that are now reeling under debt, crime, and poverty.

The restoration of something akin to a financial system, can also be retarded for weeks in the wake of the global disintegration. If the axioms prevail that all new funding must be borrowed in international competition, while the world-financial system is broke, a meaningful recovery can never occur and an escalating anarchy, by default, will become the global reality.

The difference between the two modes of response to the presently unfolding crisis becomes the determining factor between life and death for countless millions, if not billions of people. The potentially greatest crisis in human history looms on the horizon, today, while every conceivable effort is made to hide its unfolding from humanity lest sane responses should prevail.

The public, of course, will not be spared the impact of the unfolding reality. In a global disintegration crisis, when you go to your bank, its automatic bank teller machine won't dispense anymore money, or what it dispenses will be deemed largely worthless. The banks will likely remain closed, never to reopen, at least not with your account balances intact.

If this financial deprivation lasts for more than a week, law enforcement will break down. Food, can no longer be procured, at least not with money, but perhaps with violence. In such an environment will be relatively easy to speed the Empire's coveted population reduction goals. With a few well placed bombs at strategic points of the nations' electric power grids and gas distribution centers, a tiny minority of ideological extremists can end civilization in minutes. Countless people will freeze to death when this happens in winter. Evidence suggests that many frustrated ideologues are more than eager to volunteer their services for this sort of thing.

The life and death of millions will then be held in the balance of a few madmen. The modern electric power grids, for instance, are among the most highly visible and most indefensible of all the civil structures that are most vital to society. Without electric power most people will not only have no means to heat their dwellings, but will also have no means to cook the little food they may find. They will have no light at nigh, no water and no sanitation, as these systems are electrically powered, in most cases.

If the financial shutdown is maintained for weeks many millions of people will die from starvation, exposure, and violence, especially so if the disruption occurs in the winter. In such an environment of anarchy great masses of people can be destroyed with virtually no effort at all, and will likely be destroyed unless the conditions are prevented that present these opportunities.

How immensely destructive the breakdown of the civil infrastructures can be has been demonstrated during the Empire's infamous Dessert Storm war against Iraq. In this war very few direct casualties resulted from the bombing campaigns. The bulk of the more then one million civilian victims perished from the aftermath of the carefully planned strategy of bombing the nation's civil infrastructures into oblivion. People died of pandemic diseases related to lack of clean water, insanitary conditions, and from malnutrition. The hardest hit were the children and the elderly. It is interesting to note that right from the first night of the bombing the nation's civil infrastructures were targeted, especially electric power generation on which a civilized society depends.

The irony is that people have been conditioned not to believe that the financial system is in danger. They see the evidence with their very own eyes, but argue against the wisdom that would enable them to prepare a rescue package for their survival, or that would cause them to demand that a new financial platform be created according to the model for infinite economy. Thus, it is important to understanding the reality about the system that is about to disintegrate, and why it is in danger of disintegrating, in order to overcome the carefully cultured false sense of security that makes society extremely vulnerable. To most people, the system appears to be rock-solid. "Aren't the banks raking in billions in record breaking profits? Aren't the markets gaining strength?" people say.

No, they are not gaining strength. They are increasing in volatility. Sky-high stock values indicate a sick economy. They indicate that the equity base is constantly shrinking against investable resources. They represents a measure for insanity. They represent the fever that has gripped society in its disease of devoting their lives to inflating air-filled bubbles.

Sky high stock values also indicate how worthless the average investment has become. Traditionally, crashes occur when 'investors' realize that nobody is willing to pay a premium for what they have to sell. At this point they try to cut their losses and get out of the game. Except, there are no buyers flooding into a market when values are dropping. Some may decide to sell all their wares for whatever little they can get, or a forced to sell whatever they have to cover their obligations, by which values are driven down sharply.

Such crashes can be avoided, to some extend, by manipulation. Towards this end the big funds, banks, and imperial manipulators, pour money into selected elements of the market when prices are falling. In 1996 the U.S. stockmarket had been 'rescued' three times in this manner. These types of rescue operations have become almost routine by now. Indeed, it is profitable for the big players to manipulate the market when huge derivatives contracts are keyed to it, by which equally huge profits are wrought. But in times of a larger crisis the manipulation becomes less effective and tends to leave the scene open for a crash. Manipulation also fails when the volatility within the system is so great that two or three rescue operations have to be staged simultaneously. In such a case the manipulators may not find the needed money. They do already steal, beg, and borrow all there is, so that in a larger crisis they may not get enough money together to rescue anything. That's when the financial domino blocks begin to tumble throughout the system. In the financial world, where everything is interlocked, this may prove to be disastrous. A crises of such larger magnitude quickly leads to anarchy.

Does all this sound too far fetched to be true? It shouldn't. Suppose you have invited guests for dinner, and just before the dinner is served, the dog wets the carpet. This problem is easily fixed. You delay the dinner by five minutes and clean the mess up. Harmony is restored. All is under control.

But suppose, during the delay caused by cleaning the carpet the frying pan catches fire, flames hit the ceiling panels, they also catch fire, which then melt, and drip down and set the carpet on fire. Before you know it the whole house becomes an inferno. Such a crisis can unfold within minutes, right? But in such a larger crisis you do not have the resources to rescue yourself.

The world-financial system can also disintegrate totally on its own, in 72 hrs. by its interlocked processes. It may likely to do this, if the stockmarket doesn't bring it down first. Already, its volatility is increasing by the day. People are dying under austerity conditions; the global debt is becoming evermore unmanageable and unrepayable; unemployment is skyrocketing and taking its toll; the productive economy is shrinking while financial profits climb into the stratosphere; food supplies become critical; most nations have already begun to default on their obligations. The system becomes patched up by evermore imaginative schemes for refinancing the unrepayable debt obligations; soon the banking system begins to collapse under the weight of non-performing loans from real estate and stock financing; war unfolds; energy supplies are disrupted. And what happens when all these things come together? Chaos unfolds! Money becomes no longer accepted for payment in such a crisis. Then, the social catastrophe begins. In other words the world-financial disintegration can occur even without the stockmarket causing it.

Once again, this assessment may appear wildly out of the range of the rational and practically possible. Such a projection is indeed too horrendous for any moral person to contemplate, which also appears to be totally unsupported by visible evidence. A close examination, however, reveals that the exact opposite is the case to what is visibly evident.

The paradox of this age is that mankind elects to aspire to policies that assure doom, death, and devolution. Instead of reaching for the 'stars' and beyond, in terms of its economic development, which is well within mankind's present potential as China is illustrating so vividly, most of humanity is locked into a spiral of devolution. Thus, there exists a basis for hope that a reversal of the current trend may yet be achieved before anarchy takes over.

One has probably as much justification to be optimistic for a bright future for mankind, as one has justification for expecting a human catastrophe unequalled in history. Humanity is at a crossroads position today. Two choices lie before it. As always, this choice is deeply rooted in the mental domain, in the axioms that shape the policies of society, whether they be based on scientific reality or on the mythologies cultured by empires.

The choice that lies before us, today, includes several options, although these do not include an option that can forestall the end of the current world-financial system, which is doomed by its own nature. Its end is certain and imminent. Even the leaders of the financial elite have acknowledged this fact; not in words, but in action. The world's oligarchy, centered around the British Empire, has acknowledged the imminent end of its world-financial system, from which it has profited immensely, for centuries. It knows that the present speculative, feudal financial system has nothing left within it with which to maintain itself. Its response, therefore, has been dramatic and amounts to a clear admission of the fact that the system is doomed. Its response has been to switch its assets from paper equity into physical goods, hoarding gold, food, and mineral resources, especially the 'strategic' metals and minerals that are essential for the functioning of a modern society and its economy. With this shift it aims to preserve its wealth and gain an ever stronger control over humanity.

The Empire's conviction that its present financial game is over is also evident by it's evermore massive campaign to entice the public into investing all it has into the very game that the oligarchy has recognized to be doomed. This project has worked extremely well, so far. The public has jumped into the market with all it got and financed the Empire's withdrawal from speculative paper. It off-loaded the Empire's useless junk unto itself, obliging the Empire in its effort to cash itself out before the system disintegrates.

These are the realities of today.

The impact of policy decisions.

Policy decisions, more than any other factor, determine the welfare of individuals and society. In a most profound way, mankind's mental capacity affects its physical welfare. It makes little difference, in this context, whether the mental capacity of mankind affects policies of state, or affect the policies by which people govern their individual lives. The principles involved are invariably the same, and their effects are the same in that they both determine the physical state of human existence. They affect people's health, prosperity, comfort, even whether they will live or die. Global policies, of course, have universal consequences.

The society's actions reflect the various axioms that a society is taught to subscribe to, which invariably correspond to its rulers policies. Axioms are assumptions that are accepted to be true, that define a person's perception of reality. Axioms are much cruder than hypotheses, in that they are not necessarily based on any scientific process of investigation or proof. They represent merely opinions about what is real and valuable.

These opinions, even those that are deemed to be fundamental perceptions about reality, are usually artificially generated for political purposes, or to support religious structures. For instance, the axiomatic perception that the earth is flat and is the center of the universe, was once universally held many centuries ago as though it reflected reality. This perception also supported a certain ideology of the church which kept the mythology alive.

The axioms that were centered on the believe that the earth is flat had affected mankind's marine exploration for centuries, as well as its political/religious power structures, and thereby hindered its self-development. The more modern false axioms are usually centered on policy decisions that are totally out of context with reality.

The development of scientific perception, in later years, has challenged mankind to examine its axioms in the light of the higher proof that creative discoveries have established. By this process - a process that expands understanding - technologies have been developed that have raised the entire platform of physical existence, which false axioms had previously prevented prevented from developing.

The progressive understanding of fundamental principle has always been a powerful force in human existence, in that it enables the creation of resources for living which had never existed before. Nuclear energy, for instance, was not an option during the industrial revolution. It hadn't been discovered at this time. It didn't exist. This vastly more powerful technology that would have obsoleted coal based energy production was totally unknown at this age, and so was steam power unknown during the stone age.

Mankind's energy technologies, in turn, affect its agricultural potential, which, of course, determines the potential population density. The growth in world population, therefore, is directly proportional to the development of technological capability, especially in the field of energy production.

The reverse of this principle is also true. If the process is reversed by political, ecological, or financial imperatives, mankind is bound to experience an escalating collapse of its population size, such as we see already beginning. The current financial austerity that is decimating the world economies is causing millions of unnecessary deaths. Poverty is the major cause by which human life is being denied to exist on this planet. One scholar*7 has indirectly urged the creation of a formal measurement, that measures the intensity of poverty in terms of "years of human life denied."

It may well be true that more people have died in the 20th century as the direct result of faulty economic policy decisions, than have perished in all previous centuries in wars. Forced underdevelopment, economic destruction, inadequate housing, hunger, crime, drugs, etc., are all potent killers. Inversely, civilization would not exist, as it does today, without the supporting base of a vast array of right policy decisions that have created the infrastructures for living that still support most of the world-population, many of which had their root in the great periods of renaissance that laid the foundation for scientific progress through which civilization was raised to new levels.

Such periods of progress are usually coincident with a strong development in language that enables advanced communication and the contemplation of higher and more complex ideas. The works of the Greek poet Homer are a good example, who developed a language in which people could think in complex terms and examine their axioms for truth. On the foundation established by this single man the Greek Classical Period unfolded that gave rise to an impressive procession of renowned metaphysical explorers, such as Solon who pioneered the idea of constitutional law, or Socrates and Plato who may have staged the platform that helped Christ Jesus to emerge, whose ideology, in turn, became centuries later the central driving force for the Golden Renaissance. Our present civilization may well rest on a foundation that was set up by Homer more then two and a half thousand years ago.

One can find the type of development that Homer started, repeated in Italy, centuries later, through the works of Dante, on whose background the Golden Renaissance unfolded. The Golden Renaissance, in turn, gave mankind the institution of the nation-state which has been unsurpassed to date as a foundation for a people's scientific and technological self-development. The fuller realization of mankind's potential may be in part a product of what Dante has achieved in his time.

If one considers the enormous impact that mental development has had on mankind's physical existence, metaphysics comes to light as an important subject to explore, from a scientific standpoint. This involves an exploration of all the diverse areas where the effect of intelligence impacts on human existence, both in a progressive and healing manner, and in a regressive and destructive manner.

The importance of this subject is not falling by the wayside in our modern, scientific age, but is instead escalating. The dynamically increasing world-population, according to the normal patterns of unfolding life, places on mankind a growing demand for resources in food, transportation, housing, employment, health care, education, financial stability, social order, even the physical security of life itself. The impact of intelligence, or the lack thereof, in every one of these areas is enormous. It effects the entire physical platform of existence. Here, healing becomes a subject that no longer concerns just disease, but must effect attitudes and perceptions that shape the policies by which the society lives.

Disease is no longer the major problem that is effecting the well-being of humanity. Poverty, starvation, and economic deprivation, impose more agony and untimely death than all other factors combined. Mankind's approach to its self-healing must cover also this scene, not just the medical dimension of healing. Naturally, the exploration of the fundamental principles that support economic and physical existence involves also an exploration of the principles for the healing of disease. The two cannot be separated. Healing and politics combine into one single broad spectrum. They are not as separated as one might assume, since both are aspects of policy that pertain to certain underlying universal laws which cannot be ignored without consequences. The aspects of physical and economic existence, health, and intelligence, are all fundamentally interlocked in a broad pattern of metaphysical effects - the effect of man's mental capacity or intelligence on physical existence.

A series of books has been created to explore the effects of intelligence on human existence, that this book is a part of. The series explores the principles for healing that have been discovered by the leading edge scientists in the field. It also explores mankind's failure to achieve what is minimally necessary to assure the survival of it's civilization. The book series covers a broad range of topics, ranging from economics and politics, to 19th century Christian Science healing, including topics of statecraft, scientific government, and self-government.

This volume, the first of the series, is devoted to exploring one of the great paradoxes of modern times, the world-financial disintegration and its contrast to mankind metaphysical capability, by which the modern paradox may be resolved.

The paradox is fundamentally a simple one. From the moment on that early man began to develop tools and techniques for using them, man began to uplift the physical platform of his existence. Thus, a trend was established that enabled more and more people to exist on this planet by means of resources that were created, which did not exist naturally. The power of intelligence, thus, changed the boundaries of limitation. This trend has not ended to the present day. It appears to have no limit. Apart from some glaring exceptions, mankind's overall history has been one of progressive development, of advancing sciences and technologies, developing evermore and greater resources for living that have made human life easier, more secure, and longer in duration. By this dynamic development, biological life as we know it, has broken a significant barrier that had confined it to the limits of this planet for billions of years. By way of the quantum jump in intelligence that unfolded through human life, biological life has created itself a window to infinity, though which may expand across the universe. In contrast to it stands mankind's bizarre commitment towards its self-destruction.

In the most recent period of modern history, mankind's age old commitment to self-development appears to have ended. A regression has begun that has brought to light a certain paradox in economics that is becoming increasingly bizarre. This paradox has many faces. On the financial and economic front we see a dramatic collapse in the productive economy while at the same time the financial markets have achieved steep increases in valuation and profitability. The financial world no longer represents the physical reality. It represents a hyper-reality that is isolated in its cyberspace of speculative profiteering, but which has the side effect of draining the driving force out of physical economy that is essential for mankind to exist, that is essential for providing food, shelter, clothing, transportation, and whatever else is necessary to sustain life and advance education and culture. A mythology has been unfolding that is diverting the financial resources from essential areas into games of financial gambling, whereby mankind has begun, literally, to steal from itself.

On the ideological front one sees a similar paradox. One sees a growing world-wide commitment to primitive existence, poverty, starvation, and economic genocide, promoted by a financial system and corresponding political ideology which are evidently build on defective axioms. It should be obvious to rational thought, that, whatever destroys humanity is contrary to its fundamental interest and is defective by design. Mankind's interest lies in life, not death, and in the development of its potentials, the potential of intelligence to create the needed resources for living.

By a strange perversion mankind has committed itself to policies that reduce the creation of resources, and create an environment of poverty to the point at which the needed resources can no longer be developed for sustaining life because the necessary infrastructures have been destroyed, or have been allowed to decay. As the result of this ongoing economic and biological slide into poverty, one sees a weakening of the human biological system that sets up a vast breeding culture for the breeding of new and evermore exotic diseases. Another paradox is, that while all this is happening, the society's medical and biological research institutions and health-care facilities are becoming shut down in record numbers. Mankind has committed itself to a radical disinvestment in one of its most vital platforms for self-protection. In fact, we have quite a significant paradox here.

A similar paradox comes to light on the food supply scene. One sees a vast disinvestment in the world's food production capability, in order to save money. The basis for this is the same as that which is destroying the medical health support systems. The international price war in food items, that the free-trade-GATT system has ensured, has shut down all meaningful infrastructure development in farming around the world, except in the case of China and some associated nations. In the West, there remains but a minuscule amount of private investments in farming, and this little is designed to increase the looting operations by the big Anglo-Swiss cartel companies that play farmers off against each other, and the world's food exporting nations against each other. This reflects the ancient divide and conquer method by which the British Empire has imposed itself upon the world.

The year 1996 is significant in that it ushered in a sharp increase in food shortages, by means of disinvestment. Food shortages had until this time devastated mostly the poorer nations. In 1996 a phase shift has begun that will soon bring the consequences of the growing political insanity home to the dinner table of even the once rich nations of the West.

The paradox is, that mankind has committed itself to a policy platform by which it is starving itself to death for monetary reasons. Life has become too expensive to be supported! What a paradox, indeed.

Is it really possible for a people's policy to become more absurd? Hardly! Even Hitler's policy was less absurd, who merely starved those to death, in his slave-labor work-camps, whom he wanted to murder anyway. This was gruesome enough. A society's normal response, as one would hope, should be to preserve life and to develop its potential, rather than to focus on financial profits that have lost their relationship to reality, such as is the case at the present time. It is ironic that society struggles to accumulate meaningless profits by means of which its life is put in danger.

Much the same absurdity that rules the world-food

scene, can be recognized on the energy front. In this arena mankind has launched an ideological war against the survival of its civilization. While the planet's fossil fuel reserves are being depleted in some areas of the world, at an ever increasing rate, because the normally emerging new energy resources are prevented from being developed, one hears cries for conservation with a strong commitment to shut down much of the presently available energy production, even as nuclear energy development, on which mankind's future energy supply depends, is being sabotaged on the global front.

Fortunately, for mankind, the world's oil reserves are significantly larger than intial estimates indicated. In some cases the oil fields are still growing, even while extensive extraction is going on. Between 1976 and 1996, estimated global reserves grew by 72%. The great oil pool of the Middle East more than doubled in size during those 20 years. There is scientific speculation in the form new theories unfolding, about that existence of a geological process deep inside the earth where oil may be created under very high temperatures and pressures from primordial sources.*8 Indeed, the case of the primordial oil is supported by the observed fact that some planets have large concentration of methane in their atmosphere without having had an history of biological life that would account for the creation of these carbon based gases.

Nevertheless, oil alone cannot supply the energy requirements of an advancing society. It is at best a stop gap measure. Nuclear energy alone can meet these demands, except this cannot be realized without the requisite devotion to the large scale developments that will be required for it. Without large scale energy production a modern, population rich society, cannot be maintained. The type of economy that is needed to support a growing population cannot be powered with windmills and solar cells. These toy-like structures are vastly insufficient to drive the industries and transportation system that a highly developed society cannot do without. To shut down continued energy development (as is happening today) is equal to committing murder upon humanity by policy, which a crime for which many Nazis were once convicted and hung at the Nuremberg trials after World War II. They were convicted for crimes against humanity, because they were deemed to have known, or should have known, that their policies would cause the death of large numbers of thier targeted people.

The absurdity of our age is that mankind has adopted a similar policy platform against itself. Even now, as severe energy shortages are beginning to be felt around the world, mankind casts aside the nuclear energy option that can save its existence and power the global economy for millions of centuries to come, not just the few decades or however long oil and coal will last us. By its decommitment to advanced energy development, mankind has committed itself to economic devolution and to a corresponding collapse in population numbers. The paradox is, that with infinite resources at its reach, mankind has committed itself to abject poverty and massive death by deprivation.

These paradoxes are real, and they are all driven by axioms based on myths and generated believes, rather than on scientific discoveries and demonstrable proof. Even now, the present global commitment by mankind to shutting down is vital self-development in energy production threatens to have dramatic consequences in every realm of human living, because the energy sector provides the foundation for the economic machine by which humanity meets its needs. The current antinuclear hype, and the global disinvestment in developing advanced nuclear energy resources, such as fusion power, has created a volatility on the global energy scene that has the potential, all by itself, to topple the current world-financial and economic system that has become exceedingly fragile.

By its current policies, therefore, mankind has set itself on a collision course with the physical reality that it no longer regards as important. The current trends that are developing in every major area of the economy, from finance to energy, and from farming to transportation - all of which are essential for sustaining human life - show a growing fascination by mankind with fantasies and mythologies. By this trend mankind has separated itself from all that is real and supports its physical existence. For instance, while the society has chosen to halt its efforts for maintaining and developing the resources on which it depends, it cannot escape the consequences of this decommitment to reality. That such a separation from reality is not long sustainable is plain to see.

An alert humanity would recognize its need for healing in this sphere. Indeed, this may happen. It is no secret that every single excursion into virtual reality games ends at some point, usually when the game runs to its conclusion, or the power is turned off to the machinery that creates the illusions.

One cannot escape the underlying claim of reality, for primacy in all its dimension. Tragically, mankind is presently set on a collision course with this claim of reality. The fundamental principles of reality are not negotiable. They cannot be mocked my human will. They will invariably assert themselves, even if mankind collides forcefully against this assertion, as the captain of the Titanic found out.

The Titanic is sinking

The impact of today's impending collision with reality may be similar in nature to the impact which sank the 'unsinkable' Titanic when it collided with an underwater iceberg. The comparison, of course, sounds like a cliche as it has been used far too often. Still the correlation disserves to be explored for the similarities involved in a number of important aspects.

The Titanic was the crown jewel of the White Star line. It was the finest, largest, and most advanced ship afloat, a sea-going luxury hotel, a marvel of engineering, the ship-builder's proudest achievement. It was considered so totally unsinkable that it wasn't even deemed necessary to provide a full compliment of life boats for its passengers. The ship was constructed with a double-bottomed hull divided into 16 watertight compartments of which as many as four could be flooded simultaneously without endangering the ship's buoyancy.

The ship's maiden voyage, in a way, opened a new chapter in maritime travel par excellence. It became in many respects a continuous celebration that reflected the ship's greatness. Festivities were going on deep into the night. At 23:00 hours on April 14, 1912, however, while the night was still young and the salons filled with gayety, music, dancing, games, or exciting conversations interlaced with the finest foods and champagnes, a little noticed event occurred. At this time of the night only few people had retired. The ship was ablaze with lights and resounding with life. Even deep below in the great boiler room, the scene was one of ceaseless activity. Stokers continuously fed the long rows of furnaces that supplied steam for the mighty engines that propelled the 44,000 ton ship at a speed of 22 knots.

Its location was 150 Km to the south of the Grand Banks of Newfoundland, when the event occurred. She was enroute to New York. Everyone was certain the ship would arrive in record time. No doubt, activities had been planned for an early arrival and for the countless manners in which people's lives normally unfold at their destination. As it was, only a few of the passengers had heard the grinding sound shortly before midnight when the dream of the ship's unsinkability began to be shattered and the personal destination of most people aboard became an unattainable goal.

While steaming through a field of icebergs the Titanic collided with a submerged ice-formation as it travelled at a speed of 22 knots. The impact was such that the ice ripped a 300 foot gash into the side of the hull, flooding five of the 16 watertight compartments. From this moment on the ship was doomed. It could not be rescued by any means available.

Although the festivities continued for a while after the impact, the Titanic sank at 2:20 hrs. the next morning. In less than three hours the fastest and most exquisite luxury hotel on the seas; the pride of its industry; a credit to its builders; a hope come true for the travelling public - the unsinkable ship - had become a torn wreck lying silently at the bottom of the sea. It had descended to its icy grave with 1,513 of its passengers still aboard.

This utter tragedy resulted not from a failure of the leading edge technology that the ship represented. It resulted from policy decisions that failed to reflect some fundamental principles.

The speed with which the situation deteriorated for the Titanic is not unlike what may be experienced when the tightly interlocked world-financial system disintegrates. In the hours before the disintegration begins, the world-financial system will appear normal to most people, and fully functional. The values of the financial aggregates will likely be high, investors' confidence will be high, no ripples will marr the surface of the waters to reveal the iceberg that lies beneath. The markets will likely be bullish at the day's opening. In fact, few may even take notice for some time that a collision has occurred. The tremors will be 'explained' away with technical jargons as a temporary "correction" or something of no great significance. Thus, only a tiny fraction of those who have put all their equity into the markets will let this equity go and head for the lifeboats. The reality is, in today's financial world-markets there are only a few scarce lifeboats available, far, far fewer than on the Titanic.

For its 2,224 passengers the Titanic had a lifeboat capacity of 1,178 spaces, of which no more than 60% was actually utilized. Only 711 people survived the unfolding chaos.*9 When the chaos finally ended, all that remained afloat were a few tiny boats filled with a desperate lot of people surrounded by darkness and a deep silence that dissipated their sounds of agony.

Many factors had contributed to this tragedy, such as the belief that the ship was unsinkable. Are we not told the same about the world's financial system, today? The system is fail-proof.

A complete rescue of the Titanic's passengers would have been possible had the radio not been turned off aboard the Leyland liner "Californian" that was just 20 miles away from where the collision had occurred.

When the world-financial system unravels itself in the space of a few days, or even hours, there will likewise be no rescue force standing by to rescue humanity from its folly.

In a sense, the present world-financial and economic system is already sinking. It has had its bottom ripped out in a collision with the unyielding reality of fundamental principles that cannot be ignored without consequences. Like the Titanic that could not have been saved by any means from the moment on when it collided with the iceberg, so the current world-financial and economic system cannot be saved from the effect of its collision with reality, no matter how sound it still appears. The 'ship' is doomed. In fact, there are forces moving within it that threaten to blow it up, even as it sinks.

The current world-financial system can no longer be repaired. Still, no one acknowledges the fact that it is sinking. Unlike the sinking world-financial system, the Titanic's fate was not the result of any fault in engineering, design of the ship, or workmanship in construction. It was the best ship ever built up this time. Its fate was determined by a mental failure that is very much shared in today's world the captains of the world-financial system. The fate of Titanic was determined the moment its captain ignored the realities of the environment he was operating in. The moment he plotted that fateful course that would bring the Titanic through ice infested waters at a break-neck speed, the ship and its passengers were at risk. The captain, evidently believed the mythology he was taught, about unsinkable ships. Much of humanity believes the same about the present world-financial system. People believe they can ignore the fundamental principles of economics, at will, without ever having to face the consequences.

The Titanic sank as the result of massive structural damage that the collision had incurred. The same has already occurred, financially. The rapture in the Titanic's hull was so large that the ship became flooded at an unstoppable and ever accelerating rate. The same has occurred financially through derivatives speculation.

The Titanic, which was considered unsinkable by all the experts in the field, sank on its maiden voyage. Can the experts in the field of financial speculation be believed when they tell the public that their economic system is shock-proof and crash-proof, while in secret, the subject of a global systemic failure is intensively debated?

In one important aspect the present world-scene differs from the sinking of the Titanic. If one considers current developments, it is evident that a major collision with reality has already occurred. Some people actually recognize that the ship is sinking. They see evidence of its bottom having been ripped out. But, unfortunately, the raging debate that has ensued is focused on saving the ship, rather than on saving the humanity it carries.

In this, today's story differs from the sinking of the Titanic. The lifeboats are not sought out. While people are dying on the lower decks as the ship sinks deeper and deeper, the captain announces that extraordinary 'profits' are being made in the casino at the aft launch, and that the evening movie is about to start at the theatre, and pizza is being served on the promenade. Those who have noticed the shrinking distance between the sea and the promenade deck, may become alarmed, but are ridiculed and told to have their eyes examined.

Denial upon denial, of the reality and its unfolding evidence, has become the fastest growing phenomenon in today's world that is governed by a growing insanity and ever growing dangers. When the financial system disintegrates, with what shall people buy food? Without the supply trucks rolling in constantly, how long can the cities survive?

Chapter 1: A Platform for Understanding the Dimension of the Crisis

The American religious leader, Mary Baker Eddy (1826-1910), had incorporated in her works a platform for exploring significant interrelationships in a scientific manner. She had outlined a structure in the form of a four by four matrix, but had never talked about it, or directly mentioned it in her writings. Thus it remained largely unknown for over a hundred years. While its details are explored in Volume 3 of this series, a portion of it is relevant to understanding the presently unfolding economic and financial crisis. Therefore, it is briefly brought into context here.

A four by four matrix can be perceived, variously. It can be seen as a structure of four rows of horizontally interrelated elements which share a common characteristic, or it can be seen as four columns of vertically interrelated elements which may share a common purpose or development. In her outline for the structure she presents a list of four "cardinal points" which can be associated with the rows of the matrix (see Appendix A, Figure 1). These four domains, in the present context, can be associated with the four types of self-interest that are characteristic for certain types of society, as noted earlier. Appendix A, Figure 2, has this association incorporated.

In the top row, the concept of "the Word" (the Principle) "of Life, Truth, and Love" is naturally associated with infinite development. On the next lower level, "the Christ, the spiritual idea of God" relates to a spiritually alert society, the renaissance society, the outcome of which was the creation of the nation-state. While this domain is largely missing, as the institution of the nation-state is being destroyed and the idea behind it obscured, the association that presents itself here highlights the principle for reestablishing the lost domain.

The third row is defined as "Christianity." Here a dividing line is drawn, right through the center of it. This denotes the nature of Christianity which has devoted itself to great evil for religious or ideological causes, even genocides in which millions may have died. It has also been a force for immense good, for advancing civilization and ennobling the self-perception of mankind. Thus it incorporates an upward trending characteristic, and a downward trending characteristic.

Mankind's pursuit in speculation system incorporates both trends. One trend, which is financial speculation, destroys society as it drains financial credit resources away from the physical economy by which people live. The other trend of speculation, which is the original design of stock-market investment, provides an upwards trend. It is a speculative trust that puts investment resources into the physical economy for the development of society's potential. It's all done in the hope that shared profits from the developing enterprises will justify this trust. One might call this type of investment, development speculation.

The bottom row is identified as "Christian Science." Mary Baker Eddy had a problem with defining disease. She understood, in concept, that God, being recognized as the All-in-all, "infinite Mind," cannot be the author of failures (a contradiction to infinite Mind) so that the whole concept of failure exists only within the human domain. Thus a form of science is needed to deal with the human failures that God can have no knowledge of - that deals with aspects that fall outside the reality supported by fundamental Principle. The science that pursues this exploration, Mary Baker Eddy, called Christian Science. Feudalism and Oligarchism are naturally associated with this domain as they have no fundamental principle in support of them. They are artificial structures that are fundamentally failures by design, employing unnatural processes, and their existence is artificially maintained through use of stealing and legalistic powers.

Now, since the domain of speculation is divided into two halves, it becomes apparent that each half can be associated with its adjacent domain, whereby two diametrically opposite structures emerge (shown in Appendix A, Figure 3). It also becomes apparent that the two structures are in fundamental conflict with each other by their opposite natures. It becomes further apparent that both structures are powered by respective forms of 'speculative' activity, which is pivotable in distinguishing their natures. This is indicated in Figure 3.

It was noted earlier that the matrix can also be perceived as four columns of vertically adjacent elements, to represent the developmental progression of a certain idea. If one adapts this concept to exploring the nature of feudalism and oligarchism a rather interesting picture emerges, as shown in Appendix A, Figure 4.

An oligarchy has two main goals: to loot society, and to maintain its power. Each of these can be divided into two columns. The looting system has two major components: colonialization (the cartelization of resource industries and banking), and slavery (free-trade economics, debt-bound economics, money-estate economics). The power maintenance system can likewise be divided into two components, or two columns, according to the two 'pillars' on which the oligarchy's security rest: creating poverty, and creating impotence. It requires these two pillars to prevent the normal development of society that would put an end to oligarchic looting and the Empire's existence.

At the present time, poverty is created through deindustrialization, which includes devolution of education, mysticism, and deculturalization. Each one of these areas is intensely pursued. The other pillar is impotence. It is created through depopulation, which includes manipulated environmentalism, gang to gang warfare, terrorism, fascist genocide, and the denial of economic development. Another phase of creating impotence, is assassination.

Each one of these areas is intensely pursued. In fact, each of the four columns is of equal importance to the Empire. The oligarchy appears to be fully aware of this, as each of the four projects is pursued with great, and near equal intensity.

The four projects, however, are also well obscured. The most obscured, naturally, is the project of creating impotence. For this goal two world wars were created. The results, although, disappointed Bertrand Russell who complained that wars proved to be ineffective for depopulation.

Depopulation has been preached by the Empire for well over a century. Bertrand Russell was a relative late comer to the game. The foundation for the depopulation ideology was laid by Malthus, Darwin, and Galton. Their antipopulation theories, such as the eugenics theory, have furnished the excuse for the murdering of tens of millions of human beings, like Hitler's extermination of the Jewish people. Today, a new Hitler, the self-made President (dictator) of Uganda, Yoweri Museveni, is reaping another horrible harvest of death for the Empire in central Africa, under its careful guidance. Massive genocides are also planned for Russia, North Korea, Brazil, and all the western (once) industrialized nations. Different methods appear to be planned for the various nations. In Russia and North Korea a depopulation process is already far afoot through induced starvation. In the industrialized nations the depopulation goal is presently pursued by means of environmental objectives, such as through the Global Warming myth for which the use of fossil fuels is to be cut back or eliminated, without an alternative in nuclear energy production, to make up for the loss.

It cannot be mentioned often enough that without large scale energy use a modern economy cannot function. By curtailing energy production the world's population becomes deprived of its means for existence and becomes left to die. If fossil fuel pollution was the real target in the environmental game, then, nuclear energy production would have been proposed as an alternative. Nuclear energy is safe, pollution free, more efficient, and utilizes a near infinitely available fuel resource. But, this is not what has been happening. Nuclear energy is as much under attack, today, from the environmentalists camp, as fossil fuel energy use is.

Assassination is another powerful process the Empire employs for creating impotence. A single assassination can totally alter the economic/political landscape and turn the mightiest potential development process into dust, overnight. The effectiveness of this process is has been demonstrated by the death of U.S. President Franklin Delanor Roosevelt, which was officially by natural causes, but is widely believed (without proof) to have been the key assassination of the century. In other words, it was the perfect crime. No clues were left, all evidence was obscured. It is inconceivable by any rational mind, however, that his death was not caused by assassination. Coincidences with such perfect timing simply don't happen.

Roosevelt was probably the most powerful man on the planet at that time he died. He held in his hands the fate of the British Empire, which he despised. His policies had been the key factor in the defeat of Hitler. He had also declared war on the British Empire, and had made this quite plain to Winston Churchill. In other words, he was the number one death-threat to the Empire. By the time of his death (or assassination), the war in Europe had been won; the Empire was saved. America was no longer needed. Furthermore, Roosevelt would surely never have allowed the atomic bomb to be used, as it was used, for a demonstration exercise. The point is, the Empire's existence and its objectives were both put at risk by this single man. It is inconceivable that the empire would not make every effort to pull off the perfect crime when its very existence hangs in the balance. It is inconceivable that the one man who holds the key for the future just lies down and dies at the most crucial moment in history, by which the Empire was saved and the whole postwar world became altered.

After Roosevelt's death (assassination) the entire postwar scene became totally reversed. Before his body was barely cold criminal elements were at work to overturn his policies for global development. His diplomatic ties with other nations, towards this end, were dismantled literally within days. These countermanding processes proceeded so swiftly, that they had evidently been planned far in advance.

How powerfully an assassination can alter the political and economic landscape can also be gleamed from the following consideration. Imagine what the world would be like today if Roosevelt had lived and carried out his policies. The British Empire would have found no place to exist within the sphere of global economic development, the Cold War would never have begun. The grave financial crisis that the world if facing, today, would never have developed.

Assassination is one of the main security tools in the feudal oligarchic system. It was used to eliminate five U.S. Presidents to date, who stood in the way of the Empire's objectives. It was also used to eliminate most of the progressive leaders of Africa around the time of the Kennedy assassination. Whenever key objectives, or the very existence of the Empire, are threatened, assassinations are carried out that alter the political and economic landscape.

Where is the limit? you may ask. There probably is none. For an empire, to which the genocide of millions of human beings is an acceptable price for achieving its political objectives, the death of a single person causes no raised eyebrows, especially if that person represents a huge liability to the Empire. From the imperial center, no one ever resigns and lives. The same holds true for presidents who oppose it. In Hitler's days, those who went 'astray,' died mysteriously, or often not so mysteriously. Foreign presidents fit this pattern as far as the Empire is concerned.

The imperatives for the imperial goals, such as creating impotence across the world, supersede, as the Empire sees things, the 'petty' concerns of a 'lower' order. Imagine how much richer the world would be had President Kennedy not been assassinated, but had he served out his two full terms in office. The Vietnam War would have never developed; the world-wide real estate bubble would have never been inflated, which crashed into a sea of defaults; investments would have been directed towards the industrialization of the world, rather than its pauperization. Japan wanted to do this on its own in later years, but was prevented, and told to invest within the sphere of the imperium, by which process the real estate bubble was born that nearly destroyed Japan's entire banking system.

Another imperial process for creating impotence and depopulation is tied to the abuse of science in connection with environmentalism. While Africa has become a killing field and the world accepts the massive genocide, the process of shooting, clubbing, and hacking people to death wouldn't be acceptable in the U.S. and in other developed nations. Nor do such methods need to be applied, when the same result can be achieved by slowly taking away the infrastructures on which the modern economies operate, eliminating efficient insecticides, fertilizers, refrigerants, and fossil fuel energy production. People will die on their own if you destroy the resources by which they live. Environmentalism has already proven itself to be an excellent tool for advancing this murderous goal.

Gang violence is another one of the Empire's favorite tools for killing people. An example of this was the Taiping Rebellion in China, a British sponsored, a British programmed, and British armed peasant revolt against the Chinese government. The revolt erupted from the economic devastation forced upon China in the form of indemnity demands at the peace treaty for ending the British Empire's (first) Opium War. At first the Empire collaborated with the rebellion and used it as a lever to gain evermore extensive concessions from the Chinese government. But instead of allowing the rebellion to succeed in its goal of overthrowing the government, Lord Palmerston launched his own strike against Beijing (the Second Opium War), destroyed the imperial estates, and then, supported the Chinese military with his own mercenary forces, in order to squash the Taiping Rebellion from which it had greatly profited.

By this process of induced gang and 'countergang' warfare, the Empire depopulated China by several tens of millions of people who perished in an orgy of incredible carnage as the Taiping had conquered most of southern China, and in the secondary carnage that followed when the rebellion was squashed by the British who created it in the first place. The leader of the British mercenary forces was none other than infamous Chinee Gordon who eventually received his just reward during a much later British attempt to size the Sudan.

With the crushing depopulation of the Chinese patriotic movement, and the equally crushing defeat of the Chinese imperial government, the stage was now prepared to force the legalization of opium across all of China, which the First Opium War had not accomplished. This even more devastating assault on the nation which destroys the morals, the mind, and the body of its victims, unleashed a third wave of depopulation which might have been counted in the hundreds of millions had statistics of the devastation been tabulated.

The pattern by which China was crushed has been used many times by the Empire. The building up, and the subsequent crushing, of the Mau Mau uprising is but one more example. At the present time the poor people's pain in Brazil is being exploited towards similar ends. There are 40 million hungry people in Brazil, and

11 million unemployed, which the so-called Landless Movement (MST) aims to organize into a 100 million man force to seek revenge against the state, and against civilization itself, for the wrongs suffered over the years. Its ideological background is the Sao Paulo Forum, the Cuban based international terrorist apparatus whose roots come from the same 'mother' that spawned the Museveni group of mass murderers in Africa who share the Forum's believes in the 'virtues' of disorder, searing bullets, and blood-stained knives.

In Brazil, the imperial goal is the takeover of the nation which has some of the richest mineral deposits in the world. This echoes the imperial takeover of China, and in modern times central Africa. In the shadow of the 'depopulation' of China, the entire Chinese nation came effectively under British control - and this without the need for an occupying army - providing a steady flow of loot to the Dope Lords in London.

Cultural warfare.

The greatest threat to British rule in China, ironically, came not from within China, but from the republican spirit that emanated from the United States of America and found an echo in Chinese culture. As far as the Empire was concerned, that very 'dangerous' idea of patriotism had to be defeated. Because of patriotism the Empire had lost its North American colonies. It had become a force that proved virtually indefeatable. The Empire had lost every one of its three wars against it (the American War of Independence, the War of 1812, and the Civil War.) The British were fully aware that China was vulnerable to be 'infected' with the ideas of the American System which were in harmony with the long standing Chinese culture centered on the teachings of Confucius, Mencius, and their more modern extension by Zhu Xi. Thus, anew line of battle was drawn, on a new battle-field.

The battle involved searching through Chinese culture for an equivalent to the Aristotelian Enlightenment philosophy, and that of the Social Darwinists that supported the British empiricist ideology. They found Legalism, Daoism, and Daoist distortions of Confucianism, and they popularized them. They also send a particularly bright young Chinese scholar Yen Fu, to Britain, who was there indoctrinated in the most radical of British empiricism. After being sent back he became a devoted defender of immorality in science, statecraft, and economics, whose criteria for truth was found in wealth and power, rather than on the higher platform where man as a creator and discoverer opens his horizon to the infinite.

Yen Fu did not appoint his sponsors and masters. He launched an all out assault on Confucianism, glorifying Legalism and Daoism, and spend much of his life translating the writings of the empiricists and Darwinists of the West. His writings shaped the intellectual knowledge in China of what was considered Western thought. It shaped the thinking of Mao Zedong, who became a devoted disciple, not only of Daoism, but of the whole range of these destructive ideologies. The end result was Mao's great cultural revolution against rational thought, that became an orgy of persecution and mob murder which is estimated to have claimed the lives of 90 million Chinese people. This carnage, fortunately, ended the British rule over China.

During the period of recovery from the Cultural Revolution China remained receptive to western thought and suffered accordingly. It became subjected to IMF "shock therapy" throughout the 1980s, like the rest of the world. The same dismantling of the state sector was pushed upon it that has destroyed many a nation's strength: the privatization, the closures, the removal of protective tariffs, the deregulation of trade and finance, the termination of social support structures for food, housing, health-care, etc. - but soon, the Chinese rejected this outgrowth of western insanity.

China had not been spared the ideological warfare that had ravished the western world. It merely responded more intelligently. The same "post-industrial society" dogma was thrust upon it that has turned the industrial regions of Germany, Sweden, the USA, and many more, into rust-belts. It was suggested that China take a great leap forward and jump directly to the new age, to the low-technology industries of the future (the sweat shop industries for export, that were being "globalized' across the Third World). In response to this demand the "Special Economic Zones" were created that brought another wave of riches to British Hong Kong, utilizing cheap Chinese labor, but opening the country also to the western disease of financial speculation and profiteering. Thus the slogan was born: "To get rich is glorious." In reality income differentials became alarming and inflation ate away the standard of living of the vast majority of the people.

Out of this background the 1989 Tinanmen Square fiasco erupted. Intellectuals and students were out on the street demanding to be given a voice in the new China through the doors of a wider democracy. The public's support for the demonstrators was more in response to corruption in government and the growing gap between the rich and poor, than for ideological reasons. The ideological guidance came from a George Soros operated "think-tank" set up in Beijing. The demonstrators were driven by an economic crisis, but they had no understanding of what had caused it. In fact, they demanded that the IMF reforms be accelerated and intensified, which really had caused the crisis in the first place. Soon radicalism got the upper hand and scene became ugly. The brutal suppression occurred of June 4th, with the deployment of tanks and armed forces. The repression of a dispute that should have been resolved with reason, that itself arose out of a lack of political awareness by both parties, will remain a painful legacy that China bashers around the world continue to exploit, and likely will for years to come. The suppression, however, was one of the great victories over the Imperial design that China had won from this time onward. The unfortunate affair, thus, had the greatest impact on China itself, and it was a positive impact. It caused China to awake. In response to his subversion Gorge Soros was banished from China. Even, the IMF "shock-therapy" was beginning to be rejected, and the government moved away from its policy of promoting special economic zones. It made a commitment to develop the entire country.

The transformation was not sudden, by any means. As recent as 1992 a huge inrush of hot money into a poorly regulated stock and derivatives market became almost disastrous for China. But the general mood is in the right direction. Financial speculation has become severely restricted. Investment now flows into economic development, into the Three Gorges Dam, the railway infrastructures, the industrialization of the nation, and the Eurasian Land Bridge development program. The nation's commitment to 10,000 new infrastructure projects for its self-development has given rise to a brand new song of cultural optimism that was further enhanced in 1997 with the repatriation of Hong Kong. A new meaning is slowly developing for the old phrase: "To get rich is glorious." At last, this phrase is beginning to apply to the whole nation which may noon be the richest nation in the world and pull up the whole world with its progress.

The principle of the four columns

For defining the nature of the columns of her outlined matrix, Mary Baker Eddy provided a structure of four definitions that fulfills this purpose perfectly. Appendix A, Figure 5, shows these definitions in their essential meaning applied to the columns that represent the characteristics of oligarchism. It should be noted again that everything associated with oligarchy has no fundamental principle, and is therefore a negation of principle. The general column identifiers, therefore, point not to what oligarchism represents, but to the principles that oligarchism defies.

The principle for the first column has thus been identified as: "The love of the good and beautiful and their immortality." This relates to life and love which are brutally countered by the resource grabbing processes of cartelization, in the wake of which, frequently, poverty and genocide unfolds. Nothing more needs to be added here. The correlation fits perfectly.

The principle for the second column has been identified as: "The rights of woman acknowledged morally, civilly, and socially." The "woman" referred to in this text appears to be referencing the woman of the Apocalypse who represents generic man, that divine idea or image: "...clothed with the sun and the moon under her feet, and upon her head a crown of twelve stars (the stars of rejoicing)." This tall image on the divine idea (man) is totally negated by the very idea of human slavery, in whatever form or circumstance it may be pursued.

The nature of the columns is such that the outer column has its corresponding manifest in the adjacent inner column. Colonialism has its manifest in slavery. The creation of impotence, or the collapse of the natural power of society, has its manifest in poverty. Nothing more needs to be added, here. The interlinking in plain.

The principle of the fourth column, now, is identified as "divine Science" that takes the human thought and its expression, to the threshold of the infinite. It deals with "metaphysics taking the place of physics," which can be interpreted as a process in which scientific progress creates the advanced resources for human living. By this process the real power of society comes to light, the power of the human intellect as it unfolds the creative potential of the individual human being in which is reflected the nature and identity of God. A society's richest resource is always its people. Everything else is secondary. The very idea of depopulation and assassination acknowledges this principle by way of negation. The very power the oligarchy seeks to build and maintain for itself, through murder and assassination, is not power, but a fantasy that is actually a form of self-denial.

The fourth column has its manifest in the third: Impotence is manifest in poverty.

The principle of the third column is identified as "divine Science understood and acknowledged." The submission to poverty, deindustrialization, and cultural devolution involves the very opposite of what is understood in Science about the nature of man and the infinite range of his capacities as the tallest species of life on this planet. Deindustrialization, mysticism, cultural devolution, devolution of education, etc., are cruel jokes thrown into the face of humanity. They are insults. No principle supports them.

It is hoped that by shedding some light on the real principles involved, which oligarchism opposes, its nature will be understood, and its arrogant impositions be turned back and defeated, like the British fleet was turned back and defeated in the War of 1812. As presented in this chapter, the oligarchy has no real power of itself. It creates nothing, produces nothing, denies its natural strength as human beings, and can show no fundamental principle in support of its claims. It can only demand that society attributes power to its claim. It can ask for society's acceptance of impotence, poverty, slavery, and colonialization, but it cannot enforce them. Even its boldest projects that involve the depopulation of the planet and the creation of world wide poverty can only be achieved by the induced submission of the victims. It can never be forced. Every imperial war in the last several centuries, for oppression into slavery, for operations of looting, etc., could have been avoided by the application of fundamental principles that had already been discovered and demonstrated. The oligarchy's suggestions for accepting impotence, however, have been impressive and have been mistaken for power. Being devoid of any real power, the outcome of all processes built on false suggestion can be reversed. Cartelization can be reversed with nationalization in order that a nation's resources support the nation's own prosperity. Every form of slavery, as it is fundamentally artificial, can be reversed and be replaced with productive employment for creative development, raising a nation's own civilization.

The criminal methods, even the objective of creating poverty and impotence, can be dealt with in a court of law where reality counts, where fascist perpetrators have been dealt with and been hung, even in cases when they never committed a single murder with their own hands, but by policy. Likewise the creation of poverty through deindustrialization and devolution, can be reversed. No natural force in the world requires them. They are phenomena of voluntary subjections to suggestions. All of the imperial impositions can be overturned in the protected moral sphere of the nation-state, should society wake up to its potential and its right for freedom.

History presents a long chain of resistance to the British ideology of empiricism, libertinism, and Social Darwinism. At the time that Yen Fu was 'educated' in London, the pioneers of the American System of political economy, the Philadelphia Interests centered around Heny Carey, were engaged with plans to develop all of the Eurasian continent (in the late 1870's). A political alliance was being forged with leading German and Russian circles. Henry Carey was the economist who had guided Abraham Lincoln to start the industrialization of the North as a means for defeating the slavery oriented Confederate system of the South. The republican leaders and others associated with the Philadelphia Interests had even planed to extend the model of the American System of economy to Asia, Africa, and South America. Carey was the leading voice in the world, at that time, speaking out against slavery, including the enslavement of people to dope.

As it was, Henry Carey's efforts were defeated by the Empire. Carey's goal for an American, German, Russian, and Chinese cooperative effort to built a railway and telegraph line between western Europe and China across the vast expanses of central Asia, was scuttled by the British. The huge project was designed to take away the Empire's monopoly on trade, and thereby defeat it. Instead, the alliance was defeated. Still, the work of Carey and his people was not done in vain. In the 1880, a Chinese scholar by the name Yat Sen was being educated in Hawaii. He became schooled in the principles of Carey's American System of political economy. He soon discovered the fraud in the Empire's portrayal in China of Enlightenment empiricism as "Western Thought," and exposed it. His efforts did eventually break the British Imperial power in China. In doing so he became the founder of a new China. His bid for world peace, after World War I, was to utilize the European industrial machine that had supplied the war effort, for the development of China, which would have greatly benefitted Europe, China, and the world. But this bid was once again rejected. As a consequence, the West was driving itself into a deep and prolonged depression that opened the flood gates to a new global war.

Dr. Sun Yat Sen's blueprint for the development of China, that was based on the work of Heny Carey and the Philadelphia interests, is at last beginning to bear fruit. With the development of China a new era has begun in which the fundamental principles are reapplied that came of the Golden Renaissance in Italy which set the stage for the American renaissance and the discovery of the model for infinite economy.

While there is a great deal of China bashing going on today, as dirt is being dug up in the same fashion as in the worst of the West's political campaigning, one must put the bashing into perspective to the importance of the development of China in the world, at the present time - the time of an impending global financial disintegration. There exist only three major power poles in the world today. The most powerful is still the British Empire. But it is collapsing. The other two powers are the USA and China. The power-play of today is centered on what system will replace the present system after, or before, it disintegrates. Naturally, the British Empire has its own game plan, which will inevitably be an intensified version of the present world-financial system that has ruined the world-economy and is itself disintegrating. The USA, however, could force a change of course. It could reestablish its well proven model of the American System of political economy that Alexander Hamilton and Henry Carey had pioneered. But could this be sufficient to change the world? The key player in the whole game, therefore, will be China. With its long tradition in Confucian thinking and its background in the present application of the American model of economy, the likelihood is great that an alliance can be formed between the USA and China to once and for all defeat the British transworld oligarchic Empire. The future of humanity hangs in the balance in this contest of the titans.

The present intensity of China bashing, especially in North America, reveals an acknowledged weakness and fear in the imperial camp. Let us hope that this weakness is well acknowledged, for it is real. It is real, because no fundamental principle supports imperialism and oligarchism. Their apparent power is largely based on consent by the victims, achieved through manipulation, and this consent is weakening. Nevertheless, it is quite possible that the outcome of the world-financial contest will be on the Empire's side. The outcome, itself, will become the deciding factor between life and death for up to five billion people, and the continuity, or the loss, of civilization. Never have the stakes been higher in any contest.

The China bashing that is going on, today, needs to be seen in this context. The term "bashing" may appear crude and out of place in the sphere of modern civility, but it is an honest descriptor. Civility would cause one to call them: "people who speak of China in a terrogative way." Except this civility belittles the crime. And there is a crime in progress with immense consequences.

The bashers cry about China's record on human rights and democracy, but if one looks at the truth it appears that China's record on human rights is no worse than the record of the self-righteous USA, and might even be better. Thus, the hype is for political targeting and has nothing to do with rights and democracy.

In a recent report China was portrayed as a barbarian society for having hanged a man for stealing a car. Indeed, this was a barbarian act. Around the same time, however, in the USA, a convicted man on death row who was able to present credible evidence for his innocence, although the revelation of innocence came somewhat late, was executed regardless of the fact that his innocence could be proven. Not even a plea from the Pope, and from Mother Terresa, or pleas from other parliamentarians, were able to stay the execution. The man was murdered for a technicality. Evidently, it happens quite frequently that a technicality, not the truth, guides the executioner's hands.

If we look to statistics for an answer to the human rights question, they tell us that the number of people incarcerated, per capita, is roughly the same in China as in the USA. So, what is the hype about?

The China bashers also cry about Tinanmen Square, while they say not a word about Waco, Ruby Ridge, etc., etc., or the Russian's military attack against democracy, as they shot up their own parliament to rout the parliamentarians within it. And this was aided by the self-righteous West.

The reality is, there is no true justice anywhere in the world. The principle of justice needs to be relearned by humanity in the wake of the incredible carnage that people have been subjected to during the last century, that has become a century of war filled with the worst atrocities ever committed against human beings, and the stage is getting bloodier.

Actually, the worst human rights abuses are those that are not prosecuted. In this category the West is the undisputed champion. Two parallel cases come to mind which both began to unfold in the fall of 1996. One is the military invasion of Zaire, paid for to a large part of by the Empire's mining cartels, that unleashed a wave of large scale genocide that lasted for months. The death toll, should it ever be tallied up, will mount up into the millions from genocidal operations in Rwanda, Uganda, Burundi, and Zaire. The fact is that Rwanda had a population exceeding seven million before the Ugandan invasion started the first wave of slaughter in 1994. Now the population number is half that. Reports have circled the world of open air crematorial pyres burning in many places, day after day, mostly in restricted military zones, both in Zaire/Congo and in Rwanda. In this manner the dead remains of hundreds of thousands of murdered people are erases, their history stamped as though they never lived. Yet, the perpetrators of these atrocities, the leaders, Museveni, Kagame, and Kabila, are hailed as heroes in the West, rather than being prosecuted so that the crimes may end.

As for the case of democracy, China may well be a

world leader in that department. Democracy is a two way street, like speculation. Appendix A, Figure 2, shows that speculation is not a fixed thing, but unfolds into an upwards escalation into social and economic development, and a downward escalation into oligarchism and social and economic destruction. Democracy is similar to that. It can be an instrument for the self-protection and self-development of a nation, as outlined in the Preamble of the U.S. Constitution, even a protector of the Constitution itself. It can also be an open door by which a wealthy oligarchy 'buys' itself access to power, influence, and control, which, then, becomes turned against the nation. Hitler came to power that way. By this same open door the British Empire presently controls whatever is worth controlling. This is why the Empire demands the democratization of the world. This type of democracy, evidently, is a great evil and needs to be guarded against. The difference lies in the adopted model. China's process of democracy, when judged by its results, appears to be far superior, and much more protective and progressive for its people, than the brand of democracy that is pursued by all of the western nations.

Of course, this is not what the China basher's see. They see democracy as an open door to oligarchic autocracy. In fact the most praised democracies 'stink,' like hell itself. The much praised revolutionary democracy of Uganda is a single party system that tolerates no opposition; and this is being hailed as the model for Africa. Even before the single party law was passed in Uganda, opposition parties were prevented from operating, often by disruption and intimidation, but more often by the force of brutality and the gun. No pre-election meetings, posters, leaflets, or campaign signs by the opposition (to Museveni) were allowed. Even pictures of candidates printed on shirts, were prohibited, and the people who wore them were beaten. This is what is being hailed as the leading edge of western democracy, according to the praise Museveni's system receives. In this model state, the state has been at war against the country's own citizens, mostly in the north, for over ten years, in which several million people were murdered. This model democracy may be the only one in the world in which land mines are still being laid to devastate its own population, which, incidentally, might be the only commodity the country imports for its people, other than bullets for shooting them.

In the "Democratic Republic of Congo," the former Zaire, the legislature which once exceeded 700 people, has been reduced to no more than a single person, Laurent Desire Kabila, the newest dictator in Africa, the leader of the British Empire's mercenary armies, the man who took Zaire by force for his clients. The story of this 'democracy' is still being written in rivers of blood. A young boy, Pierre, testified that Kabila's soldiers came into his village, gathered together the children, then, separated the boys from the girls and began killing the boys by shooting them. He said, afterwards they cut their bodies in half, in order to prevent the possibility that some might resuscitate and walk away.*10 In most cases the operations of mass murder were targeted at the former Rwandan refugees, or the old and the very young of Zaire's own people. The death toll by mid 1997, since the invasion of Zaire began, is estimated to be between 300,000 and 500,000 people.

Similar operations by the "world's leading democracy" against its own people are reported in the press. The revelations came to light around the same time that the invasion of Zaire had begun. It began with a news expose by Mercury News in California about a well documented government operation for the importation of crack cocain into the USA by the plane loads, the proceeds of which illegally financed the Contras of Nigaraqua. In other words, the greatest dope epidemic in U.S. history was created by the country's own government in an effort to overthrow the government of another state, contrary to the direction of its legislature. The released story was further extended by EIR News Service reports in Washington, with documented evidence that points to the, then, Vice President George Bush, as the King-Pin in the operation. How many millions of lives have been destroyed by this operation is unknown.

What can be easily extrapolated, however, is the level of noise the China bashers would have unleashed if a single one of the above mentioned abuses of human rights and democracy had been perpetrated by China, rather than the West. The noise would have been deafening. This does no mean that China is an angel. It has been infected with the same ideology of Social Darwinism and British empiricism (which proclaim that man is a beast and must be regarded as a beast, exploited as a beast, even 'culled' in numbers as though humanity were a herd of useless animals). There are certain cases of gross disdain for human live in which China and the USA must be measured as equal.

China and the West also quite equal to each other in their lack of response to the immense famine that the people of North Korea are suffering after two years of flooding, followed by a drought. The urgently requested food aid in the amount of 1.5 million tones of grain has been denied to North Korea by every country in the West, including the USA, Europe, Russia, and by China. The U.S. legislature added a further insult of its own in a recent amendment to its food aid appropriation law. The amendment specifically forbids food donations to be provided to North Korea, lest the food might feed its army. The amendment was approved unanimously. In other words, in order to prevent food from reaching the North Korean army, the entire nation of 23 million people is being starved to death, which had used up its last reserves of food in the middle of June 1997, with nothing left to eat after that, till harvest time in late October. While some minuscule donations have been forthcoming from the West, not a single nation has seen fit to respond in a meaningful manner in order to prevent a humanitarian disaster of historic proportions.

The problem is not a physical one. The needed quantity of food is trivial in global terms. It is trivial even in terms of what is being wasted each year. Russia, alone, expects to loose 102 million tones (equivalent in grain) in 1997 due to the lack of fertilizers and functioning farm equipment.*11 So, the needed food is available and could be provided if there was a will to provide it. It could be delivered within days if the ideological axioms did not prevent this normal human response to a people in such dire need. The universal lack of this response indicates that humanity's thought has been universally reshaped by an artificial, political driver that has global penetration.

Indeed, western thought has been reshaped. What may be termed "western thought" has been transformed into the same narrow distortion of culture that Yen Fu had unleashed upon China, which distortion had shaped the thoughts of the founders of the Communist Party and Mao Zedong whose ideological axioms had brought death to countless millions of people. When Sun Yat Sen finally exposed the British fraud that Yen Fu had been educated for, the unfolding truth broke the back of the British Empire's stranglehold over China. The same breakthrough needs to occur again in the West and the world. Without it, there exists no moral base upon which to build a constitutional democracy that is open in its structure, but still protects; that works as a development platform, but inhibits the abuses of the freedoms it provides. A functional democracy in which human rights are guaranteed - including the economic human rights that are fundamental to life, liberty, and happiness - cannot be founded on fictions, mythologies, and distortions of culture.

What Yen Fu had achieved with his translations of the British empiricists and Social Darwinists, has been re-achieved in the modern West by the Empire's near total ownership of the world's media. The narrow minded concepts (distortions of what really is western thought), are so effective in hiding the truth that hardly anyone is privileged, anymore, like Dr. Sun Yat Sen was privileged, to learn about the republican principles that stand behind the works of the great pioneers of the American System of political economy: the Alexander Hamiltons, the Henry Careys, and the Philadelphia Interests.

Who knows about them, or even cares about the real history of the West? Who is aware of its culture in humanist tradition; in building, creating, protecting, and uplifting the world; strengthening morality, justice, honor? Hardly anyone. People know about the ideology of Locke, if not by name - the the founder of the Bank of England, who saw truth in wealth and power stolen from society at large. People also know about the Hobbes style Enlightenment empiricist ideology, perhaps not under this title, but by its effect, namely that political will can override fundamental principles and create its own reality. This type of 'enlightenment' counters all true enlightened thought based on discovery, scientific understanding, and technologies based on discovered realities.

The Hobbes style of enlightenment, unfortunately, has become predominant in modern thought, especially in the financial arena where the mythical belief prevails that it is possible to create reality at will which is overriding fundamental realities. This cannot really be done. Thus, founded on mysticism, the world-financial system is collapsing as no fundamental principles support its assumptions. Its bubble is about to pop. In contrast, the Chinese nation is advancing away from mysticism, towards a model of economy based on universal principle. On this platform, it is developing an infinite economy by which the whole of society is intended to become enriched.

The currently unfolding world-financial crisis - indeed, the impending disintegration of the entire system - cannot be correctly understood, without an understanding of the forces behind it, politically and philosophically. If it becomes possible for ideological mysticism to be stripped away, then, China and the USA will naturally unite as both nations share a common heritage and background that is deeply grounded in proven fundamental principles. When mysticism is stripped away, the remainder will become recognized, namely that the development of China proceeds on the American Systems model, which is rooted in the Golden Renaissance and the earlier renaissance centered on the Greek Classical civilization.

Indeed, Plato and Confucius are contemporaries. There unfolded a profound renaissance in China at about the same time that the first cultural renaissance unfolded in the West. The Greek Classical Period coincided with the birth of Confucian culture in China. Also their opposite trends in Aristotelian and Legalist/Taoist thinking developed at approximately the same time. The two opposing thought models, which developed simultaneously in China and in the West, have dominated human culture ever since. Both, China and the West, have experienced the pain and chaos they brought, resulting from ideologies that were in more modern times called "enlightenment" and "empiricist" thinking. Both, China and the West, have also experienced the enormously enriching effect of reality oriented thinking: the Platonic and Christian background in western culture, and its parallel in the Confucian background in Chinese culture.

The phenomenon that we see on the world political scene today, as China has begun a most profound economic self-development while the West is collapsing into unemployment, poverty, chaos, and financial disintegration, does not represent a fundamental difference in cultures. It merely represents a difference in timing in the unfolding development of human thought. China has been able to step ahead faster in the inevitable unfolding of reality oriented thinking, while the West is still artificially tied to the "enlightenment" and "empiricist" ideologies that its present world-empire imposes upon humanity as an essential platform for maintaining its power.

The first time in history when the idea of empiricist enlightenment was employed as a weapon against reality oriented thinking, probably was in response to the Golden Renaissance that had spread from Italy across all of Europe in the 15th century, that had caused all the major nations of Europe to join in a common military effort to rid the world of Venice. Venice was the leading slave trader and financial looter of the world at that time. Although the military effort to defeat it succeeded, Venetian "diplomacy" caused the Pope to relent from the intended destruction of the evil empire, by which the oligarchy of Venice was saved. In the wake of this very near extinction, the Venetian Aristocracy set out to break the power of the renaissance that had almost succeeded in destroyed it. Venice responded with its divide and conquer technique, by creating and promoting two opposing factions that would both stand in opposition to the culture of the renaissance. The two factions became known as the "reformation" and the "counter-reformation." Both were "empiricist" and "enlightenment" oriented. This total duality is possible when one operates on a platform without fundamental principle. Venice infiltrated and promoted both opposing factions. It stirred the put so skillfully that the whole scene eventually exploded into the infamous Thirty Years War which became a rampage of brutality, inhumanity, and devastation, unprecedented in history, which was superseded in horror only much later, in the 20th century.

Empiricist thinking bases its perception of reality on what the senses can see and touch, and build everything aground the limits of this sphere. Reality oriented thinking, however, embraces the discovery of things not seen; the scientific deduction of reason that develops technologies and law which manifest a broader reality than that which the senses are able to behold; that create manifests of principles that underlie reality by which tangible resources can be crated. Empiricist thinking is none-developmental. It regards wealth as limited, and focuses on stealing it. Reality oriented thinking demonstrates the creative capacity of intelligence and its infinite capacity for creating riches within the sphere of human living.

"Enlightenment" thinking, in contrast, goes hand in hand with empiricism. It disregards fundamental principles and would create its own reality, such as the notion that stealing can be made an enriching process. The welfare state must ultimately be seen as founded on this platform. The aristocracy of the world insists on perpetuating and expanding its looting. The victimized society that struggles against this scourge, is looking to the state to maintain it. Neither process can be carried on in perpetuity. The debt economy, the poverty ridden welfare economy, the deindustrialized economy, the conservatism oriented economy, are all symptoms of "enlightenment" oriented ideologies that subject the world to social experimentation that cannot possibly succeed. Each counters the fundamental principle of reality, namely, that one cannot have what is not being created.

If the above processes are pursued without end, the economies and civilization must collapse. The world is presently at a stage that has been defined by the American economist, Lyndon LaRouche, as a "boundary condition." The present world-financial and economic system that has been shaped over several centuries by a near global devotion to destructive ideologies, can no longer be repaired. Its collapse has begun, and its total disintegration is imminent, which has not yet occurred. The global society can still rescue itself from the anarchy and chaos that lies ahead. The anarchy and chaos that a global disintegration brings, have not yet unfolded and may be prevented by an intelligent response from society. On the other side of the boundary lies a dark age for humanity. The society may choose to go down with the Titanic into a new dark age. This appears to be its present choice.

The rest of this book is designed to explore the financial and economic structure of the world within this boundary condition. This structure must be understood in order that a better choice might be made by humanity in determining its future.

The Great Denial.

This modern age is not the first in history when people deny the reality before their very eyes, because what they behold challenges the axioms of their traditions and all the structures built thereon.

Such a situation is not an easy one to be dealt with with. Shakespeare understood this difficulty, Schiller understood it, all the great writers who wrote tragedies understood it, thus they endeavored to focus onto the difficulties involved in order to enable their audience to deal with the great imperatives that traditional means and concepts cannot address.

In the tragedy the heroes die. They are slaughtered because of their inability to act against traditions, against established sets of beliefs. They cannot act according to those higher demands that have never been made on them before, but which cannot not be avoided. The structure of the tragedy reveals that the hero knows deep in the hearts what the right action is, regardless of mortal danger - still the hero cannot act. The hero is not a coward in battle, or afraid to die. The difficulty lies in facing the unknown, in going against the conventional. By this the hero is doomed.

The hero in a tragedy dies so that the audience can be saved when tradition and fundamental principles are contrary to each other. In Shakespeare's "Hamlet" the hero could have saved the honor of the kingdom and the welfare of the nation of Denmark. He was thrust in a position of leadership. His own future and the fate of the nation depended on his leadership, but he failed. He simply could not do what was necessary. Thus, he perished by the very same force he had failed to deal with, and the nation suffered a loss, because of it.

In real life, however, the fate of a nation rests not with its leaders, but with itself. Its own axioms determine the political, financial, and economic climate. The values it upholds, the ideals it cherishes, the goals it strifes for, determine the quality of leadership the society seeks or tolerates. The effects that are coming to light today on the whole front of world-politics, finance, and economics indicate that the traditions on which society has depended on the whole front of its existence are dangerously wrong. People should have flocked to the lifeboats the moment the ship began sinking. The opposite is the case. But why? Why can't society act?

It is the purpose of this book to present an exploration into the background of mankind's greatest challenge to date; a challenge greater than war, pestilence, and famine combined; a challenge so severe that it will shape its future for centuries to come; a challenge that will alter the face of morality, science, technology, even the very image of man.

Future historian may refer to our present time as the great disintegration of the world-financial system of the twentieth century. Others may simply call it: The Crash of 96, or 97, or whatever the case may be. Or they may call it the great turnabout in world-history. When these phrases are heard in future times, whatever they may be, they will inevitably sum up in the minds of people the peculiarities of an era that has determined the direction of humanity for centuries to come, like World War II had, or NASA's Appolo mission to the moon, or a nuclear war might have.

What the specifics will be, of what they seen, remains yet to be determined.

The end of an era.

Future historian maý see our present epoch as a great catastrophe. Few people, today, would agree. The reality is, that a phase shift has occurred that marks the end of the present area. Actually this phase shift had already begun as far back as 650 years ago, at the very beginning of the era that is about to end. The greatest shift, however, occurred some 25 years ago around the time when financial thrift was cast out of the window and the U.S. dollar was cut loose from its backing in gold to become an instrument for speculation. Out of this background erupted the biggest financial gambling frenzy and debt bubble of all times, which is about to pop.

Momentous changes have surfaced since this time in every major economy around the world. These changes are readily acknowledged. The most profound of these is a fast growing governmental debt and a general collapse in employment and income levels, vanishing personal security, reduced profitability in industries, reduced productivity and physical production, the emergence of world-wide shortages in basic foods, the possibility of another energy crisis, and the list goes on. The major areas of growth in this period are found in crime, disease, conservatism, poverty, and stratospheric gains in the financial markets, starvation in the poorer countries, fascism in the streets and in halls of government, and wars all over the face of the planet.

The most serious of all these aspects, though they are all interrelated, is the fantastic gain in the financial markets that literally the whole world celebrates. The markets stand tall at dizzying highs in one of the longest and strongest stock market rallies that simply won't quit, until...?

Sure, the markets have gone up, and the markets have gone down. They have been at near zero, and they have reached astronomical highs. Nothing is new. It has all happened before. Indeed, is has. This is also the point that is important to notice. History tells us that with every major rally comes also a great vulnerability. The more that the stockmarkets grow, the less valuable do its aggregates become.

Oh, you don't agree! In a sense you are right. The value of the stockmarket has nothing to do with the physical reality anymore that it theoretically represents. Dividend yields matter so little today that no one cares about them anymore. All that matters is growth in share values. This is a part of the problem. The markets have become disassociated from the physical economy. They have grown in leaps and bounds while the physical economy that they represent on paper is declining and disappearing. The markets have cut themselves loose from the platform of physical production in the economy, where all real wealth is generated, and from which proceeds the society lives.

This paradox of unrestrained financial growth in the phase of physical decline in the economy reveals a very vulnerable foundation, and this not only for the markets, but for the society as a whole. By their disassociation from reality the values in the markets have become fictitious, especially so, in the financial derivatives markets that are the furthest removed from physical reality. Here, the values have become so fictional, and the profit potential so great, that the rush into these markets has created an annual global financial turnover that is pushing towards the one **quadrillion** dollar mark. This creates problems in the markets and for society.

One part of the problem is, that the profits from fictitious values are fictitious, too. This creates a problem for society when these fictitious profits are applied as claims against the physical economy, as though they were real. To a certain degree this actually works, but the process falls apart the moment that all the vast claims of the fictitious profits can no longer be reconciled with physical wealth generated in the economy, except, perhaps, by force. Such 'force' is already being applied in the arena of debt-service collection. This 'force' literally robs the physical economy by demanding from it wealth that has never been created in terms of physical production.

This interlocked relationship tends to collapse completely when the wealth demanded to satisfy financial profits exceeds what the physical economy can produce. When this occurs, debt is created.

The second part of the problem is that the fictitious system needs to be fed with ever greater inflows of real money, because it will collapse if it cannot be kept growing. This requires the nation to commit itself to constant increases in the money supply, which increases the debt. Furthermore, the ever increasing demand for market capitalization draws into the markets all traditionally existing investment funds that would normally support the physical economy The result is an accelerated economic collapse that leads to more debt.

While the debt problem that the national governments around the world are facing has become widely known, since the associated deep cuts in the nations' support structures can no longer be hidden, it is less known that the wildly growing the financial markets have created much of the debt that will eventually break the markets unless something else breaks the markets first. It is likewise, little known that every effort by the governments in deficit reduction, as a means for dealing with the debt, has resulted in increased deficits and indebtedness because of the destructive effect that conservative measures have on the wealth-creating physical economy on which the tax base rests. While there have been small temporary gains in some areas, the overall trend has been profoundly negative.

The universal effect of financial speculation.

The effect of financial speculation is felt by all people. The process of putting new money into the money supply, creates debt for the entire nation. Likewise, the looting of the productive sector through the cashing in of fictitious profits, effects all people. The same goes for the collapse of physical production when the producing industries are starved of investment funds. Everyone suffers from the drain of funds into the speculative bubbles. Even farming is effected.

Strangely, one can notice a tendency in governments to hide these negative trends. To some degree this is the result of the government's long accounting cycle by which policy actions are officially measured. In real terms, however, these figures seldom contradict the general trends which indicate fundamental errors in the society's economic assumptions. In many areas the negative trends have grown to catastrophic proportions in terms of impact on human living, where they overlap with a whole range of other disturbing trends which will be addressed later in this book.

The picture that now emerges, when one combines all the trends into a single perspective, is disturbing. It is disturbing, because the various trends become mutually amplifying. This is most visible in the financial realm, so much so that many a warning flag has been raised in financial newsletters where one reads about predictions of another 1929 or 1987 style stock market crash. The reasons that are cited are generally limited to the immediate signs in some specific area that are recognized as disturbing. There is little research evident in these letter into the underlying causes for the disturbing trends. In most cases, the newsletter writers simply blame the governments. There are complaints circulated about the government having too much debt, or not imposing enough spending cuts, or imposing too high taxes, or too many regulations, or too much government altogether,.. and so the list goes on. Such excuses are cheap shots and are far from hitting deep enough to reveal the systemic errors that effect the governments, the industries, and the financial markets together, and society as a whole.

These systemic errors are errors in the basic axioms that have become accepted by society as absolute, or as fundamental law. As the result of accepting false axioms, or sets of fundamental assumptions, a number of factors have emerged on the horizon with potentially devastating consequences for the societies of the world. Their destructive effects are likely to be severe if the policies that are based on the currently accepted axioms are allowed to play themselves out.

Most of the triggering factors that could bring the global financial house down, ironically, are not even financially oriented, in a direct sense.

One of these, for instance, is today's growing hysteria over what is perceived as a world-wide population explosion. This ideological perception has drawn immensely powerful actors into the arena of population 'management,' many of which have their own policy making capability that directly effects the economies of the world, and this not necessarily in a manner that improves the economic functioning of society. To the contrary, most these policy games are centered on economic devolution and disintegration, for these are potent weapons in the arsenal of the population reduction activists. These weapons are currently used to the full with dire effects on the targeted populations.

Another potential factor for economic devastation is unfolding out of the Middle East, in the form of a highly probable new energy crisis. The ideological architect of the 1973 oil shock has recently been put back into power, only this time more solidly than before. The last oil price shock severely damaged the U.S. economy, which was strong at the time. Another shock of equal magnitude, coming today, might kill it altogether. It would certainly the kill the debt burdened world-financial structure, and the extremely fragile global credit card debt system.

In the U.S. alone, by the end of 1996, the outstanding credit card debt had reached $4.875 trillion, with an escalating rate of personal bankruptcies (close to 1.2 million filings per year) already straining the system. There were approximately 100 million households in the U.S. in 1996, 60 million of which carry credit card debt. Of these indebted card holders, 15-20 million carry debt balances between $15,000 and $50,000 at interest rates varying between 15% and 25%.

That a large portion of this debt can never be repaid is evident by two factors: (1) that it would take on average 119 weekly paycheques to repay the obligation, and (2) that most of the credit card debt was originally created because the weekly paycheque simply is insufficient to meet the family's ongoing living expenses. Add to this shortfall the health-care expenses that the insurance system no longer covers, and the situation get grim for the affected families. Add to this, further, the possibility of dramatic fuel cost increase, which reflects itself in transportation cost increases, and food price increases, and the additional cost may well be the proverbial straw that breaks the camel's back.

Right now, many credit card companies are severely hurt by defaulting loans. Visa and Master Card took a bad debt charge-off of eight billion dollars in 1996. One of the biggest failure in the industry was suffered by Advanta Corp. of Spring House, Pennsylvania, that manages a $12.4 billion card loan portfolio. Close to 7% of its entire portfolio went bad in just one quarter.

What worries the industry the most are the bankruptcies that have not yet been filed, that could become an avalanche that the industry would not survive. Right now, the card holders who can afford to pay the minimum payments, roll over the accrued interest cost into new debt. Regardless of this worry, however, the industry has mailed out 2.5 billion new credit card applications in 1996, which adds up to 25 mailings per family.

Those who fall outside the prime lending that the credit card facilitates, perhaps because of previous bankruptcies, fall pray to the 'sub-prime' market where interest rates range higher from 20% to 160%, with an average of 35%. Most of such lending is for dire necessity, often for used car purchases, home purchases, or to pay medical bills. The 'sub-prime' market has grown dramatically in recent years. The fact that some people are willing to pay 165% interest rates, usually for small loans in the $100 range, shows how declaratively poor the nation as a whole has become.

How much of a tremor will be sufficient to bring the entire household credit market down, cannot be determined. It can be said, however, that unless the underlying problem can be solved and a global economic development begins in earnest that dramatically raises income levels, a melt-down of the entire household credit system is near. The growing disparity between the constantly shrinking household incomes, and the constantly increasing debt burden, cannot be glossed over forever. At $4.875 trillion in outstanding loans, the household debt market is large enough that its collapse, even the failure of a single part of it, could bring the entire world-financial house down.*12

Another factor that could trigger a global financial collapse, is terrorism.

One must consider that terrorism is by no means a dead issue. An insanity is developing in this arena with a frightening potential. The recent rise in large scale bombings leaves one to wonder at what point the dynamite for the explosions will be replaced with a nuclear device, or a biological device. Anything is possible against the background of the bizarre doctrine that violent death in the service of a cause assures an individual a seat in heaven. With organized crime looming over Russia, anything can be purchased with the 'right' connections and the 'right' incentive, and probably has been purchased. These purchases may well include the most fearsome terror weapons.

Another factor that could sent shockwaves through the world-financial system is the economic, social, and cultural breakdown in Russia. Russia's economy has been so severely wrecked by I.M.F. austerity demands, that a return to totalitarian control and a possible new cold war is virtually assured. Russia also poses another enormous threat. Its workforce is possibly the most underpaid and impoverished workforce in the world, which breeds severe problems in people' attitude. Now add to this background a large inventory of dangerously designed, antiquated, and poorly built nuclear reactors that should have undergone a complete systemic modernization, and you invite disaster. Then, add to the scene the common effects associated with poor equipment maintenance and the constraints that are usually associated with underfunded operations, and the probability for disaster becomes magnified. This is the current scene. If the world should experience a major melt-down, which is possible at any moment, the economic repercussions would be catastrophic.

The least of the problem would be that fallout might hit Western Europe. More severe would its effect be on public reaction against the already tarnished nuclear power industry. Such heightened reactions would most certainly force a wide-spread shutdown of nuclear power with severe economic repercussions. It is difficult to see how this would not topple the currently precariously balanced world-financial structure. The biggest impact, however, would be on humanity's future. Within a decade, more than half of the world's energy needs will have to be supplied by nuclear plants for which the most dramatic development effort must be launched in the near future.

The economic destruction of Russia, which has created this problem, that the West has so cleverly arranged to happen, might destroy mankind's future as well as its present (precarious) 'stability.'

One more factor that could bring the world-financial house down, is the Maastricht Treaty for establishing within the European union a single unified currency (EMU). In real terms the Maastricht deal is already dead as most European nations are hopelessly unable to meet the extreme demands that are made conditional for anyone joining the union. Ironically, even as the nations struggle to meet the tough demands, they wreck their economies in the all out effort to meet them. When the recognition takes hold that the EMU dream is over, the world currency balance could easily evaporate overnight and with it all the financial bubbles of speculation that are build thereon.

The world has never seen this kind of near global currency melt-down, with such extreme dislocations of value as is in the making right now. Even the slightest of such a shock is sure to cause investors to dump their paper assets for gold. This shift, all by itself, will crush the stockmarkets. It can be assumed with a high degree of certainty that this kind of shock will blow the derivatives markets out, if not the global financial markets in total.

Apart from these factors one sees a world-food crisis emerging, that has arisen out of the world wide credit crunch for agricultural production and a decade long trend of disinvestment in farming infrastructures such as irrigation, mechanization, storage, transportation and insect control. Farming has become one of the most devastated industries in the world, and the most severely hurt by cartel pricing strategies. In many areas the threshold has already been crossed beyond which production can no longer be sustained. As a result, many once productive fields remain unplanted. Deficits in food supplies, in the order of 20% - 30% (Mexico), reaching upwards to 65% (North Korea 1997) have already been registered, with no credits available in their coffers with which to finance substantial food imports. The economic consequences of the disintegration of whole nations can be sufficient to disrupt the global financial system and disintegrate it.

Another factor of this type is the strongly escalating re-emergence of pandemic diseases, out of the impoverished nations of the world. These diseases had once been regarded as conquered. Also one sees the emergence of evermore deadly new strains of diseases, that conditions over poverty enhance. This frightening trend is without any precedent in history. The severe economic austerity programs that have weakened the populations in many of the African and other Third World nations, coupled with the ban of effective insect control measures that had previously controlled insect born diseases, an ideal breeding ground has been created towards a possible biological holocaust. To some small degree, this trend is already in progress since the emergence of the HIV virus, the Ebola virus, and other less known new strains that appear at the fantastic rate of one per year.

All these factors with a possible dramatic global effect stand in the background to a severely weakened world-financial and economic system. While some of the alarmed financial newsletter writers of today see the world's financial markets near the edge of a 'cliff,' they fail to see the deep connection between the vulnerability in the markets and the steadily collapsing physical economy around the world, and the connection between these and the society's ideological assumptions and traditions.

One of the rare authors in the financial publishing world, who looks deeper into what is going on, sees an emerging insanity in the way that the volume of stock trading has risen to over a billion shares traded on the world's exchanges every single day. He sees a force driving up prices far beyond any reasonable relationship to the physical equity that they represent, which he interprets as setting the stage for a powerful crash back to reality.

Still, none of even the most alert of these authors sees the far greater vulnerability of the financial-derivatives market, the type of market in which a single bad trade had earlier taken the mighty Barings Banks into bankruptcy, and this so deeply that it simply wasn't worth to bail the bank out.

The scary aspect about the trend into derivatives speculation, especially when the banks become involved, is the sheer volume of game. Some of the great banks, the proverbial pillar of the financial system, are addicted to the derivatives game at a volume of up to 40 times their total assets. They are literally betting the bank many times over in the greatest gambling orgy ever staged on the planet. Nor are they alone. Derivatives speculation is the fastest growing financial market in the world. It has risen from a volume of $1.1 trillion in 1981 to somewhat below $100 trillion for 1995 (an increase of over 900%), with an annual turnover in speculative contracts in the one quadrillion dollar range. These figures dwarf the national budgets of even the mightiest nations. The U.S. federal budget, for instance, of $5.4 trillion (1994) appears puny in comparison to the volume of financial speculative gambling. The most scary part of all, is the rate of increase in this arena, which has not been linear, but hyperbolic, as shown in Appendix 1, Figure 1.

The most scary part of all is, that the phenomenal increase in volume that causes financial values to rise, cannot be maintained indefinitely, much less the relative rate of increase that is virtually expected by now, so that a reverse of the present trend may unleash a reverse leveraging of a type similar to that which brought the Barings Bank to its grave. Except in the coming larger reversal, in a systemic crisis, all of the world's financial players, no matter how big, are at risk, of which many will fail.

What specific cause will trigger the upcoming great crash cannot be determined. The bases are loaded. An upset in anyone of the major arenas is most certain to cause a secondary explosion in all the other arenas as well. A new Arab oil embargo could have that effect, or even a major price hike. A major 'correction' in one of the main stock markets of the world could set off a domino effect, rolling in from England and Japan. It could even be kicked off by a major epidemic of the newly emerging diseases, that impacts the physical economy which is still the only real source of wealth in the universe.

Strangely, not a single one of the factors that are threatening the global economy today, are natural occurrences. Every one of them is man-made. Some factors appear even intentionally engineered for ideological reasons. They all have one aspect in common, however, they are deadly in their consequences. In a very real way, humanity is facing the most powerfully engineered onslaught against itself that has ever been staged against human existence throughout history.

Of all the factors coming together, the financial and economic factor is obviously the most important one. The reason is, that in a healthy financial and economic environment none of the other factors matter significantly, as they can be dealt with and overcome. Unfortunately, such an environment no longer exists. What exists instead is an environment of irrational perception in an arena of a global crisis that has the potential to disintegrate the entire world-financial system, not just the stock and bond markets as many financial newsletter writers predict, but the banking system as well, together with everything that is linked into it. This may appear like a formula for utter catastrophe.

If you feel a bit uneasy, or scared, you are beginning to see the picture.

Fortunately, there are alternatives to allowing a crisis to explode. These are self-evident alternatives that have been tested in real life and have proven their worth. For those, however, one needs to dig a little deeper. In fact, in order to recognize their value, one needs to understand both the nature of the 'disease' and of the 'cure.' To some people, what comes to light as one digs deeper, may be distasteful. Indeed, the sugar coated lollipops appear sweeter, that most financial analysts put out as an enticement to gain subscriptions for their letters, though the sweetness will certainly cost many a person dearly, if not the person's life.

Unfortunately, it also costs society. We all live in this environment together in which financial speculation rules the day. We share the same world. No one can escape this fact. But it is also possible to re-shape the world from the ground up. This possibility exists in spite of what everyone insists upon to the contrary.

Not surprisingly, the process of digging for answers is actually interesting. It is certainly far less boring than to read the newspapers' financial analysis. In the papers, the central theme never varies in its unrelatedness to the realities of daily life and the struggles of people at the grass roots levels where the majority of human beings earn their living. The most interesting aspects always lie in the real world and are usually quite surprising.

Chapter 2: The link between Economy and Metaphysics

They combine, and form a single aspect that unites literally all factors of human existence onto a single basis. This basis is the human intellect, the mind that discovers, that creates, that constructs models of a reality that no one can see, that is foundational to the technologies on which the physical existence of humanity rests. Unfortunately, this basis is being ignored as a valid factor in both public and private policies, and in the respective ideologies that underlie them. Still, we see this factor evident everywhere, even at the most fundamental grass roots level. It it is lost sight of, however, at the higher level of financial conventions.

The reason why metaphysics is being ignored as a fundamental factor, may be due to the transcendental image that the concept brings to mind. Except, there is nothing transcendental about it in connection with human living. The recognition of it, or the lack of it, is manifest in the success or failure of the society. People recognize the failures of society when they impact their live in a disintegrating physical economy in the form of job-losses caused by policies for deindustrialization, austerity measures, or social cuts made by debt soaked governments. People can see the social disintegration resulting from poverty, from homelessness, hunger, crime, and from the growing wave of white-collar fascism, even terrorism, but they cannot see deeper to detect the principles that are being ignored. Thus, the cause for the failures is not recognized, so that the failures continue and the consequences escalate.

The reality indicates that no quick solution Band-Aid method can be employed that can cure the currently unfolding problems by way of some simple physical restructuring. Each single one of the factors that threaten mankind today has a mental foundation on which the physical effects are the outcome of the human genius made manifest in scientific understanding, technological creativity, and physical productivity.

The platform on which the human society exists and has existed for many ages, can therefore be said to have an entirely metaphysical basis. Everything that the society has and by which it exists - its food production, its transportation systems, its housing, etc. - rightly or wrongly, has been created by human labor that reflects ingenuity, and creativity. The genius of man, and the physical dimensions of civilization, are so tightly interlocked that they become a single aspect of man's nature and being. The capacity to think, and the capacity to act upon the recognized thought creatively in order to raise the status of living, is the hallmark of the human being. It presents a metaphysical basis. On this basis the physical platform is raised by the mental capacities of the human being.

A platform higher than primitive physics.

Metaphysics offers man a higher basis from which to create his resources for living than primitive physics can provide. It has enabled a transition in development that taken humanity beyond rudimental mechanics and ordinary processes that are associated with the 'natural world.' It is the platform on which new realities are created such as do not exist naturally, that have no primitive equivalent, that in many cases have not even the slightest basis in the natural world.

Witchcraft, shamanism, prayer, etc., are metaphysical by this definition, in that they produce physical effects in people's existence by metal processes. The same occurs through science and technologies. The technology of the nuclear fast-breeder reactor, for example, is totally a creation of the human mind that places a near infinite energy source within mankind's reach. This technology has given mankind an affordable energy source built on a resource base that can sustain the technology for twenty million centuries at twenty-five times the world's present energy production level. A whole new world opens up with the application of this technology. A whole new resource for living unfolds. A whole new reality dawns. In this case, the entire sphere of human living becomes uplifted entirely through scientific advances. Scientific enquiry has enabled not only the creation, but also the utilization, of process that have no equivalent in the 'natural' sphere, which unfold solely out of the resources of the mind.

Metaphysics combines the two fundamental aspects of human existence, the mental base and its manifest in physical phenomena, into a single aspect. The product of this combination does not exist in the natural world outside of the sphere of man, because mankind, as the most advanced part of the natural world, is itself an integrated part of this product.

With the further unfolding of this most advanced part of the natural world, the state of the natural world has evolved to higher state the moment that the potential for creativity became introduced into the system. With this a threshold has been crossed. A total phase change has occurred in the evolution of life on this planet, opening the scene to capabilities for the unfolding of life and living processes that never existed before. With the unfolding of this capability the range of biological expansion has become infinite, extraterrestrial, and perhaps even extragalatical. As the nature of life has staged for its most advanced manifest a higher plateau, with vastly expanded capabilities, a whole new reality unfolded for the promulgation of life that has never existed before.

In a somewhat different sense, this capability to advance beyond the rudiments of primitive physics has long been recognized and demonstrated to some degree. Ancient witchcraft, for instance, is deemed to have had healing influences, some of which can be explained medically today, and some psychologically, and some not at all. The utility of thought to affect physical living, to whatever degree this has been achieved, testifies to intelligent action. Technology, likewise, is the outcome of purposely directed intelligent action. Controlled nuclear fission for the harvesting of energy, does not occur naturally anywhere in the known universe, from which mankind might have learned the process. The same can be said about the intricate structures that make up a computer and its software. These exists exclusively as the outcome of the creative processes of the human mind. The capability of space-flight for exploration and spreading life throughout the near and far universe exists nowhere except within the sphere of the highest manifest of life itself unfolding its new capability of intelligence.

Nuclear power generation is a mind created process that provides for the society's development an appropriate physical energy resource that does not exist in the natural world, but which becomes appropriate as a step in the progressive unfolding that the more primitive stages of life have neither included nor required. We call this advance a process of human creativity, but it is far more than that. It is a process that is bigger than ourselves, that we, ourselves, are a part of.

What we call human capability is little more than an unfolding of life that enables us to create out of the resources of the mind a reality that has no prior equivalent, but which is endemic in the unfolding nature of life that is forever developing itself. Mankind may be seen as one of the great resources of the natural world. Mankind stands not apart from this world, no matter how strongly this belief is cherished, mankind is a part of it and stands at the fore-front of it expansion beyond the sphere of our planet. Man is a manifest of nature, not primitive nature, but the pinnacle of it. The creative capability that unfolded with the unfolding of life has for the first time in its development included the metaphysical aspect of being and the creation of a civilization that rests totally on metaphysical processes. It is certainly true, that without these processes 99.99% of humanity that populates the planet, would not exist.

The primitive natural environment of the planet, in which early man once lived in an animal type of existence, is actually quite poor and rather limited in terms of its development capability. Before the age at which the phase change occurred at which man's metaphysical capability began to be established (from between 900,000 BC to app. 100,000 BC - the age of Homo Erectus to the age Early Man) the human world population was apparently quite stable. It is believed that the population level, throughout this entire era of about 800,000 years, remained fairly constant around the one million mark. This stability was created by the limits of the harsh environment of primitive physics to which all animal type societies are subjected. These limits were absolute for them until the metaphysical capability of unfolding intelligence enabled the creation of new resources for living. From this moment on, the once absolute limits of the so-called natural world, no longer applied.

The phase change that enabled the physical platform to be raised through creativity, also raised the life expectancy of man. At the primitive stages the life expectancy was low, in the 14 to 18 year range, as life was harsh. The long term stability in the population level indicates that this tiny human population that existed, was all that the natural system was able to support on a poverty limited plain of existence. On this poverty limited platform, the human population remained in an equilibrium for 800,000 years until the metaphysical capability of man began to unfold. From this point on, things began to change dramatically.

During the Paleolithic (hunter-gather) and Mesolithic (proto agricultural) ages, until about 10,000 BC., the early effects of intelligence raised the physical platform of living to the point at which 4 million people could support themselves on the planet. Has the earth changed that it could now support or four times as many people as before, or has the human being developed a capability to create for itself what the earth didn't provide?

Since the earth has not changed, it cannot be said that the carrying capacity of the earth changed. But the nature of life changed, and its capability changed. Man had changed. A capability had unfolded in the development of man that never existed before in the entire history of life on the planet. With this capability more and more people were able to support themselves, and this with a greater security than before.

After the early stages of this new development, during what is called the Neolithic age until app. 3,000 BC. (the era of the early "agricultural revolution") the physical platform was continuously raised to higher levels by advances in the mental processes that generated certain technologies by which food could be produced at quantities that simply could not exist naturally. Through further advances in metaphysical unfoldment, it became soon possible for 10 million people to support themselves on the same planet that once supported only 1-1.2 million people. Also, with the advance in metaphysics, as life became easier and more secure, the life expectancy became increased to an average of 25 years.

Throughout the Bronze Age, the Iron Age, including the Mediterranean Classical Period to app. 500 AD (this includes the time of the Roman Empire and the Han Dynasty in China), food production became evermore organized and technologically intensive, so that the physical platform that was thereby created made it possible for 200 million people to sustain themselves on the face of the planet, or two-hundred times as many as the planet had once supported by its primitive means.

During the next 1,300 years, including the Medieval Period to the 18th century, an unfolding industrialization raised the physical platform to still higher levels, to the point that now 720 million people could support themselves on the earth, with an average life-expectancy of 38 years.

By the mid 1970s, the world's high energy intensive industrialization and farming had raised the physical platform to such high levels that now 3.9 billion people could live on the earth quite comfortably, and with a life-expectancy of over 70 years.

This development indicates that the effective, so-called carrying capacity of the earth, was constantly raised to higher levels as the physical platform was raised through intelligent processes. The earth, itself, has never changed throughout this entire period. It was mankind's capability that had changed. Mankind's mental capacities had developed and created processes that raised the physical platform of the world out of a subjection to primitive limitations, to a metaphysical environment that enabled the creation of constantly new resources for living which never existed on the primitive platform.

By this term dynamic process of life - creating constantly new and greater resources for living - mankind has been able to sustain itself in ever greater numbers on the same planet that once supported but a few. The impact of thought upon human living has been so dramatic that it enabled a 5,500 fold increase in the number of people that can support themselves on the earth, with no perceivable end in sight. As far as one can determine, there exists no fundamental limit that would end this process of unfolding.

It is a tragic error to speak of the earth in terms of "carrying capacity," a rhetoric that has become so prevalent today, representing an ideology that has inflicted severe damage onto mankind's financial and economic structure by the interjection of policies designed for reversing the dynamic process of life by which civilization was created.

The history of mankind has shown clearly that the so-called "carrying capacity," which by its own resources supports no more than a 1 million person population, has been constantly raised to ever higher levels, through metaphysical processes. It has been raised 5,500 fold so far, and with no imperative end in sight for which this development would need to be curtailed for reasons of a fundamental lack of resources, mankind's future looks bright. The only shadow over mankind is its lack of self-appreciation that allows the emergence of murderous ideologies and their effect on the society's financial and economic foundation.

Chapter 3: The Reversal of Metaphysics

That the development of civilization is the result of an intelligent mental environment is evident by the dramatic population collapse that a major insanity had effected in the 13th and 14th century. The collapse resulted from the financial looting practices of the banking empires of Florence - the infamous Bardi and Peruzzi banks, the black Gulf banking system, etc. - and the banking empires of Venice, which all together squeezed financier profits out of the European economies at levels that reflected a certain economic insanity. Profits at levels up to ten times greater than what the physical economies could produce, were demanded and collected. This process of financial looting totally collapsed the productive economies of Europe, and physically weakened the populations that the economies supported. The cumulative effect of collapsing nutrition levels in the population opened a vulnerability to diseases that set the stage for one of the most horrendous biological catastrophes in history: the Black Death plague.

The Black Death was actually created in China in the early 1330s. It was brought to Europe by the Venetian's traders who had a close 'business' relationship with the Mongol rulers of China. The Mongols' primitive culture had unleashed a two century rampage of murdering and destruction upon the Chinese people that had laid waste large numbers of cities, killed their populations (the estimated death toll is in the ten million range), and destroyed their agricultural infrastructures. The Mongols' vast herds of horses alone, some 300,000 of them, all by themselves, inflicted enormous damage onto the highly developed agricultural platform, weakening the remnant of the population. The impact of this vast herd was so horrendous, that at one point the herd grazed down all the plains of Hungary in two short years. It is not difficult to imagine what damage such a herd inflicts on a highly developed agriculture, and what deprivation is caused thereby. Out this collapse into primitivism and chaos in the physical economy, the Black Death plague emerged.

In addition to the murdering rampage of the Mongols, the plaque is estimated to have killed another 15-20 million people in the regions of southern China. The plaque had emerged out of this background of a most savagely weakened population and spread through the regions as the Mongols' looting spree drained the continent to exhaustion. A death toll in the rage of 25-30 million people represented an enormous toll at the relative low population levels of the 14th century.

A similarly weakened condition existed in the European population in the 1340s, and more so after the great financial-systems crash in 1345 at which point the Florentine and Venetian banking empires had collapsed the economies of the European basin to the breaking point. In the midst of all this disintegration, of not only the financial system, but of also the physical platform that the looting had caused, the Black Death plaque took hold and exploded like wildfire.

By 1346 the Mongol horsemen had spread the Black Death plague from southern China to the towns of the Crimea, from there the Venetian ships carried it to Sicily and Italy, from where it spread through the economically devastated regions of Europe.

The effect of the process, from beginning to end, was so devastating that it collapsed the population level by 35% to 50% throughout Europe. Although the plaque was brief in duration, Europe's population level fell throughout an entire century as the result of the combined process of financial, economic, and physical collapse. This decline reversed only after the onset of the Golden Renaissance.

The enormous collapse in population numbers that occurred throughout this period resulted from a corresponding downward reversal in the mental environment. The abandoning of reason has had its corresponding collapse in metaphysical effect.

Today, mankind stands at the crossroads once again. On one hand mankind faces a new round of unfolding insanity in the financial realm in the form of an out-of-control world-financial system that is itself near the edge of collapsing, together with political processes that have simultaneously collapsed literally all economies in the world to the point that people are dying from the effects of physical underdevelopment and related causes of biological weakening throughout the populations. The current annual death toll from this hovers near the 100 million mark. Against this background of physical weakening in the populations the age old killer diseases that were once deemed to have been eradicated, are making a come-back.

In the background to this silent dying, cries are coming out of the developed world, lamenting that the world is severely overpopulated and that mankind must shed 60% to 90% of its population in two generations.

While these are extreme positions held by some of the most powerful people on the planet, they do indicate the reemergence of the type of insanity that devastated the 13th through to the 15th century in Europe and China.

In contrast to this fast unfolding potential for collapse, mankind has a near infinite potential for a bright future, with limitless resources in energy, minerals, food, water - anything the human world desires. As for its potential in food production, mankind has not even begun to start developing anything but the crudest of the available potentials. Vast portions of the earth remain a barren waste-land, even today, while the potential of the sea remains virtually unutilized, with space-based food production not even being considered. With all this enormous potential at hand, what justification does mankind have for its commitment to a course that embraces the insane desire for a global suicide of unspeakable proportion for the perceived lack of opportunities?

A deep mental collapse.

The unfolding paradox points to a deep collapse in metaphysical capability, which points to a mental collapse. While the global population reduction programs, as they are called, are still very much on the agenda in the highest places, in terms of policy options, the actual collapse may be induced, not so much by policy, but by the dramatic decline in the metaphysical realm that traditionally manifests itself in the creating and maintaining of evermore advancing support systems for living. Mankind has stopped this advance and reversed it on a global scale. The insanity that drives this reversal is found interwoven into various ideologies that have infested the axioms that govern the financial and economic systems, as well as the social and moral culture of modern society.

This ideologically organized regression is the leading driver towards what may become the greatest financial and economic crash in history, coupled with the kind of collapse in population levels that is historically associated with these types of metaphysical reversals. The exception is, that at the present stage, the process of collapse will most likely be amplified by the dynamic multipliers that are associated with today's economic-systems collapse, such as a possible oil embargo, a possible war in the Middle East, an impending biological holocaust in conjunction with a progressing elimination of the nations' health support structures for budgetary reasons. The combined effect of all these causes being brought together during a financial crash may be sufficient to take the house down over humanity, even beyond the point of any possible recovery.

A little of the currently ongoing process of collapse is already beginning to be felt by the unfortunate segments of society that have lost incomes from employment, and are about to loose their final line of physical support as governments all over the world are driven into 'tough' budget cutting modes.

The process that is causing all this damage has been started long ago. It is interlinked with the processes that are behind the financial-system's crash. When the crash occurs, it will be but an escalated phase of what is already in progress.

One of the signs that one sees, that reveals the widely interlinked collapse, is the increasing impossibility for governments to balance their budget while financial costs skyrocket and the physical economy that provides the tax base, shrinks and sheds a great many of its productive workers, shifting the social service demands onto the governments.

The governmental budget crisis.

Since such a crisis no doubt exists in virtually every nation on the planet, and is visibly connected with the forces that drive the global financial and economic collapse. An exploration into this crisis appears useful for what it can tell us about the dynamics of the collapse before the collapse occurs. By an understanding of these dynamics, it may be possible to establish a new commitment by which the disintegration of the currently collapsing systems may be forestalled.

Science and public policy.

The question arises: What role should an individual play in response to the public budget crisis for which social structures are eliminated, hospitals are closed, education is scaled back, national infrastructures are sold off for cash?

The above question is not easily answered. The obvious answer is that any such involvement necessarily includes discovering a whole new dimension of looking at the scene than the dimension in which the problem was created. The demand is, literally, for the individual of the public to become a scientist in the search for truth. The demand for this is imperative. The scope of the collapse in progress is so vast that no one is exempt from its effect. It becomes each individual's responsibility, therefore, to contribute to the healing of society for his or her own protection. This responsibility, in turn, requires of all an accurate scientific understanding of the processes that have brought us to the current impasse that is generally known as the budget crisis.

The demand on the individual, therefore, is a demand to be more accurate than the politicians are, who run the country; to understand better the underlying principles; to see deeper; to recognize more keenly the subtle traps that endanger the society's welfare, its security, even its very existence. It becomes imperative towards this end to understand the nature of the threats that society is facing and the principles they violate. All this is necessary in order that the deficiencies may be dealt with that exist. In other words, the society must gain a clear perception of what the problem is. This step is primary in order for the public to gain a clear perception of what the solution of the crisis must be.

It is no longer sufficient, in light of the complexities and the exposures involved, to blindly vote for a government leader, and, then, sit back and hope for the best. The tragedy that mankind is facing is severe, and is a global one. The unfolding reality is not a partisan problem that a partisan solution would address, or that a different party might address better. In most cases the partisan solutions are counter productive, as they all, with variations, employ the same axioms that are responsible for the problem in the first place. The crisis that is unfolding is a fundamental problem that requires deep seated conceptual shifts to be made. The status quo is dead, and the question should not be lightly answered as to where we go from here.

The task that the scientist of society faces today is not a simple one. It involves grave responsibilities that leave little room for error. The price for error at this stage comes with a high price attached. While there has always been a price to pay for errors made, the effects of the errors have been far less immediate in the past when life was good, when the economies were strong, when unemployment and homelessness was virtually non-existent, before financial debt became a monster. Unfortunately, those days are gone.

In the mid 1960s the combined corporate, public, and private debt in the U.S. stood at below $1.3 trillion, of which the federal government carried 10% or about $0.13 trillion. Today, 30 years later, the total indebtedness of the nation has risen to above $16 trillion of which the federal government carries over 30% or $5.4 trillion, a 45 fold increase in governmental debt. A similar trend may be observed globally. In some cases the trend is more severe, and in some cases less so.

The question needs also to be answered as to what caused this momentous upswing in indebtedness. War can be ruled out, as there wasn't a major war fought during the period. In fact, the greatest upswing occurred between 1980 and 1995, when the total debt of the nation rose from just below $5 trillion in 1980 to over $16 trillion in 1995. No major catastrophe occurred during this time, but something did happen. Indeed, something has happened that the society is paying for dearly today, which has altered the way society exists, and is poised to impose infinitely greater changes yet to come. So, what happened in those years when the debt rose out of sight?

The most notable thing that occurred during this period, which began to develop as far back as the early 1970s, was a fundamental shift in the focus of attention, away from production oriented financing towards pure financial speculation. It was in this era, too, that the society was told by its elite that the world is running out of resources, and that for this reason a shift is necessary to transform the industrial economy of the world into to a service economy. While this demand was totally unfounded by the physical reality, the demand served to enable in the public's mind to the accept the deindustrialization that was planned, which set the stage for the new era in investments in which financial values are no longer tied to anything tangible in terms of physical equity or product related value.

Deindustrialization appears to be an irrational goal, and so it is. None-the-less, it was not only promoted as a concept, it was also enforced. It was put in force by Paul Volker, the very moment he became appointed to the top position in the Federal Reserve system, who was specifically selected for his commitment to the platform of industrial devolution as a desirable goal for the 1980s. The economy was said to have been overheated. He was selected to cool it off. In real terms, this 'cooling off' means destroying the productive potential by which real wealth is created for society, because such increases in real physical wealth tends to dilute to imaginary value of financial accumulations. This is why the Federal Reserve intervenes. By its choking off, of the physical economy, the creation of real wealth becomes destroyed, which leaves the field free for financial speculation to create profit.

Indeed, this is the direction in which the economy was slanted from the Paul Volker days onward. With the traditional base of the economy having been put into a death-spiral of self-amplifying collapse, a new growth industry emerged that was centered on pure financial speculation.

A double standard emerged out of this background. While rigorous growth in the productive physical economy was viewed with alarm by the financial controllers, for which the economy was choked to death, explosive growth did occur in the financial sector which set of the wildest speculation binge in history that was hailed with fanfares and announced as the panacea of economic stability.

Strangely, the public swallowed this lie that reversed the very principle of economics. By it the rich, including the privately owned Federal Reserve and its managers, became increasingly richer, and the producers of the society who generate the only real wealth in the world, lost their shirt. Today, its costs the U.S. taxpayers $2 billion annually to operate the Federal Reserve that is choking the society to death. While school lunch subsidies are cut to save a few pennies; while hospitals are shut down for lack of operating funds; while elderly people are denied the needed medical care in nursing homes to stay alive, the Federal Reserve maintains for itself a fleet of 47 private jets and has presently embarked on a major building program under which it is building all at once a $100 million building in Minneapolis, a $168 million building in Dallas, and a $178 million building in Atlanta.*13

The foundation that set up the global speculation mania had been established in 1971. It was actually in place before Paul Volker came on the scene, who was selected for his commitment to bring the power of the Federal Reserve into supporting speculation and destroying the physical economy. This actual foundation for this was created when the U.S. dollar was taken off the gold standard, which had become increasingly under attack by financial speculators. Once this reverse step was complete, the game of financial speculation was out of the starting gate. The race was on. It only needed to be supported. With increasing pressures on legislators in all nations around the globe, for a whole series of deregulations, which soon became law, the speculation game could be cranked up evermore to create vast profits. Only that 'nasty habit' of interrelating the financial profiteering with the physical economy stood in the way. Paul Volker fixed this problem. He was chosen for the top post of the Federal Reserve for his commitment to solving this nagging problem by imposing policies that would lead to a gradual but accelerating collapse in the physical economy. With true wealth creation eliminated, fictitious wealth won in the financial casinos, became ever more attractive. Thus, the most effective process for looting the public was created. The success of it has been so dramatic that the public voluntarily pours all its life-savings into the bottomless pit - it even borrows vast sums for it, in hope of a financial bonanza that it can never have. While the public can certainly be looted by the world's financial sharks, it is mathematically and logically impossible for the public to get rich by looting itself.

It is plain to see that Paul Volker has won his war against the welfare of society, as a servant of the financial power centers. He created a two tier system in which the physical economy became detached from the financial aggregates system. With the physical economy collapsing, it was no longer fashionable to focus on profits gained from increased production of physical goods. This allowed the financial resources of the society to be poured into the financial aggregates system which became more and more unrelated to any form of real wealth being produced in the physical economy.

As was noted before, Paul Volker didn't invent the trend. He merely helped it along by cranking up the 'fire' in the late 70s, that was lit in 1971 when the gold standard was abolished in favor of a free floating U.S. dollar that would yield vast speculative profits. This general trend was actually started as early as the mid 1960s, when foreign exchange trading became the big first official round in the game of creating profits without actually creating anything of value that the profits should represent. The principle of financial looting, of course, goes way back in time to the very beginning of the world's empires which existed entirely on the proceeds of looting. The process of looting was merely accelerated in the mid 1960s.

The evidence of this phase change in the intensity of looting is evident in the market basket measurement. This measurement measures what a society generates for its day to day use, that represents its achieved state of civilization. This measurement peaks in 1967, and, then, falls back to below half that level, which is approximately where we are at the present time. For this reason, 1967 is used as a comparative standard for all measurements that are designed to indicate the economic consequences that are inherent in financial aggregates speculation, which is always pursued at the expense of the physical economy.

The year 1967, therefore, also marks the start of the death-spiral of the world-financial system, the beginning on financial insanity. By 1970, for instance, foreign exchange trading had risen to 110 billion annually. From 1970 to 1980 this trading volume had increased to $5.5 trillion annually, showing a fifty fold increase. By 1990 this volume had increased to $36 trillion annually. This represents a 327 fold increase in the volume of foreign exchange trading as compared to 1970.

Huge profits accompany this speculative trading of national currencies. Here, a problem begins to develop. These financial profits represent claims against the physical economy, even though the physical economy has not generated anything in real terms which the profit claims might represent. To the contrary, the sharply escalating financial profits are stacked up as claims against a declining physical economy. It should be noted that the physical economy, alone, generates whatever real wealth exists in the economic sphere. Anything else is fictitious. This assessment, necessarily, renders all the profits from financial speculation as proceeds from looting as they are looted out of the products of the physical economy to which the speculative binge has not contributed, but has siphoned off available investment funds. In other words, financial speculation steals from society, and this theft is escalating in leaps and bounds.

The separation of the speculative profiteering from the physical platform where all real wealth production takes place, is even more apparent in the volume increase in the futures contracts market, than it is in foreign exchange trading. In the futures market, the notional volume shows a 467 fold increase between 1970 and 1990, from a volume of $0.329 trillion to a whopping $156.2 trillion in futures contracts being generated annually.

This phenomenal increase in speculation, and of course in speculative profits, would not have been possible without the dramatic devolution of the physical economy itself. The physical economy would have claimed the investment funds had it not been choked out of the competition. The double digit interest rate shock that Paul Volker had unleashed in the late 1970s, which saw bank interest rates rise to 22%, prevented any such competition. By this act, though the sky high rates were temporary, the direction of the investment game was changed.

The combined effect of the huge inflation in the financial markets and a collapsing physical economy, now set up the stage for the inevitable consequence of financial looting, which leads to a massive accumulation of debt. This debt is wrecking the financial scene today, which, once it is established, becomes self-perpetuating.

Appendix 2, Figure 1, shows the dramatic escalation in government deficits as beginning at the same time as financial speculation created a bubble of financial aggregates that became evermore removed from the production of physical wealth, which was thereby becoming depressed. The presentation in Appendix 2 Figure 1 shows that until 1970, when the great speculative binge began, there were no significant governmental deficits on the nation's slate. It shows a steady rise in governmental deficits during the 1970s when the currency looting operations began, and a much more dramatic rise in the early 80s in response to the deindustrialization shock therapy of Paul Volker's astronomical interest-rate policy. From this point on the national debt was well established so that the deficit levels remained high.

When the rulers of the world-financial games reversed the principles of economy in favor of speculative profits, they literally deceived themselves, as the fundamental principles of metaphysics on which the principles of economics are founded, are not subject to anyone's wishes or manipulation. If the chosen economic policies fail to reflect the fundamental principles of metaphysics, the economic system will fail in which the policies are applied. If the response to failures in the system is addressed with policies that are likewise contrary to the fundamental principles of metaphysics, the collapse of the system is self-assured. This is the situation in which the world finds itself, today.

The severity of the financial problems that all the nations of the world are facing today, indicates that the collapse is far advanced, and may be near the point of disintegration, of the failing system. This is true for all nations that have committed themselves to the axioms that the western world-financial system represents. The only major exception is China, which operates outside of this system, and employs policies that are more aligned to the fundamental principles of metaphysics. Here, we find a strong focus on physical infrastructure development, and the self-development of the creative potential of the population, with corresponding increases in the standard of living. This contrasts to the western trend where the social systems are collapsing for the lack of funding, and a food supply and energy crisis is unfolding.

An impossible solution:

Governmental Budget Cutting.

Let us assume for the sake of examining the problem, that a newscast reports one day that it has been determined after long debate that the government must cut its operational deficit above all other consideration. It is said in the broadcast that the government must achieve this cut by slashing expenditures in order to get its financial outflow under control.

The scenario is quite a common one. It is played out in almost every country in the world. In fact it has become a rhetoric with such a uniformity in wording as to suggest that a central agency, such as the IMF is driving the global budget cutting hysteria from behind the scenes. So, how is a scientist to react to these demands for dramatic austerity?

The most common reaction that one hears in public, is, "Yes, great! We must control our spending," or "We can't spend more than what we take in!" The question should be asked: Is this a scientifically correct reaction? Is it correct for a nation to cut spending above all else, in order to make the budget come out right, while cutting deep into the nation's real wealth, the productive capacity of its people? It doesn't make sense for a nation to destroy its income base as a means for paying off a debt.

The scientist of society must determine what principles are involved in public financing. Are these principles the same as household financing?

The answer involves several evaluations. Is it correct, for instance, for a nation to cut the social safety nets in order to balance its budget? If one answers, yes, the answer implies that the value of the human being has been discounted to zero, or near zero, compared to money. In such a case the human being is counted as a liability not worth protecting. However, is there any tangible value on this planet apart from that which the human being is producing by means of its creative potential expressed in economic activities? Even land would have no value without people using it.

Should it not rather be seen as a sign of insanity, under such circumstances, to starve the "goose that lays the golden eggs?" What gain can a society reap by starving, murdering, or otherwise destroying its people, which are the source of all value created?

Wherever the path of forcing austerity impositions is implemented, so that people become destroyed as the result of a perceived lack of resources that are necessary to maintain human life and the creative and productive capacity of the individual, the society cheats itself by eliminating the one component in the economic sphere that creates all the 'profits' that are created under the sun? Nothing else in the universe creates the slightest form of profit. All the economic value that exist under the sun is the outcome of the productive action of human labor and the scientific and technological structures that make the productive processes as efficient as possible.

By not protecting this 'profit' potential that rests exclusively with the human being, that is, by engaging in the destruction of human beings through causes of poverty, the society literally destroys itself. And this destruction is real. It is painfully felt today. None-the-less, it is still escalated. Nothing could be more a sign of insanity than this creeping voluntary self-destruction of society.

Against the logic of this background, it is a type of criminal insanity for a government to refuse to fund the support services that are essential for its people to exist, to be creative and productive, and to maintain their health, which reflects the health of society. The proper response, and indeed the only logical response in a governmental budget crises, is for the Scientist of society to determine why the crisis exists, what principles are violated, and what policies must be reversed to reverse the violation of the fundamental principles. If one pursues this process, it become immediately evident that a society cannot pay its way out of a financial crisis with moneys it steals from the tables of those which the crisis has rendered poor, nor can it generate the needed wealth through withholding supporting infrastructures that amounts to committing people to starvation and death. On this basis the budget can never be balanced, even if the entire population becomes annihilated so that the sum total of its needs add up to zero. In such a case the debt load would still remain, and continue to grow in leaps and bounds as the debt service costs are recycled into evermore debt, while the life of society has ended.

The scientist needs to determine what factors are currently starving the human system of its rightful development, and what actions are required to solve the starvation crisis without destroying even the smallest segment of the population.

If one pursues the subject in fundamental terms, it soon becomes evident that infinitely more than just budgetary considerations are involved. Deep fundamental considerations come to light with far ranging implications that relate to justice, to the principle of the nation-state, and to the metaphysical platform of mankind's existence on this planet.

Chapter 4: On Free-Trade, Privatization, Credits, Exports, and Development

A scientific determination of the causes of the example budget crisis would yield the following recognition:

.1. It would be recognized that the free-trade principle, wherever it was implemented, has made it impossible for any government to protect its nation's industries, not withstanding that protection is one of the fundamental tasks assigned to governments for which they were created. To renege on this duty to provide protection, as the free-trade principle demands, is a crime against the heart and soul of the principle of the nation-state. Because of this break of promise which the free trade principle demands from any government, many of the nations' industries have became lost, jobs have became exported to cheap labor areas, or have been replaced with slavery type jobs. In either case the tax-base is being eroded by free trade while the social support claims soar in volume. It is plain to see that this type of process is inherently unaffordable by any nation. It is also plain to see that the privatization of the nation's infrastructures and resources cannot cure the underlaying cause of the crisis which involves from a deeply underlying policy error. The reality is, that the privatization of infrastructures adds to the crisis, rather than the solution. Privatization increases the extraction of profits from the economic system, thereby further weakening the system that is already collapsing.

Would a scientist deem it wise, therefore, to cut the life-support for people who were victimized by the government's error in accepting free trade? Of course not! Unfortunately, this is exactly what is happening. A Scientist would deem it wise to shut down the free-trade practices, instead of killing people, thereby shutting down one of the factors that caused the deficit crisis in the first place.

.2. It would further be recognized that the budget crisis is also a debt crisis, and that the debt burden is unbearable. An examination of the debt burden would indicate to the Scientist that the entire financial credit system that the world operates under is fundamentally defective. Should a nation be required to pay rent (interest) on its own money? Should a nation not rather own its own credit? Why should an external private institution have the right to own a nation's credit, which the people of the nation, then, rent back from the private monetary system at horrendous cost?

It would be determined by the scientist that sky-high interest rates, in the order of 7-8% cannot be paid by an economy that produces only a 2-4% profit margin. A scientist would deem it essential, therefore, that a state owned credit structure be established for rebuilding the physical economy, and that no interest be charged for the creation of national infrastructures, education, industrial development, and scientific and technological development.

.3. It would also be recognized what the current austerity driven budget cutting really means, that it is analogous to a motorist who rips the tires off his vehicle in order the lighten the load, while the real problem is that he's run out of fuel.

The society has run out of 'fuel' and attempts to do in economic terms what the above mentioned motorist attempts, insanely, to get his machine going again. The society is determined to cut its tires off to lighten the load of its budget crisis, rather than acknowledging that it is stalled out the need for fuel. The obvious answer for any 'motorist' in such a case, is not to rip the tires off, but to get gas.

The reversal of today's global debt crisis can only

be accomplished by addressing the cause of the crisis. The fuel supplies has been cut. The entire crisis can be solved by simply restoring the fuel supply system to a healthy operational state.

There is a need for the society to take a look at what has caused its crisis, and, then, take the logically opposite action. Since the crisis is linked in part to the speculation orgy that is collapsing the physical economy, the obvious solution is to shut the orgy down and kick-start the economic development of all the world's nations as a means for generating profits for people's existence and development.

Another area in which the nations are ripping their tires off to lighten the load, rather than getting gas, are export policies. Export related issues are rarely self-development oriented, and therefore, should receive the lowest priority possible in any nation's self-development project. The first priority should always be to develop the economic potential of a nation for its own benefit. When a portion of a nation's work force is drawn out of the labor pool into slavery type employment for the manufacturing of cheap export goods, as in Mexico, the nation deprives itself of that strength of human labor that would normally be used to upgrade the nation's own economy and provide for the nation's own development requirement. That the deployment of slave-type labor for export oriented production is a detriment to any nation is evident by the desperate backwardness of the old colonial nations of the British Empire, and others that have been ravaged under centuries of colonialism. Exporting does not enrich a nation. It enriches only the traders and cartels who profit from the exploitation. This does not mean that equitable trade out of the strength of a nation's productive capacities is not beneficial. The point is, that this strength must first be built. The scientist will recognize that the opposite is happening, to the extreme. Not only do many nations export their labor, they even export their most vital resources, industries, and infrastructures through privatization. A great crime is being committed by these measures, against the nations of the world.

The scientists of society need to determine how exports may be curbed, rather than expanded, for as long as there exists the least poverty within the nation, so that this strength can be used for its own development. The focus on exports must be to first create a platform for abundance from which exports may be drawn. In fact, the economic scientist must determine the minimal platform below which exports may not be allowed. The principle must never be allowed to be repeated that was applied against Ireland during the potato blight, at which time food was exported for financial profits under military protection while the people that created the food were starving to death. One and a half million people were deprived of their life for these profits. Another million persons tried to escape the same fate by sailing to America, of which many died enroute and in the quarantine camps at their destination. Free-trade feudalism bears as ugly face. In Ireland, its parasitism almost destroyed an entire nation.

The scientist needs to understand that the free-trade principle is a weapon of empires. It is a weapon more potent than war, for the destruction of nations. Historically, this weapon was specifically designed for this very purpose. Its official creator, Adam Smith, was required by his employer to devise means for bankrupting the former colonies of North America which had dared to declare their independence from the British Empire, and to bankrupt the nation of France which had supported the American War For Independence. The principle that Adam Smith deployed, was the principle of free-trade. It was cleverly interwoven into the peace accord after the British Empire lost on the battle field. The principle worked so exceedingly well that both, France, and the newly born United States of America, were bankrupted in less than a decade.

The scientist of society must focus on the truth unfolding in universal history. A focus of this type inevitably underscores the protective and promoting function of the nation-state as the first and foremost institution on the planet that is able to protect a people against free-trade and enables a people to provide the common resources for its self-development, thus uplifting the civilization of society and to assure its prosperity.

Any scientific evaluation of this type, that regards the human being as the primary element in an economy, above all else, and recognizes man's value to society - which evaluation therefore subjugates all other considerations to this main imperative - will prove itself to be the only workable solution in the long run for dealing not only with the global debt crisis, but with any other crisis, especially the recurring crises of global financial crashes.

The dynamic nature of wealth.

The restructuring of ones focus onto reality makes some dramatic demands. It turns all conventions upside down. It has never been said throughout history (apart from a few exceptions) that the human being is the primary factor in an economy, as obvious as this may appear. But, this is the reality. The opposite ideology rules today. The current practice is to sacrifice humanity in order to keep a grossly defective economic system alive. This process may profit a few individuals richly, in a temporary sense, while it is destroying humanity as a whole. The challenge of overturning this defective focus is far greater than it may appear. It goes against the grain of the ideology of feudalism, the ideology of every Empire past, present, or future. This ideology has ruled for centuries, and still rules humanity to a far greater extend, even today, than the public is aware of or will admit. But this ideology is flawed. It defines wealth as existing in itself, as something static. If this were true, financial crashes would never occur. The reality is, that wealth is dynamic. It is something that is constantly created anew with the productive processes of society. Financial crashes occur when wealth becomes isolated, when it becomes its own thing, when it becomes disassociated from reality, when it becomes unreal. This describes the current perception of wealth.

Against this deeply ingrained ideology, that is in large measure an ideology of monetary feudalism, the type of economic solution that is based on putting the human being on top of the priority list, is not one that is easily recognized as a logical solution to a budget crisis. Under the feudalist ideology, money-rights and estate-rights are primary ("to hell with the human being"). The current thinking is that people are little more than just usable resources in the framework of these rights. This is how the world has been run for nearly a century. The world has been run within the framework of principles designed to protect wealth and power at all cost, and to advance self-serving interests. Much of the burden that mankind bears is a burden of policies designed to protect and advance these rights, falsely established, which reflect the needs of empires rather than the needs of human beings. By what fundamental right should a tiny minority of parasitical oligarchs ride roughshod over the society that constitutes 99.999% of humanity?

It is a fallacy to believe that most public policies are enacted for the public's good. Most of them, clearly, are not. But how does one choose? What criteria can be established to determine what is for the good of humanity, and what are the self-serving demands of powerful imperial self-interest groups designed to further their insatiable requirement for looting, no matter how harmful these demands may be to humanity?

Historically, the needs of human beings have been been cast aside in the interests of protecting the structures of wealth and power. The existence of such things as slavery and dope pushing (the term "narcotics trade" is too soft a term to describe the reality) proves the point. By these processes that are designed for the service of wealth, enormous wealth was created, and still is. Dope pushing is currently the most profitable industry in the world. It has become a two trillion dollar a year operation, which produces no gain for society, pays no taxes, provides nothing even to repair the social destruction it causes. It only destroys. It destroys the targeted populations morally, mentally, and physically, fuels crime, corrupts the world's financial institutions and drains vast profits out of an already collapsing physical economy.

The proceeds of this crime fuel more crime and finance much of the world's terrorism.

The bottom line that drives society nearly on a global scale is the accumulation of personal wealth, rather than the dynamic wealth of an advancing civilization.

The people who pay for the wealth that parasitism extracts from society do so with their life, while the wealth, itself, that was extracted, decays, in the unending inflation spiral that dilutes all financial aggregates as their supposed value increases. By this process civilization is ratcheted downwards into the mire of primitive existence where intelligence counts for nothing.

The same happens to what is called, wealth. What is the wealth worth that is locked up in bonds against debt that can never be repaid because the economic machine that generates all wealth has been burned out? What is any debt worth that is unrepayable? Its worth is zero.

If wealth was sought in living processes that advance the state of society and the physical platform of the world, such as scientific research, technological advances, the production of goods, food, housing, energy, transportation - all of which are living processes - and whatever supports these processes, such as education and culture, etc., the realized wealth would be forever secure. In this case the wealth would be new and dynamic as it benefits society, instead of being stale and unrelated to reality as most of today's so-called wealth is.

Ironically, the accumulated wealth of empires can only be protected from total disintegration when the human factor in economics is put on top of the priority list, as by this factor alone wealth is created, and by which it has any meaning. On any other platform the empires, themselves, are doomed. It is one of the great fallacies of the modern age that people believe that financial wealth can be protected in a collapsing economy. The fact is, that 99.99% of today's so-called financial wealth is in excess of what the physical reality supports. On the global scale as much as $500 trillion may be outstanding in financial aggregates of all types, including financial derivatives, currencies, real estate, commodity futures, stocks, bonds, mortgages, debts holdings, and others, all of which represent claims that are stacked up against the profits from the productive processes and enterprises which are becoming rapidly down sized and eliminated by a rising wave of seat shop slave labor shops in the poorer nations on the planet.

The U.S. may hold as much as one fifth of this mountain of claims, a mere $100 trillion, which must be compared to the total value added product of the nation which represents the real wealth created within the society. In contrast to this huge artificially produced value, created in 'cyberspace' as it were, stands the value produced in the physical economy which the financial value is supposed to represent. This physically produced value, however, amounts to slightly more than one trillion dollars per year. This amount represents the value added in the nation's productive processes. This value added figure contrasts sharply from the Gross Domestic Product figure (app. $17 trillion) which includes financial gains that are fictitious in nature and cannot be counted as value, since nothing of value is being produced by speculation in which investors steal from each other in their clever manipulative schemes. The value added amount represents what is physically produced in the productive economy. Its represents the sum total of the product of the society's labor. It represents the physical proceeds by which a society maintains itself, of which rarely more than 5% can be considered as free gain above the cost of production. This free gain represents the increase in wealth the society has produced for itself, which is immediately stolen.

It is stolen in the form of interest demands, and capital gains demands, which far outstrip this tiny bit of profit. A 5% profit from a one trillion dollar value of production, the society gains itself a $50 billion improvement for its existence. These $50 billion, or $0.05 trillion, now must be compared to the outstanding financial claims against it, of which $100 trillion dollars worth have been accumulated. In other words, the outstanding claims are 2,000 times larger than what is being produced. It would take 2,000 years of the society's total labor, to cash out those claims. Such a payout simply cannot be achieved in real terms, and would be meaningless if it could be achieved, since most people don't live 100 years, much less 2,000 years. Except, this doesn't include interest and capital gains demands. Let's assume that a 10% capital gain is demanded, which is far less than what most mutual funds offer, or investors demand. Given the size of the claims, this adds up to $10 trillion a year in expectations, which sum is still 200 times larger than the increase in physical wealth that is being produced.

Enormous pressures are being brought upon society, therefore, to pay out these super-inflated demands. On the strength of these claims, far more is taken than what is actually produced, by which the society becomes literally looted into poverty. Its industries become decimated, its infrastructures disintegrate, housing becomes substandard if it is unaffordable at all. Unemployments and homelessness become a national disease, and crime and ever growing scourge. On the strength of these claims, advanced research into energy technologies, on which the society's future depends, fall by the wayside. Already, 100 million people loose their life every year from causes related to starvation and prevented development.

In order to show the enormous strength of the financial claims, in Appendix 3 an attempt is made to illustrate the vastly separated relationship between the grand total in claims of financial wealth (shown in the upper part of Appendix 3), and the physical wealth being produced by the world's richest society, the U.S., in terms of profit from its labor (shown in the lower part of Appendix 3).

It has become so prevalent for the financial claimants to demand their payout in excess of all the wealth produced, that they are forcibly stealing from the livelihood of the producers of this health, even from the means that supports their existence. Since this stealing is carried so far in excess of the actual value produced, nobody cares that the looting effectively diminishes the profit creating capacity of the society. When a society is becoming aggressively looted, as all nations have become in modern times, its social structures disintegrate, its infrastructures become dysfunctional, its productive potential diminishes, thus the door opens to poverty, ignorance, disease, and death.

There is absolutely no way that the presently assumed value of the world's outstanding financial aggregates can be honored. Even if profit demands were reduced to 1%, it couldn't be done. In other words, the present world-financial system is bankrupt, its finished. It cannot be rescued by any means. It couldn't be cashed out even in 10,000 years, should capital gains demands diminish to minuscule amounts. The game is over, only the illusion continues that it is still viable.

The above, of course, is nothing more than a simplifies theoretical projection, to illustrate the nature of the process involved. In practical terms, the world's outstanding financial claims can never be honored, because the claims, themselves, increase exponentially, because of interest demands, profit demands, and continuing speculation that escalates hyperbolically. At the present time, the annual turnover for financial speculation nears the 1,000 trillion mark. If this escalation continues, the new millennium that begins at the year 2000, may start with a whopping 5 quadrillion in financial turnover in the greatest gambling casino in the world. Except, the game will crash long before this date. Wisdom dictates, that whatever cannot go on forever, will not go on forever. Right now, the world-financial bubble is severely stressed. If it isn't taken down orderly in a global bankruptcy reorganization, it will disintegrate in a catastrophic collapse and take the society down with it, or the society will disintegrate and take the financial system with it to its 'grave' as it were.

The growing disparity among financial claims.

Yes, there exists a disparity here, too. A wide disparity. This disparity exists not only between the financial claims and the physical reality, which is already infinite, but one can also recognize a growing disparity between the various types of the financial claims, themselves.

In order for a society to be able to protect itself against exorbitant claims, the society needs to become aware of the principles that govern is financial and economic systems, and what these principles represent. A submission to the "follow my lead" demand, which is issued incessantly by the elite of the financial oligarchy, is a sure way to open the door to the most horrendous consequences. Those 'helpful' demands are fundamentally contrary to mankind's requirements.

For instance, the injection of debt into the public system creates a powerful leverage with which the financial empires of the world maximize their claims of financial wealth against the physical economy, even to the point where the looting begins to kill people. Thus, debt becomes a weapon for political control, and a powerful one at that.

The debt-weapon that is required for the despicable game of strangling entire nations economically, in order for the Empire to maintain its balance of dominance over the world, can be easily generated. Indeed, it has been so generated. It has been generated in various ways, by destroying a nation's currency, like President Nixon did for the U.S. when he took the dollar off the gold standard. Debt can also be created by engineering a major upset in the physical economy by which people live, as Paul Volker did in the late 1970s as chairman of the Federal Reserve system. Mountains of debt were created when he raised the Fed's interest rate to as high as 22%, supposedly to fight inflation. The result was in the opposite. The strangulation that killed tens of thousands of businesses started the debt bubble growing as the physical economy collapsed under the weight of this looting.

The loss of society's physical wealth which is measured in the state of its civilization, always unfolds against the background of some form of speculative orgy that generates fictitious wealth leveraged up out of nothing. For this process of leveraging up the fictitious values of financial aggregates, an every increasing flow of funds is drawn out of the real world. Under this twin attack, the debt of the nations has been 'cultivated' to grow rather nicely.

Debt is a two edged sword. It becomes the primary claim against the wealth of the nations. The debt claim supersedes all other claims. It has to be primary, because under the ideology of the feudal system debt is built upon a contract that simply must be honored as a default, here, would usher in a catastrophe. Shakespeare cast the role of debt contracts well in his play, The Merchant of Venice, where contracts were deemed enforceable against life and all that it represents. Shakespeare reversed the scene, however, and upheld the primacy and sanctity of life, and labeled all contracts that act against life as crimes against the state.

This is how debt building must be regarded. For this criminal reason, everything that supports life comes under attack by means of contractual debt service demands, from social service commitments, to education, to research, to infrastructural maintenance and development, to defense, right to the very maintenance of the nation. Debt service payments have a priority protection by which debt service payments are assured, though they should logically be at the last position in consideration.

What are the principles, then, that can be observed, operating in the current financial and economic environment, and how closely are they aligned to the fundamental needs for a productive environment?

What can be observed is not pleasant. In order to hide the avalanche of financial claims, illusions are created. The standard factor of measuring the discrepancy between money and reality, is called inflation. Inflation develops when more money exists than goods, by which the price of goods goes up. This factor, however, can be manipulated, even totally hidden, as it currently is. A more realistic measurement would be found by examining the market-basket of goods that the society can buy with its earnings, or what services it receives, or what housing it is able to afford, or what type of employment is available, and what security it has for survival in case of accidents, illness, or old age. Has this market basket expanded or shrunk? The fact that many people can barely afford to live anymore, and that the governments can barely afford to help keep the disadvantaged alive, and that it cannot even afford to maintain the health and social support services at the most minimally required level, suggest that the society's market basket has shrunk significantly since the mid 60s. Some say it has shrunk by at least a half. This means that the nation is producing less than half of the goods it used to produce, and is less than half as efficient in doing so. One could say, therefore, that the economy has shrunk and that major inflation has occurred as prices have gone up dramatically in comparison to the market basket that the economy delivers.

Except, why has the economy shrunk? It should not have shrunk if we live in a zero-inflation environment? This paradox needs to be resolved.

Answers need to be found for solutions to be created. One thing is certain, the market basket has not shrunk because of any external factors. The sun still shines as it always has. The changes are due to human factors, and these mankind has total freedom to control. The only factors that exist in this realm are self-created or are imposed by other interests that are accepted. If they lead to chaos, then, insufficient alertness is indicated. So, what about our economy, then, is there no inflation as the world leaders suggest? Is there nothing that society can do to make its shrinking market basket grow? The fact is, there is plenty of inflation in the price structure, but there is also plenty that can be done about it, which is not being done now. To begin with, one's perception can become real.

The effect of hidden inflation.

The 'great' stock market crash on Oct. 21, 1929 was but a trumpet blast of an overture that played itself out into the deepest depression in modern history. The magnitude of the depression was superseded in misery only by the much earlier historical disintegration of the 'world'-financial system in 1345. In both cases, a financial crash of cosmic proportion led the way, which was followed by a near total economic disintegration. The question is, why? Why did the systems disintegrate? Had the world suddenly changed?

No, it hadn't. The depression that followed the crash, was the result of hidden inflation suddenly being acknowledged. On the way up, financial share values appreciated to sky high values, regardless of whether the respective company payed dividends, or not. This merry-go-round continued, because the financial instruments in the trading treadmill could always be sold to another bidder, at a higher price. On the way down, however, nobody wanted the stuff that was worth less every day than on the day before.

Today, after more than 66 years, the same game is till being played. The present average yield on the NYSE is 2.2%, or about half of what a T-Bill will bring, or slightly less than 25% of what a good bond will yield. Most stocks, however, provide no direct yields at all. The term "equity" should not even be used in cases when the dividend is zero. All shares are technically worthless that yield no returns. This truth becomes quite evident in a crash. Of course, once the dust settles after 82% of all equity is wiped out, as it was in 1929/1930, a lot of real equity falls by the wayside in the ensuing chaos.

Crashes occur when the illusions no longer hold up. As the illusions crash, the dream of equity in fictitious instruments crashes as well. A market that yields virtually nothing out of its productive strength, but exists only through gains from trading, is 'vulnerable.' Once bond yields exceed stock trading gains, a flood drains out of the stockmarkets into bonds. Once the 'equity' in these markets collapse in real terms, the economy collapses also, and once this happens the selling frenzy hits the bond markets as a last source for cash. After the 1929 crash, virtually all bonds soled at deep discounts, even Treasury bonds. Some went for just pennies on the dollar. However, by the deep discounting, the effective yield, if there was any, shot up.

It is hard to imagine what this interlocked disintegration will do in today's world. In 1929, the banks weren't loaded to the hilt with derivatives, the economy was booming, the government was virtually debt free, there was no energy crisis on the horizon, nor a food crisis even imagined, and the scourge of terrorism was unheard of. Today, we have all these things standing against us, that didn't exist in 1929. Non-the-less, the 1929 crash brought the country to its knees from which it did not recover until the onset of World War II when a serious effort was allowed to restart the economy.

What is deemed to be a factor for stability in the U.S. stockmarket, which currently celebrates the greatest rally in financial values in history, is an illusion. The world is in a state of crisis. The stockmarkets didn't create the crisis, they were drawn into it. They were drawn into it by the axioms of feudalism and their effect on the unwary. Japan's markets are in such a deep crisis, tethering at the edge of collapse that interest rates had to be dropped to half a percent to keep the markets together and to create the appearance of prosperity and calm. There is crisis unfolding in the European markets as well. Sooner or later, the illusion of stability, where there is none, will be overcome by reality. The markets will crash by the ideological forces that have been superimposed upon the whole world-financial and economic scene of which the stockmarkets are but a tiny part. These forces are shaping the mentality that controls the market, and those forces reflect the axioms of feudalism. When the markets crash, the real cause is not a certain insanity on the part of the investors, but is one that leads one back to the courts of empires. Here, the central control is found. Here the tune is created that humanity dances to.

Still, market crashes are quite normal, you might say - they have occurred before and will occur again. Indeed, they have occurred before, but they are far from normal. Cycles of market crashes are inherent only to the feudalist based financial system where financial aggregates become disassociated from reality in order that their value can be driven up through trading. The illusion is, that there can be value created that grows far beyond the actual value that exists in the economy in terms of value produced. This self-escalating system that grows illusions is fundamentally self-defeating as it goes through violent corrections or crashes. This gruesome instability doesn't improve the economy one bit, nor does it create wealth for society, it merely creates conditions for looting. It creates chaos. None-the-less, it is the controlling system of today.

A system built on illusions.

One of the unique aspects of the feudal system of economy, is a kind of trickery within the financial system that hides the real inflation that is building up within, that creates an illusion of calm when there is no calm. This is why the great market crashes take most investors by surprise.

This concealing feature is one of the natural characteristics of the feudal system's disassociation from reality. When a pricing bubble is artificially inflated it tends to pop at a certain point. The occurrence of successive cycles of collapse, however, demonstrates that the reality of the build-up of financial inflation within the feudal financial system cannot be hidden indefinitely. When the artificial front collapses the reality invariably reasserts itself. Collapses occur, whenever the built up inflation within the system becomes so obvious that the reality becomes recognized.

Appendix 4 illustrates this inflation as it is found in today's global financial system. The curves illustrate general trends, rather than actual values. Curves A, B, and C, in Appendix A, were adopted from an illustration presented by the American economist and statesman, Lyndon LaRouche. He described the ever widening separation between the financial aggregates (curve B) and the physical-economic input and output (curve C) as a "typical collapse function." The presentation also shows that the financial claims are infinitely inflated in respect to the physical reality.

The type of system that we operate today, operates fundamentally as a feudalist-based system that recognizes all monetary and financial aggregates as 'rentable estates' that can be deployed to generate profits that are not derived from human labor, but represent a form of looting, such as collecting interest payments on generated debt. The financial aggregates are represented by **Curve B** in Appendix 4. This curve illustrates the growth of the numerous non-productive, so-called 'investments,' such as financial derivatives, or interest earning deposits, or speculative gains from real estate, stocks, bonds, and foreign currency.

The monetary aggregates, such as cash, bank deposits, etc, are represented by **Curve A.** Most of what it represents feeds the financial aggregates system, while only a tiny portion of it feeds the physical economy.

The physical economy is represented by the curves C, D, and E.

The ratio of the profits that are generated in the financial aggregates system, all of which become claims against the productive economy, is illustrated in Appendix 3.

These profits, of course, are as fictitious as the aggregates are by which the profits were derived. They are fictitious as they are **not** derived from actual production, which is the only source of real tangible wealth. Being unrelated to physical reality, the fictitious profits become free to soar to levels far above what the physical economy produces. Since the vast majority of the fictitious profits are 'reinvested' with ever increasing leverage, the total 'value' of the financial aggregates in the system has risen to astronomical heights. This is indicated by **curve B** in Appendix 4 that trails out into space. The so-called profits in the financial aggregates system follow that same ratio of increase, which apparently has no limits.

The unrestrained growth in the financial aggregates system has created an ever widening differential between the fictitious claims that are coming out of it, and the existing monetary aggregates (curve A) such as cash money and bank deposits. This monetary system has also been rising in volume as more money had to be created by the governments to supply the needs of the rapidly growing financial aggregates market. The disparity between the two systems has created a type of inflation that indicates somewhat the uncollectability of the financial aggregates claims. Luckily for the system, the vast majority of the 'investors' have no intention of exercising their claim so that the financial inflation becomes not apparent as a reality. But when the claims are made, the inflated nature of the claims appears, and crashes follow as the illusion collapses.

The increased so-called 'wealth' that is fundamentally fictitious, which appears quite real to their owners except in a market crash situation, becomes impossible to satisfy at any time since the claim that this wealth represents is a liability against an illusion. Those who manage to cash out their claim, do so by stealing from their fellow man.

During the crash, nothing actually falls apart, but the illusion that there was wealth in infinitely inflated paper. Up to the point of disintegration the reality of infinite inflation remains hidden. The reality remains hidden as the world glories in its profits taken by theft, which profits are, then, deemed to be representative of the system as a whole. Indeed, this self-deception works well for as long as the perceived value of financial aggregates remains locked up within fictitious markets and never crosses the boundary where it must test the waters of reality. As long as the fictitious financial wealth is regarded as if it were play money in a Monopoly game (though it has no value anywhere else), the functionality of the games makes the wealth appear real.

The only kind of inflation that tends to be immediately noticed is that which affects the pricing of goods. This type of inflation is noticeable because there is a constant interchange between money and physical goods. By this routine interchange the boundary between the two systems is crossed constantly, so that an unfolding disparity becomes immediately apparent.

Curve A in Appendix 4 shows such an inflation of money volume in relationship to the volume in physical production, which is declining as shown by **curve** C. Traditionally, a price inflation results when more money is chasing fewer goods, but in a collapsing economy the earnings are also collapsing. There would be an inflation if the earnings were to follow curve A, but they don't, they collapse. The excess money supply is being absorbed by the financial markets. All this offsets the pressures on prices. Thus, the monetary inflation is cleverly hidden, once again, and the illusion of a stable financial world is maintained. The end result is, that there is no net inflation noticeable, even while the economic system is fundamentally falling apart.

The official method of 'fighting inflation,' is a process of 'managing' the required level of poverty within the system that keeps the rate of economic collapse within the rage that can be offset through free-trade price deflation. Should the economy recover and develop higher priced products, the credit squeeze is put in place immediately to shrink back this development.

By the above method the real inflation within the system remains totally hidden. It creates an illusion of a zero-inflation economy, while the actual inflationary disparity grows in leaps and bounds.

This illusion of a healthy economy appears to be extremely important to the stock market. Countless market reports from all sorts of backgrounds point out again and again that the economy is healthy because there is no inflation within it. It seems important that this misstatement be repeated as often as possible, in order to keep the 'investors' shielded from the reality. It seem important to keep them tied to the fictitious system that has little value in itself, but gains its value only in the frenzy of the trading circus, without which, stock prices would be low, according to a value determined by earnings through dividends.

The monetary aggregates system is actually divided into two trends. One portion is linked to the interchange with physical goods and services. This portion is rapidly declining with the decline in earnings from physical production. It is this portion that effects prices. The rest of the monetary aggregates are heavily tied into the financial aggregates system, as was stated before. Without this functional separation of the money flow, the decline in physical production as per **Curve C** would generate a hefty monetary, and thereby, price inflation.

In real terms, there should still have been a price inflation, in spite of the functional separation of the money supply into two groups. The reason is, that the society's income from the productive economy has collapsed faster than the collapse in production, causing a deflation in purchasing power. **Curve D** shows the decline in real earnings of the producing population. In a collapsing economic environment, the collapse in earnings always supersedes the decline in physical production as rising unemployment makes labor cheap. This resulting disparity between prices and income, that should have caused inflation in a free market environment becomes offset by deflationary pressures from free-trade imports produced in sweat shop economies, shown by **Curve E**.

Whenever the public is told time and time again that the economy is healthy, because there is no effective inflation of prices, the statement is technically true, but represents still a terrible reality. The reality is that the market basket is shrinking and has shrunk by more than 50% since 1967. The collapse that is indicated by curves C,D, and E, and the relevant portion of the money supply, is a systems-wide collapse as all the relevant elements are tied to each other so that the relative parity is maintained, even while the physical economy is collapsing. All this is necessary to keep the illusion alive that all is well.

The illusion of zero inflation, that the model shown in Appendix 4 generates, represents not a healthy state, but becomes a shattered dream when one realizes that the variances in the physical economy, though its elements remain in parity to each other, represents a deficit for society. This deficit, in turn, becomes also hidden. It becomes obscured by the fact that the governments are now obliged to make up the resulting gap through various social security programs that become increasingly necessary to keep the populations alive. At the same time, however, that the government's social expenditures are rising because of the escalating social deficit (the collapse of income shown in Appendix 4 relative to the 1967 reference point), a corresponding loss in taxation revenue occurs as the shrinking income of society shrinks the tax-base as well. Thereby, the government is doubly effected by this supposedly 'non-existent' inflation.

The social support outflow against the background of a decline in revenue creates that double deficit for the government which reflects itself in the current budget balancing debate. Unfortunately the governments around the world try to solve this problem by clinging to the illusion that cutting social support expenditures is going to make the social deficit go away. The opposite results. As the social support is cut, the physical economy collapses further, and with it, the tax revenue.

Here, the society comes face to face with one of the few real indications that the world's economic system is dangerously off track. Other indications are found in rising unemployment, homelessness, poverty, and crime. Everyone of these is the direct result of the still growing, real deficit in the physical economy, which has been growing from the 1967 reference point on, though at first faintly apparent.

This physical deficit, which to the affected people is quite visible, even to the extend that people die from it, is the only indication by which the public can see that the economic system is not working. Unfortunately, the public doesn't see what its axioms do not allow it to see. The reality is, that this visible component of the unfolding economic crash is but a minute part of what is unfolding. The reality is, that the system needs to be repaired for mankind to save itself from the impending catastrophe in the markets.

The social deficit that the government carries, which is generally called welfare, appears rather insignificant in real terms when compared to the financial demands for interest payments on the national debt. The unfortunate aspect is that the governments are quite prepared to take up the budget axe and cut off the lifeline to the poorest of the population, and consider the debt load burden as sacred. How can the government's theft from the poor save the world-financial system, or even the finances of the nation which interest payments alone are many times larger than the social support needs and have no life or death implication for society if they were curtailed or eliminated.

It should also be noted that the society, itself, had not occasioned the debt that it carries, nor its governments. The feudal, imperial system had created the debt crisis, not the needs of people. The axioms by which the empires maintain their existence, which have infested the minds of humanity, are the destroyers of humanity. They are the foundation on which debt creating process are built. But not only the debt is built, thereon. Every destructive force, policy, or action that acts against the welfare of society, even the life of humanity, is build thereon. Nor can any line be drawn that would separate the empire and isolate it as the sole offender. The minds of people at all levels of society are infested with imperial ideology translated into axioms that are fundamentally destructive to society.

One finds these axioms fermenting destruction at the lowest grass roots level of society, as for instance through the "carrying capacity" myth that defines the world as hopelessly overpopulated, under which mythology up to 100 million people annually meet their death. One also finds these axioms to have infested the minds at the highest level of governments, including presidents and world leaders. A report released in late summer of 1996, by EIR News Service in Washington D.C. presents an overwhelming amount of quite reasonable evidence that the former President of the United States, George Bush, ran the biggest narcotics smuggling business that was ever unleashed against the U.S. population, right out of the White House (as the nation's Vice President). Thousands of America's youth had not only their life destroyed in the great crack cocaine epidemic that was supplied out of Nicaragua as a part of George Bush's "Contra" operation, but many who luckily survived they physical dangers associated with high grade cocaine, are still rotting in jails across the nations for drug related crimes, such as possession of narcotics, the very narcotics which were flown into the U.S. by the plane load under operations directed from the White House. The axioms that drive such a thing are the same as those that drove the British Empire's opium wars against China during its official slave and dope trading days.

Ideally, the officers of the empires who spread their destructive axioms across the globe, should be held accountable for the crimes they unleash. In practice, this is impossible to achieve, nor would it serve any productive purpose. The countless millions of human lives that were destroyed cannot be resurrected, nor can reparations be made that come even close to compensate for the damage done. Not even the world-financial scene can be repaired. Nothing can save this system that has at its core a set of axioms which are powerfully destructive to humanity, and to itself. Even if the current Empire would be charged with the global debt load that its axioms and policies have created, accounts could never be settled. The money that would be required simply does not exist.

The nation's cannot solve the current debt problem, nor should they be logically required to repair damage which they have not created. Most of all, it should be understood that the budget problems that have arisen from the national debts cannot possibly be resolved by conservative measures that in effect increase the damage. Even in the most extreme case, by totally eliminating nation's social programs, and education programs, cutting all spending for the support of social infrastructures, right to the last penny - even by putting the entire population on the ash heap - the budget deficits won't be resolved that float on the tide of debt service demands. The debt would actually increase faster in such a case, as the income base shrinks to nothing by which payments are made.

As the tax-base shrinks, which is currently the case, and the interest on the debt keeps going up, which is also the case, currently, as the deficit in payments becomes additional debt, the deficit gets worse and worse. It is a crime to impose conservative measures in an attempt to solve this situation, which are doubly murderous, in that they kill people by deprivation, and kill the support structures of civilization.

The current world-financial crisis must be seen as a threat against civilization. It is nothing less than that. To assume that it is anything less, is utter insanity. The conservative approach to solving the world-financial crisis is a case of criminal insanity. The insanity is evident by the fact that nothing would be resolved even if the entire world-population were eliminated from the face of the earth so that no expenditures at all would have to be made for its support. Another facet of insanity is to believe that the global debt structure was even intended to be solvable. It was evidently intended to serve as a perpetual cash cow whose milk is needed to nurse a fundamentally self-destructive financial apparatus along in order that it may continue to serve its empires and prevent the scientific and technological self-development of humanity.

This little exercise shows that the dismantling of the supporting infrastructures for living accelerates the collapse of the physical economy, which it currently does, and collapses the tax revenues. It is unavoidable that this triggers a crash in the world-financial system.

The logic of the above shows that the current world debt, which is infinitely inflated in comparison to what mankind's physical economy can support, which it is intended to loot under feudalist axioms, and therefore has in real term no value at all. Whatever is infinitely inflated is valueless.

That infinite inflation has become a part of the modern financial world is evident by its huge mountain of debt that has no value to its holder. In order for the society to be able to honor its debt and repay it, the physical economy would need to grow by app. 44,000%. Within the parameters of this growth the current social deficit would become erased and the tax-base be expanded sufficiently to match the requirement for repayment of the debt. It is self-evident that this massive growth cannot be achieved on the current financial and economic platform where a 3% growth is considered inflationary and is throttled back artificially. Thus, we live as liers to ourselves: a society, dreaming as it does, hoping that its national debt will magically go away without anyone addressing the reasons that caused it.

Chapter 5: What is infinite inflation?

The curves in Appendix 4 are a characteristic representation according to recently published studies by the Executive Intelligence Review magazine. In fact, **Curve B** cannot be completely represented as the paper is too short. The growth of the financial aggregates trading, which includes the bond and stock markets, the financial derivatives markets, and international currency speculation, is represented by Curve B in a composite conceptional manner. Appendix 1, Figure 1 shows a more accurate representation of a single one, of the major elements. It shows the world wide total of all the financial derivatives in the system averaged out for a given year. This growth pattern matches that of Curve B in Appendix 4. In reality Curve B may be somewhat conservative.

Several of the other elements within the financial aggregates system have increased much more rapidly. For instance, between 1966 and 1990 a whopping 613 fold increase in foreign exchange turnover for profit has taken place, which is an explosive growth by any standard. Is it any wonder, then, that the currencies of entire nations suffer from this ravishing trade? The growth in futures turnover was somewhat less, which has grown only 493 fold during this period. These figures are huge. They represent a 61,300% increase, or a 49,300% increase respectively. The total annual turnover in financial aggregates between 1966 and 1995 has risen from $1.69 trillion to $500.00 trillion, for a 300 fold increase. These are enormous values involved in these increases.

If one compares the value added product to the total financial turnover, one finds the latter to be 440 times larger, which represents a separation of the financial world from the physical world in the order of 44,000%. In the mid sixties, the two aspects were close to even, which means that financial turnover was tightly linked to the exchange of physical goods. In today's situation, however, the financial world is highly inflated (App. 44,000%) in relationship to what it represents as an interchange medium to facilitate commerce. The effective inflation is actually worse than that, if one compares the generated claims (called profits) within the financial aggregates system to the free profit of the productive industry. The disparity may be as high as 90,000% and more. This figure, however, is still conservative compared to reality, because it doesn't include the debt load that the nation carries, which requires interest payments to be made that shrink the free-gain profit that the nation has realized in the productive industries, and turns these profits into a negative net amount. In other words, the financial claims are infinitely inflated in comparison to what they represent, as claims against the free gain in the physical economy.

The result of this infinite inflation that is not recognized, is an illusion of monstrous proportions. On the surface it appears that no inflation exists in the system, except a lot of wealth, while in reality the perception of so-called wealth has been inflated to astronomical levels. The illusion, of course, does have the desired effect of raising, what is called "investor's confidence." It is this confidence that causes the citizens of the nation to empty out their savings into the infinite sink-hole of financial aggregates, which is happening every day at a rate of 10-25 billion dollars per month in the U.S.A. alone. What we see here, is a modern day gold-rush, operating in reverse.

The inflation figure of 44,000% is based on an estimated $25 trillion in financial gains realized in the U.S. markets, which are are fundamentally claims against the nation's value-added production, which however, amounted in 1994 to only $1.3 trillion. If one subtracts from the value added production figure the cost of labor, the necessary taxes, and the cost of the business operations required to achieve the production, a net profit of 4-6% remains, which is a high figure for any productive industry around the world, so that the total free gain profit of the nation's productive effort amounts to something in the order of $0.0585 trillion. This free-gain is the profit to society that is achieved by its labor above the cost of production, against which all claims must be measured. In real terms, no other wealth creating processes exists than the productive activity of human labor. Even claims against real-estate property, for instance, have ultimately no meaning unless an income stream exists to satisfy the claim, which is in turn derived from productive activities.

When the financial claims of the debt of the nation, and those arising from the stockmarket, some $25 trillion, altogether, are measured against this free-gain derived from production. The paper claims become meaningless in enormity. These $25 trillion in paper claims represent a claim against the $0.0585 trillion in actual wealth produced. This makes the paper claims 43,000% larger than what can be satisfied. The percentage may actually be slightly more as the typical profit margin of the productive industry is constantly declining in a collapsing economy.

These values are the inflation differential that is

indicated between points B and C in Appendix 4. It is important to note, here, that the indicated inflation value is meaningful only as a theoretical measurement under the assumption of a **zero interest rate** environment. If one adds the interest demands to the equation, the differential becomes infinite.

In a zero interest rate environment the differential between paper claims and production generated wealth, is theoretically rectifiable. If no new claims were generated, it would require a pay-out period of some 440 years to settle the current paper claims in physical value by applying the total of all the profits of the productive economy to this purpose for a time span of 22 generations. In practice, this would never happen. But this is what an inflation of 44,000% in claims over real profit means.

The inflation figure of 44,000%, of course, is meaningless in real terms, since the real world evolves around debt service costs which present a higher claim on the wealth produced by society. Since the current world-financial system operates on a feudalist platform, interest demands become a central factor that shifts the entire equation to the point where everything becomes totally meaningless.

On the feudal platform, financial aggregates are understood as **rentable estates** that are required to bear earnings. Therefore, we must now include this feature of the feudalist-based economy, called usury, or income generated from indebtedness, into the equation that measures the claims against earnings. The result is a deficit, rather than a profit, in the wealth produced by society. So now, we have deficits in earnings, rather than profits which might become available to repay debts or cash out fictitious stock prices. And those deficits are huge.

Since a nation operates as a single economic unit, and the total U.S. debt stands at $16 trillion, the corresponding annual debt service cost, at 5% interest amounts to $0.8 trillion, which is all by itself 15 times greater than the total free-gain profit derived from physical production. This tiny $0.8 trillion in debt service demands, now has a rather amazing effect on the $25 trillion in outstanding financial claims, in that it invalidates them all.

If one applies the debt service costs against the free-gain from the productive economy, what should remain as profit to advance society, turns out to be many times too small to satisfy the debt service claims. In other words there is nothing left over by a long way for the repayment of the debt or to cash in fictitious financial aggregates from the stockmarkets. The end result is that these financial claims simply cannot be satisfied.

The reality is, that no one can satisfy a claim with an income drawn to zero, or with an actual deficit in income. All claims, therefore, that were measured against the free-income in Appendix 4, are in reality claims against a non-existing resource, or a negative resource. This means that all the claims against this resource have become effectively uncollectible and thereby valueless. In reals terms, the effective financial inflation, therefore, is infinite.

This type of infinite inflation may be likened to what happens to the value of an oil well once the hole is gone dry. An income gone negative, is a dry hole. In such a case, the value of the oil well (not counting land and equipment) is zero. In doesn't matter in this case whether the book value of the oil well is one dollar, or ten, or ten million. In every case, the book value is infinitely inflated above the real vale, which is zero. No sane person would spend ten million dollars, or even one dollar, on a dry hole.

The above situation accurately describes the value of the mountains of debt that the nations carry, whose incomes are become negative under the yoke of feudalist debt service demands. The world's income has become a dry hole, and the book value of the world's debt is not up in the tens of trillions, but is substantially zero.

All this means, that since neither the financial claims, nor the debt itself, can ever be paid off, both are simply rolled over into becoming evermore debt or ever greater financial paper, both of which are infinitely inflated even as they grow. In other words, the value which they claim to represent, is pure fiction. It doesn't matter, therefore, from a standpoint of value whether the Dow Jones Industrial Average stands at 100, 5,000, or 25,000. Once the 'well' that delivers the real value has gone dry, the value of whatever represents a claim against it, is zero.

The above interrelationship represents not only what is true about today's stockmarket, or bond market, or the debt that the nations choke under. It also represents what is true about the world's currencies.

The very moment that a nation's free-gain from production becomes a deficit for the nation (which is possible only under the feudalist system), from that moment on all financial inflation becomes infinite so that the actual size of the debt that has accumulated, or accumulates thereafter, becomes an inconsequential factor. Once the inflation is infinite, the value of the aggregate is zero. It may appear to have value. It may even sell as if it had value. But it has really no value at all. The same is true for the debt. It appears to have value to the holder who collects debt service payments.

But when it comes to the cash-out stage, its value becomes related to the dry hole.

Any increase in debt within this relationship is therefore irrelevant to the debtor, since a debt that is unrepayable, remains so no matter how big it grows. In other words, the whole financial process has become meaningless. This is what happens under extreme feudalism, by which debt service demands quickly grow out of context with reality. This, in short, is what infinite inflation means.

This is also the platform on which the present economy operates. The principle of the usurious platform assures that the debt can never be repaid, by which the empires hold sway over their realm. Nor is there anything built into the modern system that would prevent the Federal Reserve from cranking up its interest rates back into the 22% range, to tighten the belts, or "cool off the economy" as they put it, as was the case under Paul Volker's reign. Nor would it actually matter if they did. It would simply increase the already unrepayable debt and bring us nearer the point when the shape of reality dawns and book values resume to represent real values, which are largely zero. The great crash, therefore, is but an exercise in realization. In reality, the financial crash or disintegration has already occurred.

The above calculations that show a negative income for society from its productive activities, were made intentionally simplistic to illustrate a point. The present GNP is currently four times larger than the value added product from manufacturing. This differential reflects the relative size of the service and financial industries, both of which produce next to nothing for the raising of civilization.

Appendix 1, Figure 4 shows the profit to debt relationship that has unfolded in the U.S. economy, as somebody else sees it. A writer for the Executive Intelligence Review News Service, John Hoefle, commenting on the unfolding disparity between debt and actual profit in the economy, writes: "Currently, for every dollar of so-called profit, we loose $2.50 and incur $4 in debt, for a total of $6.50 per dollar. That's like going down to the store and buying dollars for $7.50 apiece, and then taking that dollar, and calling it profit. Furthermore, the guy we're borrowing the money from to buy these dollars, doesn't have any money either: He steals it from somebody else. That "somebody else" is the rest of the world. We are stealing money from Ibero-America, from Africa, from the former East block countries, looting their populations and our own, to keep the bubble afloat."(Executive Intelligence Review, March 10, 1995)

Now, since the income of society is so low that the debt can never be repaid, and since the feudalist platform makes it impossible to generate the required economic expansion by which the income is increased sufficiently to pay the debt, it doesn't matter how much further the debt grows. This fundamental fact appears to be a difficult pill for 'investors' to swallow, for they keep on pouring more and more money into paper instruments that finance the debt. In order to sanitize the insane process, the investors will create for themselves the most far fetched arguments they can think off to deny to themselves that infinite inflation exists, and that it means that the differential between paper values and physical values has grown to absolute irreconcilability.

In the light of this, it is rather astonishing how staunchly people are denying the fact before their very eyes, which any student in primary mathematics will confirm, that once financial aggregates have reached the threshold beyond which they have no practical value, it really doesn't matter how great an amount one owns of them. The result will be zero in all cases. In other words, whatever in the system represents a claim against something that does not exist, is irrelevant, except for trading purposes and make-believe games. There is a reality of the background of today's financial scene. It is a most tragic one. This reality is evident in the suffering of the people whose economies are looted to the ground by financial claims, whose currencies are devaluated, whose industries are collapsing, whose economic life-blood is sucked out of the physical system and is poured into the fictitious aggregates systems by the lure of fantastic gains. The reality is, that the financial system has become dysfunctional and worthless, and the society that supports it, is dying.

Developing a solution.

The solution begins with recognizing the symptoms and acknowledging that a problem exists. Once this is done, the problem is half solved. Were a physician treating this case, the physician would acknowledge to himself that the case requires a radical solution. If a physician saw a patient dying because a vital organ has become dysfunctional to the point that it cannot be repaired, he would recommend to the patient that the patient give the organ up for a new one that functions properly. Failing this, the patient would die.

This type of radical surgery is equally necessary in the economic and financial realm in order to save mankind from a similar fate. This fate is unfolding rapidly as the world-financial system, which normally functions to support the development of the physical economy and the advance of civilization, no longer fulfills this type of function, but causes the opposite. Since a vital organ of mankind's economic system has become deeply dysfunctional, so much so that it cannot be repaired, which the reality of infinite inflation indicates, steps must be taken to replace the failing organ with a functional one.

A physician knows from experience what a functional human organ looks like, and which organic defects can no longer be repaired. This type of skill is severely lacking in the economic and financial arena. It existed centuries ago when the Renaissance unfolded for this very reason, or the American Revolution was launched that eventually led to the establishment of the most powerful economic system ever created in the planet. Today, this skill needs to be relearned.

The scientist of today needs to relearn the principles that underlie the American System of economy, the most successfully functioning system that the human intellect has created so far. Astonishingly, it is a very plain system. Its focus is on raising the status of society and the state of civilization by enhancing the creative capacity of human labor, rather than enhancing speculative profits (oh how antiquated! how wonderfully functional!)

The infinite model of economy.

The infinite model is shown in Appendix 5 Figure 1. The model has three elements. It consists of a physical economy that creates profits in terms of real tangible wealth for advancing the standard of living of the society. This advance in civilization is the third element in the model. The advance in living standards raises the platform of civilization, which represents scientific and technological progress, achieved through culture, learning, advanced research, etc.. This advance, in turn, enhances the productive capacity of human labor so that the interchange between the second and third elements becomes self-amplifying. This progressive development has no inherent limits, or conditions for cycles of collapse. It represents an infinite development system.

The first element of the model is the principle of the nation-state. Under this principle the nation creates for itself a currency and extends to itself interest free monetary credits for industrialization and the creation of infrastructures, such as transportation facilities, water development, electric power development, energy resource development, education, etc., that get the physical economy operational and provide essential services for it. The economic return that the nation gains by extending to itself interest free monetary credits, is not measured in increases of aggregate values. It is measured in increases in the profit generating capacity of the economic system that supports the life, happiness, and security of the nation. By this process economic gain becomes multiplied.

This system is essentially centered on productive private enterprise (in contrast to private speculative looting). It is focused on creating profits for society under conditions that enhance the society's creative and productive potential, which are the foundation of civilization. This self-amplifying process constantly increases the 'energy' that unfolds within the dynamics of the infinite system, so that the system can be carried on, literally, to infinity.

The feudal financial system, contrasts sharply with the infinite system. the feudal system is a terminal system. Nothing is ever created or produced within the feudal system of economy. Its focus is on looting whatever wealth exists until the strength of the human system is drained to zero. In the process of looting, it destroys whatever strength a society has; it destroys the society's infrastructures and industries. The post-industrial society dogma, is feudal dogma. The looting process, of course, cannot develop to infinity. Thus, the feudal system is a terminal system by its very nature.

In the infinite system of economy, which is progressive and development oriented, the role of the nation-state becomes one in which protection is high on the agenda, and support for the processes by which human beings realize their potential. These processes include education, science, advanced technologies, but also art, music, drama, creations of beauty, etc.. As the society grows richer under the infinite model, it's chosen political platform becomes inherently less-taxation intensive. Taxation falls away in proportion as the functional interchange between the economy and civilization becomes evermore self-amplifying. Taxation may ultimately disappear. In the infinite model of economy, taxation becomes displaced by the creation of new money. In a dynamically growing economy, the money supply must be increased constantly to match the increase in physical product. In this environment the recycling of money through taxation becomes structurally unnecessary.

It is extremely difficult for today's modern society to comprehend the principle of infinite development, because the society's thinking is too narrow and too small, even in its wildest imagination. Having been steeped for centuries in conservative ideologies, under the rule of feudalistic axioms, the society's imagination has been infested with axioms that breed the acceptance of limitations as a final reality. The result is, that even in such cases when the society allows itself to think big, it thinks in small terms, none-the-less.

In terms on nuclear power development, for instance, thinking big might mean a five fold increase in the rate of construction, over the next five years. The contrast of this still largely conservative approach, in its comparison with the real need of society, is profound. It is a stunning contrast, because realistic thinking would embrace a scope in energy development that has the objective to enable the total replacement of oil as a motor fuel for all forms of transportation, with hydrogen fuels produced from nuclear power. For this goal a technological and industrial development effort is required that pales all development efforts in history into insignificance. A growth in development by several orders of magnitude is required to achieve this goal. But it must be achieved, because the world's oil resources are finite and depletion is already taking its toll.

Mankind thinks far too small when it fails to look beyond the oil stage. The shrinking oil resource puts it into a stranglehold. Oil is like gold. Gold will never become a useful currency because it cannot be expanded in quantity, proportionately to the unfolding patterns of life. If gold were a currency, its limited supply would keep an economy stagnant. The same is true for oil. Oil is too limited a resource to meet the transportation energy requirement of an economy that expands according to the dynamic pattern of life. There just isn't enough of it in the ground.

It is a simple economic fact, that if the needed expansion in energy supplies cannot be achieved, human life must contract. The creation of large scale resources requires large scale energy inputs. Anything less puts us back onto a more primitive level of existence, with primitive lifestyles, toil, poverty, and starvation. Nuclear energy, converted into hydrogen fuels is the only option mankind has to overcome the present energy bottleneck that oil represents. It is also the only viable option for avoiding a total global energy supply failure in the future when the oil wells begin to run dry.

In agricultural terms, too, mankind thinks far too conservative, even when it dares to contemplate the greening of the desserts. Sure, the desserts can be made green, and if this is done, what then? A naturally developing society that maintains itself at a healthy nutritional level requires increases in food supplies which are again several magnitudes greater than what mankind dares to imagine today. Even now, the requirements of the present world population is for twice the supply than is currently produced. Naturally, these increases can be achieved. Mankind has not even begun, but to scratch the bare earth and plant seeds in it. Only a fraction of the world's available land is used for food production, and only a tiny portion of that is irrigated, and absolutely no large scale production is done in climate controlled, multistory, indoor facilities.

When mankind thinks big in terms of metals, the giant open pit mines come to mind that exist in some parts of the world where ready made ore is simply dug out of the ground. This primitive type of mineral production is once again a bottleneck that chokes off expansion of infrastructures. This primitive approach, that was great centuries ago, hinders the development of the society according to the dynamics of life. It lacks the parameters for infinite development.

Realistic thinking in mineral production embraces efforts in nuclear fusion as an essential path to the technologies required for the decomposition of rocks into constituent elements, most of which are compounds of metals and silicone. We need to think of types of resource development that are several orders of magnitude greater in scope than anything ever produced on this planet. And we need to do all this just in order to survive as human beings, with a civilization that bears witness to the grand capacities of the mind, without which the earth would be primitive and desolate, and mankind would be bound to the harsh limits of nature and become throttled by its poverty.

We need to think big in terms of energy, food, and material resources with which to build, or humanity is finished and collapses into impotence. We need to industrialize food production in science intensive processes and energy intensive facilities to free the human being from toilsome trudgery. Right now, the farm sector still imposes the most toilsome labor and the most dangerous working conditions on the planet, and pays mankind the smallest return for its labor. The current state of farming, therefore, amounts to a brutal waste of human resources - a waste of the most precious resource on the planet.

In order to survive on this planet, the human species must think in terms of infinite development, embracing even space based living, farming, and manufacturing, so that the earth can be devoted to cultural pursuits, translated into 'gardens' for beautiful living and for the exploration of the development potential of the natural world.

The functionality of the infinite model of economy must now be judged against the current model of economy.

The first thing that becomes painfully obvious as one begins the comparison, is the utter inability of the present feudal system with all its interest demands, its debt building schemes, and constant looting, to generate the financial resources for development efforts of the necessary magnitude. The feudal economic system is a parasite that takes three bytes out of humanity for every step of progress that mankind still makes in spite of the impediments put in its way.

The present system is not only economically impotent, it is also self-destructive. It has been built upon usurious inflationary trends that lead to cyclical crashes at intensities proportionate to the inflation developing within the system. At infinite inflation, as we have it today, the intensity of a potential crash is proportionally high, and so is the danger that mankind may be deprived of its place in the sun by the senseless destruction that the disintegration of the total feudal world-financial system necessarily brings.

It appears at a glance, therefore, that the infinite system of economy is operational only within the setting of the nation-state. This certainly has been true throughout history, but it is not fundamentally true. In fact, the opposite is true.

In order to explain the last statement one needs to take a closer look at what the nation-state represents.

The nation-state and infinite development.

The nation-state represents the highest state of political economy ever developed. It was the first political structure in the world in which a collective society recognized itself as human beings, rather than property to be enslaved, owned, or exploited by emperors or empires. This collective set up the conditions most ideal to human development. Instead of slavery it established education, instead of subjecting people to servitude it created the potential for the self-development of each individual. Instead of imposing toil it built infrastructures for scientific discoveries, and for technologies that embrace the use of energy and intelligent processes to produce the goods and resources for living.

The first nation-state was set up in France in 1461, by King Louis XI, on the wave-front of the Renaissance. It lasted for a precious few decades. As the dark ages returned to Europe, the idea of the nation-state remained like a beacon against the background of dark ages that mankind had suffered through. It became the hope of many who sought to reestablish this light on the shores of the new world, the American lands. Out of this hope a thriving republic unfolded, of citizens who were better educated, better protected, and more efficient producers of wealth than all the subjects of the old empires of Europe ever were.

In this process the institution of the nation-state became a protective bulwark against the parasitism of the empires and their so-called nobility and Aristocracy. It became a sanctuary for sanity in statecraft and economics. Herein lies the strength of the principle of the nation-state, but not its limit.

The enormous tasks that a reasonable redevelopment of the world imposes on mankind, such as replacing the limited energy resource of oil with nuclear energy for transportation and industrialization, even the industrialization of farming, cannot be accomplished by a single nation in a sanctuary type environment. The nation-state platform is too small for this. It was an ideal platform for the age in which it appeared. It provided the absolutely vital spark in mankind's self-perception that marked the beginning of the end of the imperial ages. Such a breakthrough could only develop and blossom in a sanctuary for scientific and moral growth.

One must acknowledge, however, that the dynamic unfolding of life on this planet has changed the scope of the physical development need that has become the requirement for the future. The limiting boundary of the nation-state, therefore, becomes an impediment. Infinite development, which is the object of the infinite model of economy, is not reconcilable with boundaries. Infinite development embraces a wide view and a daring in thought that is bigger than what the conventional imagination might allow.

The thought is tempting, therefore, to assume that a United Nation's based world can provide this larger platform that is essential for infinite development. This is not the case. The very opposite is the case. The United Nations organization has created an artificial unity in which no one is free. It has taken the world a step back in development. It has removed the boundary in which a nation-state could operate for the self-development of its citizens. It has imperialized the world in that it promotes the old axioms of the empires of dark ages, and enforces the policies that are inherent to these axioms. Nor is this the only damage that the United Nations Organization has inflicted on humanity. It has also created a false sense of unity.

In the early stages of the developing republic on the shores of North America, the citizens of this republic had many supporters. For instance, the unfolding republic might not have survived the attack by the British Empire in its fight for independence without the strong support of the French nation. This principle of fundamental unity between nations, expressed in the mutual support of each other in efforts for self-development is gone. It has been smothered under the cloak of an artificial unity by U.N. contract, which is in real terms a contract of self-enforced isolation.

Infinite development requires a globalism based on a unity among mankind that is based on the universal recognition of that principle that was first manifest in the development of the nation-state out of the darkness of the dark ages. We must not mix up the principle which is fundamental and the product which results from it. The principle is absolute, like the infinite principle of life. The product, however, is subject to development. The principle that is reflected in the nation-state is the hope of the world, and must at length reflect itself in a type of international association where globalism is not artificial but is drawn by the imperatives of this principle. In this scientific globalism for infinite development, the nations will inevitably respect each other in the role of 'citizens' of a world community, and find their greater strength in mutual support. In this context nations prosper, even as the individual citizens of a nation find and realize their strength my means of the utility of the supporting infrastructures to which the people of the union have made a common commitment for the common wealth of all.

Infinite development cannot place on any other platform than the global extension of the principle of the nation-state, as a supportive platform of unity among the nations. Any other platform is too small to achieve the vital advances that are a part of the necessary development of civilization. Infinite development is both necessary, and natural. It is necessary, because a reversal of this process means disintegration of civilization. The reverse of development does not lead to a gradual, linear, devolution. It involves disintegration. A tree that is forced into reverse development, dies. Mankind has only two options for its future: infinite development or disintegration. There is no middle ground.

Infinite development, also, is the natural state of economy. The reason for this has been recognized ages ago.

Infinite development is native to the nature of man.

Nothing is more fundamental to the nature of man than the factor of infinity. There are no limits to the scope of discovery, to scientific understanding, to the potential for unfoldment. Animals are limited by the parameters of nature which they lack the means to control. But man is not an animal, or a worm, or even a higher ape. Man is endowed with a mind that unfolds a horizon with infinite potentials. We comprehend what no ape can see, or engineer what no ape can dream of; we can stand upon the stars and look from them onto the universe and know that there are no limits to were we can be, or what we can accomplish, or what we can make of this world and this universe. We can make models of thought and discover with these the minutia of the tiniest fragments that constitute the physical world, or the human body, and use this knowledge to create platforms for freedom. To rational thought, limits are unknown.

It is not surprising, therefore, that the factor of infinity has become associated with the perception of man as a divine idea, as created in the image of God, or the reflection of God as an infinite idea of infinite Mind unfolding in life. Nor is it surprising that the factor of infinity is associated with mankind's perception of what it recognizes as God. Divinity, infinity, and man have become linked. The surprising part is the timing of this development. The recognition of this link goes back centuries upon centuries. However, if one looks closely, the surprise fades away.

One of the most profound demonstrators of the higher dimension of infinity was unquestionably Christ Jesus. He demonstrated a capacity that lay beyond dreams, but was real. He demonstrated a facet of mind that defies the imagination, even today, although the processes are repeatable and have been repeated. He demonstrated no miracles. Miracles do not occur in the real world. He demonstrated the potential of principles that no one could see, which became therefore bound into the religious context to be acceptable. He demonstrated the principles of infinite being, of man's power over nature in a whole range of metaphysical dimensions. In a spiritual sense he was the 'son of Plato,' though he excelled beyond what even Plato had seen. Christ Jesus called himself "the son of man" but also defined himself as the "son of God."

Christ Jesus came onto the scene at the pinnacle of the Greek Classical period, which may be the first period in human history in which the factor of infinity became interwoven into human culture, both in scientific understanding and practical technologies, and in the cultural dimension of beauty which had its first profound expression in the art of that civilization. Beauty is a dimension of infinity. It is unquantifiable.

This also brings the focus back to physical economics. The strength of infinite development is a spiritual focus that finds riches in the unquantifiable. The proposition that is set forth in the Preamble of the Constitution of the United States speaks of a higher identity and self-respect that is not quantifiable but involves infinite factors that are open to boundless development: "We the people..." "for a more perfect union..." etc., involves such higher platforms as justice that embraces the principles of common defense and the right to freedom in the pursuit of happiness and self-development.

The ideology of the Preamble is attributed to the work of the German philosopher and scientist of this period, Gottfried Leibnitz. It sets forth in essence the same principles that Christ Jesus had demonstrated, who had elevated the image of man to the divine heights of infinite value. No one had understood the value of the human being at the time of the American Revolution better than Gottfried Leibnitz had had understood it. He had put the human being on top of the heap, having dominion over all, just as Christ Jesus had demonstrated the great potential of man's dominion over the body. A few decades after Leibnitz, America's pioneer of the science of Christianity, Mary Baker Eddy, defined God as infinite Principle, Mind, Life, Truth, and Love, and man as God's image and likeness. This perception became the platform for a new epoch in Christian healing.

Now, let's look at where we are today.

Whereas the infinite system of economy focuses on the infinite and unquantifiable as a driver for the boundless self-development of society, the feudal system of economy focuses exclusively on the quantifiable, the limited, and the limitable. It focuses onto the factors that are inherent to disintegration.

What all this means in terms of down to earth reality cannot be determined, except that we have reached the threshold of what might be the biggest disintegration in history. We have no historical data with which to illustrate what this process involves, since nothing even close to the current level of financial inflation has ever unfolded throughout all history, which is now ready to collapse and evaporate. The point is, that once the fascination of mankind is locked onto the quantifiable (even if it is an illusion), it looses its grasp of infinity. The resulting catastrophe may well be several orders of magnitude greater, in human losses, than any other catastrophe in history. We face a choice that may shut the door to the potentially brightest future in all of human history, and open it to a New Dark Age that rivals the worst ever. Here civilization may end altogether. This is the price that mankind pays for loosing its grasp on infinity. The price is huge. Ironically it results from mankind's lacking ability for thinking big in terms of unfolding potentials.

The realistic approach is to think big. The realistic approach is to focus onto the unquantifiable, for infinity is unquantifiable. Out this mental background physical riches evolve that supports the growing society. We need these riches to survive. Much is at stake in this arena where the role of the game is all or nothing. And this truly is the rule of fundamental principle. We cannot mock this principle. We can only move with it or suffer the consequences if we fail to respect it.

How does our current model of economy compare to the infinite model?

The foundation for the worthlessness of today's financial claims was set up in the 1970s when the platform for the national debt was created and the door was opened to ever broader financial speculation. As is well known, this decade started with a deep plunge of the U.S. dollar that was cut loose from gold early in the decade and was made into an instrument for gambling. On top of that crisis came the oil shock. A low and bear market followed. Then, near the end of the decade the infamous Paul Volker interest rate shock took the economy even deeper into chaos and debt. Once this the direction was fixed, the 1980s became a decade of economic collapse, financial deregulation, and a speculative binge that gave rise to a real estate bubble, a derivatives bubble, and a banking crisis in which 711 banks were wiped out in the mortgage oriented thrift industry.

This powerful economic collapse was evidently

intended. Officially, the collapse was created as a means for "cooling down" the economy. It appears that Paul Volker was specifically appointed to the top post of the Federal Reserve System for his known commitment to economic disintegration. Once he was in control, this commitment translated itself into an official policy structure that opened the financial scene to a brand new era of speculation insanity, the likes of which has never existed before. In the shadow of his infamous double digit interest rates, that rose as high as 22% at one point, tens of thousands of businesses were bankrupted, which could not afford to pay loan-shark rates for credit while their productive enterprises produced no more than a 5% profit, over all, if that.

It cannot be determined whether Paul Volker intended to render all financial aggregates within the system worthless, by setting the stage for infinite inflation within the system, or whether the explosion in financial aggregates was not anticipated. It may well be that the developing crash potential was intended for ideological reasons in the service of the oligarchic empires that traditionally profit from the dysfunctionality of mankind's development.

Well, whatever the reason was that triggered the 'avalanche,' the crash came in 1987. At first the stockmarket got hit, then, the economy. The result was a creeping depression that led to business closures, mergers, takeovers, and layoffs. The cycle still continues to the present day. Paul Volker had certainly achieved his goal of economic disintegration. The financial disintegration is yet to come, in the near term. The stage has already been set.

There remain many more questions to be explored about the paradox why intelligent people commit their nation's livelihood to a self-defeating system in the first place, and regard the disintegration of its prosperity a virtue.

The illusion that is created today that all developments are for the good of society, and that everything is under control, is created mainly for the public. The bubble of illusion would pop, if the above questions about the modern paradox were explored. The illusion that all is well, while the system teeters at the 'edge of a cliff' is created for the public with the aim to maintain the public's confidence in the dying system. Under this guidance, the public relishes its near zero inflation environment and its 'glowing' investment 'opportunities,' even while the system is rotten to the core and is about to take a tumble.

The illusion that is dished up for the public is evidently designed to hide what is going on deep within the system, for the processes that create and maintain the illusion are astonishingly complete. The control is so complete that it successfully hides even the inflation that should be noticed, that exists between the market basket that the society can afford, in comparison to what the society was once able to afford in the mid 1960s. As was pointed out, some of this deficiency is overcome through the free-trade looting of other nations. The process of hiding is actually so well orchestrated that it may yet have a still deeper purpose. It should be noted that all efforts by responsible people to repair the collapsing system have been thwarted, who had tried to revert the system back to a functioning type of economy many times in the past.

The irony is that the bulk of the presently endangered financial aggregates can still be saved from destruction by a recommitment to the infinite type of economic system that has actually performed such a rescue once before. The irony is, that the very notion of such a rescue is rejected out of hand as such a rescue process would spell the end of the feudal monetary world-system that the reigning Empire of the planet needs as a ready cash cow by which it maintains itself.

As was stated before, the difference between points B and C in Appendix 4 represents the inflation within the financial system that we would have to deal with if the system were converted at the present moment to a zero interest rate environment. Such an environment is a fundamental prerequisite for setting up an infinite system of economy in which no interest is charged. The question arises: Would people be cheated, if a conversion to the infinite system were to take place?

Surprisingly, the answer is, no! In such a system, the settlement of all currently outstanding claims is fundamentally possible. The pay-out may be spread over long periods of time, and become possible only after a massive revival of the physical economy with investments into revitalizing infrastructures, energy production, reindustrialization, and farming. But the pay-out is possible. In fact it may be quite painless once the productive capacity of the nation has been brought back to life by which real wealth is created with which to settle claims.

It is likewise evident that such a rescue of claims is totally impossible in a feudalist based environment in which monetary and financial aggregates are considered **rentable estates** that are lend out to procure earnings without production (erroneously called profit), or are deployed to drain value out of the economy through speculation, which altogether makes the feudal system parasitical in nature. Now, when the debt service claims, by themselves, exceed the profit yield of the productive economy, there is nothing left with which to pay off the debt. Thus, the entire debt becomes uncollectible and therefore worthless.

It is interesting against this background, to note the deep dedication that exists globally, to the self-limiting and self-destructive feudal system. The system is so widely, and so relentlessly defended, as if it were sacred in nature and cannot be altered even if the survival of society is put at risk for it.

It may be that the society's failure in dealing with the axioms that underlie the feudal system rests with the lack of perception in public thought of the nature of transcendental values, such as infinity.

The existence of infinite inflation, such as has been created within the financial-economic system, is physically unrepresentable on paper. It can be hinted at, but it cannot be shown. An infinitely large piece of paper would be required. The same difficulty exists in representing the measure of the illusion that is artificially maintained by maintaining the dying world-financial system. The fact is, that neither the illusion, nor the inflation that the illusion hides, can be maintained, or should be maintained. No one should even attempt to rescue them when they crash, since such a rescue is inherently impossible. Unfortunately the dying system is being maintained today at a great cost in human life and by shady means of behind the scene manipulation, by which monumental efforts are made to rescue the system from its impending fate. This precariously upheld complex of mutually amplifying **illusions,** or in reality, **self-delusions,** is by far the grandest con-job ever launched in the entire history of mankind.

When the fictitious nature of the superinflated value of the financial aggregates is realized, the market collapses. At this point it can no longer be saved. The financial claims, therefore, become devalued to near zero. It is ironic, that under the feudal financial system, which is centered on creating and protecting private wealth, the very wealth that is to be protected, is doomed from the beginning.

The current differential between fictitious wealth, and the physical reality, can only be resolved within the infinite system of economy which alone is able to provide the massive investment into growth that is needed to jump-start the economic productivity of the nation and the world. A minimal real growth in the order of 88,000% would likely be required to match and surpass just the inflation that exists within the system that separates the outstanding financial claims from reality, and the same again to create profit for the advance of civilization.

Since this kind of growth cannot be achieved by a self-defeating system that can barely achieve a 2% growth rate at the very best of times, the entire fictitious system is doomed to disintegrate as it cannot correlate itself to reality, nor uplift the physical reality to where it matches the financial value system that supposedly represents reality.

The practical result is a crash that puts everything back to near zero! This means that during the cycle of disintegration, the output of the productive economy suffers the same shock wave. In graphic terms, this means that level C in Appendix 4, will likely be at a far lower value than it is at present, since any general disintegration tends to decimate the physical economy. A collapse in the order of twice the current inflation within the system may be a reasonable result. Of course, the moment that one gets into such astronomical levels of collapse, as near the 100,000% range, the effect will be immeasurable for all practical purposes. In short, the total disintegration of the world-financial and economic system may yield unimaginable consequences for human life on this planet.

The astonishing part is, that the catastrophic collapse, when it occurs, does not actually represent a fundamental change, but merely reflects a more accurate recognition of the reality that already exists. It is the illusion that crashes in cycles of inflation driven financial collapses. Reality, itself, never collapses. Reality remains unaffected by periodic crashes in the markets when the bubbles of illusion burst. Herein lies a great danger, but also the logic for a choice. The choice is, that the equalization does not take place by default and unleash an catastrophe, but is done by intend and by intelligent means so that humanity can be protected from the anarchy that follows a total global financial collapse.

The currently promoted choice is inaction on the society's part by which illusions are upheld. These include the illusion that the feudal system is invincible and fundamentally benign. It may well be that this illusion remains intact even after the impending crash has occurred and the civilization of mankind has been reduced back to levels comparable to that of the dark ages.

The term "inaction" is really a contradiction in language. There is no such phenomenon as inaction. There is either development or disintegration. There in no such middle ground were nothing happens. Only in the world of big finance is inaction conceivable, as in this realm nothing is truly related to reality. Unfortunately, this exception is woefully exploited.

The political imperative for creating illusions.

The bottom line is, the so-called wealth of the rich cannot really be protected by the system that created the illusion of wealth. The process of creating the illusion of wealth where there is none, is a powerful political tool for destroying civilization. Whether it has been used in this manner as a means for advancing the population reduction objectives of the oligarchic empires that historically operate on a platform of strategic poverty to maintain their balance of power, cannot be determined. What is evident, however, is that virtually all governments on the planet have been maneuvered into playing the very game that is most powerfully destructive to themselves and their populations. This should cause one to ponder what may lie behind this global strategy. The strange coincident exists that the governments of the world act almost in unison in this regard, like a synchronized chorus, proclaiming virtue in fascist austerity measures as they wield the budget axe against their own populations, and thereby against themselves.

The fact is, that not the grandest illusion ever staged can hide the reality that the only actual wealth in existence is that which flows from the profit of the productive economy created by human labor. Whatever has been created by financial speculation and manipulation, should not be called wealth. 95% of it should be seen as fictitious, and the rest be regarded as proceeds from theft.

The global debt crisis is therefore not a budgetary problem, but is fundamentally an ideological problem that has enabled the quiet destruction of the nation's wealth producing processes by which the population lives. The global debt crisis is not a problem of governmental overspending. It is a problem of strategic misspending, of bolstering non-productive financial industries that drain the productive industries of affordable investment funds, that also drain the governments of funds needed for infrastructures, for advanced scientific research and education, and for equitable employment that is needed to strengthen the population and its purchasing power.

Today, the oligarchic demand is in the opposite. The demand is for some real life blood to be shed, by imposing ever harsher financial austerities that put whole segments of the population onto the scrap heap, especially the unfortunate segment of the populations that the destruction of the productive sector has put into poverty.

The governments' growing refusal to fund the deficit between trend D in Appendix 4, and the 1967 base-line, necessarily causes a further collapse in the physical economy, as poverty has never been a force for economic booming. The tolerance of poverty, wherever it may be found, portents a tragic loss to the society as a whole.

The opposite to this loss is found in the principles of the nation-state that represent a commitment to the common realization of the creative potential of the human being. This potential, of course, cannot be realized while the society' strength is drawn out of the population by an 'industry' that thrives on the financial looting of the population, its productive economy, its infrastructures, and its governments. The strange coincidence that the world is facing today shows a combination of an accelerating decline throughout the world's productive economy while at the same time the financial so-called 'profits' have risen to an all-time high. Both processes need to be reversed.

The bubble economy: a feature of the self-destructive system.

What passes under the name of economy, today, has actually become quite surreal. Very little in this arena reflects the fundamental principles of economics anymore. The shakeout of this surrealism that has noting to do with reality, except by name, falls, as always, on the shoulders of the poor (the growing masses that are made poor by the system). The trend of collapse that is shown in level D represents the typical effect of the currently adhered to principle of economics. In reality, the decline of the curve may be much steeper than shown. The actual experience has been, that every conservative measure of spending cuts for balancing budgets has increased the collapse of tax revenues in the long run and raised the deficits in a greater measure than what the savings amounted to. It is an illusion, therefore, that a nation can balance its economic budget by running up a secondary deficit against the strength of its population, that is, by starving the very element by which real wealth is created. This destructive trend of accelerating conservatism in the real world, together with an increasing insanity in the financial world, can be observed right across the planet. It leads, by its own dynamics, to an eventual shutdown of the nations and a collapse of its population, numerically and physically.

There are no circuit breakers possible for disabling the principles of reality.

While great efforts have been made to make the markets crash proof, these measures are quite superficial and have primarily a psychological effect. One financial analysts laughs at the flimsy nature of the so-called circuit breakers that have been put in place to prevent cashes in the stock markets.

Since not a single one of these superficial measures changes the underlying axioms that drive the collapse of the economies, the effect of these measures will be no more than superficial. Right now, most "circuit breakers" in the financial exchanges consist of measures in delaying trades. By this method the circuit breakers effect the timing of the impending crashes, but not the force that drives them. The delaying tactics could easily make the crashes more severe and their effect a great deal more damaging. The mere fact that no major crash has occurred since 1987, after which the 'circuit breakers' were introduced, does not mean that the sea is calm. The fact is, the 'bases are loaded' for a great 'home-run' of all financial values (to near zero)

Three major bubbles are likely to burst simultaneously, when the crash is unfolding.

One bubble has grown in the banking system. The banks are loaded to the hilt with financial derivatives speculation, which is likely to go against them in a crash. They had no choice in this, of course, as the physical economy does not support the rates of return that the banks must provide in order to stay in business.

The second bubble has grown up in the stock markets which have reached the highest stock price values in the markets' entire history, while the industry that the markets represent is giving extremely low yields (2.2% at the TSE300, 2.3% for the Sstocks, with dividends ranging as low as .8% paid out by the once mighty blue chip giants, such as IBM).

The third bubble has grown up in the arena of derivatives speculation. In this part of the industry, financial leveraging and volume has reached astronomical proportions. Irrational leveraging was deemed to have been a major factor in the great crash in 1929. Because of this problem, the leveraging of trades had been subsequently limited to a ratio of 10:1. Today, leveraging in excess of 40:1 is not at all unusual, and may reach as high 4000:1 for some index options. At the same time the yearly turnover in financial contracts has reached a global volume near three quarters of a quadrillion dollars, and is likely to exceed that figure, which is already tens of times greater than the combined gross national product of the entire global economy.

Deflating the bubbles.

When the world's giant financial bubbles pop, and they are likely to pop simultaneously, how safe are the pension funds, the bank deposits, the income portfolios, the mutual funds? How safe are the corporations who have shed large portions of their workers into early retirement while the funding for these obligations has been contracted out to the fictitious financial system, even though the final liability for the pensions remains within the corporation? In fact, how save is the population itself, in terms of its physical food supply?

During the great depression following the crash in 1929, the city populations obtained a reasonable flow of supplies from the network of family farms in the surrounding country side, which was the local supply network at the time. Today's food supplies, in contrast, flow through a centralized system of processing plants and distribution networks operated in large parts by foreign cartels, which may become dysfunctional in a financial breakdown crisis.

The fact is, mankind cannot afford to allow these bubble to pop, as they will. The bubbles need to be deflated and the system that created them needs to be replaced with one that works. These steps, however, cannot be taken unless the mechanism is fully understood that created the bubbles, so that the practicality of the infinite economic system, as shown in Appendix 5, that is able to deflate the bubbles, becomes evident.

Appendix 6 provides an overview of how the current bubble economy works, which is a self-limiting and self-destructive system. It is made up of five elements. Two of these are identical to the model of the infinite economy. They are: the physical economy, and the society which operates the economy with its productive capacity. The feedback loop still exists by which the society applies its productive labor to create a profit for itself with which to enrich its living. However, a great deal of this profit gets drained off from the productive process, so that little remains, if anything, to advance the society's technologies, and to raise the status of civilization. By this drain on the society's strength, the self-escalating development of society becomes broken.

A portion of what is drained away feeds the fictitious bubbles (path D). The bubbles, themselves, are self-amplifying, but they must be fed to be kept growing.

The bubbles are also fed by the state (path G). In order to keep the bubbles growing, the governments are persuaded to increase the money supply. The process immediately creates debt for the state, that the state is required to pay interest for. Likewise, when industries require capitalization, more debt is created, which the society must bear the cost for, in some fashion. Whatever flows into the bubbles through paths D and G, becomes debt for the nation in one way or another, as the flow takes away a vital portion of the nation's income stream for living.

The essential function that the nation had taken on under the American System of economy (the infinite model) - that of creating its own currency and low cost credit for industry and infrastructures - is usurped in a bubble economy by the debt centered private financial structure owned largely by a tiny oligarchy. The three types of bubbles that are shown in Appendix 6, grow at the expense of the physical economy and the welfare of society.

Each of the three bubbles that are shown in Appendix 6 has a loop by which it recycles it's so-called profits within itself through speculation. By means of this loop, and large inflows into the bubble, the bubble inflates itself. The intensity of the recycling depends partly on the leveraging of the capital within the system. The leveraging in the stock markets is driven by the intensity of trading. The leveraging is usually low in such areas where the market is still focused to some degree on physical equity. The average gain is also low, in the 15% range, which is many times greater than the profit to society from the productive physical economy.

The leveraging force in the banking system is the competition for public funds. The funds are used by the banking system primarily to drive its own derivatives gambling operation through the financial and equity markets. The true gain of this system is well hidden, as it is largely a self-serving system operated by a controlling oligarchy.

The third bubble is the financial aggregates system of pure speculation.

These various bubbles grow as they feed on the proceeds of society. They grow through contributions from the society by way of interest payments, or through voluntary contribution by society in response to the illusions the markets offer, of multiplying profits. The bubbles are maintained by a steady inflow that must exceed the outflow, which difference, then, becomes magnified through the leveraging mechanism of the system. Once the flow stops, or the differential becomes negative, the bubble collapses into thin air as the illusion it represents evaporates. This means that the entire system comes into danger when the physical economy is drained to the point that the flow differential can no longer be maintained. That is where the world stands today. That is where it stood in 1929, and in 1987.

On only two occasions, in the entire history of mankind, has the inflationary self-limiting feudalist-based model of economy been replaced with the infinite model. The first occurred as the result of the Renaissance. It occurred in France in 1461 when the institution of the nation-state was pioneered. The second occasion occurred at the end of the 18th century after England had bankrupted the Unites States of America through imposing free-trade under the peace accord by which England surrendered its official claim on its renegade American (former) colonies. The free-trade environment had caused a massive rise in governmental debt through the normal channels of the feudal system. This debt explosion caused an awakening, however, within the nation. The, then acting treasury secretary, Alexander Hamilton, turned the whole trend around, virtually over night, by causing the nation to own its own currency and its own credit, which became available to it at near zero interest as an investment into itself, creating physical infrastructures, creating education, developing science, technologies, and industries with which to increase the productive power of the society. The result was, that the three financial bubbles were instantly replaced by a governmental function that the nation carried out for its own benefit. The result of this low or no interest rate financing was such, that the nation's potential in creativity and productivity was not inflationary, but had the opposite effect. The result was an explosive economic upturn, that was so great the the huge accumulated debt was paid off with very little pain, while the nation prospered immensely. It was said in these days, that "the national debt has become a national blessing."*14

The dynamics within the infinite model of economy.

Appendix 5 shows both the flow and the dynamics involved in infinite model of economy. The flow diagram has only three elements, because the banking system and equity markets are functionally in unison with the physical economy. They are a part of it, so that the creation of real wealth, which is initially funded by nationally owned credit for the creation of infrastructures and the development of scientific and technological progress, is carried forward by the economy's own resources. This is possible, because the free gain profit of the productive effort of society is reinvested by the society into its further self-development, rather than being siphoned off. This type of economic model operates penalty free. Its investment credits become an asset, rather than a long-term liability.

The fundamental feature of this model incorporates a funding source that is owned by the nation for investment into itself for the purpose of developing its productive potential and creative capacity. The wealth within this system is generated by the secondary effect of increased productivity, rather than in the form of monetary or financial gain. By this system, the inherent wealth of the population - that is, the power of its labor, and the riches of its creativity - are being unlocked. By enhancing this potential, by maximizing its effect in real terms through free advanced universal education for the purpose of enhancing creativity, through scientific and technological progress, etc., revolutionary increases in the productivity of mankind's labor is achieved, and this naturally with corresponding increases in the income of the population.

This increase in physical productivity is the fundamental factor that prevents the occurrence of social deficits, such as the governments carry today. Also, the government's revenues are constantly increasing under this system, with which the society funds advanced scientific and technological research and development. In the infinite system of economy all this is possible, even against the background of ever decreasing levels of taxation. This is the type of foundation on which the newly formed nation of United States of America was able to pay off its national debt without pain, and without hindering the momentum of its economic development.

That such a system is not inflationary is evident by the natural trend under which incomes and productivity tend to coincide in a healthy economy (shown in Appendix 5, Figure 2), even in a sharp upwards trend, while the differential between income levels and declining prices widens. This provides a deflationary effect resulting from increases in the creation of goods that represent real profit for the society in a well functioning economy. The proof of the pudding is in the eating. A feudal economy, on the other hand, is always inflationary as the focus is shifted onto the increase of money and away from the production of products that support human life and civilization.

Increasing money without inflation.

In the infinite system, large increases in the money supply are obviously necessary. These increases, however, remain in context with the production of physical wealth for society which corresponds with a sharply growing industrialization on all levels of the physical economy. In the infinite system, money is an interchange medium, instead of wealth. The fundamental principle of economics dictates that the money supply must grow in proportion to which the economy expands. This is required in order to facilitate the increasing interchange. This is why a gold-based currency won't work, because the gold supply cannot be expanded sufficiently to meet the constantly increasing currency needs of the infinite system of economy.

The two factors, the money supply and the physical economy, must always remain matched. If they are not, inflation or deflation results. Money must never be used as an instrument to stimulate the economy, or to throttle it. In the infinite system the economy is driven by the need for development. Money is expanded to supply for this need.

Factors, other than greed, should drive the society's development. These factors are manifest as intelligent control. Money is not wealth, and should not be elevated to such a position. When the illusion prevails that money is wealth, then, money is put ahead of the economy, rather than being regarded as merely a servant of it. When this happens, the money supply and the physical economy grow out of proportion to each other and inflation or depression occur. This can never happen under the infinite model of economy where the physical needs of society drive the economic game, and the money supply tags along.

Today, the opposite happens.

The fallacy of using money as a tool.

The nation's money supply is routinely used as a tool to stimulate or retard the economy in order to maximize financial gains, to manipulate the markets, and in some extreme cases to keep the financial system from collapsing.

For instance, until the middle of 1995, the money supply was kept tight. This was said to be necessary in order keep inflation low. Then, suddenly the printing presses were turned on all over the world. In Japan new money flooded into the system to rescue the crashing markets. The money supply was abused to force a rescue operation. The biggest national banking system in the world, the Japanese banking system, had suffered losses in excess of a trillion dollars. In order to affect a rescue, new money was pumped into the monetary system at a prime rate as low as 0.5%. One should applaud such a generous offering of credits, except this credit was not earmarked for infrastructural development that would have created an equivalent in physical wealth. It was pumped down the bottomless pit of the financial aggregates system that had begun a melt-down spiral. Nothing was devoted to infrastructural developments. This arena continued to collapse and with it the state of the physical scene of civilization which the financial system is supposed to represent.

From a standpoint of metaphysics, the cheap credit that was poured into the market did in fact destabilize the financial system more, that it was supposed to salvage.

Naturally, the society will be demanded to pay a heavy price for keeping the market bubbles alive. Much of the same has already happened in the U.S., although the prime rate didn't drop quite as far. The markets have indeed responded to the cheap credit, and rallied to ever greater valuations. Except, those values are factious. Here, good money is thrown into a basket that has no value at all, or extremely little at best.

The new money that is printed in the U.S. is deemed 'necessary' for still another reason. It enables the U.S. Federal Reserve (which has no money of its own) to 'buy' the U.S. Treasury debt that the commercial markets can no longer absorb. By this process, the governmental debt that had lived up to this point in the realm of the financial aggregates, has becomes monetized. The result is, that the same hyper-inflation that exists in the financial aggregates system is now beginning to spill over into the monetary system, by which money becomes progressively valueless.

At the moment, the U.S. Federal Reserve doesn't own very much of its government's debt. It is believed that the Fed owns lightly less than 8% of it. However, even this small amount is a huge sum that represents a significant chunk of the total U.S. money supply, which is also quite small compared to the nation's debt. Once the financial markets begin to collapse, the Fed may be forced to 'buy' an increasingly larger share of this debt, which means that the money supply continues to increase, so that the value of the monetary aggregate becomes increasingly worthless, and so does the value of everyone's savings account, if anyone still has one.

These are the wonderful 'advantages' of the feudal economic model. It is, indeed, hard to find a logical reason why humanity clings so tenaciously to this dying system - why it is determined to go down to an icy grave with the sinking ship.

The increase in money that is killing us.

The current problem with printing more money, is, that the money isn't spend for wealth creating infrastructures, such as industrialization, or new scientific and technological developments that raise the physical platform of society and provide new resources for living. Instead, the new money is spent on issues that are dead before the money is even printed. This money is for all practical purposes wasted before it even rolls of the press. This insanity must now be looked upon in the context of the collapsing social platforms where the poor of society, the elderly, and unwed mothers, are progressively denied the means to exist. Here, a tiny fraction of the newly created money would prevent the death of countless thousands. Except this is not what is being done. The general trend is to embrace fascism and force whole classes of people into situations that spell certain death, while the financial system is flooded with money by which its inflation becomes evermore rampant. We are presently at the beginning of what would become the biggest inflationary spiral in history by which the world-financial system moves towards total disintegration, while the society is put into a parallel physical death spiral.

The problem is that the feudal system is by its fundamental principles incapable of supporting the kind of infrastructural development that raises the wealth-creating capacity of the society's labor and creativity. Its parameters for measurement doesn't allow for a valuation of the potential physical productivity of society's power of labor. The feudal measurement system measures only that which has inherently no value, and maintains processes for multiplying the valueless aggregates at the expense of destroying the physical processes by which society must ultimately maintain itself. This, now, is what is called security.

The nation-state is not a 'welfare state.'

The model for infinite economy does not provide for waste. It's principle does not support the creation of a welfare state in the sense that big government meets out a living to society. By design, the nation-state is a state that promotes the welfare of society by enabling protected economic activities, supported by the required economic infrastructures. The nation-state is designed as a welfare state only in the sense that it provides the conditions that unlocks the potential of society in which the society finds its infinite wealth and welfare. This development process can never be inflationary. Nor will this process ever lead to a stockmarket that grows at a rate of 15% a year, compounded, while the productive economy shrinks. In other words, the United States of America do not presently operate according to the principles of the nation-state. Its people have become insane. The people of this nation are presently throwing money at the stockmarkets by the barrels full, as if it was the only game in town. The insanity in moderns society has grown to such proportions that a full 90% of its liquid wealth is now "rolling the dice on the biggest speculative stock market ever."*15 The society has emptied its savings accounts in the bottomless pit. This is not how a nation-state functions. In earlier times this figure was near the 10% mark, now its in the 90% range. The sad part is that these 'investments' are essentially worthless the moment they are made, while the public loses its ability to care for one another and for itself.

The model for infinite economy is capitalistic in nature, in contrast to the current model which is financially oriented. The capitalist approach looks for tangible profits from physical production, which are reinvested into physical production. This process has the potential for infinite continuity and provides abundantly for the needs of human living. The modern approach to economy, which is financially oriented, is its opposite. Here, greed demands greater returns, and the door to the fictitious world of financial magic opens up where any level of profit can be achieved for as long as no one tries to correlate them to any form of the physical reality.

The capitalist element of the infinite system for economy, is a self-strengthening system that can be carried on in a pattern of infinite progression. Financial aggregates are not included in this system, as Appendix 5 shows, as they are meaningless in a functioning economy and are easily shut down by regulatory and taxation measures should they occur. In the capitalist system, there will still be a stockmarket, but one that focuses on yield rather than on the insanity of speculative trading.

Speculative trading is a sign of extremely high levels of monetary inflation over physical equity. It is the classic case of too much money chasing too few goods. In a collapsing economy where real equity is shrinking, as we have it today, financial inflation is inevitable. This applies even to the stockmarket, where the bidding war for what is left of the physical economy drives prices to the stratosphere, regardless of the fact that there is virtually no yield forthcoming from the super-inflated investment. Whatever yield there was in the beginning, has been watered down to infinitesimal levels by the vast price increases in the greatest stockmarket rally of all times.

For instance, a share that once paid a $6.- dividend per hundred dollars invested, provided an excellent return of 6%. Now if the same share is presently valued at a thousand dollars, even as it still yields the same $6.- it yields a pitiful 0.6% return on investment. The higher the market is valued, as more and more money is poured into it, the less is the ratio of return. The currently high market values are no cause for celebration. They should cause tears. They should cause investors to flee that market in droves.

The richest markets, in real terms, are always found in the infinite system where market values tend to remain naturally low and yields high, since the market is constantly expanding. In a rapidly expanding market where the equity expansion is high, prices remain low as there is no bidding competition going on. This makes for one of the lowest priced stock markets, ever, but also the richest and most secure, in terms of return.

In real terms, financial aggregates never represent wealth. They are fundamentally a factor of the feudal economy. They represent a bubble of illusions that some are able to exploit, but which is doubly destructive to most people in that it not only causes periods of market crashes, but also causes the physical collapse of the economy. Financial aggregates are a part of a system that has an inherent tendency to redirect the focus of attention away from productive activities towards paper-backed values that have no inherent relationship to reality other than that of an illusion.

An enormous bubble of illusion has been building up in recent years, which is getting bigger and bigger, and which is actively promoted as a panacea. There are presently more stock mutual funds chasing the market than there are companies registered on the New York Stock Exchange. According to the nature of the game that is played, their day will be just about over. Reality dawns. Someone is bound to see the light. "Never has a speculative market blow-off burned so much money. Never has it involved such a large number of participants. Never has it gone so far that it threatened the global financial system," writes Nick Guarino of The Wall Street Underground.*16

There exist only tow models for economic-financial systems: The self-limiting feudalist model of the bubble economies, and the infinite model. The task, therefore, is one of choosing. The infinite model has been highly successful for the brief period in which it was implemented in the United States of America by Alexander Hamilton during the George Washington administration. The self-limiting feudalist model, on the other hand, has never created a successful and productive economy in the entire history of mankind, but has led to inflation upon inflation, crash upon crash, and a society drained by by successive cycles of social catastrophes and a long chain of wars that it necessitated. In other words, we have a paradox, here.

Logically the infinite model should reign, but the feudalist-based model reigns instead and has put mankind in great danger. Why does the paradox exist, and what does it mean? The question may well be asked, what has torn the infinite model of economy down to the ground so that it is no longer used?

The answer to that question lies in the historic background against which it was most successfully established, and by which it was defeated.

Chapter 6: A Paradox in History:

The War Between the Infinite, and the Self-Defeating Model of Economy

The self-defeating model of economy is centered on usury. Usury is an ancient concept that has long ago been recognized to be destructive, which has therefore been incorporated into the taboo system under which it was declared by the church as a sin. Originally, this taboo applied against the demand of interest payment for monetary lending. In fundamental terms, usury defines all economic conditionalities by which profit is drawn from processes that do not actually produce anything, such as lending money. The profits, then, become a claim against the wealth produced from physical production. The feudal system is fundamentally a system of usury. Under the feudal system, the lord, who has received or purchased land from the King, 'rents' the land to the peasants which produce physical wealth by their labor. The lion's share of this wealth is, then, demanded by the land's lord for the use of the land. This is usury.

It has long been recognized that this system of usury has a self-limiting effect on economic activities and becomes outright destructive to society in that the profits from human labor are not used to raise the status of civilization and improve the productive capacity of society. Under the feudal system the produced wealth is simply used up. This system gives nothing back to society. The wealth is drawn out of the productive system to feed luxurious living and a bubble of manipulative systems that the monarchy and the oligarchy maintains. This type of system has lost its relationship to productive processes, except for purposes of looting them.

The great financier empires of the 13th and 14th centuries, of Venice and the city of Florence, bypassed the anti-usury taboo of the church by attaching monetary lending to conditionalities through contractual arrangements which in some cases drew net-gains of up to 40% per year. The banking houses of Venice and Florence not only created the major currencies in use throughout Europe, but had also manipulated their value and owned the credit capability with which they first supplied, and, then, looted the nations. This sounds familiar, doesn't it?

As this type of economy is self-defeating, it consequently collapsed, like any system must that operates contrary to the fundamental principles of metaphysics by which, alone, wealth is obtained. The collapse of the Venetian system lead to the great crash if 1345, the only total crash of a world-financial system that has ever occurred in history.

Naturally, any power structure or empire that lives from looting, embraces the usurious system. It does so, even though the system has the tendency to crash. The usurious system happens to be the only system by which the feudal oligarchy can draw wealth out of the productive processes of the nations, by which it maintains itself. For this reason it became imperative for the oligarchy, and for its representative the monarchy, that the usurious system be maintained at all cost.

The unfolding of the Renaissance and the subsequent creation of nation-states introduced a grand departure from the usurious system. This, evidently, was the main reason why the oligarchy has ever since tried to prevent the infinite system from becoming established. This was especially true at the time the British oligarchy was dealt its severest blow when the American colonies declared their independence. Total war became necessary to prevent this from becoming a reality. Still, it appears that the war was not so much fought as a means for the empire to regain the loss of its colonial territory and the tribute money that it brought in, in the form of taxes and exploitative trade. It appears that deep down at the root level, the war was more fundamentally necessary as a means for preventing the infinite economic system from becoming reestablished throughout the world that the Renaissance had represented and had conceptually introduced.

After six years of fighting the War of Independence, the oligarchy was defeated on the battle field, but even as it conceded, it created a new war on the economic front. For the purpose of winning this new war, the British Empire commissioned one of the foremost of its elite, a certain Adam Smith, to create a strategy for bankrupting the newly created nation, and the nation of France that had helped the American's to rebuff the British.

Adam Smith's response was a clever one. It was an idea that seemed benign, but was a killer in reality. He created the principle of **free-trade.** The idea was quietly attached as a conditionality to the peace process by which the newly created American nation was ceded its independence. And indeed, as expected, by applying the free-trade principle the new nation was quickly bankrupted.

As it was, the oligarchy failed, however, in this second attempt the bring the new nation to its knees. Rather, it caused the opposite outcome of what it had intended. Instead of crawling on its knees, begging the Empire that it be rescued from its financial woes, the United States created its own financial system based on the infinite model that was pioneered during the Renaissance. On this basis, because of its dramatic increases in productivity, the newly created economic system put the feudal system far into the shadows. In response to this rebuff, even greater efforts were now made by the British Empire and its oligarchy to defeat the United States of America by any means at their disposal.

The first efforts resulted in another war, the war of 1812. As this war failed again, still another strategy was concocted. The new attack was unleashed through the southern slavery states, which, throughout the colonial days were most closely aligned to the feudalist Empire. The targeted states where persuaded by diplomacy and subversion to break away from the American Union of states. The obvious aim was, to set into motion a process that would lead to the destruction of the U.S.A. as a nation-state, and leave the spoils to Britain. After this scheme (the Civil War) had also failed, still another shift in the war against the infinite economic system was initiated. President Abraham Lincoln, who stood at the helm of the nation, who was defending the infinite system, who had successfully resisted the slave trading Empire that ignited the Civil War, was simply assassinated. Here, the Empire finally gained its victory! From this point on, whichever President stood in the way of the British Empire and its drive for recolonializing the U.S. back into the British feudal system (at least financially) was shot in short order. Three presidents were shot in this process, in quick succession: Lincoln (1865), Garfield (1881), McKinley (1901), and one more a half century later: Kennedy (1963). Some also believe that F.D. Roosevelt was murdered by aggravating a natural condition of illness (1945).

The recolonialization became effective around the year 1875 through the Specie Resumption Act that legally tied the U.S.' financial system back into British hands. From this point on the nation was doomed to a destruction from within that has never stopped from this time forward. The new, feudal economic system drove the nation into a series of financial crashes that has not ended to the present day.

After the turn of the century the transition to the feudalist system of economy was firmed up with the creation of the U.S. Federal Reserve System, a private organization that was given the power to own and control the nation's currency and credit on a platform that reflected the British / Venetian feudalist ideology. By this the oligarchy's victory in North America was total. Now a new war began, the war of the feudalist system against the population.

The great banking crash of 1907, in which people saw their life-savings evaporate, and the 1929 stock-market crash that brought the entire economy to its knees, testify to the destructive power of the self-limiting, self-defeating feudal system that was now fully in control.

The feudal system has never been challenged from this point on. Whenever a U.S. president had even hinted at such a possibility, he ended up dead. By this process, rather than being challenged by mankind, the feudal system became the standard for the world. It became globalized through the 'services' of the U.N. organization and its financial arm, the I.M.F..

The sad fact, that this defective system presently controls the world, and holds it at ransom, does not imply that the system is the best available platform of economy that humanity has created. This is far from being the case. It merely means that the oligarchy that requires this system as a platform for its looting has been able to so befuddle the world into adapting this system, that it has now become universally accepted. The universal acceptance of this destructive system, in spite of the pains it causes, demonstrates that the system is being promoted and protected by an immensely powerful oligarchy that depends on it for its existence, while the infinite system of economy on which the survival of society depends, has been quietly pushed into the background of history where it rots, and is not even recognized by society as an option, much less is promoted and demanded to be implemented.

The paradox of choice.

In order to explore the paradox why society embraces a self-destructive system, rather than one that has been proven to be beneficial, it becomes important to understand that at the present stage (which may not last very much longer) the people of United States still have the political ability to re-adopt its earlier, successful model of economy - the infinite model that by its first, complete, and successful implementation in history is rightfully called the "American System of Economy." It is also important to understand that the European nations no longer have this ability. They lost the right to select the financial and economic system of their choice because of their commitment to the Maastricht Treaty for European Union. All European nations that have committed themselves to this treaty are prohibited under its terms from adopting any other model for economy and finance than the self-limiting feudalist model. They are prohibited under this treaty from creating for themselves direct national credits for investment into infrastructures for the nation, for improving education, for advancing science, technology and industrial development. The evidence suggests that the oligarchy had won another round with this provision, that prevents any nation from creating investment funds for its self-development, that demands that all investment funds be 'rented' from the oligarchy's world-financial system.

With this, we have a paradox to resolve. Why would any nation commit itself to close the door on its freedom of choice?

This paradox is actually no different in nature than the paradox that one finds in the U.S. which still has the legal right to choose, but refuses to choose the best available system, devoting itself instead to a system that is self-limiting, that is detrimental to its livelihood, even destructive on a global scale?

Paradoxes invite scientific enquiry?

For the paradox at hand, one might explore what assumptions are built into the choices, and what is the driving force behind these assumptions. One might also explore what principles they represent, and what the fundamental principles of metaphysics indicate about the reality involved.

The Maastricht paradox:

To get back to the Maastricht Treaty paradox; the treaty commits the nations of Europe to the universal adoption of the oligarchy's self-limiting, feudalist model of economy, which already rules at the present time. One might say that nothing is actually lost by adopting the treaty. This is not true. One cannot say this. The reality is not that simple. A great deal becomes lost by implementing this treaty. The future of Europe becomes lost by it. The treaty prevents the most tragic mistake in history from becoming corrected, which has been committed by all nations. It appears as if the people felt that a commitment to unity in error could magically make the failing erroneous system functional.

It is certainly possible to adopt by common commitment the proposition that $1 + 1 = 7$. It is even possible to built an entire economy on this platform. Except the force of commitment to an error, no matter how universally it is adapted, does not change the reality of the error and the effect of a people's commitment to it. There is no wisdom in a universal commitment to erroneous doctrine.

The creation of a universal European currency has no fundamental economic advantage in terms of improving the productive and creative potential of the societies that are committed to having a united currency. However, it creates enormous disadvantages. The Maastricht process achieves one of the oligarchy's main objectives, that of dismantling the sovereignty of nations. It disables the means for protecting individual societies and their developed economies. This opens the door to the free reign of destructive looting. Nor does the damage end here. The treaty also forbids a nation to issue directed low-cost credits for infrastructure development and reindustrialization. The Maastricht treaty dictates that all credits must come from the private feudal system. This stranglehold becomes a death collar.

By their innocent commitment to the Maastricht Treaty, the nations of Europe have, as far as can be determined from exploring the functioning of the feudal model of economy, committed themselves to their self-destruction, and are pursuing the process vigorously with the corresponding result becoming evermore evident. The mass strikes that have been erupting in France and in other nations, as the result of this commitment, are testimony that painfully destructive moves are already being made on the social front for no other reason than to maintain the prescribed commitment to the feudal principle that the Maastricht treaty imposes as by force.

It is also important to understand that the United States is presently in the final stage of becoming forced to commit itself to the same fate. The insanely irrational conservative revolution of the Newt Gingrich phenomenon is fundamentally not a political movement at all, concerned with balancing governmental budgets, as the rhetoric goes. Rather the whole conservative movement constitutes a unified ideological front that has infiltrated the governmental structure. The goal, evidently is not to meet the needs of the society, the constituents, the requirements for national development, but to carry out an ideological commitment towards destroying the political institution of the Presidency and the principle of the nation-state. When this coveted goal is achieved, the structure of government will be totally altered and decapitated. At such a point, the political capacity may no longer exist for the nation to adopt the infinite model of economy that can only be implemented within the framework of the nation-state.

It is one of the great tragedies of modern times that the principle of the nation-state is so poorly understood. It is not surprising, however, that this trend has developed. The principle of the nation-state and the principle of the model for infinite economy, are one principle. Neither can exist without the other. By adopting the feudal system of economy, one of the pillars of the nation-state has been destroyed. The fundamental principle of the nation-state has been rejected. It is not surprising, therefore, that one sees a commitment to conservatism unfolding that spells out clearly that the nation has rejected its constitutional commitment to self-development, common wealth, common protection, and has instead embraced a commitment to poverty and self-destruction.

The Malthusian background, an economic issue.

In modern years the institution of the nation-state has become increasingly under attack by the agencies of the oligarchy which is still fighting the same war against human development that it had fought when its platform of feudalism and colonialism was first challenged by the American Revolution. Ever since that day the nation-state has been laid to siege by the Empire: attacked by its terrorism, wrecked by its indirect and direct political intervention, weakened by its poverty, destabilized by its environmental demands and related myths that are directed against the support structures of human living. Moreover, this war has become a global one against the whole of humanity.

Many of the forces that are currently deployed against the principle of the nation-state are deeply intertwined with the oligarchy's demands for a collapse in populations levels around the globe. The Empire drives these demands by shutting down mankind's economic activity at an ever increasing rate, together with its food and energy production.

One might sense a conspiracy, here. Indeed, there exists a conflict of ideologies. The conflict between the infinite model, and the feudal model of economy, is but a subset of this larger conflict to which the oligarchy has committed itself and the forces of its Empire. In this respect, conservatism is a subset of the Empire's Malthusian ideology. All the ideological structures of Malthusian nature operate from, are safeguarded by the Empire, and support its feudalist oligarchic system.

Under the principle of the larger conflict between the infinite and the oligarchic, feudal system, the Imperial systems are contrary by their nature to everything that is essential for the effective development of the human potential by means of metaphysical processes. Any serious commitment to develop the creative and productive potential of mankind necessitates a commitment to the infinite model of economy and a break with feudalist model that operates hand in hand with Malthusian oligarchic ideology which provides the cover for the Empire's looting.

Metaphysics and infinity are fundamentally linked and are the counterpoised to oligarchic ideology. In order to prevent any possible meaningful commitment to human development, the oligarchy's imperial forces have gone to great length to destroy the fundamental identity of man as a metaphysically capable being. Great efforts have been made, and are still being made through ideological structures, to tear the status of man to the ground, to equate man with the image of a worm.

This is achieved in several ways. It is achieved by attributing to mankind animal attributes rather than metaphysical attributes. The animal attribute is promoted through the "carrying capacity" mythology that defines the planet as too small for mankind in the manner that a meadow can be too small for cattle or sheep as it becomes overgrazed by too many animals. But man is not an animal. The mythology that puts man on an equal plane with animals denies that fact that the resources by which mankind exists today on this planet have all been created by mankind out the resources of the human mind. These resources were not found on the natural plain. The 'carrying capacity' mythology that would have people believe that the earth is too small, denies the fact that mankind is presently 5,500 times larger that what the natural plain could support by its own primitive resources.

The spiritual fact of a creative intellect that identifies mankind by demonstrated accomplishments, says something about the nature of man that cannot be said about any other species on the planet. This metaphysical platform, is an infinite platform. On this platform, one sees no discernable limits to mankind's continuing unfolding, such as limits imposed by the nature of available physical resources. Such limits do not exist. The limits that are promoted in front of the tired gaze of humanity by its oligarchy, are myths that incorporate outright lies.

Great efforts are currently made by the oligarchy's Empire to cause mankind to commit itself to a massive collapse of its population levels in order (so the oligarchy hopes) to prevent mankind's vast development potential from becoming recognized and realized, which would shut down the feudal system that is totally incapable of supporting any meaningful development. This is evidently the reason why Japan was prevented in recent years from initiating economic development efforts throughout the Third World nations, and the reason why its vast flows of money were subsequently channeled into real estate speculation that created the infamous real estate bubble that has already collapsed, which has severely damaged the Japanese banking system in the process.

Several more, similar, mythologies are incorporated into the oligarchy's effort to shut mankind down as a progressive force. These efforts include the creation of the "ozone depletion" mythology that has been contrived to break down mankind's refrigeration capabilities; and the myth that the DDT based pesticides are dangerous.

These myths, which have not a glimmer of truth that a serious scientist can detect, have been created to shut down mankind's capability for survival. The priority target appear to be the poorer regions of the world. Here, the production ban of DDT has shut down mankind's fight against malaria and the insect infestation of its crops. The production ban of the CFC refrigerants is targeting the refrigeration chain in poorer regions which cannot afford to replace their refrigeration systems. The death toll is expected to reach upwards to 40 million people per year, as the result of the CFC ban. And there is more to come. The myth of "global warming" that is currently promoted around the world is used as a basis for shutting down mankind's economic activities altogether, that are almost totally dependent on fossil fuel energy.

That this multipronged complex of attacks against mankind is nothing more than a conspiracy against human life is evident by the fact that every one of these myths originate out of the wide channels of the Empire - the same Empire whose oligarchy controls the world-financial system and profits from it.

One cannot fault the oligarchy for this, for its existence depends on the looting feudal system being kept alive and well. The oligarchy has maintained itself throughout the ages by a keen self-interest in systems for looting, which it needs, that go back to the slave trading days, to the days of the opium wars, and farther back than that, to the financier operations of the Venetian Empire and the banking Empire of Florence which together brought the house down over Europe by means of excessive profiteering.

The modern oligarchy follows the ancient path, though it employs the most advanced ideological and psychological means to protect its looting systems on which it depends. The Venetian oligarchy drained gains in the order of 40% per year, and more, out of the economies of the European area that provided barely a 2-4% profit. By these inflated profits, the Venetians and Banks of Florence, collapsed the economies of Europe to the breaking point. The famous 1345 collapse of the world-financial system (such as it was at this time) was the biggest and ugliest world-financial collapse in history.

Half of the population of Europe survived the chaos, and so did the oligarchy. But, the oligarchy didn't repent. It couldn't repent. To repent, meant suicide. Nothing could have caused the oligarchy to reverse its platform built on looting. It hasn't repented to the present day, as the same process the brought the house down in 1345 happens still. The evidence can be seen in the huge imaginary profits that are being built up into 'paper mountains' of financial aggregates, from which the organizers of the game draw substantial monetary profits. The buildup of worthless paper that results as a by-product of the looting operation portents an enormous catastrophe that may take the entire world-financial 'house' down and possibly end civilization as we know it. It may even hurt the oligarchy to some degree. Except, the coming crash will not likely cause the oligarchy to repent, either. There is nothing that the oligarchy could create that it might substitute for its looting system that it needs to maintain itself. The oligarchy's only other option is to restructure its own nature into becoming partners in human development. This option, however, has been consistently rejected thy the oligarchy throughout history.

The massive accumulative effect of the financial inflation that the Venetians had staged in the 14th century, unfolded in the form of a general disintegration of the economies of Europe. Virtually all of Europe's wealth evaporated in the crash, together with half the population that perished through the resulting poverty and the plague. The oligarchy is not moved by such catastrophes, nor can one detect any evidence that it has altered its game. It appears to be as totally committed to its system, by which it exists, than it was in earlier times, regardless of the consequences to other people, of its commitment to the looting of society. And why not?

Why should the oligarchy not be committed to its system? Why should it change? It has the financial resources to create the networks and institutions to uphold its looting system for as long as it desires. The oligarchy 'owns' the ideological authors that create the required ideologies, and it owns the grass-roots supporters that promote the ideologies globally. It also owns whatever else is needed to assure that the feudalist system survives in spite of its inherent cycles of crashes. The Empire is committed to maintain its system even if 60% - 90% of the global population must be eliminated to assure the system's survival. Should the oligarchy be expected change its position for humanitarian concerns? This can hardly be expected from a people whose tradition is rooted in slavery, slave trading, dope pushing, setting up wars, destabilizing nations, looting the world through colonialism and subversive games. Why should the oligarchy change now?

The onus to fight for the survival of civilization rests not with the oligarchy, it never has. This responsibility rests with society. It lies totally in the society's own court. Mankind has more than sufficient resources of intellect to protect itself from oligarchic aggression and ideological lies, and to achieve the scientific and technological development that can erase the desperate poverty that has been created all over the world. The society alone carries the responsibility to replace the feudal model of economy with the infinite model that has already proved itself whenever it was employed. It is the society's task to replace its poverty with prosperity, and, then, to protect itself from the revenge of oligarchism when this step is taken.

The infinite model of economy exists, and mankind's metaphysical capability exists by which mankind has the means to develop itself far beyond its present state. The fact that mankind has achieved a development that has taken it to a population level that is 5,500 times greater than what the natural systems of the planet could support, proves that there are no inherent limits poised against the development of man, except the limits that are self-created by little minds. These limits appear only in thought, in mystical ideologies that render man with an animal nature and deny the creative and productive capacity of the human intellect. The so derived conservatism may artificially conjure up limitations. The limits may even appear quite real, though they represent but a consequence of development being shut down and infrastructures collapsing. At this point, the self-imposed limits may appear absolute, even though they are pure illusions.

When mankind's development platform becomes sufficiently collapsed by the destructive ideologies that are pure illusions, the self-created limitations become real by effect, and by mankind's acceptance and are thus understood as final. Such a perversion may take place in the not too distant future and result in the effective renewal of the world-colonial system of economy on a feudal platform, possibly under a formal U.N. dictate to replace the nation-state with the resulting loss of hope for any rebirth of prosperity and civilization on this planet.

Globalizing the economic collapse.

It is not the least remarkable, considering the oligarchy's need for a feudal background and the power to enforce it, that the very system that has proven itself throughout history to be inherently self-limiting and self-defeating, has become the universally accepted global system, and that the infinite system that has none of these faults, has been put totally out of the picture. This irrational commitment by the whole world to a defective system, has been achieved through wide-spread efforts by an immensely wealthy oligarchy working behind the scene, which operates in the name of ideological 'guidance' that is controlling people's thoughts. The Empire has also has achieved direct political control over the governments around the world by means of its infiltration into high places, thus developing for itself a position of great power within established governments and international organizations, which it virtually owns. Another path to attaining a global commitment to the defective system is through instigating wars wherever a resistance to the globalization of feudalism may develop.

On the surface, the remarkable success that the oligarchy scored in all these efforts, accounts for its success in keeping the single most destructive economic system alive, on which its existence depends, and to impose it globally regardless of its destructive nature. This remarkable success by the oligarchy, however, rests more solidly on the political apathy and the political disinterest of the world's population, than on any other factor of the oligarchy's own creation. The oligarchy has no real power in itself. Its Empire is but a shell. It succeeds by bidding the society to discard the principles underlying its own prosperity and adopt the feudal principles instead.

The potential downfall of civilization rests, therefore, with mankind's failure to take its responsibility serious, to protect its own vital self-interests.

The fundamental metaphysical fact that **man is free** is of no avail to anyone unless it becomes the platform for action, a platform for taking responsibility, for developing the infrastructures for existence that mankind has proven to be capable of developing and by which it currently exists. The oligarchy, with all its self-assumed wealth and power, would be powerless against mankind's recognition of its own identity in infinity. The oligarchy can only suggest the self-devolution of humanity. It can never actually impose it, though it appears to have been remarkably successful in imposing it.

The oligarchic British Empire had no power, for instance, to set off World War I, but it was successful in doing it by creating the adversarial positions among the European nations for which the nations destroyed themselves in violent combat against each other. Conspiracies and manipulations are powerful weapons, but they are ineffective in an environment of alertness. They are effective only through mythological idealism that misdirects alertness and causes the devolution of reason.

Against this background, the universal acceptance of the self-limiting economic and financial system, in-spite of its fault, is not really a surprising phenomenon. Nor does the universal acceptance of the faulty system prove anything about its worthiness. All that the universal acceptance of the deeply faulty system proves, is the universality of political apathy that can be found throughout the world population, which the oligarchy merely exploits, quite professionally at that, and aims to maintain and increase.

Creating a financial monoculture.

The impending global collapse of the faulty world's-financial and economic system has the potential to be catastrophic in its effect, but it represents nothing more than the natural effect of the global political apathy that has always existed, or was created where it did not exist, and is becoming more widely exploited. In this vacuum, the oligarchy has spread its ware and created a global financial monoculture. A global collapse cannot occur without a global commitment to the dying system that has no strength in it, nor underlying sanity of reason. The globalization of the feudal financial system that has been achieved to date is similar to an artificial forest made of nothing but spruce trees. As soon as the spruce budworm arrives, the forest becomes infested and overwhelmed by it, and, then, dies. The same exposure exists today in the world-financial system which has become an element of a global monoculture. The global financial and economic situation is similar to a disease having infected every part of a planet-wide monoculture, as the same ideology has been impressed on every nation operating under the IMF system. Thus, the devastation will be global when the disease takes its toll. The 'spruce budworm' has arrived and is thriving everywhere. Soon the consequences will begin to appear. When free-trade and deindustrialization (the post-industrial society doctrine) were imposed, they were imposed universally. When in consequence governmental debts were created, they were created globally. When the money became tight because of debt service loads, it became tight globally. Once the printing presses were turned on to lighten this load, they were turned on globally. Likewise, when the financial system falls of the cliff because of the unfolding insanities, it will do so on a global scale. The financial experts have a technical phrase that defines this, although the phrase doesn't indicate what the global financial and economic breakdown means in real life terms. They call the breakdown a "systemic failure." This is hardly a fitting phrase for the potentially greatest social catastrophe in human history.

Monocultures, however, are not a natural occurrence. Very few survive in the real world. The man-created monocultures in forests and agriculture are vulnerable to sudden collapse, by infestation and changes in environment, and must be carefully maintained. The same holds true for the world-financial monoculture. There is not a single financial and economic system on the planet that functions according to the fundamental principle of metaphysics. China comes close, but not close enough. It is still tied quite deeply into the world-financial system, although not to the total extend that the rest of the world is tied into this system. There exist presently very few nations whose financial system functions differently from the rest of the world. In other words, the fundamentally defective, self-limiting, and destructive feudal financial system that the IMF represents, has been 'adopted' to rule the world. According to the nature of monocultures, this world-financial system will take the entire world down with it, when it disintegrates. There are no safe harbors in a monoculture environment, where one might weather the storm. China, by being only loosely tied into the world-system, is therefore the only major nation on the planet that may survive the global crash, economically.

A productive monoculture based on universal principle.

As was said before, the universality of the feudal system that largely rules the world today is by no means a proof of the worthiness of system. Monocultures have a validity only in cases when the universality reflects the universality of fundamental principle. Principle is absolute; its applicability is universal. The universality of life, or of the infinite system of economics which may some day become universal, are examples of the universal reflection of a fundamental principle. The resulting 'monoculture' strengthens whatever it supports, whereas the universality of fundamental error, such as feudalism in economics, exposes the scene to corruption and disintegration. The effective globalization of the free-trade principle and financial feudalism has made humanity depended on a defective monoculture. Herein lies the great danger. Monocultured forests are open to the predatory action of insect infestation, and therefore represent fundamentally a defective monoculture. The feudal financial monoculture is likewise open to predatory action, with the results mounting up. Thus, the 'spruce budworm' is having a grand time in the 'forests.'

The reality is that our global financial system is about to collapse, just as a monocultured forest is liable to collapse once predation begins. These collapsing systems are about as far removed from the infinite model of economy, shown in Appendix 5, as anything can be. They are the total opposite of the infinite system, by which their dysfunctionality is explained, including the certainty of collapse. The collapse, when it comes, will be as 'spectacular' as any monoculture collapse the world has so far experienced. That collapse is the natural fruit of the One-World dictatorship ideology.

The point of the impending collapse of the current monocultured world-system can almost be predicted. It is the point at which the illusion that the system is working, can no longer be maintained. This, typically, is the point when reality hits home; when the flow of real wealth into fictitious financial aggregates system can no longer be made large enough to keep the fictitious financial and monetary systems growing. This is the point when the populations begin to die, physically, through imposed poverty; the point at which the physical deficits can no longer be hidden. This situation exists today. Hospitals are being shut down for lack of money; health-care and research services are shut down; social collapses occur; rampant crime unfolds in the streets; disrespect for the law and fundamental principles becomes common place, involving both the government and the population; anarchy begins - but facing all this, the governments are bankrupt for a solution.

Everyone knows that printing more money doesn't solve anything, except no one has a better idea. The feudal system cannot afford a solution to this crisis. In a monoculture there exists no strength to deal with a crisis. There exists not a single economy on the planet today that is operating on the platform of the infinite system, and is thereby save, except possibly China.

Since the modern system of the world's economy functions as a whole, the disintegration of the financial aggregates that has been rather minute in the past and more isolated, will not likely remain isolated in the coming crash, nor will the upset of the physical disintegration, by itself, cure the underlying problem. The feudal platform will likely remain in force, in spite of the physical collapse, until it becomes universally replaced. The great crash in 1345 that wiped out half the population of Europe, did not replace the feudal system or cure its inherent defects, nor did the consequences of the feudal system ban it from ever being applied again.

In today's world, history is about to repeat itself, and it is unlikely the end result will be any different, only bigger. In fact, none of the financial crashes in history have ever cured the underlying defect that caused the crashes. The only effect that has been observed, is that the crashes tend to be larger in proportion to the magnitude of the financial inflation that has built up within the monocultured system of which the world-financial, economic, and political system is presently the largest in history.

The global unprincipled monoculturalism.

While the world celebrates the 'strength' of its global financial markets, it has in fact no cause to celebrate. The more the financial markets grow, the more devastating will be the collapse of the system on the populations. The growth in the markets and the size of its value reflect the vast extend of the monocultured game. The size of the unprincipled pursuit reflects little more than a measure of the liability and volatility that has been built up by the globalization of defective axioms. The intensity and extend of the current globalization is not a measure of strength, but of globalized insanity. The more the market grows, the weaker the markets become. The more they grow globally, the more volatile the world becomes. Every time the stock markets blast off to new all time highs, the yield per investment drops lower since the size of physical industries that the market represents, remains the same or does in fact decline year after year. Without a global input into these markets, the dangerous values would not exist.

For instance, in the month of January 1996 $24.5 billion of new money poured into the U.S. stock mutual funds. This figure represent a record. It marks the greatest monthly inflow of new money into the funds in history. Now, this inflow also came on top of the peak of a multiyear "bull market." In fact, according to reports, a huge portion of this inflow went into aggressive growth equity funds, the highest risk category on the market. There is nothing healthy about this rush into equities on such a huge scale. There is nothing healthy about the public throwing such vast sums at the market at its most perilous point. This advancing insanity would not likely have been possible without a carefully created monoculture in attitudes. After all, if the whole world is playing this game it must be all-right, people are telling themselves. According to reports, stocks and equity mutual funds have become the American public's most favorite vehicle for holding its savings. A greater share of its assets is thrown into this market than into any other for of investment, surpassing bank deposits, treasury bills, bonds, real estate, and anything else combined.

There are more stock equity funds in existence in the U.S., some 7,000 of them, than there are stocks listed. Most of these are managed by 'kids' barely 30 years old, who have never experienced the devastation of a deep crash, like the 1929 crash from which the market took over 30 years to recover. What do they mean, when they say, "invest for the long haul?" Most have only been in business for a few years, yet the public throws its money at them. Some actually do deliver 20% to 30% gains, but at what risk, and at what cost to the society. Like members of a herd, they compete with each other, but they all play the same game, they have to, the investing public demands that they do.

The fund managers, like the investing public, are part of a peculiar monoculture of mutually supporting insanity that drives evermore 'air' into an inflated bubble. Sure, there are extreme paper profits registered from this inflow, which don't mean anything. The monetary inflow drives the market values higher and higher, even though they are selling the same old stuff that is actually decreasing in value as the economy that the stuff represents is collapsing. Thus, they are driving the bubble closer to the point at which the bubble pops.

The trading mania that drives stock values up, is really a facet of monoculturalism. Suppose there are 100,000 shares of a certain stock on the market that are valued one dollar each. The next day, 10,000 of these are traded for two dollars. The trade required a monetary input of $20,000. Now, since the game is a universal one, everybody assumes that the new price applies to all shares, so that the market's value has suddenly gone up from a value of $100,000 to $200,000. In this case, a $20,000 inflow caused a $100,000 increase in market value. This vast 'profit' that is suddenly chalked up, is the value by which the financial funds are measured. This measurement is meaningful in an environment in which everybody thinks alike, acts alike, perceives reality alike. It means nothing to those who understand the reality of the situation, and it means even less if the funds that intentionally throw money at some worthless stock in order to create profit through inflated market values. If in the above example the 10,000 shares were sold between departments of a single fund, the increase in market value was accomplished at no cost at all. The profit, therefore, is meaningless, as it has no footing in reality.

The underlying axioms that cause cyclical market failures, have up to the present, never been tarnished. The glitter of the market shines in the eyes of the people. A promise of a 15% or even a 20% return on investments, glitters in comparison to the dull 7% that the banks pay, or the tiny 2% that the physical economy generates. This, also, is where the problem lies. The tiny 2% that the industry generates, is real. All the other profits represent a wonderful dream that pops with the rude awakening when the upwards leveraging ends that drives the markets into the stratosphere. Of course, there are some who have managed to monetize the paper profits, and in so doing they steal from the unwary. In the overall real world, however, the market produces no profit at all, but expenses and opportunities for gargantuan losses.

This reality, nobody likes to talk about. The axioms that drive the systems to ever greater highs are protected by the universal 'religion' by which the global feudal system operates.

This does not mean that the required departure from this trend cannot be achieved. It is certainly possible for a nation, especially a nation with the tradition of the United States of America, to pull itself out from under the yoke of the feudal monocultural system, and declare it bankrupt (which it is), and to replace this bankrupt system with a new system according to the infinite model of economy that operates totally in the real world. Nor is this system an experimental novelty. It has served the nation for many decades during the first century of its history. Under this system national credits were created by a national federal bank. Nor were these credits used for speculation, were credits cause destruction, but were directed specifically for the economic development of the nation, by which the USA became the most prosperous nation on earth. It became the envy of mankind, and a model to be copied.

It is certainly within the range of responsibilities for the officer of the Presidency of the United States of America to protect the public from the great financial, economic, and social harm that a chain reaction crash of the entire world-financial system may unleash. The President, therefore has the power and the responsibility, according to the design of the Presidency, to protect the nation by putting the entire Federal Reserve system into a bankruptcy reorganization as a measure to forestall the crash. It is certainly possible for this supreme officer of the nation, being charged with such great responsibility, to initiate for his nation that has already suffered greatly from the dying feudal system, the reestablishment of the infinite system of economy. In doing so, the President would be opening the door to the creation of six million jobs per year. Unemployment would become a forgotten word in the resulting environment of protected industries of the type that Alexander Hamilton had pioneered, that had featured prominently in the nation's history. From a position of real strength in the physical economy, some of the markets may actually survive, and those that don't survive will cause little damage in a dynamically growing economy. On this platform, the nation will survive the death of the feudal system, and the IMF system that represents the feudal system.

There is no reason why any nation or person must subject itself indefinitely to the potentially most disastrous social, economic, and financial system of all times that the current world-financial system has become. The reality is, that man is free to act rightly. The nation is greater than the forces that would dictate its destiny. The option to act wisely can be exercised at any time.

Today, the U.S. President still has the political capacity to take the required steps. None-the-less, the officer of the Presidency has little hope of succeeding without the backing of the society at large which cannot be spared the responsibility of standing up and be counted, demanding its its rights to be acknowledged. As this fundamental requirement is far from being met at this present time, or even recognized by the public, the wealth of the nation and its citizens cannot be protected, nor can the global crash be prevented, or civilization be safeguarded.

One begins to wonder in this context what role the vast quantity of 200 million publicly held guns will play in the environment of anarchy that the greatest financial crash in history is sure to unleash. The question must be asked who is ready and willing to live in a world where people begin to eat by the gun? Who is willing to pay this price, and for what?

The monoculture of public thought, and its effect on the market.

Public thought reflects many of the characteristic of a monoculture. And this monoculture is real. Public thought has been carefully channeled to take on this characteristic. It has become a monoculture of singularized cultivated opinions. The arrival of the baby-boomers created the foundation for this monoculture, as the baby-boomers formed a large singular block of people. This foundation has been utilized, transformed by subversive 'guidance,' and universalized. Now, the end-product has arrived at the markets. The so derived monoculture big and single minded.

The currently installed 'circuit breakers' that are intended to prevent the crash of the market, such as the infamous crash in 1987, are hopelessly inadequate to even slow the coming crash that is driven by this tremendously large single minded culture of directed opinions.

The circuit breakers work as follows. When the Dow drops 200 points below the last day's closing, trading is halted at the New York Stock Exchange for one hour. This is intended to allow things to cool down. When the Dow drops another 200 points below that, trading stops for yet another hour. After this, the game is wide open. After these two one hour stops, no more impediments are imposed. It is difficult to belief how a two hour halt in trading alters the 'programming' of the monoculture that drives the market. When the market reopens after its one hour shutdown, all the held up trades are likely to become a torrent that floods the trading floors as if the gates of an overfilled dam are thrust open. After the second hour of of market closure, the market is allowed to crash to any level whatsoever, without further intervention. The reality of the game is, that nothing can save the market that is driven by a type of programmed insanity.

The futures markets have somewhat different trading curbs. When the Slooses 500 points the futures market goes "lock limit down" for ten minutes. This means, no sales are allowed for ten minutes at lower prices. When the market hits the 1200 point drop level, the lock limit down is imposed for 30 minutes, at the 2000 point drop level the lock limit is imposed again for thirty minutes. At the 3000 point drop level the lock limit down goes into effect for the rest of the day, while trading for higher prices is still allowed. The same occurs on the second day, except that the market is allowed to fall 5000 points before the lock limit down goes into effect for the day. The one day drop that is thereby allowed before the trading is shut down for the day, is actually greater than the crash in 1929, or the crash on Black Monday in October 1987.

The established crash barriers are puny. They are little more than speed-bumps. The delays they impose may actually heighten the selling frenzy and increase the losses. When the Sdrops 1200 points (equivalent to 120 points on the Dow) a condition called "side car" switches on. This means that the big arbitrators can no longer trade electronically. They are required to go to the trading floor and wait for the buyers to arrive who may bail them out; and even then, their orders must sit five minutes before they may be executed. All this is imposed upon the big boys while the market continues to drop. These delays virtually guarantee the big funds huge losses. The end result will be, that it makes their anxiety worse, which adds to the selling pressure, and may even trigger a total downturn. In other words, the circuit breakers are powerless to prevent a real crash. They may slow it, temporarily, but tend to make the crash worse when the so restrained orders are released.

A real crash in the financial markets cannot be prevented by these devices. The crash is powered by a totally different driver, such as financial inflation and a mind-set that ignores the reality. When the inflation becomes so obvious that it flips the mind-set that ignores reality, the monocultural dimension will cause an unstoppable run on the markets. Crashes occur in the markets when the reality of financial inflation becomes recognized and becomes responded to. Procedural 'circuit breakers' cannot stop this avalanche that unfolds when the reality comes to light and deflates the bubbles of illusions.

Circuit breakers cannot save the markets from the recognition what should have been obvious to everyone at the outset, that in a declining economy the only growth industry that can exist, is the one that thrives on illusions. Crashes occur when the illusions evaporate. The circuit breakers cannot deal with that. Nor are the crashes necessarily confined to crashing stock values, indexes, and bond values. The entire social and economic structure of the nation tends to crash as well, through the after-effects.

The circuit breakers may have a different effect, which may actually be intended. They may break the crash up into a series of cascading collapses which invariably drive the total crash deeper as the intersystem effects begin to be felt that expose the illusion of financial wealth more powerfully than a single quick drop might accomplish. The intersystem effects have deep ties into the banking industry as Japan has found out, and into the insurance industry as London found out, and into the currency markets as Mexico had learned, bitterly. They will also have deep ties into the real estate markets, the commodity futures markets, the bond markets, the precious metals markets, the oil markets, even the Treasury debt markets.

The infamous stockmarket crash of 1929 must be seen as a baby crash in comparison to what is at risk today. It must also be recognized that the 1929 crash caused none-the-less the greatest social collapse in the history of the U.S. nation. The effects of this crash persisted for many years until the production requirement for World War II opened the gates for a strong, although temporary, economic recovery. It must further be recognized that this horrendously awful crash in terms of its effect on society occurred under circumstances that were nearly ideal for the society's survival. The 1929 crash occurred at the height of a strong economy, and against the background of a healthy agricultural system, a healthy banking system, and a flood of real physical wealth flowing from the newly developed oil resources. The crash also occurred against the background of a well functioning government that had little debt on its books. Still, in spite of all these ideal circumstances, the crash caused an enormous catastrophe that is still remembered as the Great Depression.

Today's background is infinitely worse. The impending crash comes at the time of a severely weakened economy; of an emerging world food crisis; of a banking system that has transformed itself into the gambling empire of the century; of a dangerous dependence on oil imports with a possible price crunch or total embargo on the horizon; of a government that has been crippled by debt and ideological attacks, which may be forced to default on it obligations; of a governmental budget crisis that is destroying the social support structures of the nation; of a growing insanity by the population itself that is throwing its savings at financial aggregates that have no inherent value; of record deemployment in the productive industries that throw people into early retirement positions with pension funds which ride themselves on the disappearing financial aggregates; and of a rise in fascist attitudes throughout the nation that is armed to the hilt with anything imaginable, from hundreds of millions of hand guns, to tens of millions of automatic military assault weapons. No one can determine with any kind of accuracy how deeply this immensely fragile background is going to be stirred by the chain reaction effect of a financial crash in which trillions of dollars worth of assumed equity gets wiped off the big boards in the U.S. and elsewhere, in the biggest financial disintegration in history.

The 1929 crash is useful as an indicator in that it has demonstrated the principle that no one is isolated from the after effects of such a calamity that arises out of the feudal economic system driven to its extreme, and amplified by the monoculture of thought that has practically universalized the society's response (or no response) to its deepest failures.

A monoculture in political direction.

There has not been a fundamental turning point on the world political scene in the last hundred years. The world is still as deeply founded in feudalism as it was a hundred years ago. Whenever there was even a hint of such a turning, it was quickly eliminated. President Franklin D. Roosevelt had planned such a turnaround and had made significant progress. This trend ended abruptly with his death. The reversal of Roosevelt's policies, which were based on the infinite system of economy, was swift. The reversal was thorough, and global. The traitors had stood ready and acted fast.

President J. F. Kennedy had a similar reversal planed and had initiated it to some degree when he was eliminated from the political scene by assassination. Whoever dared after that to even speak the word "development," disappeared. Thus a political monoculture was created by brutal fascist attacks that still rules the political minds of humanity today. The so created political monoculture had even been given a name. Its focal point has been called "the new world-order" which indeed it had become on a global scale.

The reality is, that mankind is constantly effected by the destructive nature of the feudal system. Its effect is not only evident in the financial markets, but also in the policies of nations where a new wave of fascist doctrine guides the policy makers into channels of such austerity that people are beginning to die under the weight of it. Only half a century ago, people were convicted and hung at the trial of the Nazis in Nuremberg, Germany, and this for the same crimes against humanity which are now imbedded into public policy. They were convicted and hung, not because they actually killed anyone, but because they had known, or should have known, that the policies they imposed would lead to the wrongful death of the targeted segments of the populations.

The question must now be answered of whether this criterion applies to today's policy makers. Governor Ridge of Pennsylvania stands publicly accused of the same crimes by policy decisions that cut over 200,000 people off the most minimal public assistance, and this at a time of an accelerating collapse of the physical support structures by which society normally maintains itself. The governor stands accused of throwing away the life of people in favor of a tax relief for the very rich. He stands accused for not imposing a speculation tax on speculative financial turnover which would fund many times over the social funding cuts for which people, especially the elderly and unwed mothers, are shut out of the system and left to die. In real terms, however, the whole of society suffers from this fascism. Nor is Governor Ridge alone in enacting Nazi style policies for which he stands accused by the population. These styles of policies are found in many nations, and they are fundamentally driven by a single factor: The IMF austerity ideology which has discounted human life far below the value of financial aggregates for which the human lives are sacrificed.

Appendix 1, Figure 4 shows one of the secondary effects of the feudal economic system that is impacting every person of the society. Figure 4 shows the devastating relationship between the debt created under the feudal system, and the economic profits of the physical economy. As the debt rises the profits disappear and become negative, by which the debt increases. This interrelationship is destroying the economies. It will not go away with any crash in the markets, but will likely increase its devastating effect, because that axioms that underlie the escalation are rooted in a monocultural ideology that drives the public policies which defend the rights of feudalism above all else.

Debt values cannot evaporate in the crash of the markets. Their claims remain. They may partially tumble in a series of after-shocks, but only to be re-established later. Appendix 1, Figure 2, presents the growth in the world's foreign debt, versus interest paid. The striking feature is that the world debt grew by nearly the exact amount of interest paid and did not deviate from this trend at the time of the 1987 stockmarket crash. In other words, the interest charges that the debt service demands impose are consistently rolled over into new debt since they can't be paid. A stockmarket crash, no matter how deep, won't effect the ideology that keeps the system going by whatever means can be invented, even if this includes the indirect murder of whole segments of the populations. Today's trend that exposed people to a certain death for budgetary reasons, will most certainly be magnified beyond anything ever imagined in the wake of the crash of the world-financial system.

Fortunately, the recycling process works only for as long as the debt obligations can be recapitalized into new Treasury offerings, or be monetized by printing more cash. At this point the true value of the debt will become apparent.

The capacity to refinance debt obligations, by which the system is currently maintained, will likely vanish in the wake of a crash. This means that the global financial system falls apart at the deepest level, the moment a crash unfolds in the markets. Here the governments' reaction is crucial. Will it defend the debt system and revitalize it in some for as the feudal ideology dictates? Or will the governments shut the entire feudal system down. This crucial reaction will determine the life and death of civilization after the crash. At the present moment, it appears that the feudal system may be saved at the demise of humanity, so strong is the political monoculture that is controlling the world scene today.

There is a great fear being created about governmental defaults. It is being said that defaults will make future borrowing next to impossible. The history of governmental defaults has indeed been an ugly one. When the newly formed Soviet Union defaulted on the previous government's debt, it closed the door to any chance for new bond issues on Western financial markets. The same happened three decades later in China when Mao Tsedong defaulted on the previous governmental debt, which sealed off China from Western financial markets. The fear in all cases is centered on a supposed need for "Western Credits."

The default scare carefully avoids the crucial factor that any meaningful redevelopment of the world cannot be accomplished on the feudal platform of which debt is a central factor. If the debt factor crashes to zero in the dynamics of the market place, this intelligent realization should be accepted and not be overturned artificially by revitalizing the debt by governmental policy in an effort to save the feudal world-financial system after the markets crashed.

A global governmental default is actually unavoidable under the globalized feudal system. In fact it is an ongoing policy that unfortunately does not bear the correct name.

When President Nixon abolished the Gold backing for the U.S. dollar in 1971, under oligarchic pressures, the interrelationship between the Deutschmark and the Dollar, that had remained steady up to this point at four Marks to the dollar, was simply turned off. The dollar dropped like a stone, then, recovered briefly, and quickly dropped again, further and further to the 1.4 Mark level where it sits today. The huge loss that the nation suffered by this policy, and all nations who owned dollar assets amounts to a governmental default on its obligations. By its surrender to the pressures of speculative feudalism, the government defaulted in its responsibility to protect the welfare of the people and the life-blood of its economy. The dollar's default was as a matter of policy. One financial analyst said it looks like the dollar rolled of a table, bounced once, and, then, died. This is the weight of feudalism that the governments are coerced to bear.

In real terms the drop of the dollar represents a crash in value that is just a bit less than the 1929 stockmarket crash at which 88% of the market's value was lost. These 'fluctuations' represent gargantuan variances, but they may all appear a like child's play in comparison to the unfolding 'fluctuations' when a default crisis erupts all over the world, simultaneously, as a matter of ongoing policy.

It is highly unlikely that a global default crisis of much greater proportion can be avoided in the wake of the currently impending stock markets crash, unless the feudal financial and economic system that caused the cycles and dynamics of crashes and defaults is being abandoned.

No amount of pain that would, then, be imposed upon the population, or new investments that would immediately flow into the new markets, can help, here. Mexico presents an example for that. Mexico's operational deficits have grown year after year, regardless of the deprivations imposed on the people, and in spite and the vast flows on international investments that were flowing into the country's markets during the early 1990s. Appendix 1, Figure 3 shows the rise in Mexico's yearly deficit in relationship to the rise and fall of international investment into its financial markets. They almost match each other. The greater the feudal investments were, the greater was the national deficit.

These deficits won't go away until the system is abandoned that causes them, nor will the problems cease that are associated with this system. The fact is, Mexico could roll over and die completely, and the deficits wouldn't go away, but would continue to get bigger. Nothing can be done about this increase under the feudal system. Not even its own flood of investments can help it, but tends to make the deficits worse.

The nation-state, a bulwark against financial and economic monoculturalism.

It is tempting to suggest that the universal establishment of the infinite system of economy would in effect create a new monoculture across the world. This would certainly be true if this were to be dictated from the top down through the channels of the U.N.. But no monoculture syndrome results when the development comes individually and naturally from the grass roots up, within the economic unit of the individual nation-state. The resulting monoculture would be one that is founded on the universal recognition of fundamental principles, rather than reflect a universality based on threats, coercion, and deeducation.

When universality is achieved on the platform of fundamental principles, the so established universality merely reflects the conditions that are inherent in reality and are absolute in themselves. This universal recognition does not necessarily reflect itself in a universality in detailed implementation of the fundamental principles. Here lies the great difference, and the value of national sovereignty.

In the monoculture based on fundamental principles, the global scene may include a universal international development assistance that is occurring individually, rather than by the force of clever contracts, as nations assist each other out of the recognized value of fundamental principles. There is a world of difference between the feudal and principle oriented monocultures. In the principle oriented monoculture, national cultures, national needs, national aspirations, may all be preserved in a multicultural adaptation of a single underlying fundamental principle by which humanity profits collectively but still remains individual and sovereign.

The argument may be made here that this approach would open the door to new Hitlers, by allowing national sovereignty to regain a heightened importance in the relationship between nations. But what hope does mankind have on its present platform of feudal monoculturalism when the central dictatorship that the U.N. aspires to become, is controlled by a new Hitler who enforces fascist and genocidal policies against the masses of humanity? Indeed the U.N. is showing a strongly fascist and dictatorial face in its many operations, ranging from economic sanctions that destroy civilian populations, to the protection and abetting of genocide, to the brutal austerity policies of its IMF organization, to its draconian environmental demands that have little or no scientific basis. Close to a hundred million people per year are paying with their life for the result of the present fascist monoculturalism that is gaining evermore strength. There is no security for any person in a world ruled by a feudal and fascist political monoculturalism.

The only security that can be found lies in a multifaceted approximation of the infinite system of economy, translated into the global sphere. This natural monocultural globalism would be based on the application of fundamental principles that function naturally, that have proven their worth within the setting of the nation-state, that are able to raise the status of man and society to the higher plane where man's metaphysical capability can be developed out of its own inner resources. This puts the infinite system that has several times been operating within the sovereign nation-state, miles ahead in security, wealth, and morality, over the feudal system of economy that is currently preparing a New Dark Age for mankind, if not its grave.

Chapter 7: The Society is Cheating Itself

Humanity has adopted many avenues for cheating itself, as for instance through free-trade; through war; through cultural, economic, and financial disintegration; through deindustrialization; through shutting down energy and infrastructural development; through shutting down health protection, justice, and humanist education; and of course, through the stockmarket.

Appendix 11 illustrates the nature of the stockmarket. This market has a monetary inflow, and a monetary outflow, which are always equal. Contrary to popular perception, **there is nothing IN the stockmarket,** no matter how much money is poured **into it.** The following is the reality about the market.

The marked doesn't take anything.
The market doesn't give anything.
The market doesn't create wealth.
The market doesn't accumulate wealth.
The market doesn't take away wealth.

The market is a flow-through channel. Whatever flows in on the buying side, flows out on the selling side (less commissions.) In practice, a lot of the outflow instantly becomes new inflow as the returns from trading are generally 'reinvested,' less taxes and commissions. Whatever 'profit' is generated by this process is not generated in the market. There are no profits generated in the market. The so-called 'profits' from trading in the market are a type of loot generated in a con-game by which 'investors' steal from each other within the process of trading, or in most cases are stolen from by the professional sharks.

The only real profit that can be gained through the market for investors, is the dividend "yield" that represents an investor's share in the profits from productive processes of the companies whose stock the investor owns. This profit, however, does not come from the market, it comes from the physical economy.

When a crash occurs, the process indicated in Appendix 11 does not become altered by one single bit. There will still be an inflow of money into the market, and a corresponding outflow, minus commissions. The in and outflows still remain balanced. The only thing that changes during a crash, is the investor's perception of the value of the financial instruments sold in the market.

The process is similar to the game of selling hats. The following is what one might see in a hat-trading market. The buyers and sellers appraise each other's hats. Those who buy hats may wear them for a day and sell them tomorrow. The various store-keepers, or 'investors' all sell high fashion hats. At the high point of the market, they get a high price for their hats from each other, and from the public. But there also comes a point when hats fall out of fashion. By this change in perception, the store-keeper's entire inventory get devalued to scrap. Naturally, some store keeper may find a few hats in their inventory that have some utilitarian value, like keeping the rain out of one's face when working in the garden. A few may even be lucky enough to sell their useful hats for a price that accords with the actual utilitarian value.

The same happens in the stockmarket.

The prices in the stockmarket may shoot up into the stratosphere when stocks are valued exclusively for their 'growth' potential through trading, but as the market values get bigger as stock-prices escalate, it also becomes necessary that ever greater amounts of monetary inflow are drawn into the market to maintain an attractive relative 'growth' which happens to be the only factor of interest, to 'investors.' As the game continues, there comes a point when the relative inflow of capital that is required to generate a perception of 'growth' is so large that the required capital can no longer be attracted into the market game. At this point investors look at their purchases and say to themselves: Why have I invested so much money into these 'investments' if I cannot get a decent return for what I have paid? This becomes especially agonizing if the banks or bonds begin to pay better returns. Consequently, the investor sells - that is, everyone sells.

It should be noted that today's 'investors' are a part of a near global monoculture. They think alike, and act alike. When it is time to flee the markets, they do it together. At this point, nobody want's the old stuff anymore that pays next to nothing in the trading game, or even looses money when the perceived stock values are slumping.

The buy and sell mechanism still continues at this point, but on a lower level. There are still buyers and sellers in the market during a crash. There is still money flowing into it and flowing out, only the 'instruments' that are sold are suddenly deemed to be of lesser value. Indeed, a share that yields only 0.7% (without trading 'profits') has not much value as an investment, has it? Since this is all the profit that a share may bring if there is nothing to be gained anymore through the trading mill, the tendency is to get rid of the investment - to sell it. Here, the market adjusts itself to reality. The investment, suddenly, sells for what it is worth, which is next to nothing.

Here, reality becomes important again. Once the trading fever is over and a $150 share drops in value to $15, with the dividend amounts remaining the same, the profit yield of the share suddenly rises. It may rise from 0.7% to 7%, which makes the devalued share a useful investment again. In this case, however, the income represents a share of the profit from the productive activities of the company that the share represents an entitlement to.

Market crashes occur when the realization takes hold that the "Emperor has no clothes on." The pretending ends, and reality becomes important. The 'investor' (gambler) looses dearly at this stage. Actually, the 'investing' society always looses, even if the game is going well. A huge volume of commissions do flow out of the trading system every single day, which support an enormous industry that produces absolutely nothing for the advance of society. The cost of maintaining this industry is, of course, paid for by the 'investor.' Furthermore, the financial industry consumes some of the most talented people and corrupts them as they become professionals in the game, in which 'investors' are stealing from one another, which they regard as a virtue.

The sheer size of the modern 'bull'-market that the industry celebrates as a sign of strength, is really a measure of the immorality involved by which junk is pushed for extremely high prices. It is not hard to imagine how much more advanced the world would be today if the talent and resources that are devoted to this game of organized theft, was devoted to the advance of humanity. Imagine how much could be accomplished if the focus was on mutual support, instead of on stealing from one another! This change in focus would strengthen the productive environment by which civilization as a whole becomes elevated.

The problem is not that humanity is inherently corrupt. The problem is that it has been forced to adopt the feudal system of economics that is inherently corruptive. The stockmarket is not inherently a bad thing. In the environment of the infinite system of economics, the stockmarket has such a wide base in physical representation that it absorbs easily all the investments it can get without diluting share values through escalating prices. Here, the investment process aids the progressive development of productive industries and processes.

In this kind of market, the public actively participates in its own development. Under the feudal system, however, "development" is a bad word, so that the physical economy shrinks and contracts by which its financial representation becomes super-inflated. A market of dreams begins to develop which is good for the sharks who want to steal from the public, which they do. The public actually gets looted twice in that the market process that loots it, consumes tremendous resources in manpower and monetary funding which are drawn away from the productive economy and become wasted in processes that produce nothing.

This doubly collapsing process is inherent in the ideology of feudalism that has become the cash cow of the empires that promote it. Every empire that has ever existed by some kind of system of feudalistic looting. The last and greatest of these empires, which is still in existence, is the British Empire. It's agents have persuaded the whole world to subject itself to the feudalist game. Feudalism has become globalized. Nor has the game ever worked 'better' for humanity, than it does today. It has always looted mankind of its substance and corrupted its very soul, destroying reason, honor, and humanity.

One might assume, here, that the world should welcome a market crash. This reasoning is flawed. There are too many factors tied into the stockmarket game, at the present time, which make a crash highly dangerous. One factor is the simple fact that 90% of the public's life-saving is currently 'invested' in the stock and bond markets. The huge amounts so 'invested' can never be drawn out. Any large scale redemption would cause the whole market to collapse. The collapse, therefore, is not something one should look forward to. Nor is a collapse inevitable. When the collapse occurs as the Dow opens one morning 500 points down, countless voices will advise which public to stay in the market "for the long haul" while the big houses that promote this advise are dumping their wares by the barrels full, lest they become worthless in their keeping. Of course, by the time the public catches on to the came, there will be little left in terms of stock-value.

What the result will be when the public realizes that it is loosing 80% of its savings, and nothing can be done about it, is hard to imagine. No tragedy has ever been sadder. The fact is, a tragedy of this nature has never happened before. Traditionally the public has been invested in stocks by no more than ten percent of its savings, not 90% as it is today - 90% of which appears to be doomed. When 88% of the stockmarket lost its value as the result of the 1929 crash, the public as a whole was not severely hit by the losses, as it would be today.

Another factor that should cause everyone to wish that a stockmarket crash would never happen again, is the simple fact that the feudalist game that has destroyed one of the finest capitalist tools that a society can have for its self-development, has become a feeder of a secondary industry that is many times bigger and has a global inter-tie into the world-financial system that has set this system at the edge of a cliff. When the markets crash, this system will tumble with it.

The monoculture of financial feudalism has drawn much of the world into the financial derivatives 'circus.' The trading in this circus operates on the same principle as outlined in Appendix 11. Again, there is an inflow and outflow of equal magnitude. The public buys and sells financial gambling contracts to each other. These contracts are traded in an atmosphere that would prevail if bets in a horse race were traded among all the betters while the horse race is in progress. The difference is that the values of the financial bets are huge, with an annual turnover that is 100 times larger than the entire stockmarket that the bets are based on.

The relationship between the stockmarket, the derivatives market, and the size of financial instruments involved, is shown in Appendix 12. The two figures of the financial derivatives market in the USA and the total annual turnover have been adjusted to show the modern amounts. However, their graphic representation has been left as they were in the mid-1990s, representing $40 trillion and $500 trillion respectively. Today's financial derivatives games that are played by the commercial banks alone add up to slightly over $94 trillion. This figure does not include the games played by the hedge funds and the over-the-counter market in derivatives. The total worldwide annual turnover has been reported to be above the $8.5 quadrillion mark. To represent this amount proportionately the right column of Appendix 12 would have to be four times as tall for the USA alone to represent the annual volume of derivatives gambling.

As one might expect by the size of the game, there are big players involved. All the banks are addicted to the derivatives game, as they are a part of the world wide financial monoculture. The banks have become gambling casinos. The game is rigged, of course. As everyone knows, the 'house' sets the odds by writing the contracts. Usually the writers of "options" (as some of the betting contracts are called) profit by the game. The 'house' always profits in a casino operation. Statistics tell us that 80% of all options sold in the market expire without claims being exercised against them. In a crash, when the game doesn't go by the rules of the house, the big 'casinos', including the banks, may be doomed.

This carnage will hurt society. Since the banks are involved, the public will suffer the loss of its savings which may be still in the banking system. If one translates this type of exposure into the global context, the logical projection is that the world-financial system disintegrates. Money, itself, may become worthless in the process, by which all commerce presently operates, including that which facilitates food supplies, energy supplies, transportation, law enforcement, etc.. The reality is, that civilization as a whole is threatened. Such a collapse has catastrophic consequences.

As far back as 1993, when the derivatives bubble was still small, the American economist Lyndon LaRouche, warned about the danger this bubble presents, and suggested that it be eliminated through taxation. The world scorned him, but it would be a great deal safer today if his warning had been heeded. Oh, how the society is cheating itself in the grandest style possible!

Apart from all this, there is still another and even more dangerous game afoot. This game is currency speculation. In the stockmarket and the derivatives market are always two players involved, a buyer and a seller. Both act voluntarily, although the society suffers the consequences. In currency speculation only a single player is involved. The targeted nation has no choice. It cannot abstain from the trading of its currency, even though its daily living depends on a stable currency. In a feudal setting, any individual is entitled to buy and sell currency, which the banking system gladly facilitates for a fee. Thus, a single player can hold an entire nation at ransom, which happens quite frequently. The investment 'hero' George Soros, for instance, is credited with having devalued Italy's Lira by 30% in a single handed attack on the currency. By his action, an entire nation lost 30% of the value of its money, and all this for the profits of one single man and his "Quantum Fund."

Still, George Soros's trading is but a mild case of the game. The private controllers of the International Monetary Fund and the World Bank, control vastly more than just the currencies of the world, they also control the life of virtually every citizen of every nation on the planet. By the force of financial conditionalities they control who eats, and who doesn't, which country develops (if there still is one) and which doesn't, and how many people will die of starvation, and which country is allowed to import food. They've literally got the whole world 'in their hands.'

If there is a crash in the world-financial system, one can assume that these players will expand their powers of global dictatorship. Already, they are acting under the cover of the U.N. with a request outstanding to have their own armed forces and global taxation rights, and further legal rights for global governance in areas of population 'management', food production, energy production, and environmental issues. If these rights are granted, which is likely in the aftermath of a crash, these players will have amassed the power to shut down, or severely curtail, the use of fossil fuels, food production, and refrigeration. The tools for this are already set up in the form of environmental mythologies, such as the "global warming" myth that everyone believes in so deeply, or the ozone depletion myth, or the myth that the world is overpopulated and must shed between 50% and 90% of its people, depending on who makes the demands.

When even the lesser demands are achieved and energy use is severely curtailed so that the economies can no longer function, many more hundreds of millions of people will die of starvation, than are dying today from causes of forced economic underdevelopment. Just imagine what kind of world will unfold when the fuel source on which mankind presently relies for its farming, transportation, industries, heating, cooking, etc., becomes curtailed to a trickle or is being eliminated is some areas of the world!

It may seem unimaginable that anyone would take away mankind's energy resource without replacing it with nuclear power, but this is the goal. The fact is, this goal can be met with ease, with the stroke of a pen, under certain circumstances. It can be met by a process that has already been established and proven to work, such as the process by which the PCBs, the DDTs, and the CFCs were all eliminated. So far, the public hasn't even bothered to stir its stumps in its self-defense, much less roused itself in the defense of humanity as close to 100 million people a year are already being wiped out by means of financially imposed underdevelopment.

Herein lies the greatest tragedy of the feudal market system, and the catastrophic potential of the feudal world-financial system in its tendency to disintegrate, thereby opening a political vacuum by which the feudal Empire achieves its coveted world dictatorship status and mankind pays the price with its very life. By its inaction at preventing the ensuing financial disintegration on the basis of replacing the feudal system with the infinite system of economy, mankind is cheating itself out of the brightest future that ever lay within its grasp, and surrender its very life instead.

It cannot possibly be overstated what levels of chaos are attached to the stockmarket crash that is currently being set up at neck-breaking speed. All the stops have been pulled in order to assure that the stockmarket will keep on growing to galactic valuations by which the crash will be the more spectacular when it comes and drive the world into anarchy that its Empire needs to grasp total control.

Towards this singular goal, although this is tightly covered up, the printing presses are presently running at full speed in nearly all the major financial domains around the world, printing evermore money for feeding the fictitious markets. If the crash cannot be prevented by intelligent processes, it will be the biggest splash of chaos in human history, unleashing the greatest cry, and, then, a whimper in a world of 'silence.'

A political monoculture: Made to order.

Feudalistic monoculturalism has become the most deadly force that humanity has ever faced, and the most hidden that was ever created. No, it didn't unfold naturally. It was created. It was build step by step, although exploiting an ideal situation. The end of World War II created the biggest baby boom in history. Whatever the boomers touched upon became a big thing, from diapers to schools, and from dental procedures to cars and suburbs. When the Vietnam quagmire was at its worst and the peace-movement was unleashed. Then, the boomers were in their late teens, in their most impressionable years, and they were 'tutored' well. They were carefully guided by the best professionals in an ideological game by which they would loose their touch with reality. This conditioning was deep and has remained. In fact it has been carried now forward onto the new generation, so much so, that the current Western society acts as a single monocultural team that is more associated with dreams and with cleverly created illusions than with the real world. In the tradition of such mental conditioning this monoculture supports everything that the built in axioms dictate to the human consciousness. It is not by accident that games of fantasy have becomes super-exciting, the unintelligent is being promoted, and the fundamentally real is labeled unexciting, dull, and of no value. Now, that the boomers have hit their biggest earning years, the markets are not just superinflated by their obedient devotion to the game. The markets have become a dream-world all of their own, which is celebrated with fanfares.

There are a number of immensely dangerous false beliefs that are currently held universally, on this platform. They are:

.A. That profit can be generated through trading stocks, options, and currency.

.B. That prosperity can be generated by ignoring the physical economy.

.C. That society can find political and financial security in a global political and financial One-World dictatorship setting without sovereignty, without the sovereign nation-state, without scientific, cultural, and technological development.

.D. That individual health can be maintained while huge portions of the society are forced into conditions of diseases through underdevelopment, poverty, and starvation, which create an ideal biological breeding ground out of which evermore exotic and incurable super-strains of viruses emerge, like the HIV virus, the Ebola virus, or possibly some newly emerging strains of the flu.

.E. That environmental demands can be forced upon mankind (often for the flimsiest excuses) without serious economic repercussion by which the infrastructures that support mankind's existence on this planet become eroded and eliminated.

.F. That there is a future for mankind without an aggressive focus on scientific and technological advances.

.H. That any meaningful large scale scientific and technological development is even remotely possible under the feudal system.

.I. That a nation's farming industry can survive and be productive without the protection of a parity payment system.

.J. That freedom and prosperity is a gift to humanity that doesn't need to be earned.

.K. That the present world-empire, the British Empire, has the interests of humanity at heart.

.L. That any empire's feudal system and free-trade doctrine, by which looting they exist, are a good thing for humanity.

.M. That governmental budgets can be balanced by starving the population, as during the age of the Poor Laws where social assistance was totally overruled by the state. - Are there no work houses?

.N. That fictitious financial profits can be created out of thin air, and, then, be monetized at infinitum without imploding the fictitious system, and with it, the real economy?

So, the list goes on, and on.

The great baby-boom monoculture of today has achieved a kind of self-deprivation that is second to none. This result is not by the boomers own choice. A great deal of prior development effort has gone into its creation. Had the boomers of today experienced the 1929 crash that caused people to jump out of windows, they might be less inclined to roll the dice on the markets with 90% of their savings riding on the outcome. But all this has been negated by the wonderfully glowing game in which the boomers themselves are made the central element.

Had they gone through the long blight of the Great Depression that followed the 1929 crash, they might be more interesting in upgrading civilization, than upgrading their pocket books by stealing from each other. Had they experienced the dynamism of even a remotely functioning economy, such as the one that was allowed briefly in order to rescue the Empire in World War II, which had pulled the U.S. out of its deepest depression in history and established it as the greatest military and economic force on the planet, the boomers might have opted for setting up a new economic Renaissance for humanity, instead of the greatest death trap that the present world-financial system has become.

The reality still remains, however. What has been achieved and created by humanity is never lost. What is built if fundamental principles is always operational and implementable. In contrast, not a single fundamental principle supports the myths that the feudal global monoculturalism has been created to represent. The entire feudal mythology can be collapsed overnight by a mental restructuring of humanity onto a platform of reality. Feudalism, itself, has a crash potential in that it exists without a footing in any real fundamental principle. Its so-called principles are created illusions.

So what if the British Empire was successful in shutting the U.S. back down after the war was over, with its tool of feudal monetarism. A people who have experienced the power of the infinite model of economy should not have clung so tenaciously to the worst system ever created and have selected it to govern its economies. This error can always be corrected. No fundamental law demands that a people must forever tie itself to a value system based on irrationalities.

Had the new generation been touched by the pride and optimism that was felt back in the 1950s when the world's greatest industrial nation had committed itself to explore the new frontier of space and set foot on the moon to explore it on a routine basis, they would not be so eager today to bow their head to oligarchic demands for devolution and deindustrialization, but had kept their head high by advancing education and scientific research in energy projects and new physical principles, instead of shutting them down - instead of turning highly productive industrial jobs into unemployment or menial employment as hamburger flippers, bicycle couriers, or stock brokers serving the financial Empire that is tearing humanity to the ground.

It is unfortunate that all this rich experience was withheld from the new generation, by creating an ideology of detachment from reality, and attachment to dreams. Their life had blossomed at the time when the U.S. nation was maneuvered into the Vietnam war, which was was designed not to be won. It was designed to destroy the U.S. nation from within. President J. F. Kennedy was shot for this purpose. He was shot two days after his order was given for the U.S. to withdraw from Vietnam. It is being said that there exists proof that the President's order was countermanded while the President was still alive, as if the countermander knew that an assassination was but days away.

With Kennedy out of the way, the flood-gates of American 'assistance' were opened wide. Year after year the agonizing load of the mightiest war machine on the planet grinding against a gentle rural people would impress itself upon the moral conscience of America and the world, especially the young. Then, at the height of the agony, the same official in government who countermanded President Kennedy's order to withdraw, began organizing the youth of the nation into a peace movement. Except, the peace movement was not organized on a platform of expounding the truth that lay behind the war. It was organized on a platform of psychodelic withdrawal from reality by which not only the youth's foundation for the future was destroyed, but the veterans of the war and all the values of society and what had been accomplished prior to the war, were branded as outcasts, criminals, and morally degenerate, so that the experiences of the past became lost to the unfolding generation.

This may all seem far fetched, but if one considers the thread that ties the historical developments of the time into one, a great consistence comes to light that cannot be considered to have come about by mere chance as too many details are involved. Consistent coincidences do not occur.

Just as the generation that fought the Vietnam war had failed to protect itself against the forces that shot their President and turned the brightest achievement of the age into dust - that had turned pride into shame and shut down the nation's future - so the baby-boomers had failed to protect themselves and their future against a far more powerful manipulative force, so the the people has not only lost control over their destiny as human beings, but had been turned into pawns for the manipulator's game, who were then empowered to run the world, as they do to the present day.

Sadly, but truly, the Empire has claimed the life of the postwar generations, but it can never erase the potential that still exists for the deprived generations to regain their reason and claim for themselves the brightest future a people could possibly ask for which is in their grasp.

The potential exist, even now, for the greatest catastrophe that has ever been prepared in human history, to unfold, or to be overturned.

It all comes down to a matter of choice and to a matter of swift action as there is little time left to halt the unfolding default that comes from inaction, which unfolds with the great crash that is certain to take mankind towards a new and ugly dark age which may well be its final state.

Chapter 8: The ugly face of feudalism: Fascism

If the differences between the feudal system of economy and the infinite system were limited to financial inflation, their effect might be tolerable. This is true, because the financial aggregates, themselves, even before they crash, are largely unrelated to reality. But there is much more lost in the feudal economic and financial system, than what evaporates by its recurring crashes of financial values.

The divergence that is indicated between points B and C in Appendix 4, which indicates the size of financial inflation, should not exist. This creates a whole new social situation. We see a growing deficit on the physical platform where we should see a net-gain. What we should see is indicated by the positive curve shown in Appendix 5 - the curve of "Real income and Physical production" that should have followed the monetary curve that also represents physical inputs and infrastructures. Curve B in Appendix 4, which represents purely financial aggregates, should be a steady zero.

The question may be asked, here, what has this to do with fascism?

The answer is not obvious, but it is a fundamental one. It is best discovered if one explores the loss suffered by society under the feudal economic system. This loss must be measured by its effect on society in terms of lost productive capability. The differential between curve B in Appendix 4 (which should represent the society's physical product, but represents financial aggregates instead) and curve C which represents the present state of the physical product, indicates the incurred loss to society that results from its adherence to feudalism. This loss is huge. It translates itself into immeasurable social destruction, even large scale loss of life. Loss of life, by act of policy, defines the very heart of the nature of fascism.

The deficit that exists between the "Real Income" curve in Appendix 5 (which shows where mankind should presently be according to the natural dynamics of unfolding life), when compared with the dramatic drop that has occurred under the present feudal economic system (shown in Appendix 4 by curve C and D) represents the measure of suffered that is imposed upon humanity world-wide.

This suffering has many faces. Each one is tragically real. Each one is felt daily, on a global scale. Nor will this difference be automatically erased by a sudden crash in the markets, because the axioms remain that create the differential. A sudden crash in the markets tends to increase further that already huge gap between real income and the potential income under the infinite system, that the parasitism of feudalism has created. The truth of this is born out by the deep depression that followed in the wake of the 1929 stockmarket crash.

The real dimension of the losses which the world currently suffers under the yoke of feudalism, cannot be imagined. This dimension necessarily includes the loss of a prosperity that is inherent in the infinite system of economics, which humanity has been prevented from experiencing. The society is certainly able to measure the loss in the size of its market basket, which has shrunk by half since the mid 1960s. Except this loss is puny, compared to the real loss that includes the unrealized potential under the yoke of feudalism. And even this figure is puny if one takes the projection backwards in time to the beginning of feudalism on the planet. It is conceptually impossible to gage the size of the real loss that is suffered because of feudalism, as this loss must also include the dynamic multiplier of all real progress, compounded over many centuries, the effect of which has been prevented. That status of civilization always unfolds in proportion to the dynamics of the unfolding of life, unless this self-development is prevented.

Since the scope of mankind's real loss, because of feudalism, is impossible to imagine, it is best to shift the focus onto minutia of the measurable losses that have been suffered in recent years, and are still being suffered.

The deficit in income and production, because of feudalistic policies, that affects the world-population today is not measured in percentages of monetary differentials. Indeed, one is tempted to make such a measurement which would miss the real point altogether. This deficit must be measured by its effect in terms of starvation, in the escalation of disease, in levels of imposing death. For the nation of Mexico, the current deficit of income and production translates itself into the death of 300,000 children, annually, which die from illnesses that result from to severe malnutrition. This figure was compiled by UNICEF. Fascism is not only measured by the murdering of people in concentration camps and their gas chambers. It is also measured by other types of similar policy impositions that lead to the mass murdering by soft means. Whoever enacts policies that deprive a people of food, and the means to create food, commits murder as surely as if he or she wielded a club and bludgeoned people to death. The mass murder of human beings, by any means, is a crime against humanity, and is fascism, pure and simple.

In order to understand the insanity behind the tragedy mentioned above (which is not an isolated case), one needs to consider another factor that also enters the feudalist equation. This factor acts like a multiplier of fascism. It increases the losses that mankind suffers because of feudalism. This factor is responsible for some of the most bizarre situations that have unfolded in modern economics.

For instance, during the 1980s, Mexico was pressured by the I.M.F. to embrace the free-trade market 'magic.' It was pressured to turn to turn its attention to the world-market for its food needs, instead of pouring money into farm support credits which its growing agricultural industry needed. Mexico bowed to the pressure. The result is, that today, a few short years later, Mexico's once proud farming sector lies in ruin while the nation lacks the funds to import the food that its farming industry can no longer supply. The result is a severe deficiency in food resources that is weakening the strength of the nation and is killing its children by the hundreds of thousands. Nor does the tragedy end here. It has a global dimension, which reflects itself in no food surpluses being available in the world markets, to be bought, except for a huge premium that the poorer nations, like Mexico, cannot pay. Adolf Hitler was a Boyscout fascist, by comparison, in his crude methods of murdering people that were also thinly disguised. Free-trade feudalism is much more effective, and apparently totally honorable.

This dimension is best explored by looking at the case of Mexico once more. Here, we have quite a different fascism unfolding than the kind that Hitler had pursued. Its operation is clean. It unfolds in the arena of High Value Commodities exports, which feed the richer nations at the expense of the poor of humanity. In this arena, one sees a glimmer of the true fascist face of free-trade.

The Mexican food deficit that has been created out of the country's loss in basic food production capability under I.M.F. austerity conditions, must now be seen in relationship to the country's growing food exports that are mounting up against the background of the country's food deficiency and outright starvation. In this setting, profit oriented free-trade exports drain food resources out of a country in which the population starves. The Washington based newspaper, The New Federalist, reports that most of these exports are drawn out of the country under the control of a tiny number of London centered international food cartels. The food exports are in the form of cheaply produced "High Value Commodities" (HVCs) such as "frozen cauliflower ('Green Giant' brand, owned by London-based Grand Metropolitan), canned mangoes, fresh fruits and vegetables."*17 Under this market driven magic of free-trade, food exports steals from a nation that suffers starvation and sinks irreversibly into poverty and biological disintegration for the monetary gain of foreign empires. Adolf Hitler never murdered with such ease and efficiency.

Much the same is also unfolding in Russia, where fertilizers are exported that should be used by the country's own farming sector. In this case, the population is being starved in order to raise money for meeting the I.M.F.'s conditionalities and debt service demands. Of course, some of it may also flow into the pockets of the various Mafias, while the producers of the nation starve and die. The death spiral from the effects of feudalist predation is so severe that the country reports of the fist time in recent history, a population decline.

Nor are the cases of Russia and Mexico in any way unique. They are but examples of a world-wide dilemma, with world-wide consequences for the human population. According to the Canadian Hunger Foundation and the U.N., as many as 30,000 children under the age of 5 die every single day, from causes related to economic starvation. This adds up to 11 million children being put to death annually under the feudal economic system. Since children under the age of 5 represent 10% of a normal population, the effective annual number of deaths by economic starvation around the world may be near the 100 million mark, year after year. Adolf Hitler was a failure in the realm of fascism. The horrors of his death camps are superseded today a hundred fold on the global scene, nor is there the slightest protest forthcoming from humanity against the fascist system of today. The actual global death-rate from economic devolution may be slightly lower than a 100 million annually, because in the poor countries, such as the Philippines, very few people (a mere 3-4 out of 20) survive to the age of 50 years.*18

The unfolding deficit in world wide food production may soon become noticed also in the rich countries. The current world wide deficit is believed to be in the 60% range, below the norm that constitutes a good nutritional level. It is also believed to be 15% below the minimal nutritional level. This rather large deficit is mainly leveraged against the Third World nations where it manifests itself in large scale starvation and related causes of death.

The world food deficit does not, however, reflect an underlying lack of agricultural potential. The potential exists for vast increases in production. This lack of financial commitment to food production, appears not be unintentional, since the outcome reflects the oligarchy's commitment to its population reduction goals which are best realized by undermining the physical and metaphysical basis of civilization. The withholding of financial resources stifles the creative and productive potential of mankind. Consequently, people begin to die. The feudal Empire's world-financial system is ideally suited for promoting this type of breakdown. Feudalism is always two-edged sword of evil. It is always parasitic in its looting practice, and destructive in its policies. It is fascist in nature, and supersedes the fascism of Hitler, which seems hardly possible.

It is conceivable that the entire physical platform of society becomes eliminated by ever tighter and tighter funding, so that very large numbers of people will die, far in excess of the hundred million people that are currently sacrificed each year by this process. With this destruction already going on, it is certainly impossible to fund scientific and technological development. A society cannot develop itself and feed a dominant parasite at the same time. Thus, the feudal system of economy becomes a potent weapon in the empire's war against humanity.

Let us not be mistaken about the fact that there is a war going on against the life of mankind, on a scale immensely greater than Hitler's war. Prince Philip of the British Empire states in a foreword to a book*19 that, if it were possible to be reincarnated, he would ask to come back as a "particularly deadly virus" in order that he might kill off vast numbers of human beings to help reduce the world population. It appears that the feudal world-financial system has become such a virus, which the empire promotes and protects, which has grown increasingly destructive since the mid 1980s. Its destructive looting has become especially effective against the Third World nations, most notably Africa. There, the destruction of the human population by economic means is already widely implemented under the I.M.F. austerity doctrine.

The Empire's commitment to a dramatic world-population reduction, as a policy objective, is far more real than one may think. While the elimination of large masses of people cannot be legislated or be debated in any parliament, it is quite easily implemented, unilaterally, through clever financial maneuvers. This process seems to be well under way.

Actually, the idea of introducing dramatic population reduction measures is not a new one. It was lauded long before the present wave of starvation was created that is ravishing the world population in this modern age. The idea that genocidal murdering of human beings is a good thing was promoted some decades ago by the Empire's Bertrand Russell, one of the major pseudo scientific driver of oligarchic ideology. He lamented bitterly about the growth of humanity, and how little anything effects it. He writes about it: "War, so far, has had no very great effect on this increase, which continued through each of the world wars. (War) has been disappointing in this respect..." And he adds, "but perhaps bacteriological war may prove more effective.... The state of affairs may be somewhat unpleasant, but what of it? Really high-minded people are indifferent to happiness, especially other people's."*20 Didn't Adolf Hitler display much of the same attitude?

The interrelationship between austerity and diseases.

The boundary within which the current world food deficit is destroying the lives of human beings is beginning to shift. Until now, artificially induced starvation has affected mainly the Third World nations, like Mexico and the African nations. Soon, these will no longer be alone in this arena, as the lower economic layers of the (once) industrialized nations are fast joining their ranks. The first to be affected are the poorest segments of the so-called 'rich' nations, as social protection programs fall by the wayside. The categories that are already hit by this first stage of the ever widening sphere of austerity, are the children, the elderly, the disadvantaged, the jobless, the homeless, the disabled, etc.. Nor with will the expansion of the imperial attack on humanity end there. As the boundary of austerity continues to shift under the pressures of financial parasitism, evermore people find themselves suddenly on the side of the boundary where deprivation takes its toll, as the productive economy collapses deeper and deeper into devolution.

The rate of this 'progress' into a slow and painful dying is accelerating parabolically, as the population base is shrinking that supports the looting parasites. Herein, the parasite, itself, is doomed. The Roman empire collapsed out of the poverty it created. The Bisantine, the Venetian, and the Ottoman empires collapsed for the same reason The wild growth in the looting of the populations has doomed every empire to date. Thus, the current world-financial cannot be rescued by any means. It is doomed to disintegrate out of the poverty it imposes, and the point of this disintegration is near. Fascism always destroys itself.

Now that the end is fast approaching for the

current Empire, one looks for visible signs, which are inherently fascist in nature. The Roman Empire had grown absolutely fascist before it disintegrated. So we look for signs of fascism, and, then, we look for signs of its bankruptcy. The Roman fascism was bankrupt. It had looted all, destroyed all, perverted all. It had nothing left with which to hold itself up. The same is evident today in the dramatic decline in the Empire success in looting. There simply is nothing left for the parasite to gouge out of the living processes of society. A good example is found in the stock markets. The inflow of funds that the North American public had been enticed to pour into the Mutual Fund markets (instead of into its self-development) has declined from more than $25 billion per month at the beginning of 1996, to less than $4 billion at mid-year. Also the rate of growth in index values compared to the rate of inflow has dropped. The same amount of inflow that gave the Sindex an uplift of 32% in 1995, has produced less than a 4% uplift in 1996.*21 Moreover, a large portion of this 'uplift money' that was poured into the markets, which produced only a minuscule uplift, was actually borrowed by the Mutual Funds against their portfolios. This borrowing by the funds, though it may be insignificant in the larger sense, illustrates the principle of the feudal system that deprives the society of the much needed development resources for upgrading the physical platform that supports human existence, which is, then, poured into the bottomless pit. In real terms, todays fascism is bankrupt, which may be the reason for the dramatic increase in world terrorism (supported by the Imperial machine.)

The tragic effect that feudalist looting has had on the once rich society, is similar to the tragedy to which Mexico has been committed, where people starve to death while food is being exported in order to generate profits for foreign corporations. The Mexican tragedy, in turn, may even be considered worse than the tragedy by which 1.5 million people were starved to death in Ireland, during the Potato Blight when food was exported under military force to protect the free-market looting. The crisis in Mexico appears to be worse from a moral standpoint, because the financial profits for which the children in Mexico are forced to die, are worthless the very moment they enter the financial aggregates system that is itself disintegrating. Here, the lives of human beings are sacrificed in a large manner, for profits that feed an empty bubble. The profits are actually meaningless in the infinitely inflated world of financial values, but not so are the lives that are lost.

This increasing insanity that is unfolding, reminds one of the insanity that marks the final stage of every empire in history.

If those who live by this wildly inflated so-called wealth were alert to the realities that they deny, they would realize that the boundary of the growing deficit that the feudal system has created, has already embraced them, too. Fascism has no boundary. It respects none. It is benign to no one. It destroys universally. The effect of the superinflated financial system that is destroying humanity is embracing virtually every human being that lives under this system, and under the sun.

Fascism also has a medical face. Its destructive rampage leads to an accelerating growth and spread of pandemic diseases coincident with the world-wide collapse in physical development. This process has been going on for five decades already. The biological culture of large masses of severely weakened people poses a biological threat that likewise respects no boundary, not even financial wealth. The HIV virus that causes AIDS is understood to have resulted from the natural processes inherent in weakened populations, so that the normally blocked mutation of animal viruses into the human domain becomes enabled in proportion as the human strength subsides. Normally, this crossover mutation is blocked.

Also the viral mutations themselves, accelerate, in environments where cross-infection between species has begun. It is not surprising, therefore, that the HIV virus emerged out of Africa at a time when the continent suffered under severe physical depression resulting from wars, forced underdevelopment, and increasing austerity demands by the world-financial institutions. The financial profits that were squeezed out of this impoverished continent, and still are, come at a terrible price that is to be paid by all mankind. In this case, the parasitic looting steals from the life of humanity on a global scale.

One might find it strange, to realize, that out of the over 40,000 law-suits that are started each day in the U.S.A. alone, not a single one of them seeks restitution for damages resulting from the biological consequences of parasitic Imperial, financial, and economic looting. Actually, the phenomenon is not so strange at all, as fascism has a tendency to embrace even the minds of people, and not just their environment for living.

The phenomenon may not be strange, but it is frightening! Regardless of what people think about it, the world-wide biological collapse has begun and is accelerating as the conditions that have caused it, are worsening. And what is more frightening still, is the fact that the world is shutting down its most vital biological defense systems in order to save money, which is demanded to support the looting. Under these conditions a biological holocaust of huge proportions becomes a definite possibility.

Even the so-called war against AIDS is a disgrace. We are still in the upswing phase of the disease, with a strong, ongoing, proliferation. In the background of this 'explosion' few efforts are made in terms of biological research, scientific education, social policy responses, which together might avert the escalation towards a social catastrophe. Here, too, there is no money available for any serious effort that matches the severity of the disease. Also, more dangerous than AIDS is the growing potential for new diseases, or new strains of the once deemed harmless diseases, such as the common influenza. The new strains that have been unfolding in recent years have become increasingly deadly and drug resistant. Just imagine what havoc a deadly strain of the flu virus could unleash, which is by no means impossible, or a strain of the Ebola or HIV virus that spreads itself, airborne, like the common cold. It is an act of utter insanity that the world closes its eyes to this danger by shutting down the relevant research institutions under the pressure of "market forces."

The reason for this insanity is simple. It is derived from the axioms of feudalism which carry the seeds of fascism within them. Since fascism has no intelligence and no relationship to the functions of mind, its proliferation is not under anyone's control. It infects all, when not resisted.

How far the health support infrastructure of the world has been collapsed by this creeping, feudal, fascism, is indicated by the events surrounding a three day conference (Dec. 11-13, 1995) in Bethesda, Maryland, which had been launched by the severely struggling biological research sector, or what is left of it. The conference was called under the heading: "Preparations To Meet The Reemerging Threat of a significant Global Influenza Outbreak." It was acknowledged at this conference that while the growing biological threat is indeed serious, the means simply do no longer exist to deal with the threat, and the few means that do exist, are fast being dismantled.

An indication as to how deeply the health protection budgets have been decimated around the world can be gleamed from the fact that only 14 of all the world's nations were represented at this conference. The reason, obviously was money. The participants had to pay for their own travel costs, their own lodging, and their own expenses.

Against this growing poverty in so vital and difficult a field as disease prevention, the potential exist for new pandemics to unfold that may far supersede the ferocity of the 1918 swine flu pandemic that had infected 2 billion people, world wide, and had killed 20-40 million. Under today's conditions a single such outbreak has the potential to be far more deadly than all the wars of this century combined. This is the real face of the cost of the parasitic financial systems, and its fascist face that promotes the looting of society until it collapses into its death. It is impossible, at this point, to determine whether Prince Philip of the British monarchy realizes that his deepest wish, to be reincarnated as a "particularly deadly virus," is on the fast track to becoming realized.

What is unfolding here is a paradox in itself.

One sees a war being waged against mankind in the biological theatre. At the same time one sees the essential defenses being dismantled by the budget squeeze that had traditionally been established against such a threat. What general, in any war situation, would shut his defenses down the very moment an attack is launched against his forces? No general, of course would do this, but mankind is doing just that, and it is doing it in a theatre in which the consequences are far more horrific than they are in theatres of war.

Nor has this war against humanity only biological consequences in the form of diseases and an engineered collapse in global food production. This was is also directed against energy production, education, scientific and technological development, and every imaginable facet of the platform on which human existence depends. Feudalism, with all its horrendous side effects, may be the most potent 'disease' with which a society can be infected. It is a virus by which humanity becomes destroyed unless the virus is understood, so that mankind can begin to protect itself. There exists no other option for survival. And even here, this vital option, is fought against by the Imperial machine. The Empire has turned the most vital element for mankind's survival into a sham phrase: Protectionism! With every ounce of its strength it fights the idea of self-protection. It promotes free-trade as a weapon and demands a nation to open itself to economic destruction at its very root. The entire pyramid of lies that surrounds the feudalist ideology must be understood and dealt with, which involves a total reversal in all cases. Self-protection is not a sham process. It is a vital process. The total reversal of all feudalist axioms is absolutely necessary to defeat its fascism. Nothing less will do.

One must judge, therefore, at this point, whether

the disease of feudalism was imposed on mankind for its destructive potential, or whether it was imposed by the Empire, unintentionally, or by default as no other platform existed by which to maintain its opulent life style. One must also judge where the greater fault lies for the globalization of the disease. Does the main fault lie with the Empire that has no other means to exist, or does the main fault lie with the human society which has the mean at hand to cast off the most threatening parasite that feeds on it, and focus on its self-development?

The paradox of mankind's refusal to rescue itself from the disease of feudalism, and its fascism, indicates not so much an unfolding insanity among mankind, as it indicates a certain blindness to reality that its mental perversion to its feudal ideology has created. The paradox is, that this hyped up commitment to the self-limiting feudal financial and economic system has created among the world population a commitment to commit suicide. And no one dares to awake for this commitment. Just ask anyone about the likelihood of a world-financial disintegration and its consequences, and you'll be declared an idiot. No one want's to awake. No one dares to awake. The reality is too frightening to contemplate. Thus, the paradox continues.

The cleverly created commitment by society to its shiny illusions has blinded humanity with lies, so that it cannot hear the truth. Humanity believes more religiously in its financial gains than any priest has likely ever believed in religious doctrines. This fatal belief persists in spite the fact that no such thing as a purely financial profit can truly exists. On the basis of this belief, mankind has undermined itself with infinite inflation in a financial aggregates system whose nature it cannot see. This illustrates somewhat the tenacity of the error to be overcome, and the depth to which the reversal must reach. How can mankind even hope to meet the far more difficult challenge of overcoming the root of feudalism which can never be seen or felt, when it cannot see the most obvious evidence of it that has decimated its own physical existence and its civilization.

Against this background, the differential between curves B and C in Appendix 4 represents not merely a measure of financial inflation in real terms, but it represents also the measure of vulnerability that humanity has created for itself in terms of its failure to respond to the death 'weapon' that Bertrand Russell had insisted long ago would be desirable, which he suggested should be one of 'bacteriological' warfare. This weapon has been created. The bacteria, however, are mental, counteracting the metaphysical capacity of mankind.

Against its unfolding death-spiral stands the infinite system of economy, founded solidly on metaphysical principles, it enables the development of the inherent strength of humanity. Metaphysical principles are mankind's natural immune system against feudalism, and it parasitism and fascism. The metaphysical effect will never cease, in which mental development through a commitment to scientific and technological progress, uplifts the physical scene and the state of civilization. Its principle is absolute. One cannot mock it by opposite axioms and escape the consequences. But one can apply it and utilize its potential. Whenever this, so founded, mental development takes place of which humanity is totally capable, its reflection will be immediately manifest in infrastructural development, in advanced transportation, in great projects of water management and flood control, in energy development based on new physical principles, in agricultural revitalization and development, and in a new platform for health built on the native strength of the human system. Civilization will be uplifted by this process that unlocks the riches that exist within the creative and productive potential of the human being. A new and brighter civilization will brighten the scene.

This projection of process may appear utopian and idealistic. Far from it, it reflects the fundamental principles of metaphysics which include a self-escalating dynamism. The metaphysical foundation is a foundation that supports the dynamic nature of the development of life. There is nothing utopian or idealistic about its scope. The problem is, that mankind's imagination has been bound to feudalism for too long, so that the most fundamentally natural appears to it as miraculous and idealistic. The feudal foundation is a foundation of darkness. It scope is the self-elimination of humanity. Its measurements can't be applied to measuring reality.

The above consideration, to some degree, addresses Point 3 of the scientific enquiry for addressing the problems of the governmental budget crisis that is plaguing every nation.

Chapter 9: Governmental Budget Balancing:

Can It Be Done Conservatively, with Fascism Standing in the Wings? - Focusing on the Process of Healing.

Today's focus in political affairs must be on healing. In the metaphysical context, healing means becoming aware of the truth about what is real, peeling away the lies that hide it.

A nation's commitment to scientific envelopment reveals a certain commitment to the infinite dimension of the human being, as a recognized truth. The unfolding of reality, is what this nation is aiming for. Such a nation looks beyond the much tooted smokescreen of balanced budget conservatism that is cutting back on everything that supports the strength and potential of society. Can infinity be aimed at conservatively? Of course not. The two are contrary to each other. Infinity is reflected in life and intelligent existence. Life cannot be expressed conservatively. The result would be death. Political healing, therefore, means achieving a sense of reality in the face of feudalism and its fascism. It means achieving a sense of life in the face of conservatism and murder.

Since the guiding motive in this volume is focused on national budgets, one must acknowledge that these budget simply cannot be brought into balance without this fundamental healing. To address the problem on any other fundamental platform, always translates itself into supporting the type of illusions and fascist policies that created the imbalance in the first place. Let us look, there, at all the elements that create an imbalance in the economies of nations by which their stability is eroded and fascism becomes enthroned.

The platform on which imbalances are created has four elements. The four elements are shown as four columns in the flow diagram in Appendix 7.

A. The first element of imbalance is centered on the creation of debt. Debt lays the foundation for fascism.

History supports this statement that financial debt supports fascism. Without the enormous debt load that was heaped upon the shoulders of Germany in demanded reparations for the British Empire's war against Europe, created the seed bed for Adolf Hitler's fascism. Likewise, it was for debt service goals that the fascist concentration camps were created, which were originally conceived as slave labor camps for profit. Later, they served the war industry, until they finally became nothing but absolute death camps.

The creation of debt is a natural element of the feudal system. Whoever lives by this system becomes its servant and is strangled by it. Under the feudal principle, a nation **rent's** its money from a privately owned bank. If that nation requires to expand its money supply to upgrade its industries and infrastructure, the newly created money (which the private bank creates) becomes a debt to the nation, for which the private bank demands interest. And so, the development of that nation is strangled at the outset.

The principle is fundamentally defective in that it is inherently the nation's right to create its own currency. The feudal system is fraudulently assumed, in that it overturns this fundamental principle, taking away the rights of society, and assuming these rights for itself.

The, so, fraudulently created debt, in turn, becomes immediately a tax burden on the population, as large amounts of interest payments are demanded in return, which are called "debt service charges." The tax burden, in turn, acts against the strength of the productive economy which generates the real wealth for the nation, by which the burden of indebtedness becomes multiplied.

The principle of feudalism is designed to facilitate the creation of private wealth through public debt, including individual debt, and corporate debt. This is a process of looting. The looting is further made worse by a parallel development in the stock-equity markets where illusions of wealth are created were no wealth is generated at all. What drives this loop that creates bubbles of debt and illusions, is a staunch denial by virtually everyone involved, that a problem exists. This attitude is created by a total denial of the infinite system of economy, as if this system did not exist. By this denial, the feudal system appears as the only system there is, and who would even murmur against it if there are no alternatives in sight?

The second step in the healing process, beyond recognizing that a problem exists and it represents, is documented in a similar flow chart which describes the infinite model of economy, shown in Appendix 8.

The principle of the infinite system of economy enables the creation of wealth for the society as a whole. This necessitates a protective environment designed for increasing the creative and productive potential of the population. Whatever the society creates for itself, then, becomes an investment created into its own well-being. This is the original principle of the nation-state. The differences a subtle, but deep. The feudal system is build an a created perception of general poverty, which the bank overcomes by lending wealth, for a fee, of course, which actually amounts to theft. The infinite system, in contrast, is based on the scientific discovery of infinite riches imbedded in the nature of man by virtue of the human intellect. In this recognition, nothing needs to be borrowed. The door is open to create infrastructures of finance, energy, learning, and technological industrialization, by which the inherent riches of the human being are realized. The mental transition that creates a phase shift in thinking, stepping away from the poverty oriented system of lies, towards the infinite system of reality, is a process of healing.

The functionality of this principle was experienced shortly after the American Revolution. It proved itself well, as a structure for protection against feudalism and its debt-creation. Without this infinite principle, national debts can never be erased, budgets can never be kept in balance. Under this principle, Alexander Hamilton created a structure of economy that enabled the society to experience its riches. These riches proofed to be so immense, that the national debt that was designed to choke the nation, was paid off with ease, and worthless investments actually gained substance. This is the process of political healing that can save the modern society also, which is choking desperately under feudal indebtedness.

The loop in this system, as shown in Appendix 8, escalates the wealth of the society that everyone benefits from. This system is not focused on creating a screen of glowing illusions that hides the looting practice of the owners of the feudal system, that everyone suffers from. It does the opposite to creating illusions. It creates prosperity. This prosperity has traditionally set the American System apart from the fascist system of slavery camps, work houses, and human extermination centers.

The budget crisis fundamentally arises from futile attempts to equalize illusionary aggregates with the physical reality of an economy that is collapsing under the weight of the looting that is needed to continously inflate the financial bubble. The creating of imaginary financial wealth is literally killing the global society, yet it cannot let go of this empty promise. The process is as deadly as the Malaysian Monkey-Trap. The monkey who takes hold of the peanuts inside cannot withdraw his hand without letting go of the peanuts. This it cannot do. It could walk away from the trap empty handed, and thus save its life, but it can't let go of its price, even though it cannot possibly have it. The monkey trap is designed utilize this inablity, by which the monkey is caught and dies. The modern society has been carefully educated to behave in the same manner, and this 'education' has been enourmously effective. It keeps humanity trapped even when the pain becomes nearly unbearable and people are beginning to die as the societies' rulers resort to fascism in a vain attempt to keep the illusions alive that the destructive system is beneficial.

In real terms one cannot turn illusions of wealth into physical equity that raises a people's status of living. Illusions are dreams. The world is dreaming that the feudal system generates wealth and prosperity. I reality it does neither. There is no productive element within the feudal system that is based on a platform of stealing. All its elements are various forms of fascism. These, society accepts, adopts, and is willing to die for in its stuper of educated insanity. It would override fundamental principles by force of will or wishing. But reality always ends the dreaming. Principle is absolute. It cannot be mocked by human will. Nothing can ever be gained by enforcing a system that is bankrupt at the outset. The result will be the fascist self-destruction of society.

Appendix 9 shows the relative relationship of expectancy in the dream world, compared with the physical wealth being generated in the real world. The **unsupported profits** necessarily become destructive claims as they involve various degrees of parasitic looting which is starving the economy. The destructive effect, of course, increases with the growth of the markets in which it occurs. This growth is forced to occur, by clever means of deception. Here, false claims are grown. The relative size of the markets is shown in Appendix 3, including their relationship to the profits that are generated in reality.

Those who would balance the budgets must realize scientifically that the vastly inflated value of financial claims that are represented in the upper portion of Appendix 3, cannot be equalized with the value of the real profit that is generated in the suppressed physical economy, shown in the lower portion of Appendix 3. In the infinite system of economy the relative sizes are reversed.

Governments must realize that counterproductive processes, such as the debt building system, cannot succeed in creating wealth. Evident impossibilities cannot occur or be enforced by violence or law. Debt cannot create prosperity. It simply can't.

The process of draining the physical foundation of the economy, thereby weakening the strength of society in order to satisfy illusionary claims, cannot balance anything. It can't balance budgets. What can't work, won't work, no matter how hard this is pursued. The first step that is required for equalizing governmental budgets, is an equalization of the financial claims with reality, which cannot be done on the feudal . Consequently this platform must be left behind on the road to progress. This platform is invalid.

Here, healing is needed. Healing, or restructuring one's action onto a platform aligned with reality, fundamentally, causes no destruction. It causes progress.

B. The second element of imbalance is centered on creating speculative pressures. It is a fascist process that dulls the minds of humanity.

Some say that the opposite is true, that speculation adds stability. Nothing could be further from the truth. Financial speculation is one of the major factors involved in debt-building and in eroding the physical economy through disinvestment. Disinvestment in agriculture, infrastructures and industries is killing people in Mexico and in many other nations, right now, and had been killing people in Africa for decades. Financial speculation is a death trap that destroys society, by robbing it of its development resources, which are, then, wasted in none-productive processes.

Adolf Hitler must be understood as an amateur fascist, in this sense. He murdered with the gun, with poisonous gas, with explosives, or burned people to death. How messy! The murdering done so much 'cleaner' today, and far more efficiently. Who needs poisonous gas when one can take a people's money away by which its economy operates? People will crawl into dark corners and die quietly when they can no longer support their existence. And they die in much greater numbers on a global scale. Murder by financial policy is many times more effective than Hitler's policies ever were. And at the root of it all, lies financial speculation that is looting the world for the masters of the game.

A fundamental principle exists that shows that the money supply of a nation needs to expand with the expansion of the economy. This expansion is required in order to facilitate an expanded flow of commerce. In the infinite model of economy, this increase in the money supply causes no burden to both the government and the people, but becomes a boon in that it increases the wealth creating activities of physical productive processes.

In the feudal system, the same need exists also, for an ever increasing money supply. However, in the sphere of intense financial speculation the increase in the money supply is not devoted to increasing the production of goods the physical economy and to expand the society's infrastructures for living. Instead, the new money is channeled into processes with which to heat up the 'trading' fury in the financial markets. This is a double killer. It spurns on disinvestment, but in the feudal system of economy any increase in a nation's money supply is accounted as debt against the nation's balance sheet, for which interest is demanded by the financial industry. Thus, the 'trading' in the financial markets, which produces absolutely nothing in real profit for society, becomes a substantial liability in that it creates debt and debt obligations for which social support structures are destroyed. Thus we have a double acting fascist element unfolding from financial speculation.

The reason for which the money supply needs to be constantly expanded in the feudal system is inherent in speculation. The fictitious aggregates must be kept growing, otherwise no 'profits' are generated and the market dies. As the market increases on 'value' it is only natural that ever greater inflows of money are required to achieve the same proportional gain. This fundamental need of the speculative system to be constantly fed with ever greater inflow of funds creates a the competition for investment resources that literally starves the physical economy to death.

The social security liability to governments, that arises from a dying economy, naturally translates itself into evermore debt. The national debt crisis is fundamentally a revenue crisis of a kind that secondarily demands increased expenditures. To treat it merely as an expenditure crisis, shutting down social supports, reveals the underlying fascism of the feudal system that seeks to prevent economic development at all cost. The result is that people are dying under the budget axe, while the debt still mushrooms, and real cause of the dilemma remains not only unaddressed, but is actually protected from becoming altered. The feudal platform of economy will never disallow financial speculation, or even hinder it with taxation. By this commitment, humanity is doomed.

While the governments appear to have committed themselves to default on their social obligations, the liability won't go away that they owe to society. The default will come back with a vengeance through increased crime, an escalating economic decline, and a further decline of the tax base.

The fact won't go away that a nation cannot reap prosperity by means of an ongoing disinvestment in physical production and infrastructures. Once humanity is eliminated, there is no sources of wealth left. One cannot kill the goose that lays the golden eggs and still expect to harvest riches. Once the goos is dead, it is dead.

The fact remains that no amount of budget magic can overcome the divergence from reality that financial speculation forces in society. Whatever is bled from the economic progress is stolen from the strength that should advance civilization. In this sense, the financial speculators, literally steal from society's future, and seal its fate.

In order to heal the process the growing divergence must be reversed, not by conservative budgetary means, but by a fundamental recommitment to the infinite system of economy in which speculation has no place. Speculation is only useful on a limited platform, where the same aggregates must be traded back and forth in an endless progression for ever higher prices. On the infinite platform, the investment opportunities are infinite, so that trading affords no advantage. The only gain that an investor can hope to realize in the infinite system, therefore, comes from the production of physical value through investment into physical processes that benefit society. Here, no damage is done and the platform of civilization is raised. Fascism has no root in the infinite system. On the infinite platform society is healed.

C. The third element of imbalance is centered on free-trade, as compared to equitable trade. Its fascism lays the foundation for slave labor camps.

The principle of the infinite system of economy rests on national investments into infrastructures that enable the society to realize its inherent potential. These infrastructures protect a nation's industries and advance its capability. Political infrastructures, such as tariffs, protect the pricing structure that is necessary to allow for sufficient taxation with which to pay for advancing education, advanced research for future resources and technologies, for the needed transportation systems, for energy development, etc., without which the nation has no future.

The free-trade ideology introduces an element of imbalance into the equation. It breaks down the self-protection capability of the nation, on two vital fronts and throws the whole self-supporting system out of kilter.

One front that free-trade hits in the developed economies is the balanced pricing structure that is adjusted to national needs and geographic conditions. This pricing structure is invaded by free-trade dumping that kills established industries on one side, and opens slavery shops on another. Thus, the whole physical platform is dragged down into the dirt where the cheapest slave labor rules the day. On this regressive platform no social, moral, scientific, and technological progress can be achieved. It is impossible to build civilizations on slave labor. The advance of civilization requires advanced technologies to create the needed resources. The technologies, in turn require a stable support base that the wealth of society provides through its productive activities. If this self-feeding loop is broken, in which free-trade act like a virus, the whole system becomes dysfunctional. This is why free-trade was set up by Adam Smith for the British Empire, as a means for bankrupting the new American nation after it won its War of Independence with the Empire, and why that nation was bankrupted by means of free-trade destruction within six years. Free-trade is a fascist system. Its design is to kill, to enslave, and to loot. The sweat-shops of Mexico steal from that nation the strength of its labor for destructive exports. Hitler had a similar thing going in his ghetto and concentration camp industries.

Healing from the free-trade holocaust cannot be achieved merely by saying that free trade is bad. The Empire won't allow this vial aspect of its feudal structure to be overruled or to be negated. Nothing can be achieved on this front without taking the entire feudal structure down, and this means a total commitment by the nation to the infinite system of economy and whatever is associated with the infinite platform. This platform is build on the recognition of man as the tallest manifest of life on the planet, with a creative potential that opens a pathway to the stars. Slavery exploitation cannot be tolerated on this platform. Here free-trade becomes equitable trade that raises that status of civilization across the planet.

No other healing is possible to free a nation from free-trade impositions.

It is self-evident that a nation will never be able balance its debt dominated budget without first dealing with the free-trade imposition that helps to destroy its revenue base and that of its partner nation. No nation can balance its budget while its physical wealth creating capability being undermined. Ironically, this is precisely what the governments have committed themselves to do. In other words, the world is far from being healed. Slavery and the system that supports it, still reigns supreme.

It should be noted here, that the absence of free-trade does not mean the absence of any form of global trade. It only assures that such trade is equitable and has the potential to raise, rather than lower, the status of all parties involved. Tariff protected trade has always been equitable trade. Without maintaining and enhancing this potential, that is without protecting its own investment into itself by which economic riches are created, a nation has nothing to offer in trade that raises the status of civilization universally. On any other basis, trade becomes a process for looting, which it has largely become.

Only on the infinite platform can universal healing be realized.

D. The fourth element of imbalance is centered on the destruction of the infrastructures of society: The post-industrial society dogma, a fascist dogma.

What the British Empire had achieved by instigating World War I, and World War II, is being pursued in modern times in a much more efficient way as a matter of ideological imposition. It has actually been possible to induce a nation to voluntarily destroy its industry and be proud of the process. Industrialization and industrial development have become bad words. We live in a post-industrial society now, in an information age. Who cares about about developing new energy resources? We'll shut down the need for energy. We create a society powered by wind-mills and solar-cells. Who needs infrastructures such as power grids, water supply systems, transportation networks? We'll go back to nature and live off the land. Who needs industrial products and industrial jobs? We'll create service industry jobs and pay each other, and live in a healthy, clean, and more simple style.

The above, is the modern face of fascism. The post-industrial, energy lean, primitive world is not a utopia in which life is beautiful, but a world of deep poverty in which only a tiny fraction of the present world population can survive. Without energy and fertilizer intensive farming, agricultural yields will drop dramatically, and of that which is grown, much will be wasted in deficient storage, transportation, and processing. A 90% drop in population levels will result, because without food, nobody can live, and without efficient infrastructures in energy, transportation, and industrialization, the needed food cannot be produced. The post-industrial society doctrine is therefore a supremely fascist doctrine that requires the elimination of five billion people from the face of the planet.

It is interesting to note that the post-industrial society doctrine has originally been promoted by the Empire's elite who has also promoted the carrying capacity myth and numerous associated population theories that argue for a sharp depopulation of the planet. If the feudal platform remains in control of humanity, this goal will most certainly be reached in the near future.

Healing, here, rests as always, with establishing the infinite system of economy, and whatever is associated with its fundamental platform.

It must be understood the ground of the earth is poor. The only riches that a society has, are those created by its people. If this creative process stops, poverty and death reigns on the planet. Natural resources are valueless until the work of people turn the resource into products that raise the status of civilization. Even the most precious of the natural resources, such as water and farmlands, would be of no value to a nation if the knowledge and skills did not exist to turn the virgin lands into productive fields for which irrigation may be required.

Population theorists sat that we have reached an impasse in this arena. They see nations with no significant agricultural potential requiring food, and other nations, like China, whose vast potential is utilized to the present limit, which is likewise in need for more food. They theorize from this, that mankind has reached an impasse that is resulting from a carrying capacity limit of the earth? Mankind must stop its population growth, they argue, and cause a regression from the present population levels, in order that the demands for more food go away?

The option of killing people by starvation, certainly opens possibilities for curbing population growth. But this is not a viable option for a long list of reasons. The only viable option lies in shutting down the post-industrial doctrine and re-employing the same processes that have been used from the beginning of civilization for meeting the human need. These processes are centered on creating new and evermore abundant resources of a type which have previously been inaccessible and therefore inapplicable to the problem.

The almost chronic shortage of fresh water, especially in the best growing regions of the world, can be easily overcome with a decisive increase in effort. Many of the world's great rivers simply flow into the sea in the form of an open sewer. The fact is, the sewers can be cleaned up, and a global water distribution network can be created. Nuclear powered desalination of seawater can be employed. The tasks involved may be enormous against the background of today's poverty in financing, but they pose no fundamentally insurmountable problem.

The fulfillment of this task requires two main components, a vast resource of people, and a vast resource in metals and energy, all of which are abundant on the planet. The human resource is primary, however. Without this resource nothing happens. It is a resource of intelligence, scientific knowledge, and technological capability. The other resources, such as metals and energy are but a technological step away.

The point is, mankind lacks nothing. We are sitting on top of an infinite energy supply, and supply of metals. The entire mantle of the earth is made up of metallic silicates, mostly orthosilicates of magnesium, iron, and nickel. The molecular bond that binds the metals to silicone and oxygen may not be easily broken, but they can be broken. The technology for this can be developed, and the energy resource to drive the technology lies also within reach. All that is required is a dedication to the process.

With sufficient water, energy, and building materials, the world's desserts can be made to bloom with ease. Undoubtedly, a whole raft of technologies need to be developed along the way before wheat can be grown on the Sahara. One needs to develop technologies for soil creation, for environmental protection, protection from infestation, etc., all of which can be achieved. It cannot be achieved, however, without industrialization.

With infinite energy resources available, and infinite amounts of glass and metals, large portions of the world's agricultural production could even be moves indoors into multistory growing centers, leaving the naturally productive lands once again free for the development of natural diversity.

Ironically, the main impediment against this development is the one resource that has no natural limit whatsoever, which is money. What prevents this development today is the feudal platform on which money regarded as a lendable 'estate' which must be rented for a kings ransom. On the feudal rentier platform no financial development resources can be created of the size that becomes necessary for humanity to maintain its existence.

In a newspaper article around the time of the 50th anniversary of the end of World War II, a writer focused on the apparent paradox by wondering how it was possible for mankind to create this immense war fighting machine that covered the globe with the most advanced technologies and innovations ever amassed on the planet in so short a time, and how it had been impossible just months earlier, for a college graduate to find a job with sufficient income to support a family. The writer didn't recognize that the apparent paradox arose out of an ideological difference in perceiving and utilizing money.

During the war years, when the oligarchy's existence was on the line, the direct creation of monetary credits for industrialization was allowed. In other words, the infinite system was allowed to operate for a season. For this brief period the ideology of feudalism was lifted. During this period the normal potential of the human being could be realized, by which a war machine was created that saved civilization from a potentially global fascist nightmare. Except, the moment that victory was sealed, the old feudal platform was quickly reestablished.

Still it provided an illustration of the enormous potential of the infinite system of economy.

Another such problem hangs in the wings today for the United States and the world in terms of dwindling oil resources. America's oil reserves contain no more than a ten year supply at present levels of production (See Appendix 10), while the nation's production capability has fallen. Already the U.S. is 50% short of what it needs. With the rate of production declining, and energy requirements going up, a very large deficit will soon arise that could have catastrophic consequences, especially under a new oil embargo.

Again, the problem is not an insurmountable one. It can be easily solved with the application of technology. It may require a national effort to create the technology. The fact is, that even without creating a single new technology, the presently operating nuclear fast breeder that is safe and creates no appreciable waste and pollution (unlike old nuclear plants) can open the door to the production of hydrogen fuels which could eliminate oil as an energy source within a very short time. This could leave the remaining oil to be used as feed stock for the medicinal and chemical industries.

The only factor that is blocking such an effort, again, is money. For the love of money (which cannot be created under the feudal system) the nation is throwing away its future.

Feudalism, actually, not only retards development, but it also steals whatever resources does exist. It was obviously over access to oil, that the Dessert Storm war was fought. When will the next oil war erupt, and how many people will have to die for it? This answer will be determined by how tenaciously mankind clings to its beloved feudalism, and its self-limiting ideology. Wars will never cease for as long as the feudal system is holding its ground. Wars will only cease against the background of universal, infinite development, the very opposite platform to what the post-industrial doctrine demands.

For the sake of money, mankind is throwing its development potential away. It is literally destroying itself by denying itself the resources that are within reach for its continued development.

It is a fundamental factor of metaphysics, that a nation that destroys itself as a people does this by destroying the infrastructural platform by which its wealth is created, by which it maintains its existence and civilization. The slightest devolution of this platform means not only death to ever increasing numbers of people, but leads to the collapse of society itself. A society and its people are one.

The society and its people live as one, and they die as one. A nation-state is nothing more than a people bound to a common commitment. Anything that does not reflect this commitment to common wealth, common achievement, and common defense, is contrary to the platform of the nation and should be discarded. This principle has been understood 500 years ago when the idea of the nation-state was born. One of its fundamental platforms is **common defense,** which includes the defense against poverty, disease, slavery, ignorance, etc., for the promotion of life, liberty, and happiness. Any would-be budget cutter who ignores this platform destroys the nation by destroying the people, which ultimately inflates the budget deficits in leaps and bounds and destroys the government as well.

The irony is that this principle was well understood 500 years ago, while in the modern age of scientific advances the whole world pursues the insanity of self-destruction by adhering to a feudalist financial system that makes the nation impotent in terms of development, that makes it debt ridden, and is causing the physical destruction of its industries and the life of its people.

This fascist based insanity has now become globalized, with the global promotion of the budget balancing insanity that goes beyond deindustrialization, that cuts profits directly out of the life of people, which in the end profits no one. The insanity has become so gross, however, that the nations are fully prepared to sell their future for the dollar. Indeed, they insist on it.

Chapter 10: The Mathematics of The Budget War

Factors of Fascism

The currently most widely accepted platform for cutting deficits is to slash expenditures. The money that doesn't come in cannot be spend. Right? At least, so the argument goes, and out comes the budget axe. Any family budget is brought into line by this method, so the politicians tell themselves and the public. They say that the pain that is suffered today makes it easier "for our children in the future." But, is this assumption correct?

The reality is, that the exact opposite is true.

The majority of individuals and families are constantly engaged in an effort to improve their status of living. They do this by raising their income, either through better education, or through acquiring broader skills, or through advancement in job-levels. Without these constant efforts, the stage is set for a trend into poverty. No parent will tell a child: Eat less, and you'll be secure for life. Instead, parents encourage their children to develop their potential. In some families, a large portion of the family budget is devoted to this very goal, even at the expense of taking on loans as a means for assuring a bright future for their children. This is how family budgets are run in reality.

The notion that a nation must drive itself into poverty to assure a bright future for its children results from a certain axiomatic insanity. Every increment of shutting down the nation's productive potential leads to more poverty. It brings up the specter of death for the future, rather than life.

It was this process of shutting down the potential of the nation that evolved out of the "post industrial society" dogma that was focused one earlier. It did its part in creating the debt problem in the first place that the modern budget cutting mania intends to address by budget measures. It is impossible by any standard of logic to address such a problem by escalating the very process that has generated the problem. By such a process the problem becomes multiplied. Four plus four equals eight, not zero.

Whichever financial forecaster makes mathematical predictions that show a balanced governmental budget in 5 years, or in 7 years, by the force of the budget axe, totally ignores the powerful collapse-multiplier of the budget axe, that cuts deep into the wealth producing potential of the nation, eroding its tax-base even as it expands the social service demands.

Cuts may be useful where enormous waste exists, but apart from this, they are counter-productive. Any industrial accountant will agree that a deficit in accounts cannot be erased by shutting down the production plants that create the revenue. An accountant might suggest that investment into new products and production has historically increased the cash-flow, by which accounts might be balanced with new income streams.

A business, certainly has the option to shut itself down and declare bankruptcy, should it cease to keep its product line vital. A nation, however, cannot afford to to this, for this bankruptcy means death.

We have two opposing ideologies represented in the arena of the budget war. One ideology is based on collapsing the economic process and accepting poverty as a savior and bankruptcy as the outcome. This is the fascist model.

The second ideology is based on the development of the economic potential of the human intellect. It comes as no surprise, therefore, that one sees the two contrasting ideologies, the infinite and the feudal platform, represented by two contrasting models for economy and finance. The collapse oriented ideology that heralds conservatism as a virtue unfolds out of the feudalist model. This this model has become accepted globally, the budget cutting mania has become a global phenomenon. The feudal system that drives the budget axe is also the foundation of the globally imposed world-financial system. The two phenomena are linked.

Conservatism towards the human needs, as a means for maximizing the profits of a parasitic minority, is an age old platform that operated throughout all the ages of feudalism. It can be traced back to the Roman Empire and beyond. It is the platform on which every empire in history has been founded, and by which the empire collapsed. The toll in human life is too horrific for this game to continue. Unfortunately, the game is accelerating rather than slowing down.

The development oriented ideology that heralds

growth as a virtue, in contrast to the model of empires, is championed by all those who cherish the realization of the human potential, who see the foundation of civilization as resting on the Renaissance of ideas, the power of caring, the potential of scientific advances, the efficiency of technologies, even the beauty and strength of the human soul that sees beauty and strength in all living processes and supports them. Here, humanity finds its strength.

The nature of money in a feudal setting appears in a totally different context than it plays in the infinite setting. In one sphere it is seen as a rentable 'estate' that is lend out for draining profit from an economy. In the other sphere money is seen as a nationally owned catalyst for human development.

One of the two spheres will prevail in the long run. The choice will ultimately be determined by the system's potential for serving the human needs. Logically, this choice should be made now. The greatest potential should be applied presently, towards solving the present governmental budget crisis.

The process of evaluating choices.

Mankind appears to have a choice at this present stage, to choose between two opposite systems. Contrary to opinion, nothing is cast in concrete, so that fundamental choices are possible. So, how, then, shall we choose today?

What our choice will necessarily be is determined by the imperatives of the future? If we, the society, choose to continue the present course, we may soon find ourselves in a most uncomfortable, if not impossible, position. What this implies, needs to be considered now. On a scientific platform the logical requirement for the future determines the path of the present.

Is this, however, really the way the world is run. Let us assume the impending crash in the financial markets occurs tomorrow, in the U.S. (which could indeed happen), and let us further assume that the crash is a mild one in the order of the 1929 crash (which is not likely), and let us also assume that the crash remains localized, and that much of the current banking and financial system survives so that the current trend may continue (which is not likely either), what effect would such a crash have on the U.S. government's position relative to its debt? The most likely effect of a major wipeout in the equity markets would be a dramatic rise in interest rates as a measure for keeping the remaining wealth in the country. The moment that a substantial portion of the present market capitalization has been lost, the free money that may still exist will likely flee the country for greener pastures. A lot of countries, like Mexico, Venezuela, Argentina, etc., have already gone through devaluations by which interest rates have gone through the roof, in some cases into the 100% range, and higher.

Let us further assume that interest rates in the U.S. will rise to about 12% or possibly 15%. What effect would this rate hike have on a nation that is carrying a 16,000 billion dollar debt? The carrying cost would suddenly rise to $2-2.4 trillion, against the background of an unfolding and severe depression that always follows a major equity wipe-out in the markets. In 1929, the after-shock was so severe that no recovery ever occurred from the resulting depression until the economic phase shift occurred at the start of World War II.

In a situation of high interest rates, together with a collapsing economy, and a severely depressed credit market, it will evidently be impossible to refinance the $2.4 trillion in debt service demands by any means. The result will be an inevitable chain of defaults which will most certainly include the government's Treasury debt. Already, the U.S. government is technically in a default position, which is presently addressed by monetizing this default position by means of printing new money in order to keep the lid on the problem.

Also, there is another area of interest. It is an area in which the governments around the world do already default on their obligation to their citizens, and this at a tremendous cost in human terms. These defaults come in the form of shutting down vital infrastructures, protective measures, scientific, technological, and bio-medical potential, education support, health support, etc.. The current default position will necessarily be increased monumentally, once the governments are forced to carry a three-fold increase in financial obligations against the background of sharply reduced revenues. Also, there is not anything left to be cut in terms of administrative waist, or equity to be sold by privatization of state enterprises.

The accelerating defaults will hit everyone, even if there is official approval given for unlimited borrowing in the markets. The Treasury bond won't buy anything in the markets when it is tarnished by defaults, nor could the markets be able to supply the needed cash to fund the social deficits associated with a collapsing physical economy.

In response to these various types of default, the price of the U.S. dollar will likely crash and put the whole international currency market in to an uproar, by which the effective size of the nation's debt will explode, because of foreign components of the debt. What, then, will balance the budgets? Also, what money's will the corporate debt be financed with, or the private debt of the nation? The words, bankruptcy and default will be written in capital letters.

The feudal model of economy could actually collapse under this crisis, together with a social collapse that may destroy many a nation. It is evident that the feudal model must be abandoned before this point is reached.

The wisest choice would be to unhook the nation from the feudal death spiral before the impending crash in the markets takes place. This could be accomplished by adopting the development oriented model. Under the infinite model, that is centered on boundless development, the budgets that are strained to the breaking point, today, will most certainly become payable, indeed, and the debt in governments and industries will become re-payable indeed, None of this is currently possible to do, by any means. As for choices, the nations of the world really have none other, if their goal is physical survival. The choice that exists is between survival and suicide, which is not a choice as between valid options.

By the society's current commitment to budget cutting, it has put itself, ignorantly, on the path of committing suicide. Because of its refusal to deal with the underlying cause of the economic and physical collapse that the budget crisis is a symptom of, the industrial world has reduced itself to the status of a pauper and a thief, because the feudal system that currently dominates mankind's axioms does not only prevent development but also loots whatever equity may still exist, anywhere on the planet.

It should be noted that the above scenario represents an ideal case. The real magnitude of the currently impending world-financial disintegration and its effects will likely be much worse. This seems hardly possible. Still. it is.

The society's budget cutting commitment totally ignores that the entirety of the fictitious monetary and financial aggregates system, for which the cuts in the life of the nation are necessitated, has no actual value. This may soon be recognized. Therefore, the mathematical algorithms in budget projections, have no value either as they do not deal with real factors, and are doomed to collapse in the crash of the bubble of fictitious values.

That a great insanity currently reigns the world-financial system, is evident by the demands for capital gains tax cuts that are made by the rich, supposedly as a means of spurring on the 'economy' (the fictitious value economy). If these demands were adopted, the result would further increase the momentum towards the impending collapse and the destruction of real profits. By these measures no one would gain, while they would further increase the devastating magnitude of the collapse when it comes. The financial growth (in fictitious aggregates) is fundamentally a negative growth. It represents as much a liability for the nation that supports this growth, as it represents an illusion of value to the holder of the fictitious financial (so-called) wealth.

It is a myth that a nation can balance its national budget while its government reneges on its responsibilities to create a nationally owned currency (vs. the assumed rights of privately owned currency); to protect national industries (from free-trade looting); to curb speculation with regulatory and taxation measures (instead of removing regulations and granting capital gains tax reductions); to support the population on a platform of common defense (instead of affecting its destruction through imposed poverty). The responsibilities of government within a nation-state are defined by the principle of the nation-state. If these responsibilities are ignored, as they are today, the potential of prosperity that is inherent in the platform of the nation-state, is lost. The collapse of civilization to the pre-nation-state level is inevitable if the principles of the nation-state are cast to the wind. If this happens, it will take society back to the status of the dark ages of the early 14th century and before, in which 95% of all people, on all continents, lived as serves, slaves, or worse, and the world, itself, had very few people and few comforts for those who lived in these times.

Can a capital gains tax cut create prosperity for a nation?

The answer has already been given. It is a resounding, NO. But only a part of the reason had been explored. To discern the deeper aspects requires a little detective work.

We deal once again with a paradox that obscures

the real situation that nearly all nations face. The paradox is related to the measurement of the nation's income. On one hand we have a physical economy that measures itself in terms of Value Added Product, which is the total value produced in physical production. In the U.S. this amounts to slightly over a trillion dollars a year. This measurement does not include the product of mining and farming, which usually adds add another 20% to the value of things produced, for a total figure of production in the physical economy of significantly less than $1.5 trillion.

This figure must now be compared to another measurement that the government tallies up, which is the Gross Domestic Product (GDP) that measures everything, including services and whatever else makes up the tax base. For the U.S., this figure exceeds the seven trillion dollar range. This means that the none-productive industry which produces no physical value is five times larger than the productive industry. The bulk of this unproductive value, evidently comes the financial industry where much of the total product measures fictitious gains from bloated values derived through speculation and trading. This is the portion that is subject to capital gains taxation, which is already substantially less than any other tax on income. Since the speculative process starves the physical economy of its vital investment resources, the speculative process causes a measure of social destruction that far exceeds the value of capital gains taxation. The society, therefore, carries a substantial deficit that arises from the processes that provide speculators gain. Which means that the taxation is actually insufficient by a very large measure.

Now, if the capital gains taxation were to be eliminated to satisfy the wishes of the financial industry, speculation would increase substantially, and so would the loss to society that arises for the process of speculation. The social losses would likely increase substantially, increasing the poverty and pain of the population, and the size of the national debt.

Tax measures that increase speculation, therefore, have fundamentally a negative effect. Whoever argues that such measures increase the wealth of the society, does so ignorantly or lies outright. It is self-evident that no value is produced for society by trading financial instruments from one hand to another for ever higher prices. Real taxes may be collected from the fictitious gains in the value of aggregates traded, but these taxes are no gain to society either in that they offset only a small portion of the economic damage that the fictitious value system inflicts on society. It would be a gross injustice to society as a whole if the government were to waive its right to these reparation payments no matter how insignificant they might be in size to the whole problem. Without these taxes, the problem would accelerate even more, and so would would the resulting liability to the nation. The society (taxpayers) would have to food a double large bill out of its continuously shrinking resources as the physical economy contracts under pressures of disinvestment.

Logically, the opposite of the proposed tax cuts should be enacted. A platform of taxation should be set up that stops speculation altogether. This goal, unfortunately, is impossible to achieve in practice. So far, it has not even been possible to enact a financial turnover tax of one tenth of one percent of the notional value of instruments traded.

The pain that society suffers from the disease of speculation can never be cured on the feudal platform of economics where values are limited and all investments must be 'rented' from so-called investors, which leaves the physical scene depleted and the horizon open to the excesses of financial speculators. This pain can be healed, however, on the infinite platform of economy which operates on a platform of direct investment by the nation into infrastructures and industrialization. In this environment private capital finds boundless opportunities to create profit for society, in which it shares. In such an environment of unfolding riches the 'grounds' becomes increasingly infertile for speculation.

There is a great need for this healing to occur quickly, before the world-financial crash occurs in which everything disintegrates.

It should be noted that the very rich of society would gain the most by this healing. If the fictitious system disintegrates, all is lost. If a shift to the infinite system of economy is achieved, some investments might be saved and gain real value in the resulting boom in the physical economy. This had been the general experience in the past when the infinite system of economy was enacted by Alexander Hamilton and George Washington at the time the U.S. nation was bankrupted through free-trade. In fact, a special tax cut could be initiated under the infinite system that actually enhances the wealth creating capability of private capital in the physical economy.

The nature of ^wealth-enhancing^ tax cuts.

The only type of tax cut that can benefit a nation is that which enhances the physical, scientific, and technological development of the nation, and its industrialization, such as an investment tax credit, a research tax credit, a technology cost tax credits, and tax credits for wage earners who invest in their education and advancement of skills. These are the only tax credits possible that can enhance a nation's real wealth through enhanced productivity. All other tax credits are destructive.

Under the infinite system, wealth-enhancing tax cuts might be implemented initially with corresponding types of capital gains taxation (with no capital loss write-offs) that shuts the speculative markets down and refocuses the attention of society back onto productive processes for earning profit in real terms.

Naturally, such a transition to the infinite system of economy would blow the entire financial aggregates system apart, which has no real value in itself. Illusions loose their value when the focus is shifted back to reality. The current flood of monetary inflow that drives the fictitious system would stop overnight. The flood in capital loss tax claims that would destroy the feudal system in a financial collapse through the tax loss claim forwarding mechanism that exists in many a country, wouldn't touch the infinite system of economy where all accounting is based on reality.

The effect of the collapse of the fictitious bubble would actually be minimized through an orderly general bankruptcy reorganization and refinancing of industries that would otherwise disappear. In this case, as the nation takes back control over its money, the creation of development credits at zero or near zero interest becomes a boon for all segments of the economy, to rebuilt the economic machine. The financial crash would be a soft one under such circumstances, in that the revitalized physical economy would take the pain out of the transition from the feudal system, which has no value but illusions, to the infinite system where real value is generated.

If the unfolding world-financial disintegration takes place under the feudal platform of economy, no structures exist that can pull the society out of a total collapse that is likely to draw all values to zero. In this situation, the word "depression" will not apply. The reality will most certainly be unimaginably worse.

The economic reorganization of a nation onto the infinite platform would no doubt cause some pain as the illusions of immense financial wealth evaporate in the context of reality. Except this would no be the deeply destructive kind of pain that the society as a whole is moving towards when an uncontrolled disintegration of the global financial system takes place that looms on the horizon. When an intelligent reorganization takes place, onto a platform that works (as it has already proven itself) it may be said again as it was said when the infinite system was enacted in the early years of the U.S.A., that "the national debt has become a national blessing." This saying resulted when the nation responded in its early years of independence from the British Empire, to a desperate situation that had been created for it under free-trade economics. The nation responded with an awakening of its intelligence that quickly turned the Empire's intended defeat of the new nation, by means of the free-trade weapon, into a momentous victory.

By this process, the nations' budgets can once again be balanced. It is totally possible to revive the productive economy with the same intensity and effect through strategic policy measures: through credits in taxation, through national investment into infrastructures, through revitalizing the nation's platform of strength from which its debts can be paid with no pain, and the targeted portions of it population will survive which the budget cutters of today are committed to relegate to the scrap heap.

The current budget deficit crisis is not a hard one to resolve within the infinite system of economy, once the erroneous platforms that have created the deficits and debt, are recognized and dealt with.

Yes, there is a difference between what is officially called ^the economy,^ and the ^actual^ or ^real economy^ that is providing a living for society...

...and the sooner that this difference is recognized, the sooner will the world's budget problems be solved. The real economy is measured by looking at the market basket, according to the LaRouche method, which measures what the average person's income buys of the productive economy. This also provides a measure of the real productivity of the nation.

If one takes 1967 as a base year, the production of

the U.S. economy for the U.S.' market basket has fallen by over 50% and is declining at an evermore accelerating rate. For some items, the drop in what the nation produces for the market basket is over 90%, with a corresponding losses in employment. The deficit in the nation's production for the market basket is made up in part by imports, and is offsets in part through reduced consumption.

Contrary to the GDP measurement which has increased by leaps and bounds, the size of the nation's market basket (imports included) has shrunk by 25%. This reduction reflects reduced income levels from employment, even though the number of workers per family has increased. In other words, the U.S. economy produces less than half, with a greater amount of manpower, than it had produced in 1967, while the population is consuming 25% less. In some areas the drop in production is so severe, that it would take a 500% increase in employment, like in the textile industry, to produce a 1967 style market basket in today's world. In other areas the needed increase is somewhat less. A 300% workforce increase would be needed in the shoe and steel industries, for instance, to get these industries back to the 1967 production levels.

This dramatic decline in production, now needs to be seen in comparison to the Gross Domestic Product (GDP) that measures the total economic activity of the nation. The trend of this figure shows the very opposite. It shows a dramatic increase from $513 billion in 1960 to $7.113 trillion in 1995. Since both, the production of the market basket has shrunk, and the market basket itself has shrunk, rather than showing an increase of 13,000% as the GDP calculation indicates, a gross error is made in the evaluation of the GDP figure. It is certainly true that the average person does not own 13 times as many cars than in the 1960s, or owns a house that is 13 times as large, nor has the population grown 13 fold. One must conclude, therefore, that the 13,000% increase reflects a conceptional error that reflects the inflation that has taken place in monetary value compared to physical activities.

In other words, when governments speak of **the economy,** they rarely mean the actual physical economy that provides for the living of individuals. This portion of the economy has shrunk by 50%. What the governments refer to, therefore, is that portion of the GDP has has indeed grown 13 times in perceived value, so that the real economy that effects the living of the populations and their market basket, represents but a small portion of the total of the measured national product.

The remaining portion of what is termed **the economy,** which is not a part of the economy that provides for the market basket, represent a combination of factors. These include in large measure the inflation of the bubble of built up capital and financial products. Since the latter factor represents the lion's share of what is measured as economic activity, it is this factor that is actually quite unrelated to actual living, that is referred to when the money controllers say that **'the economy'** is "overheated."

This terminology, "overheated" does not mean that a meaningful increase in employment has occurred, or an increase in physical production has taken place by which the size of the market basket of the population has increased. No, it means that the capital factor is overheated that measures the discrepancy between physical reality and monetary representation. Usually, in such situations, interest rate increases are applied to curb the capital factor, which of course, hurts the real economy the most. But, then, who gives a hoot about the real economy that amounts to but a small fraction of the GDP in terms of the inflated measurements?

It appears that the controller's interest rate interventions in **'the economy'** have nothing to do with improving the physical living of the society, but are primarily directed at preventing potential blowouts in the capital and financial markets, or to spurn on new activities in these market as may be needed to maintain the increase in capital gain. Usually, interest rates are lowered when stockmarket indexes are in decline, which causes alarm bells to ring. Thus, a financial mechanism is applied by which the greatest stockmarket bubble in history has been 'managed' whose 'performance' hides the state of the real world.

In spite of official rhetoric, it is certainly true that today's stockmarkets, and the related financial aggregates markets, are the most manipulated markets that ever existed. Since interest rate controls are determined by the banks, like the Federal Reserve bank in the U.S., one also wonders at the striking coincidence that exists by which the big banks just happen to be engaged in gargantuan financial derivatives speculation, especially in interest rate derivatives speculation in markets that they control, in which area the banks just happen to be highly successful. There has rarely been a more tightly rigged game than this, although it is now totally legal thanks to deregulation. And the size of the game that the banks play is big.

By mid-1994, the U.S. banking system has held $17.9 trillion in derivatives instruments, which amounts to seven times the combined value of all the banks outstanding loans, or 53 times the banks' combined equity of $335 billion. Appendix 2, Figures 2, shows the size of this relationship between assets and derivatives for the nine top U.S. banks. Figure 3 shows the further relationship of the derivatives gambling for one of the banks' own equity. Since 1991, when the derivatives game got under way in large measure, bank profits have risen to record highs and bank failures have become a rarity, while the real economy suffered its worst period of bankruptcies and workforce layoffs, in possibly its entire history. The two trends simply do not match. In other words, the banking system has cut itself loose from the physical reality that it once served, and has drifted off into the cyberspace of gambling casinos where wonderful paper profits are made.

The same trend away from reality is reflected in the rise of the Dow Jones average which is loosely tied to the rise in derivatives speculation. As the Dow has climbed steadily upwards, it is being said that speculation has brought stability to the market. The reality, however, in in the opposite, and is quite scary. There are on average several million derivative contracts traded each single business day, in the U.S. alone. The value ratio between purely financial speculation, such as interest rate contracts, as compared to commodity based speculation, has also widened. This ratio stands today in the order of 10:1. The stock and futures derivatives game, of course, is not the only game going. There are huge financial trades in bonds going on, in government securities, and in national currencies. The total financial turnover for speculative processes of all types, including the off-balance sheet processes, is so enormously huge that it is estimated to amounts in the U.S., all by itself, upwards to $500 trillion annually.*22 This amount of speculative financial turnover is 69 times greater than the also vastly inflated value of the Gross Domestic Product. The sheer size of it is so huge, that it dwarves everything else. For instance, it is 450 times larger than the total M1 money supply of the nation. Because of its massive size, gambling constitutes the largest component of the world economy. Even in international currency transactions, the speculative component is huge. It is conservatively 200 times larger than all the world's transactions for the sale of physical goods.

When one hears talk about **'the economy'** doing this or that, it is this game that is being referred to. What is being said about **'the economy,'** therefore, has absolutely nothing to do with more food being put on people's table, or shoes on their children's feet. This is also why the desperately sought after capital gains tax cuts are deemed to have an enormous impact on **'the economy,'** even while they would hurts the life of the people in the real economy where the resources for living are created which are shrinking evermore.

A study by the Heritage Foundation in the U.S. reveals the skewed nature of the benefits of the proposed tax cuts for the rich. These tax cuts are deemed, according to this study, to create an increase of $32.1 billion in disposable income for speculators, spread out over seven years (averaging $128 per person of the U.S.A.). However, this single increase of $128 per person is deemed to cause a spending increase of $66.2 billion (or $264 per person) and in addition to that result in $88.2 billion in new investment (or $352 per person), and in addition to all that, it would also create 103,700 new housing units (a $25 billion investment, averaged out to $103 per person). This accounting magic that turns a $128 increase in tax savings into an $719 increase in spending is only possible in the realm of dramatic financial multipliers in an 'economy' that has lost all connections with the real world.

The presently occurring increase in the M3 money supply reflects such an explosive growth pattern already, that matches the growth pattern of speculative insanity that has left the real world far behind. The 1995, the increase in the U.S. money supply has been nearly 5 times greater than the average rate of growth of the money supply since 1990, and represents the sharpest increase in over 20 years. The sad part is, that the economic projections that the society likes to see, can grow only in the land of illusions. The reality of the disintegrating real economy remains unaffected and unaltered, if not accelerated.

Insanity in economics reflects insanity in politics.

Yes, there is a distinction between the real economy that puts food on the table and shoes on the feet, and the 'economy' of run-away insanities that have no relationship to the processes that support human existence.

It is a type of advanced insanity to create an 'economy' that is fundamentally centered on pure speculation. Unfortunately, this is what the society professes to love. It doesn't even seem to matter to it that this type of 'economy' is inherently debt-ridden, super-charged with impossible values, and is ultimately self-defeating. Society has lost sight of the fact that the aim of an economic system is to raise the status of civilization through productive activities by which a nation becomes wealthy. Instead, the society has focused on a system that is designed for draining the wealth of a nation into a few private pockets. The greatest insanity is in believing that this process of draining wealth from the economy is a promotive rather than destructive enterprise.

It is a fallacy, therefore, for the private monetary regulators, such as the Federal Reserve, to believe that stability can be created by such monetary measures that keep the fictitious system growing by such means that strangle the productive economy and the population of which unspeakable sacrifices are demanded for this. Oddly this insanity appears to be justified in the minds of the financial regulators, if only they manage to keep the fictitious systems artificially alive whenever they shows signs of collapsing. The insane belief that this induces stability and security, cannot forever hide the reality.

The reality is fundamentally quite simple. If twice as many financial aggregates are created than physical equity, than the financial aggregates are only worth half their face value. If the financial aggregates increase tenfold, while physical production declines to half, as has been the case since the 1960s, the financial aggregates are worth but a 20th of their face value. And so the progression goes to infinity where it sits today, so that the speculative gains that are chalked up on the big boards, are a total illusion.

This describes the financial aggregates, and much of the current stock-markets. Most stocks that are traded on the exchanges represent to the bearer a part ownership of a company. Many of the company's traded today pay no dividends whatsoever, have never paid any, and may never intend to pay dividends, or pay only minute amounts. The current average yield stands at 2.2%. In most cases, dividend payments are insignificant factors in determining the value of shares. This means that shares are bought for the hope that another 'investor,' at a later date, will pay even more for them. With each increase, the value of the share - which was zero to begin with in such cases when no dividends are paid - becomes inflated by an imaginary escalator. If a share that pays no dividend, was never traded, its effective value of zero would become immediately apparent as the realized return from the 'investment' would be zero.

The fictitious nature of the speculative value system is also apparent when one considers the stock of the best companies in the system, like that of the blue-chip giants, such as IBM. At an average share price of $120.00 a share, the share earns presently $1.00 in dividends per year, which is considered a good return under present economic circumstances. This means, that without any fictitious value increase through trading, the bearer of the share will have to wait 120 years to get his capital back, assuming that no taxes are paid on the 'income.' If taxes are included, an investor may have to wait for 150 years to see his money returned if the share was never traded.

It is only through the process of trading the share on the market, by which a dramatic rise in value can be realized, that profits are made, although no actual increase in value through economic activity has occurred. By this process of driving the value up in a buying and selling competition, the 'investors' literally steal from each other as they demand payment for value that does not really exist.

Now, since the imagined increases in value occur only through the process of trading, an entire industry has been created to promote this trading and to make it as profitable as possible. This industry has become an essential part of the fictitious value system, because it, too, produces nothing but an imagined increase in value of equities that are traded. This, this industry has a life only when it becomes possible for the bidding system to carried on at infinitum, driving the imagined value to ever higher levels by drawing new 'investors' into the game. Except this infinite goal cannot be achieved.

Not even an equilibrium can be achieved. Once the inflow of investment stops, that is, once the imagined value can no longer be increased through trading, the entire system looses its value, that has value only because of trading. Once this point is reached, when no trading increase is accrued, and no dividend profits are realized, the shares in the system become useless, as indeed many are, and were from the beginning. At this point the market is considered to have crashed, though nothing has actually happened to the economy or the companies whose equity the market represents.

The sad part is, that huge portions of the nation's savings and pension funds are invested in financial aggregates of this sort that are fundamentally valueless, or of minute value, in terms of real return on investment. Still, it must be said that the stock market is non-theless the most sane of the fictitious systems. It is, after all, tied to something that is related to economic activity. If all shareholders of a company voted to have the profits of their company paid out, they might see a 1% return, or a 3% return in rare cases.

Any return that is expected above this level is based on some illusion on the buyer's part, that the share is worth more. Through these self-escalating illusions, the book value is driven up, which however is not real. Still, it must be noted that this escalation of value has a positive impact on the equity system. The inflated fictitious value of the stock equity system determines also the sale price of the companies that the stock represents. If the share price would be in a range that brought the company's dividends into parity with bonds and other investments, the industry would fall prey to the ravages of corporate raiders, because the physical investment would have to be highly undervalued to generate high rates of return. The corporate raiders would win, because in the modern economic climate real earnings for actual physical equity are extremely small. In the physical economy, the rate of earnings per equity invested is currently to small for an 'investor' to be contend with. Without capital gains, the share prices would adjust themselves to create the expected earnings, which makes the sale price of a company small compared to its equity. Consequently the corporate raiders will enter the game, and through asset stripping have a glory day.

This protection against corporate raiders that high share values create, is bound to evaporate in a crash of the markets. In other words, the coming crash will expose the productive economy to the most severe predatory action imaginable. The corporate raiders will have their best time ever, in America. Unfortunately, again, the society looses. But what of it? The society loves its feudal system, at least it pretends to.

The reality is, most people are told what to love, and they do so, rarely realizing what is is that they devote their life to.

The above exposure does not exist in the high profit arena of a fully functioning economy, based on the infinite model, where sanity reigns.

Far more insane than the stock market is the financial derivatives trading. It speculates on the effect of speculation. Its aggregates are contracts on the future values of stocks, currencies, indexes, or interest rates, all of which are themselves the outcome of speculation. One can, for instance, at a fraction of the real price buy a contract to purchase gold at a certain price at a future date. If the market price is higher at this date, one wins. The person who buys the contract bets that the market price will be higher at this future date, so that a 'profit' is made by buying low at the contracted price and selling the proceeds at the higher market price. But this is not all. The futures game also creates profit when the market is collapsing. By buying contractual options for the right to sell a certain commodity at a preset price, a substantial 'profit' can be made when the market goes below this price. Such a contract enables the 'investor' to buy low at the market and sell the purchase back at the higher contracted price. This process of profiteering from an economic crash is only possible in the wonderland of cyberspace. In reality, nothing is gained in the process that raises the platform of civilization.

This gambling on the effect of other people's gambling, appears to be a harmless game on the surface. People say, "What is one man's loss is another man's gain, so that everything comes out equal." In theory, the game can even be put to some practical use. In the above example the options game can be used to take the risk out of investing in gold. In fact, the options game was invented to reduce price-fluctuation-risks in the commodities markets. For instance, for a price, certain investors were willing to put their money on the line in order to reduce the risk of price fluctuations for producers or purchasers. In this respect the game fulfilled some useful function, even though the profit that the game created was not derived from the productive process itself, but was looted out of it.

But what about interest rate derivatives, which are futures contracts on interest rates levels, or rate fluctuations? The phenomenon that can be observed is actually quite frightening. The further these derivatives become removed from the physical equivalent, the more enormous the sums tend to be that are involved, and the greater the ensuing risk and profit potential. The point is, that by this contract trading venture vast profits are chalked up that lure investment funds out of the productive economy into leveraged speculation. The annual world turnover of such instruments is estimated to be in the $700 to $800 trillion range. The profits of the game, like in any other financial game, are self-multiplying, and ultimately represent a claim against the products of the real economy, the same economy that the fictitious values of the stock markets are also claimed against.

In other words, the derivatives trader is in a double jeopardy. While the profits are invariably fictitious, though taxable, the loss potential is real as there is simply not enough real value in the world to pay out the paper profits.

The other component of the fictitious capital market is the bond, the T-bill, and bank investment market. Neither of these markets bears any relationship to the actual profits created in the economy through the metaphysical effect of human ingenuity and labor. Fictitious values and profits are inherently 'metamythical' in nature, rather than metaphysical.

Since a society is not supported by myths, the deficit between the myths and reality will inevitable re-assert itself. In other words, the markets will crash, and whatever is tied to them will crash with them. The only hope that a nation has in protecting itself, lies in bringing its value system into an equitable relationship with the productive capacity of the nation which rests on a metaphysical platform.

Chapter 11: The 'Metamythical' versus the Metaphysical Platform

Mankind's War Against Feudalism and Fascism.

The metamythical platform is currently collapsing on all fronts. The stock market values have risen to such highs that the slightest upset on the political scene tends to cause huge swings in the market. There are warning signs recognizable, like a sudden 50% loss in the arena of high-technology stock issues. This has already occurred. Except what we have seen is merely one front of many fronts that are all in a near state of crisis.

We face an ensuing world-food crisis, a possible new world-energy crisis, and definitely a world-debt crisis. We also see a crisis of global political instability. We face a political crisis in Russia, created by IMF austerity conditionalities and privatization, and an unfolding political crisis in Europe, created by the Maastricht Treaty conditionalities, and others. And besides these, there is the Conservative Revolution crisis unfolding in the U.S. that aims to destroy the functioning of the U.S. government, it Presidency, and the spirit of the constitution, even the nation-state itself. It doesn't even shy back from bringing up the specter of a governmental default on the debt.

Another crisis unfolds in the economic and monetary implosion in Ibero America where interest rates have spiked into the 100% to 200% range, with food production lagging at a 30% deficit in some staple commodities, and with a financial system so deeply in shambles that it offers no hope of averting a debt default from blowing the whole fictitious global debt-structure sky high.

Such defaults become inevitable from a certain point on, when it becomes impossible to squeeze credits out of the international community, or more blood out of the population. There comes a point beyond which the population begins to die, as is already happening in Mexico where large numbers of children fall victim to malnutrition while food is being exported.

With six potential crises unfolding, it is unlikely that a major breakdown in the financial system can be contained. Another oil shock, for instance, will kill the world-financial system. The magnitude of the impending breakdown may affect every category that is currently in a near crisis state, and may spread globally in such a manner that the ensuing catastrophe may be the most tragic in all history.

What such a catastrophe really represents is nothing more than the accumulative result that has been stored up in the background through a long term discounting of the metaphysical platform for human existence. We are standing at the edge of a cliff. A mental phase shift has occurred over the last 15 to 20 years, that has put us there, that has put the focus more and more onto on adopting the feudal economic and financial platform which operates on what may be defined as a 'metamythical' basis. A mental bubble has been created of shiny lies. A rapidly growing set of illusions has gripped the minds of people which cause people to believe that the society can exist without the physical component that supports life, and without the metaphysical foundation on which the physical component is created.

The physical component is vaguely recognized as essential. Reluctantly people agree that mankind cannot live without food, water, clothing, shelter, transportation etc., all of which are taken for granted today. Because of the growing disinterest in the physical structures that support human existence, the focus has shifted away from what has traditionally driven the creativity and scientific breakthroughs that are essential to maintain the needed productivity in the physical realm. It has shifted into cyberspace.

From a metaphysical standpoint, mankind has made virtually no progress in the last hundred years, especially not in the last 50 years, apart from a few minute exceptions in the world of electronics. Not a single fundamentally new energy resource has been developed in the last fifty years, although this is clearly within reach and is desperately needed as the whole economic platform is depended on high rates of energy production. Nor have any new types of mineral resources been developed that match the growing requirements of an expanding population, although these are likewise but a technological step away. We still live like a gatherer society in this respect. No new approaches to agricultural production have been developed, either, although the possibilities are endless. No major water resource development has taken place, although the need is great and the resources exist aplenty. Mankind has wasted its attention on wars instead of developing the processes it requires for living. It is as if mankind has switched itself off. It has fallen into the deep sleep of feudalism that allows no awakening, no development, no scientific and technological progress, nor anything else except that which lines a few pockets with gold.

It has been said that Adolf Hitler was the century's foremost fascist. This is not true. Mankind as a whole is far deeper entrenched into the game the Adolf Hitler ever was. It has totally committed itself to shut down its future, globally, which is something that Hitler may never have dreamed of as being possible.

Mankind has dabbled with nuclear energy for a while, even developed a system with a near infinite potential in affordable energy production and resources at hand that are sufficient to last for 200 million centuries, or however long the solar system will remain inhabitable. Mankind has even built for itself demonstration facilities to prove the practicality of such a system and has experienced its potential, and then...., suddenly, progress is stopped. Suddenly, utopia is brought onto the scene to replace rationality. It is brought into the financial markets in the forms of fictitious gains that have nothing to do with the platform on which mankind earns its living. The real platform, then, suddenly, becomes neglected and decays, while the utopia that grows into a great bubble gets all the attention, all the support, and delivers nothing but empty dreams.

This dreaming has become most dramatic since the beginning of the 1980s. In the U.S., for instance, financial mutual funds have increased in numbers nearly ten-fold since 1980, while their assets, collectively, have increased more than 30 fold.

Ironically, the size of the stock market itself is trivial, compared to the speculation it supports. Still, this is where the people's hopes for their future are based. What insanity! The nation's debt is already three times larger than the stockmarket, and the financial derivatives market is nearly ten times larger than the debt, while the value added production of the nation's industry amounts to but a pitiful fraction of all this, in the order of a tiny fraction of 1%, yet that is where the society's physical support comes from.

A remarkable 'correction' occurred in 1929 in this interrelationship between hope and reality, when the stock market suddenly lost 88% of its book value. It took the market 25 years to recover from this single drop. It took until 1954 for the stockmarket to get back to the break even point with its 1929 value, and 14 more years after that to get back to the same ratio to the GDP that it had when it crashed. Today, we have reached that same ratio once more.

The physical economy by which mankind lives, is in real terms much more benign in returning profit to society than the fictitious markets are, and so it should be. The fictitious markets are a part of the feudal system that is focused on looting rather development. They destroy the wealth creating capability of society. The physical economy, in contrast is a component of the infinite system.

The physical economy would be far more advanced than it is today had it not been put severely under pressure by the feudal system, for decades and centuries. The feudal system that demands a kings ransom for investment funds cannot support the scale of investment that is necessary to develop the new energy, mineral, and farming resources that are required for humanity to maintain itself in the near future. Mankind is already in a severe deficit position in its achieved development compared to what would be normal for an infinite development system.

Naturally, far greater investment resources are required within the infinite system of economy, than even the huge resources that currently flow in the financial markets for speculation, which don't produce anything.

In order to address the world's current needs, and the requirement for the near future, the presently existing development deficit needs to be overcome as quickly as possible. The needed development resources for this recovery can only be provided through a decisive commitment to the principle of the nation-state. It cannot come through feudalism. The feudalist game must be called off if mankind intends to survive. Mankind has no choice here. The requirement is dictated by fundamental principles.

The feudal oligarchy's answer is to forget the future, to stop all meaningful development on the planet, to let the population starve, get sick, and die back to a low level of population density and civilization for which no new resources need to be developed. In such a case the oligarchy would reign supreme over all, for eternity. Even right now, this oligarchy has the upper hand, and its game is to let humanity die.

The ideology that this oligarchy embraces, such as deindustrialization, shutting down development, scaling back resources, enforcing disinvestment in agriculture and infrastructures, creating depopulation through poverty and the escalation of diseases, are all in the forefront of implementation, and are widely accepted by mankind as a supposed necessity. One can hear the key-phrases spoken everywhere; "There are too many people on the planet... We are raping the land... We are destroying the earth...."

The only growth industry that is encouraged under the new ideology is the financial aggregates industry that produces nothing except illusions, debt, cyclical crashes, and looting profits for a tiny minority, while it drains the physical economy that still exists towards the utopia of 'depopulation.'

In the face of the potentially most devastating disintegration of the world-financial system, the devolution into a New Dark Age may gain its biggest boost soon, that could set mankind back 500 years in terms of normal development, if not forever. The sad part is that this is forced upon mankind in such a manner that the underlying insanity has become totally accepted without hardly anyone realizing what it is that has been accepted. Mankind, literally, has made a blind date with the potentially greatest disaster in its entire history.

The great social and economic crisis that mankind is facing, which may be the most horrendous in its history, is fundamentally little more than a crisis in self-perception translated into political philosophy. It is a crisis in separating national policy from the fundamental principles of mankind's economic existence which is totally metaphysical in nature.

A refocusing onto the metaphysical basis of society's existence offers the only hope mankind has to restore equity into its value system by which society is able to adopt the infinite economic model and survive. Without this, the currently impending disintegration of the world-financial system will unfold merely as an opening note of an overture of regression that will take humanity back to the dark ages from which the Golden Renaissance once saved humanity. At this point, the potentially brightest era in human existence comes to a close before it even begins. Whether mankind survives the disease vector that corresponds to such a vast biological collapse cannot be determined. We face a potential onslaught similar in nature, but much larger in scale and mortality, than the Black Death plague. Some may survive such a biological holocaust.

The fallacy of separating physics from metaphysics.

Since the first man shaped a stone into a tool some 2.5 million years ago, the human intellect has raised the physical platform for living to a constantly higher state of civilization. By this principle all true wealth is created. By applying intelligence to raise the physical platform, mankind follows a separate path than the animal world. This path, however, requires that mankind does judge itself accordingly. No other species on the planet, than man, is able to create physical resources that do not exist naturally. The creative, productive intellect of man is the foundation of man's civilization. It has its manifest in the physical sphere. Here, the proofs of the metaphysical potential unfold. Here, as always, the proof of the pudding is in the eating.

In other words, human civilization must be measured in terms of the ingenuity and efficiency in the production of physical goods by which human life is sustained on this planet, and is protected and culturally enriched by a purposefully created orderly environment. In this sense, civilization is the manifest of wealth created by human labor that raises the entire platform of living. 99.999% of today's humanity exists by this wealth. Without the metaphysical capability of man, a capability that no other species on the planet has, the human population on this planet would number no more than a million. People would exist under poor living conditions with a short life-span.

The mere fact that 5,500 times as many people support themselves on this planet, today, than the earth had been able to support in the pre-stone-age period before the age of intelligence, is a testament of the wealth-producing capacity of the human mind that raises the physical platform through new discoveries, creativity, and technological productivity. This capacity is manifest in food production, quality of housing, education, energy use. The earth does not provide this kind of living for man. Far from it. The fruits of nature are small, scarce, and primitive.

Life, itself, and its nature are in no way small or poor. The natural world is extremely rich in itself (which includes the human potential), although it does not offer its riches on a platter. The riches of life are found through discoveries. In the discovery of fundamental principles lies the key to new resources, and the security for life.

In agriculture a small new revolution is afoot that aims to develop the inner resources of the natural system as a means for overcoming the developing deficits that the chemical intensive industrial agriculture is experiencing. Except, far too little is done. The fact is, mankind has barely begun to make a decent effort in the arena of exploring the riches that exist and the potentials for productive development. We still live on the main crops that were developed in ancient ages, of grains, rice, and potatoes, and we still grow these in the open fields. We literally haven't bothered to put our money where our mouth is. We haven't even begun to explore the possibility of large scale indoor food production, or to make the desserts productive. We rather let people die of starvation than to stir our stumps to make even a minimal effort.

For millions of years mankind's growth has been limited by the physical platform as its mental capacities had been poorly developed, much less understood, by which its potential remained totally underutilized. For 2.5 million years mankind's numbers had remained stable in the shape of an animal type herd, limited by poverty and a lack in understanding that imposed additional physical limits. The resulting platform has been infinitely small, compared to today's platform that feeds 5.5 billion people. Man has learned to create his own physical platform, not by dominating nature, but by exploring the world and utilizing its strength, and developing it. On this basis mankind has created a platform that does not exist naturally but which has a foundation in the nature of life and its reality that is infinitely rich. The history of mankind has been one of **positive development,** of exploration, of stepping beyond the limits of ignorance.

On this platform mankind still exists today. This platform must be maintained and be constantly advanced. It is an intelligently created foundation for living, the product of the mind manifest in physical form. Withdraw this foundation and civilization collapses accordingly, together with the number of people and the quality of life, to whatever level the reduced physical platform can afford. It is not sufficient, therefore, to create merely renewable resources, because life is dynamically expansive. The focus must be on expanding and self-developing resources, and a shift to an ever greater quality of life.

It has also been observed that the population growth tends to level off with an increasing quality of life, which is the result of positive development. To limit population growth by the brute force of increasing poverty is a dangerous game of roulette that can collapse the whole system. The feudal financial and economic systems imposes such a game, even as its own game is currently collapsing.

The metaphysical foundation of human living cannot be replaced with a 'metamythical' foundation, no matter how hard this is tried. It may be possible for legislators to enact statutory regulations that contravene all fundamental principles, which the legislators wrongfully call laws and demand people to live by as though the were laws, but it is not possible to built a civilization on this platform.

It is not possible to live outside the sphere of reality and its laws. It is not possible, for instance, for society to profit by contravening these laws, nor is it possible for mankind not to prosper when these laws are applied. The very idea behind law-enforcement is irrational. Enforcement may have some meaning in respect to faulty regulations under which penalties are applied to create results as no natural principle supports them. Fundamental law, however, is self-enforcing, like the law of gravity. No one can escape from it. It benefits all. Whoever stands on the pinnacle of a citadel and pretends that the law of gravity does not exist or does not apply, will quickly find out that it does exist as he jumps.

Today, mankind stands at this pinnacle with the same pretension in terms of its chosen model for financial and economic policy.

Mankind has accepted the myth that deindustrialization raises the status of civilization by lowering the physical platform for human living. The contradiction should be self-evident. Mankind has further accepted the myth that slavery-based economies, such as those raised by the free-trade doctrine, enrich the physical platform of human existence. Erroneous dogmas, however, cannot combine self-evident impossibilities with the wished for experiences. The recurring crashes in the financial markets are of this sort.

Mankind has also accepted the myth that wealth can be created outside the metaphysical sphere, through non-productive processes. For instance, mankind believes that wealth can be generated by trading financial aggregates rather than by physical production. It is believed that it is possible to mark up profits many times in excess of the profits of the physical productivity by which society raises its status of living. This impossibility in real terms, is possible only in the make-believe environment of mutually agreed upon pretending. The Venetian financiers of old pulled 40% in profits out of a physical economy that generated no more than a 4% gain. By this relocation of wealth, rather than the creation of wealth, the economies were looted into a collapse by the Venetians, whose looted profits became largely meaningless, too.

Mankind still believes it to be possible to create profits without producing. The whole world now believes in this myth. Mankind believes this myth so deeply that vast segments of people of the United States of America have devoted 90% of their savings acquiring stock in companies that pay no dividends at all, which are thereby worthless for all practical purposes except for trading - and traded they are! This game of creating make-believe value, where there is no value, is possible only in the environment of mutually agreed upon pretending. It exists wholly apart from the metaphysical basis of human existence, which basis it denies and hinders from being utilized and developed.

With the further introduction of financial derivatives into arena of financial schemes, the 'game' becomes evermore removed from anything real. The fictitious profits appear real, and have become huge and the potential exciting. Indeed, the game works wonders in the sphere of mutually agreed upon pretending where the game is played. The 'investors' of the world stand at the pinnacle of the citadel, indeed, shouting to the people below: Look at us, isn't it marvelous what we can do, we can fly!

As always, there are self-evident clashes with reality. Whenever the metaphysical principles are ignored, whether unwittingly or through regressive 'education,' the result will always be a clash with reality, or a 'crash' in the markets. The great stock-market crash of 1929 was but one example.

It is interesting to note how far the game of make-believe has become separated from reality, for the world is in a far worse shape today than it was in 1929, and the 1929 crash was quite a catastrophe. Their catastrophe may seem remote today, and hard to imagine, but people did jump out of windows in 1929. The collapse was so deep and devastating, it was literally unbearable. Once wealthy tycoons became beggars and jumped, other sold tooth paste or apples on the street corners. The greatest depression in the nation's history followed that lasted for years and years.

In terms of today's crash potential, the 1929 crash was a baby one. The 1987 crash was already more volatile. The 1987 crash came within a hair's breadth of collapsing the entire financial structure of the U.S.. The sheer volume of the collapse was such that several of the major brokerage houses could no longer meet minimal capital levels as required by the stock exchanges. A few were actually bankrupted, which were bailed out afterwards. This touch and go situation may not be repeated again.

Neither will the 1929 scenario be repeated again. In those days the U.S. was strong, its financial scene calm. Off-balance-book gambling hadn't hit the financial industries yet. The $500 trillion annual financial turnover for gambling lay still far in the future. In the days of the 1929 crash speculators had leveraged their 'investment' by a factor of ten, at the very most. Even this was deemed excessive. It was deemed so excessive that after the crash, speculative leveraging was limited by law to a ratio of two to one. The bitterly learned lessons of the depression years brought with them also a flood of safeguards to protect investors, "so that this will never happen again."

Today, mankind finds itself not only in the midst of the biggest gambling spree of all times, but it also 'liberated' itself from the safeguards that had been created to protect society from such insanities. With today's trading in options, indexes, index futures, and a long list of other derivatives, 'investors' can 'borrow' their investments at a fifty to one leverage, even thousand to one, in some cases, and more.

In today's game, however, the individual 'investors' are not alone in being exposed. The entire banking system is exposed. The banks have become addicted to the game of leveraged 'investments' in derivatives at the tune of upwards to 460 times their equity, and up to twenty times the assets they control. And even this appears to be not enough for some. Enormous pressure is brought upon the government to repeal the Glass Seagall Act that was created in response to the 1929 crash, which in those days had been made worse by the bank's direct involvement in the stockmarket. The banks played their customer's deposits on the markets to generate profits, and had lost fortunes. The same happens again, through the banks' addiction to financial derivatives gambling.

The Glass Segall Act had created, what is called the "Chinese Wall" effect, separating the banking system from the stock markets. This wall is about to crumble officially, even as it has already crumbled through the derivatives game.

The chairman of the Federal Reserve supports the insanity of repealing the last protection the public has against irresponsibility in the nation's banking system. Those who warn of the consequences are discreetly silenced.

By all appearances, the banks run the banking system exclusively for their own profiteering, with no regard for the economic well-being of the nation that the banking industry is intended to serve. The banking system has become the biggest casino operation on the planet, and aims to get bigger, still. The day's are long gone when savings deposits helped fuel the economy of the nation. This may have been true up to the 1970s. Today, the opposite is true. Bank deposits have become a portal for money to be drawn out of the productive sphere of the economy, to fuel the financial aggregates games.

In some of the games were the banks play with the depositor's money, the banks win decisively: such as the derivatives game that wiped out Gibsons

Greetings, or the Orange County treasury in rigged deals which earned the banks huge profits. Some of the games the banks also loose, though rarely, like that which killed the Barings Bank which became so thoroughly destroyed by a single bad trade that no financial rescue was feasible. Other banks have died more quietly or were deeply shaken by their losses. The losses, however, are minute, since the banks control the game and the outcome is predictable for as long as the 'markets' blossom. A sudden reversal, as in a crash, will almost certainly turn the markets against them. With today's huge leverage, such a reversal could wipe the entire banking industry of the map, with losses far greater in proportion than that of the Barings Bank that simply could not be rescued from the scrap heap that it had put itself on.

The deregulation mania that has been thrust upon society by devious operatives has demanded deep changes throughout the entire financial sphere, not just the banking system. It has made the industry self-policing, which equates to a free licence to loot the public by any means possible. In other words, the most scrupulous are now controlling the game with total freedom for maximizing their profits in any way the see fit. With the banking system now also controlling their own brokerage houses, the public's broker may no longer just facilitate trades, but may in fact be an adversary to be reckoned with. It is said that there exists evidence on tape in which banking officials brag about "nailing" their customers, and about how they "roped" their clients into deals and then "raped" them out of a lot of money. This is certainly possible under today's setup in which the industry is given a fee hand to promote its interest.

The financial deregulation has had already devastating effects, without a crash even occurring. It has created a departure from reason. Ten years ago the stock markets traded 100 million shares a day. This figure has now risen to close to a billion shares traded a day. In 1980 futures trading amounted to 5.5 trillion dollars in the U.S., by 1990 this had risen to 152.7 trillion - a 27 fold increase, and a 1000 fold increase since 1956. The loss of reason has translated itself into increased vulnerability with a devastating potential. In real terms, the financial games have no longer anything to do with investing in economic processes. The age of investment has ended. A speculative orgy has begun. The NASDAQ exchange, which offers the most speculative, the most leveraged, and the most bizarrely priced market on the planet, has become the darling of the financial world. More shares are traded on the NASDAQ today than on all the other exchanges combined. The NASDAQ's average trading volume is in excess of 500 million shares per day. The 1929s were clam on the financial front compared to what is mounting up today when seen in perspective.

Another thing that was absent at the 1929 crash, that looms in the background today, is the explosive debt burden that far exceeds in size and demands the wealth producing capacity of the economy. Between 1970 and 1990, the total U.S. debt has increased seven fold. Today, it stands at over 16 trillion dollars - more than half a million dollars per worker of the productive economy.

The world is facing a crisis of historic proportions. Nothing close to what is mounting up today has ever occurred in the history of mankind. There is not just one storm front on the horizon, there are a dozen of them, each with the potential to trigger a total collapse of the financial system, world wide. What such a collapse means in terms of impact on individual living may be judged by the catastrophe that would occur if just 20% of the worlds banks, stocks, bonds, industries, etc., went under, which could easily reach as high as 100% in the more volatile areas, such as banking, derivatives, stocks, and bonds. Mexico stands as a grim reminder of what a preferred client of the Wall Street houses looks like after the game gets into full swing. It offers a look into the future. In a few short steps Wall Street and Co. has set Mexico back 100 years in its development, with the corresponding consequences on the life of its people. The nation is in the deepest crisis in its entire existence, with the crisis getting worse by the minute. There is great suffering in Mexico, and not superficially. Wall Street's tricksters have wiped out the economy, and they are now feeding on the spoils. The country's choices properties are now sold in foreign lands at auction for discount prices that border on plain robbery, and in the background of this demise of a nation hundreds of thousands of children are starving to death or are dying from malnutrition related diseases. These horror stories are real.

Mexico's pain should be judged as unbearable, though the global crash has not even occurred. Officially, the country is said to be recovering and showing strength. The reality is that the country was lucky to have been able to borrow two billion dollars on the Eurobond market with which to meet its $750 million dollar interest payment, in response to which it got an extension on its $22 billion principle that its owes to the U.S.. The amazing thing is, that these paltry sums that amount to no more that a single hour's volume of a single day's 'trading' on the financial markets of the U.S., are still large enough to have such an enormous impact on an entire nation. This brings into perspective the enormity of the scope of the games that are being played, and are being encouraged by the governments that need the taxes derived from the incomes of these games. This also brings into perspective the vast differential between the physical reality - the sphere in which people live, work, eat, and support their existence - and the financial 'mysterium' that has been created in a make-belief world which cannot possibly be reconciled with the real world.

The case of Mexico should be regarded as but a minor glitch, though people are dying from the result by the hundreds of thousands. It cannot be considered as anything more than a glitch, compared to the potential global crash that the world is racing towards. Few people, if any, have the capacity to put $500 trillion speculative games into the context with the reality of life at the grass-roots level of the nation where unemployment has reached record highs, homelessness is appalling, and poverty and crime have both become a national disgrace. We have a case here where life, itself, is depressed to the breaking point, and insanity is evermore accelerating.

Now, if this presently gross physical depression is the normal stage of affairs, at a time when all the essential aspects of society are still functioning to some degree, no one can image what ensues when the entire financial system on which the economies are still founded, evaporates world-wide in a giant crash. It will make the 1929 era appear like paradise in comparison.

And this coming crash is a certainty. Only the timing is still uncertain. The differential between the physical economy and the financial insanity can no longer be reconciled by any means. From that moment on at which the financial system has separated itself from the physical economy, the foundation for its doom has been laid.

The world-financial system will die also because of a number of other factors.

One of these factors is the global debt crisis. The U.S. nation carries a $16 trillion dollar debt with a carrying charge of a trillion dollars per year. This system has no hope of surviving since it imposes a claim which is 20 times larger than the nation's profits from physical production. While the unsatisfied claims are being rolled over into new debt, it is self-evident that the process cannot continue for long as the entire debt-structure becomes increasingly meaningless. This discontinuity is even more likely to occur in consequence of the current attempts, world-wide, to increase the debt-service collection through fiscal austerity measures, which have a destructive effect on the physical economy, thereby widening the gap between claims and payable resources. A crash occurs when the entire debt structure becomes universally understood as being meaningless, when 'investments' into debt are understood as worthless, when the trading of the debt stops and defaults sweep the field.

The occurrence of this default is currently accelerated by the idea that a nation or a business can balance its budget by cutting back on expenditures. It is said that all household budgets are balanced this way. Except, is this true? The fact is, this is the worst option a household can choose. Cutting expenditures (apart from waste) deteriorates the earnings potential. A hungry, sick, and impoverished person cannot work, and so the budget ends up in worse shape as the result of cutting back. The proper course is to increase education, individual's skills, strengthen health, improve personal appearance and whatever else is necessary in order for the wage earner to become more gainfully employed. While the success of this approach depends on a functioning economy, the principle remains valid in every situation. It applies not just to households, but to nations as well. Spending cuts that destroy the productive capacity of a business or nation, destroys the earnings capacity and makes the deficits worse.

Reality bears this out. The last five years of escalating speculation in the markets have been the worst in history in terms of bankruptcies, unemployment, economic collapse, and sky-rocketing debt. Where the budget focuses on austerity, it should focus on development, and on scientific and technological progress. The success of this process, of course depends on the creation of supportive policies, unlike the free-trade policies which destroy any hope for development.

Since the budget cutting mania is escalating universally, it may very well be the trigger that brings the house down as the economic system grinds to a halt under austerity impositions. Collapse is an unavoidable characteristic of the fictitious aggregates system. Once defaults disrupt trading in one sector, the trading collapses throughout all sectors. Without trading, the value of the financial instruments evaporates. A share of a company that pays no dividends is worthless once people stop offering money for it. This rule also applies to debt, and to every other aspect of the fictitious financial system.

This type of "mud-slide" has actually been going of for some time already. The Carter-Volker interest rate shock that set off the spiralling increase in financial aggregates, has already killed 771 banks of the Savings Loan system. Government regulation had set up a low interest rate structure for home construction loans, to be financed through the Sthrift banks. The banks had no choice but to fail. Their loans where in a low interest rate sphere, while the 'deregulated' deposits demanded returns that reflected the rising markets which the Fed drove up into the 22% range. It is impossible to maintain a long-term low interest rate loans portfolio while the government offers depositors rates of return three times higher than the loan rates it had imposed under law.

A few banks survived this crushing betrayal. Some survived through a massive, in some cases illegal, rush of secondary investments into speculative ventures. Most of the affected banks, however, simply died. The fact is, whenever public policy and reality become divorced from each other, economic collapses occur. The fact is, in this single case the Federal Reserve system's private manipulators, at their pleasure, caused the destruction of the entire thrift banking system. This single policy move by one man has costed the nation and its government more in bail-out money than the entire cost of the Vietnam War, and many times more than the total cost of nation's space program from which all of humanity has benefitted.

Another factor that may trigger the coming crash is the emerging new oil-shock and world-food crisis. King Fahd of Saudi Arabia, America's best ally in the Arab world, has suffered a crippling stroke and passed on the reigns to his half-brother Prince Adbullah, the radical nationalist who had engineered the first Arab oil embargo. Should there be a repeat, which could easily be staged centered on the Arab world's hatred for the West, the impact will be much worse. The U.S. is presently importing twice as much oil than it did in 1973. Please note Appendix 10. In 1973 the U.S. imported 25% of its energy needs, today it imports 50%. If the Saudis were to turn the faucet down, say 50%, the shortage would send prices through the roof and earn them actually more income, worthless as it would be.

A partial oil embargo is by no means unlikely. The U.S. is in a vulnerable position. It lies open to blackmail, as never before. It has virtually no stockpiles with which to weather a storm, and all its easily extractable oil is gone. It has an estimated 23 billion barrel reserve in the ground, enough to last for ten years. Some of this is in sensitive ecological regions, in deep waters and in permafrost where the ecological movements have made exploration and production nearly impossible. Also, some of the reserves cannot be extracted economically unless prices double. The Middle East, in contrast has 662.9 billion barrels in reserves (28 times of the U.S. reserves), all of which is inexpensively producible. It has enough in the ground to last for 100 years at the present level of production. The Middle East, literally controls the energy use of the world, and thereby mankind's economic well-being, including that of the U.S..

Without a large scale crash program in nuclear energy development, the U.S.'s national political independence is history. Without it, the U.S. is a beggar at the mercy of the most brutal economic and political blackmail. Tragically, the environmental movement is doing its utmost to assure that this vital energy development that might save the nation, will not be accomplished. Naturally, the environmental movements which prevent this development are largely controlled and financed by the British Empire and its agencies which together form the world headquarter of feudalism and underdevelopment ideologies.

In today's climate of astronomical financial inflation and a collapsing physical economy, the onset of another oil shock may very well crush not only the U.S., but also crash the whole world-financial system and the global physical economy. Before 1973, when the oil-shock was unleashed, governmental deficits where virtually non-existent. The U.S. and its economy had little debt and a strong income. Her corporations were the biggest and the strongest in the world. Her banks and financial markets were sound. Non-the-less, the Arab oil embargo brought the nation to its knees, simply because it had failed to protect itself in the most vital of its economic foundations, its energy supply. Thus, a tiny country of 20 million people was able to dictate terms to the economic giant of the world. It's conditions unleashed a financial phase-shift.

Now the U.S. is the biggest debtor on the planet. Its citizens, its businesses, and its governments alike, owe vast sums. The nation is vulnerable. Its foreign reserves are drawn to zero. Its corporations, too, have no financial cushion left with which to soften the blow of another embargo. The stock and bond markets are vastly separated from reality. Another oil embargo may well be more devastating than a nuclear war. Russia has already lost a greater portion of its industries to financial disintegration under the IMF austerity program, than it had ever lost to Hitler's bombs.

Another key element in the ongoing world-destabilization is the growing food production deficit. This trend is NOT the result of shrinking farmlands and a rise in world population. Most people in the populous nations eat far less than they did in past years, since they can no longer afford to buy food. The growing deficit is the result of a decline of investment into farming and farming infrastructures such as pesticides, irrigation, fertilizer use, and low cost production methods that are said to be destructive to the environment, to the soil, and to water systems. The required investment to increase food production in an intelligent manner, simply is not being made. To the contrary. A dramatic disinvestment in food production has occurred that has large scale consequences that are not instantly reversible, not that anyone wants to change course at this time and invest in farming again.

Together with a shrinking world-food supply and a constantly weakening population, especially in the

Third World nations, the economic collapse has set the stage for the alarming comeback of a whole roster of diseases that were once considered wiped out, together with the emergence of new viruses such as the HIV and the Ebola virus. This renewed onslaught of diseases is quite dramatic in literally all corners of the globe, and it occurs at the precise moment when health care and viral research institutions are being shut down at an alarming rate under budgetary pressures. A major epidemic could sweep across the world and cause massive damage on the population. This, all by itself, could cause a financial crash to occur.

There is only one thing that can be said with certainty in this uncertain time, namely that the crash cannot be avoided. The effect of the crisis can be dampened to a large extend by an intelligent response to the crisis before the crash occurs, but, all-in-all, the system as it stands today cannot be saved. Only humanity can be saved, if the feudal system is into bankruptcy before the crash occurs. Failing this, humanity and its civilization will crash as well. It cannot save itself on any other platform. The game is coming to an end.

The potential crash that humanity is facing is the lawful, natural result, of a negative growth system that has run its course.

Chapter 12: The Dynamics of Negative and Positive Growth Systems

In order to better understand the dynamics of the negative growth system, let us first explore the dynamics of the positive growth system. The positive growth system is best illustrated by the dynamics of the unfolding of life. The positive growth system is therefore a natural system.

The positive growth system: The dynamics of life.

A gardener puts a seed into the ground and in due time there emerges a plant in tender shades of green, forming a bud, blossom, and fruit. In its growth it creates color, shapes, substance - none of which exist in the ground. It unfolds these out of its own resources. It grows, and as it ripens, its fruit can eventually be harvested to sustain life elsewhere, or become seed again to create new plants. And so, life expands in all possible dimensions.

Mankind is a part of this dynamic process. The human society represents the most advanced stage of it. Here, the dynamics of life come to light in a type of development where the application of intelligence has enabled discoveries of fundamental principles and have paved the way to the stars and the building of civilizations. Here, too, life is a strongly dynamic thing. It becomes manifest in constant development, in unfolding intelligence, in creating and discovering, and in building. Civilization is a complex and dynamic thing of life. The entire human sphere is a living structure that has unfolded out its own rich inner resources. It's strength is in understanding, and in utilizing the nature of life and its expression that the human sphere is a part of.

Since mankind's development began, mankind has followed a pattern of constant growth, a development that has taken us far beyond what the dust of the earth contains, or 'nature' could provide.

Mankind lives by the principles of live, and so does anything that unfolds and develops. There is no such thing as static life, or zero growth, or negative unfolding in real terms. 'Static life' is a contradiction in language and impossible in reality, and so is the modern economic equivalent, the much promoted concept of a 'zero growth' doctrine that an oligarchic elite is trying to impose on mankind.

A 'zero growth' state cannot be achieved in real live, nor can it be achieved in the economy by which mankind lives, which is itself a thing of life. If a plant is starved into a 'zero growth' state, it dies. Life grows and unfolds, or ceases to be. The 2.5 million years of primitive existence during which the human population levels were quite stable, were not a period of zero growth. They were a period of a murderous conflict in which the dynamics of the unfolding of life were continuously crushed by the limits of the poverty within the primitive system. Life can't attain a 'zero growth' state at any level.

The impositions of a 'zero growth' economy manifests itself as disintegration. Human society is a living structure in all its aspects and cannot be forced into a 'zero growth' process that is contrary to the dynamics of life without enforcing the global collapse of the system. This holds true physically, economically, scientifically, and spiritually. Whatever is connected with life must grow, must develop, or it collapses. Has anyone ever seen a flower in a state of zero growth, or even growing smaller as it unfolds? Life exist only in the form of constant development. Apart from this positive growth or positive development, there is but death and oblivion. Not even animal societies exist in a zero growth state. They live in an environment of conflict where the development of life is constantly being poised against death, either through starvation that reflects the poverty of the limits of the ground, or through predation, or through the natural vulnerability of life at low stages of intelligence where effective protection from physical hazards is not possible.

The nature of life is growth. The animal kingdom is in constant association with death, as the mental resources for infinite development have not unfolded at the animal stage of existence. Mankind, however, has achieved this capability for infinite development. The fact that the planet is currently inhabited by 5,500 times as many people than the planet could support in an animal sphere of existence, is proof of this capability. The human system is sustained not by the resources of the dust of the ground, as the animal world is sustained, but by scientific and technological development.

Currently, no perceivable limits exists that would prohibit this development from continuing, which has the potential to go on literally to infinity. There exist no true limits in energy resources, in mineral resources, in farming resources. Whatever limits are paraded in front of the public's eye are imaginary or are based on political doctrines designed for maintaining exploiting empires.

Two major doctrines of this nature are currently promoted. One doctrine was mentioned earlier. It is that which is currently used to promote deindustrialization. Its focus is centered on promoting the idea of dwindling resources. The focus is being sustained by artificially generated proof that is found in the result of a world-wide destruction of the scientific, technological, and industrial capabilities, through which normally the new and ever greater resources are brought on line.

The second major doctrine designed to halt the development of human life on this planet, is the "carrying capacity" theory that aims at reducing the world-population by 60-90% in two generations. The project has the appearance of reflecting a major insanity, but it is non-the-less promoted by the world's most powerful institutions and individuals. Both these counter-development doctrines employ what may be called a 'negative growth' system of economy, with which to achieve these goals.

The nature of negative growth systems.

Logically, **negative development,** or **negative growth** should be an impossibility, for all true development is positive, unfolding according to the dynamic pattern of life which manifest positive growth. Unfortunately, in a world steeped in mythologies of all sorts, **'negative development'** is possible, resulting from what may be termed **'negative growth'** systems. Several of these systems have been created. On the surface, they all present the dynamic patterns of growth, but this growth, by its nature, is inherently destructive.

These **'negative growth'** systems have distinct faces, but one aspect unites them. On the surface they all appear to be benign. The mythologies that generate the illusion of positive growth, therefore, makes their true nature hard to detect. Still, one needs to become aware of them so as not to fall victim to the effect which is the effect of 'negative development.'

Negative development can be understood as a development based on faulty assumptions. It is a development which generates a certain type of growth which is destructive to life. This 'negative' growth is quite different in nature from the growth of a liability that an accountant might accumulate in terms of unpaid bills, which can certainly be paid to settle accounts. Negative growth is typified by a dynamic growth that is fundamentally suicidal, like a cancerous growth in a body, or like the growth of certain types of financial aggregates as we find them in today's world financial system. Here, as was noted earlier, we find an enormous growth in capital aggregation that has no relationship to the physical reality, but which is ultimately destructive to the physical economy that it pretends to serve.

For example, if one owns a share in a corporation that is bought at fair value, then, there there exists a physical equality between the capital value of the share and the physical value it represents. If the share is subsequently sold at an increase, while the value of the company remains the same, that increase in the value of the share is a fictitious capital value that has no physical equivalent, either in terms of any value to the society, or in terms of value to the owner of the share. However, this increase, which is a fictitious capital value, is financed with real capital by the purchaser. The fictitious capital growth, therefore, while it registers real growth, is destructive, for the process of acquiring fictitious capital value draws real capital away from the physical economy into fictitious assets that have neither real value in themselves nor afford any tangible profit for the advance of society. The result is, that the productive development of the society stagnates as capital resources are drawn out of the productive economy into the fictitious markets. At the same time the fictitious markets grow inflationary and become thereby volatile to disruption like a highly inflated air filled balloon.

If in turn, the fictitious capital value (the increase that has no physical equivalent) is traded through a financial system that exists exclusively for the purpose of trading fictitious aggregates, then, the whole structure involved becomes fictitious, though it grows in leaps and bounds, while it is constantly increasing its toll on the physical economy. Soon, its base expands into a conglomeration in which the entire aggregate of the fictitious system becomes leveraged upon ever smaller relationships to anything real or of actual value. The most powerful markets, today, trade nothing at all that is real, but trade pure speculation.

At some point, when the growing bubble has become sufficiently volatile, the leveraging begins to act in reverse. Typically, the reverse action is triggered when the fictitious aggregates are required to cover loans that created them, or when situations arise through which it becomes apparent that no value, or very little value, does actually exist in real terms. When this reversal sets in, the whole development structure tends to collapse due to the tightly interlocked nature within fictitious bubbles. The result is a collapse with powerful, even catastrophic, negative effects. The end result is, that the entire development that has taken place, has in effect been in the negative.

The main mechanism within the system that forestalls the natural reversal into collapse, up to a certain point, is the dynamic growth in the fictitious market that mimics the normal patterns of life. For as long as the fictitious bubble grows, it appears healthy and keeps on growing as people pour money into it. By the same token, for as long as this system can be kept growing artificially, or the appearance of growth can be created, the built in tendency to unleash a reverse leveraging can be contained and be held in check. This principle is exploited in the form of aggressive manipulation of the markets. The central banks control the game by means of interest rate manipulation that enables more or less capital to flow into the fictitious system, by which to spurn its growth, or to prevent it from exploding into thin air.

Growth is the fictitious system's life-line. The fictitious system can be maintained only by drawing ever greater amounts of real capital out of the physical economy with which to drive the trading in the markets to ever greater levels of financial inflation. Without this infusion of cash that creates profit for some, there is no incentive for trading in the fictitious capital markets. Once the cash infusion stops, the trading stops. And as soon as the trading stops, the financial instruments traded, which usually have value only through trading, become suddenly valueless, as fictitious capital aggregates are.

The growth potential of this self-leveraging 'negative growth' system is phenomenal. It is phenomenal, because it is decoupled from the physical economy or anything real. The growth in the fictitious system can be made infinitely attractive to the 'investors' as its profits do not depend on what is physically possible in the productive economy. It unfolds in a dream-world where the imagination is the limit. This is why it is possible to achieve a hyperbolic tendency in the growth of financial aggregates and resulting profits. Appendix 1, Figure 1 illustrates the hyperbolic tendency in the world-derivatives growth.

Naturally, as this growth is progressing, the vulnerability within the system increases in like manner, so that we have also a hyperbolic growth tendency in vulnerability. Eventually, when the growing of the system can no longer be sustained through new inputs into it, the vulnerability becomes paramount, which at this point has reached a precarious state and reverses its leveraging by which the whole thing disintegrates.

The system may be termed a negative growth system, because its growth has an accumulatively destructive, or negative effects. It is a suicidal system. In financial terms, the system first loots the productive economy on which it feeds, and, then, destroys the remainder, when it collapses. It displays a growth pattern that is both real and enormously dynamic in its development, as some 'investors' that draw profits from it can testify. Except, this development, being contrary to life, develops towards a catastrophic termination, rather than towards infinity. Herein lies the main difference.

Some people call such a system a cancerous growth system, for the growth of a cancer is equally destructive to that on which it feeds. It is self-evident from this description that the nature of such a system is totally contrary to the platform that must be established for advancing civilization and for securing human existence on this planet.

An example of the 'negative growth' system.

Today's financial scene illustrates well how the 'negative growth' system works in real life. Let's go back to the hyperbolic growth pattern that was mentioned earlier (Appendix 1, Figure 1) of the world's globally outstanding financial derivatives. If one plots the growth pattern of these values, one finds that the pattern matches the curvature of a hyperbolic horn, such as a trumpet. This curvature is almost flat in the beginning, as Figure 1 shows, but soon rises and increases its upwards trend evermore sharply until it flairs out steeply, like at the wide opening of a trumpet.

Our current position in this growth pattern of the world derivative market, as shown in Appendix 1 is right at the flair-out point that represents the wide opening of the trumpet where a minute increase in distance from the mouth-piece corresponds to large increases in the opening of the horn. The illustration shows that in 1993 the globally outstanding derivatives amounted to roughly 15 trillion dollars. The market had risen to that point over the preceding ten years. However, a single year later, this 15 trillion dollar volume that had mounted up over the span of a decade, suddenly tripled in a single year to the gigantic 45 trillion dollar mark. In 1995, it rose equally as sharply again.*23

Now, at the same ratio at which this growth unfolds, the system's feed capital requirement increases, by which the growth is maintained. The feed capital requirement, therefore, likewise approaches the same flair-out point on the hyperbolic function. The point of disintegration is the point at which the feed capital requirement for keeping the system growing, exceeds the capital resources that can be pulled out of the real economy of the nations. Since the society's capital resource is constantly shrinking, as the productive economy is collapsing, a discontinuity will be reached, at which point the growth of the bubble stops and the bubble implodes under reverse leverage.

The crash of such a system can be predicted with a fair degree of accuracy whenever accurate figures can be obtained. At some point along the flair-out stage, typically when the demands for feeding grow by leaps and bounds, but at which point the available feed capital resources become exhausted, the process goes into reverse. Since the vulnerability within the system has increased in the same proportion, the system's instability will reach a state that which the slightest reverse leverage sets off an avalanche into total disintegration. If the financial avalanche is big enough, which it is when a single market bubble reaches a volume in the $100 trillion range, the entire world financial system gets swept along by the avalanche, especially when the banking system holds a major portion of the disintegrating market.

The nature of any 'negative growth' system is such that it will disintegrate. If the disintegrating system is electronically interlocked with the investors that drive it, as all financial markets today are, the disintegration may happen extremely quickly. The markets may be still surging upwards when the first minor upset occurs, like that which killed the Barings Bank, that sends shockwaves through the system that start a chain reaction. Then, puff, 72hrs later, or in less time than that, the entire system lies in ruin.

Every major financial crash in history has unfolded quickly, and this happened without the high speed communications facilities and computers that we have today. What goes, puff, in such a globally interlocked crash - in a blow-out of systems that trade close to a quadrillion dollars worth of instruments annually - is the total-world financial system - banking, pensions, mortgages, commerce, investment - everything that is connected with money.

The coming crash is likely to be global and total, because the whole financial system is more tightly integrated into the fictitious capital market than it ever has been. In real terms a new era has begun that has been created out of the movements of the 1980s and early 1990s. Appendix 1, Figure 1, shows that when the last big crash occurred in 1987, the infamous Black Monday in October, this new era of insane negative growth that we are in now, had not even begun.

The disintegration point in a negative system is logically near the beginning of the flair-out point of the hyperbolic curve. We are actually somewhat beyond this stage already. In a natural setting the current system would most likely have already crashed. Instead it has been kept alive for intensified looting, by driving more and more capital resources into the markets, artificially, by the mutual funds who borrow against their portfolio to manipulate the markets. Isn't everyone told in the papers and newsletters, and by the bank's brokers: Buy equity, buy equity, buy equity... look at how the funds grow?

The enormous pressure that is put on governments to cut spending, even if the cuts destroy the life of countless people, must be seen in the context of the controllers of the system endeavoring to raise feed capital from around the world with which to feed the dying world-financial system. That such measures do not cure the underlying problem is self-evident. At the very best, they delay the crash, as we have it today, and in delaying the crash the manipulators are making it worse when it finally hits.

One's immediate reaction, most likely, is that the governments won't allow this to happen; that they will resist it. The reality is that the world-financial system is under private control, and that the governments are as much a victim under the private world-system as everyone else is, and have fundamentally no control over it.

What the result will be in human terms, when the system dies, cannot be determined. Catastrophe, may be too mild a term. The impact on humanity depends on the actions taken by society at the moment of collapse, or before. The kind of global disintegration that we face today, of a whole range of interlocked markets blowing up together, has never occurred throughout history by which the possible impact of it might be judged.

It will no longer be a mere stock market crash, what we are facing, such as occurred in 1929 and 1987. The potential has been built up for something much greater than a single market crash. A new term must be used to define it. The term, disintegration, might apply, but will it be just that?

The only thing that is certain, at this stage, is that the disintegration will occur unless the system is taken down orderly in a global bankruptcy reorganization throughout the entire world-financial system. While this is impossible under the feudal system to ever happen, it is easily done within the infinite system of economy, although this is not likely to happen either, since 99.99% of humanity isn't even aware that an infinite system of economics exists.

The moral and spiritual foundation to drive the needs phase shift in thinking has not been developed, either; not in the public's consciousness of the United States of America, nor in the world abroad. The present reaction in high places, according to all evidence, is panic. Most people who are familiar with the current system see no way out of the dilemma. The public is actually better off. The public is told that the system is "crash-proof." If the public knew what sad shape the system is in, it would have crashed the system long ago.

The intend is clearly to save the system at all cost, rather than to save the society from the enormous danger that the collapsing system poses.

It is a fallacy to believe that a 'negative growth' system can be saved, as the controllers of the feudal system insist. It cannot be saved because of its underlying nature as a looting system. It cannot be saved beyond a certain point. This point has evidently been crossed, as the required looting is killing more and more people, which once were the grass roots donor of the loot. Nor can the system be artificially curtailed through strangulation, as is attempted at times. It cannot be forced into a zero-growth state where it may operate forever. The very moment that one begins to curtail the growth of a 'negative growth' system into some kind of equilibrium, a reverse leverage sets in and the disintegration happens immediately. The only way that the society can save itself from the impending collapse of the system, is by taking it down orderly before the collapse kills a lot of people on a global scale.

A negative-growth system is a self-collapsing system.

The mental 'negative growth' system.

There are actually quite number of different variations of the 'negative growth' system operating in the world. The world-financial system is but one of them. The mental equivalent to it, may be termed an **'enlightenment'** oriented system, where the fictitious aggregates are ideologies that grow in leaps and bounds and govern the society's actions without them having any foundation in reality. The resulting erroneous actions, in the end, destroy humanity. This effect, defines these ideologies as a 'negative growth' system.

The growth in this system is driven by a blind zeal that undermines a people's sensitivity to the physical infrastructures for human living. The effect of this type of negative development, in the metal sphere, is that the mentality that is being nurtured by this system, which likewise grows in leaps and bounds when it is professionally promoted, forces a termination of the scientific, technological, and moral development of humanity, which is followed by the devolution of the very support structures on which the physical existence of humanity depends or civilization has been founded.

The growth pattern in this mythological, so-called **'enlightenment'** system is similar to that of a financial bubble. It is built on dreams that are just as hollow and fragile as a soap bubble is, which naturally disintegrates. This mental 'negative growth' system is as destructive to those who are devoted to it, than the financial 'negative-growth' system is. Its is therefore similarly as suicidal in its effect.

The mental form of the 'negative-growth' system is probably the most destructive forms of all the 'negative-growth' systems that have ever been unleashed against mankind. It has itself many faces and is many times more powerful in its destructive effect than war. In fact, wars are created by one of the lesser applications of this system.

In its grosser form, it is a system that grows at the expense of human development, causing devolution in morals, culture, education, science, industry, technology, farming, health-care, transportation, energy production, land use, even political ideology, elevating instead irrationalisms. Its growth is leveraged, of course. The leveraging is derived from the devolution of all rational perception, which it achieves.

The reverse leveraging, however, leads not to a

restoration of reason. The collapse does not trigger a positive growth. It triggers anarchy and chaos.

The reversal of the mental 'negative-growth' system is triggered by a somewhat different process than that which disintegrates the fictitious capital growth system. The disintegration of the so-called **'enlightenment'** system is triggered by the breakdown of the physical support structures for human living that it promotes, such as the breakdown of food production, and energy production, etc.. The disintegration point of the 'enlightenment' system is reached when the fictitious ideologies themselves become meaningless in the face of the catastrophic breakdown of civilization.

The mental 'negative growth' system follows the same hyperbolic pattern of increase that is typical for all such systems. Its increase is measured in the aggregates of destruction, like the destruction of human beings for ideological or eugenicist purposes that Adolf Hitler had pioneered with his genocidal move against the Jewish people.

Another example of the mental type of 'negative growth' system is the poverty based 'depopulation' ideology of modern times, for which economic underdevelopment is spread globally. Under this 'enlightenment' system, at the current rate, close to 100 million people are put to death annually, according to U.N. figures and equivalent figures released by the Canadian Hunger Foundation. These reports indicate that currently 33,000 children under the age of 5 perish each single day from underdevelopment related causes. The death rate for the total population may be extrapolated from this.

The disintegration of this 'negative growth' system likewise takes place shortly after the flair-out point of the hyperbolic growth pattern. One of the early signs of negative leveraging in this type of system is the development of such diseases as AIDS and the numerous new and exotic diseases that come to the surface at an astonishing rate. AIDS, the dreaded effect of the HIV virus, is widely recognized to have evolved out of the background of a collapsing physical environment that is artificially weakened by financial policies. It is believed to have resulted from a viral species-jump, from a species of monkeys to human beings, in the poverty stricken, weakened, populations of Africa. It is not surprising that the HIV virus came out of Africa, because the African populations were among the first, and the most severely targeted regions on the planet, under the population reduction doctrine.

Another major type of negative growth system is the **oligarchic** economic system. The most striking example of this type of system is the old Venetian model of economy, which is entirely centered on looting.

The Venetian negative growth system.

The Venetian model is possibly the best example that can be found to illustrate the nature of the **oligarchic** negative growth system. It is ideal as an example in that it has played itself out over several cycles of collapse. The first cycle was centered on slave trading and financial currency speculation for looting. The economic collapse that it generated led to global financial systems crash in 1345. The destructive effect of this negative growth system was such that the entire population of Europe was physically weakened and depressed to the point that the Black Death plaques, which had developed in China for over a decade at this point, under the ravishes of the Mongol Empire, and had broken out into the European arena, spread with an explosive force that destroyed half the population of the affected nations.

After Europe recovered from the destruction of this particular negative growth system, the development of a positive growth system began that became known as the Golden Renaissance. The looting oligarchic empire of Venice now saw itself threatened with extinction by the forces of the Renaissance. In response to this threat, the Venetian oligarchy determined to destroy the Renaissance, in order to save itself. It accomplished the task by instigating and promoting two separate 'enlightenment' systems that were contrary to each other, known as the Reformation and the Counter-Reformation, through which it created a havoc among the nations of Europe that set the stage for the infamous Thirty Years War. This war was so effectively destructive that in some areas three quarters the population had perished. The economies lay reduced to a shambles and the country side turned into a waste-land.

Still, Venice felt insecure and without a viable base for continued looting. The true reasons will probably never be known, but it transplanted itself around that time into the northern parts of Europe and into England. From there it began in earnest to loot the world under the flag of the British Empire that became the greatest colonial power, slave trader, dope pusher, and financial looter the world had ever seen. 75% of the global slave trade was carried out on British ships.

The fate of empires, however, is to collapse and to disintegrate. An empire is itself a 'negative growth' system. Every empire that has ever set itself up on the face of the planet has collapsed and disintegrated. History teaches us that. Still, history, only records the visible facts. It leaves out the underlying reason. It does not record, for instance, that the fate of empires is the natural result of a 'negative growth' system going into reverse leveraging.

Today, the British Empire is ruling the world through its far-flung ideology impositions, and through its financial and political policy impositions. But in spite of its vast power and influence, its mode of operation reflects the typical pattern of a 'negative growth' system. Its ideologies expand globally, but they are highly destructive. They are policies for deindustrialization and the removal of the most vital support systems for human living. They are also the driving element of the depopulation doctrine. They are the central force (and financial support) of the resource depletion myth that demands depopulation, the ozone depletion myth that promotes depopulation by destroying refrigeration, the global warming myth that promotes depopulation by shutting down the use of fossil fuels, etc. etc.. In short, the oligarchic 'negative growth' system has become a system of war against humanity that aims to hinder normal human development at all costs, so that the feudal system can be maintained.

All these developments, over the last decades, have shown the typical hyperbolic increase in the intensity of the manipulation with which the oligarchy fights its war against humanity. The negative growth within this destructive system may well be nearing the flair-out point of the hyperbolic curve, indicating that a major collapse of the system is near. The poverty, misery, destruction, and death, that this system has spread throughout the globe is becoming increasingly recognizable as being totally without value or merit. Still, the ideology of depopulation is not yet recognized to be as fictitious in its nature as a stock certificate is, of a corporation that has decided never to pay dividends.

The collapse of this 'negative growth' system may coincide with, and may in fact be triggered, by the collapse of one of the other 'negative growth' systems, such as the financial aggregates system. There may be an inter-system leveraging occurring by which all built up 'negative growth' systems disintegrate in a chain reaction that will put an end to a 650 year cycle of history that has held back mankind's self-development.

If one considers the dynamics and the collapse potential of the world's interrelated 'negative growth' systems, it would be most surprising if the upcoming financial crash remains limited to merely the stock-market, as in past times, against which a whole range of immensely powerful systems are now leveraged. A global disintegration of the world-financial system is much more likely to occur. The current world-financial system, being feudalist in nature, interestingly enough, also happens to be one of the foundations of the British and other empires, so that its disintegration fits also into the collapse process of the 'enlightenment' and oligarchic 'negative growth' systems.

A 'negative growth' system may be likened to an airplane. An airplane flies quite well, though it is immensely heavier than air. It flies perfectly until its fuel runs out. Without fuel, it will crash. When this happens before its destination is reached, what rides on the plane will crash with it. As for its destination, the 'negative growth' system has no productive destination that it aims for, except to maintain an illusion, even as it destroys its own resources and supports as it lumbers along.

Every 'negative growth' system creates a bubble that appears wonderful on the surface, but is an illusion throughout. In the case of the airplane, the illusion is that heavy metal flies. This illusion is well understood. It is understood in terms of technology and energy use. The process is relied upon. It is intelligently exploited as a means for transportation. Great care is taken that the bubble is maintained until the plane arrives at the desired destination. Financial bubbles, in contrast, are much less understood. Nor are they benign in their purpose. Those who understand the processes exploit them for their advantage, and of course, take care to keep the bubble afloat until their personal goal is reached, at which point the bubble is allowed to bursts, which may happen soon.

The anatomy of a financial bubble.

All bubbles are created. Bubbles do not occur naturally. The last commercial real estate bubble serves as a good example. It began quietly, it grew, it popped, and it left a big mess behind. Its cycle is complete.

The great real estate bubble began to form when the normal expansion of the productive economy was shut down under the deindustrialization doctrine. What started the bubble, was a puzzle: What to do with the money that would normally flow into industrial expansion and the advancement of the economy?

Japan was especially hard hit, with its booming economy. Japan had consequently set its eyes on the economic upgrading of the Third World nations. This was prevented by a fearful oligarchy who might have seen a new Renaissance in the making. Under the so-called Plaza Agreements of 1985, Japan was persuaded to channel its investments instead into the U.S. markets. The persuasion apparently was easily accomplished, since Japan depended on America's nuclear 'protection' during the Cold War years.

As the productive economy was to be scaled back, real estate came to light as the big opportunity to make the excess money grow at head-spinning rates, and this without having to go through the traditional bother of earning profits by expanding production, which profits are usually very much smaller than what speculation can achieve.

Another flood of funds for the real estate markets was the newly created tide of narco-dollars, which flowed into the system in great bundles. The narco-dollars, too, were looking for a profitable home. In response to this financial inflow the real estate markets exploded. They exploded in the U.S., in Japan, in Europe, creating an enormously huge global bubble. The market had no option but to explode to ever higher values, with the vast inflow of money chasing a limited physical market base. There was only so much commercial real estate in existence that could be bought or be built up, and what didn't exist was created whenever there was the slightest opportunity.

In the process of the resulting competition, prices rose out of sight. With this, the construction boom began, and still prices went higher into the stratosphere. The problem is, that a real estate boom, apart from a temporary boost for the construction industry, adds very little to improve and advance the productive sector of the economy, but adds extra costs so that the boom became a parasite that drained wealth out of the productive sector, the same source of money by which the boom was created in the first place.

Eventually the bubble collapsed when the oversupply that was created became noticeable, by which the monetary inflow into the commercial real estate market could no longer sustain any growth in value. The collapse began at first with a rising tide of profit taking which drove the prices down. With lower prices, a wave of insolvency unfolded that leveraged the collapse even further. The sky high value that had been leveraged up in the real estate market at great expense, that was celebrated as an economic miracle, suddenly became an investor's nightmare. The banks were caught up right in the middle of it all when the values crashed, and so were the big real-estate giants like Canada's Olympia and York. Nearly everyone of the major banks around the world was hit by the collapse of the bubble. Japan's banks suffered loan losses in the order of close to a trillion dollars in the game.

Most banks turned to pure financial speculation in the aftermath, by means of which some recovered their losses. Those who played the derivatives game well survived, but became addicted to it.

Pure financial speculation has the advantage that it has no direct dependency on physical equity against which investments might be measured. When the commercial real estate market collapsed, huge sky scrapers stood empty as they became too expensive to sell or to rent. This can't happen in the pure financial aggregates market where nothing represents anything real, where everything is based on levels, rates, indexes, or amounts of change, etc..

The only problem is, that this 'cure,' to which the banks have become addicted, which saved the banking system from its real estate losses, has created a new and vastly greater bubble of bank gambling in the financial derivatives markets. The result that we face today is a type of insanity in which the effect of one error is cured by committing a greater error.

Thus, a much greater bubble has now replaced the bubble that had burst, and this folly is hailed as progress. The bank loans that went sour during the real estate collapse amounted to only a small portion of the banks' total loan portfolios. The new bubble, however, has built up exposures that are may times greater than the depositors' assets, and immensely greater than the bank's own equity.

In a very real way, the banks are not banks anymore. The days are over when bank deposits were functioning as a means for concentrating capital for economic expansion. In today's world, bank deposits have become deposits into gambling funds. There are exceptions of course, but generally, economic lending has fallen by the wayside, as it must, in a era of deindustrialization.

The unfolding new bubble has fundamentally restructured the banking industry. It has created a new image for it, though the old names remain. In operation, the banking system acts like Ceasar's Palace where money is made from gambling. The depositors lend their money to the game, and are thinly rewarded for it. In the old sense, the banks are not banks anymore as the traditional relationship to the depositors has been altered. The old image is still alive that equates the bank with the Rock of Gibraltar, but in reality the security is paper thin and should be seen as such.

In theory all bank deposits are insured by the various deposit insurance corporations. This system works well in times of individual bank failures. The insurance funds are usually sufficient to cover such exposures, with governments taking on whatever losses remain. This system can't possibly work, however, when the bubble pops, and bubbles don't deflate slowly. Just like a soap bubble, they tend to pop. In technical terms, a systemic crisis erupts. It means that the numerous interlocked contracts that are floated within the financial system cannot be honored. This should not surprise anyone. Not even a magician can pay with money that does not exist. The systemic crisis is a fundamental characteristic that is built into the nature of any bubble economy, in which the values that the system represents, are not real. The banks' contracts with their depositors are paper thin, as these contracts become inherently invalid in a systemic crisis, as do all the other contracts that are tied into the bubble economy.

The great danger to society from the bubble economy is three-fold. One danger is the obvious crisis of the systemic collapse. The other crisis erupts silently in background in terms of human destruction as more and more blood is demanded from the population in an effort to keep the bubble growing at all costs.

This pre-collapse crisis, that has been ongoing for some time, manifests itself as increasing austerity, which we have world wide today, even to the point at which it is killing people, beginning with the elderly and children, and generally all those who are caught up in the physical collapse spiral that is associated with any financial bubble economy.

The third exposure is, that it is very difficult for the average wage earner to protect whatever assets and savings the individual may have. With the banking system having become vulnerable to collapse by its speculative exposures, and stock market values having become highly fictitious, where does a person put the few savings that might exist? Into Gold? Indeed, there is a massive buying of Gold in progress as the big 'investors' are getting out of the fictitious paper markets into something real. Except the precious metals market is likewise overpriced in comparison to the collapsing physical economy, since the ultimate value of the gold is derived from its value as input for commercial production.

There is no safety in bonds either, as they depend on the continuity of the organization that issued them. Even the government's Treasury bonds are exposed to a great volatility, the volatility of the government itself, and its ability to redeem the bonds from incomes out of tax receipts, fees, duties, and services.

The fact is, in a bubble economy, the 'cancer' invades all the healthy structures of the nations and corrupts them with its rampant inflation. There is nothing that remains secure, healthy, and productive. The moment that financial values become separated from the values produced in the physical economy, the spiral of collapse begins. Statistics indicate that the collapse accelerates as the separation between physical and financial aggregates widens, leading to an inevitable disintegration. The disintegration that occurs as the bubble collapses, that causes much of the social damage, is actually but a correction that brings the economic scene back into some realistic relationship to reality, or close to zero.

One can get some glimpses of the depth of the physical collapse that is currently taking place, by observing the world food supply. One sees agricultural production declining because of lack of investment into agriculture, resulting into production losses in some cases of 30%, even 50%, so that many of the nations that were once exporters of food, can no longer sustain their own populations, nor have the funds to import food. Russia and Mexico are prime examples of what is taking place, though in the overall scheme they are but like the tip of an iceberg. In Mexico, one finds fields left unplanted for lack of investment into seeds, energy, and fertilizer, and other fields withering in the sun for lack of irrigation while people are starving. At the same time one sees the farmers' incomes drained away by ever lower price offerings from the cartels, for their products. By this gauging, the little bit of strength that may be left in the farming industry, is being drained into the speculative markets by the profiteers, where the returns are higher, though the losses are often total.

Another phenomenon that unfolds in a bubble economy is a growing hatred of the government, with efforts being made to chop the governments to pieces. Numerous financial newsletters are floating throughout the nations that deride the governments; that complain about governmental debt and high taxes. Unfortunately, hardly a word is said in these newsletters about the origin of the debt, which is the direct result of the explosive growth in speculation.

Now, in order to sustain this growth in speculation which is officially called "a recovery," the governments are required to add to the nation's money supply that is in circulation. The addition to the money supply, however, is charged as debt to the nation. Bubble economies invariably create debt for the governments. The borrowing of funds for bailing out the banking system repeatedly, created evermore debt for the nations.

The bubbles generate debt when they grow, and they add to the debt when they collapse.

And still, there is more debt generated by the bubbles while they last. As the bubbles inflate, the physical economy decays. This decay creates social deficits that must also be funded by the governments, which ultimately adds to the debt. By all these effects, the debt becomes a bubble in itself.

Of course, the financial markets reap a king's ransom in interest charges, called debt services charges. Since these charges all by themselves are greater than the profits in the physical economy, they are refinanced, and thereby turned into more debt. The common tax payers have cause to complain, for it is their sweat that now must pay the bills incurred by all this speculation, and bear the pain that the financial bubble economy imposes.

With the pressures that are now mounting globally, the aim to shut down the governments in the name of decentralization, localization, or tribalization, the last structure that supports the existence of the society becomes eliminated. If this occurs, who, then, catches the debt that the bubble economies impose upon the nations?

It is surprising to note how broad based the disdain of governments has become, the very structure by which society maintains its existence. The cries that demand the shutting down of governments or governmental actions are suicidal, but are growing louder. One wonders who is driving the noise.

It has always been the attitude of the rich feudal aristocracy, throughout the ages, to let the sick people die, the poor starve to death, the homeless to succumb to their fate on the streets. This trend has not changed. Wherever feudalism exists, the destruction of humanity exists. Wherever cancerous economic bubbles are created, the destructive trend becomes rampant, for the bubble economies and feudalism are one.

In order to deal with the cancer, one needs to deal with what causes it. It is impossible to address the global debt crisis, or the governmental budget crisis, in isolation, by for instance, the governments slashing support for the society by means of increased conservatism. Can a society cure its hunger through starvation? Of course not. The bubble economy is parasitic in nature. The more it grows, the more it causes starvation. Nor can the cancer really be cured by surgical means. But it can be cured by a systemic change.

Suppose it were possible for the President of the United States to take the personal initiative and shut the cancerous system down, to put the Federal Reserve through a bankruptcy reorganization and reestablish the Fed on a healthy basis as a federal bank, and restructure the nation according to the model of infinite economy as Alexander Hamilton had done, recreating the American System of economy - would this cure the problem?

Fundamentally, the answer is, NO! It would avoid a great catastrophe and buy the society time for the fundamental healing to occur. But the healing must come from within. The bubbles of false ideologies that have been promoted through the 'enlightenment' 'negative-growth' systems, cannot be erased by governmental policy changes. They may be exposed for what they are, and so be cured, and be neutralized by growth in intelligent observation, honest enquiry, and through scientific and educational processes. But this takes time. It takes a strong devotion to the task, and a great deal of effort.

Like a biological cancer, the economic cancer of a bubble economy grows around a catalyst that invades the systems of healthy growth. Today's medical methods of cancer treatment are largely ineffective, because a focused eradication of the cancerous cause is not yet possible. Cancer treatment is focused on a process of localized general destruction of the biological tissues, in the hope that the healthy tissues will show a stronger recovery. That is a brutal approach, but the only one there is. An effective treatment of the economic cancer is more readily possible, through advances in metaphysics. By being able to recognize the parasitic principles that drive the bubble economies, and by acknowledging the connection between the effect of these principles and the unfolding social chaos, such as the debt-related destruction of society, it becomes possible for society to give up the destructive principles, to build safeguards against them, and so to heal itself of the disease.

That the society has not even begun to move in this direction is evident by the fanfares with which the cancerous growth in the financial markets is celebrated as an economic miracle. Once it becomes thoroughly acknowledged by society, that the more the cancerous system grows, the more the society is doomed, some hope exists for a real healing.

At the present time, the feudal ideology and its expression in a feudal financial and economic system, is embraced by society as a boon to civilization and hailed as the key to progress. Much of the society's commitment to the feudal ideology may have been generated through many decades of directed advertising and through strategic handouts of some tidbits of unearned profits that tend to wet the appetite of society for more of the same.

This artificially cultured commitment of the society to feudalism can be reversed, however, by focusing on the principles of healthy growth, developing the real strength and real wealth of the society. The contrast between healthy growth and cancerous growth, must be recognized in order that the healthy growth becomes sustained and the cancerous growth becomes eliminated. Once this step of progress is being made, the feudalism that is driving the cancerous game, is understood by its nature as the destroyer of mankind, and will be abandoned. Until this step of progress is made, the sad and tragic outcome of the society's commitment to feudalism will take its toll, even as its cancerous bubbles grow.

Today, the toll is escalating as the society if offering continuously more and more of the substance of its living and its future at the altar of feudalism. The reality, however, cannot be side-stepped, that this process of the society's escalating decommitment to the platform of healthy growth leads to a vast disintegration of the entire world-financial and economic system that necessarily engulfs even the so-called rich. And this is the stage where we are at today.

Chapter 13: The Impending Collapse of the World-Economic System

In summing up the vast dimension of the phenomenon that unfolds behind the scene of the governmental budget crises, we need to look at the globalization of the collapse.

The illusion which has been created by the modern trickery that hides the real inflation in the financial system, has allowed a buildup of inflation in monetary values to an enormity in size and volume that is far greater than anything that has ever been encountered in any crash in human history. The effect of this enormous and wide-spread inflation has the potential to cause a crash that covers the entire sphere of human living.

The enormity of the delusion that has been created, not only financially, but in other economic and social aspects as well, may be likened to a belief in the seismic stability that has been experienced for decades on top of the San-Andreas Fault, which hasn't moved much over the last decades except for a few minor tremors, but which has stored up tensions within its formation of an unimaginable magnitude in earth quake potential. When the financial quake is triggered, by whatever cause may trigger it, the global financial system is bound to collapse into the vacuum of its hidden inflation. The physical collapse of the world-economies will likely be tied to the financial collapse, so that far more than just the financial markets are doomed. The banks are most certainly doomed that are tied into this system. The pensions are doomed, by which countless people live today. The entitlements that the governments and industry maintain, are doomed. Even food distribution is doomed. Food distribution is currently concentrated in the hands of a small number of cartel companies, owned by the oligarchy that has no interest whatsoever in the welfare of humanity. Even the biological health of society is doomed in this crisis which has the potential of staging the largest biological collapse in the history of human existence as the food production and distribution chain becomes disrupted, which is already stressed and is paper-thin.

Every value that has been established in monetary relationship, in physical equity, in food security, and in physical stability, is doomed. The already substantial deficits that exists in everyone of these areas, will likely escalate rapidly, especially in respect to the nation's capacity to provide physical support for their populations.

Already many ugly aspects of this unfolding collapse are noticeable, though the real crash has not even begun.

A strange situation has arisen in the way the society responds to what it sees. While the unfolding evidence is quite ugly in many parts of the world, everyone in society endeavors not to see it. A grand denial is taking over where sensitivity should reign. This response may be instinctive, perhaps, as people may realize that the unfolding ugliness of today they may appear like paradise in comparison to what lies ahead, which in itself is so incomprehensible that the response of denial is actually a natural response, as irrational as it is.

What will trigger the crash that causes global disintegration cannot be determined. A whole range of developments compete for the 'honor.' It could be triggered by a new oil shock, an epidemic outbreak of disease, a default in the world-debt system, a political upset like the breakup of Canada with the separation of Quebec, or something as minor as an interest rate change by a central bank that starts the chain reaction of disintegrating collapse. Japan's central bank, for instance, has felt it necessary to drop the prime rate to 0.5% in order keep the financial system alive. Japan is fighting to keep itself alive against the background of a collapsing physical economy with corresponding losses in the banking sector that is still reeling from the real estate losses. Also, its situation is made worth by the decaying value of its dollar oriented investment in U.S. treasury securities of which Japan own a lot, as the dollar is dropping in value. The problem is, that the Japanese central bank must raise the interest rate at one point, because all the interest-free money goes straight into building new financial bubbles instead of fuelling healthy economic growth. Once the rate goes up, an outflow out of the bubbles could cause a collapse with world-wide repercussions. So highly unstable has the world-financial system become.

But why can't society give up its love of cancerous growth.

An uncontrolled disintegration is never a pleasant thing, especially when it happens globally. Though it is easily avoidable, it is unlikely that it will be avoided. This paradox result from the underlying illusion of the bubble economy that defines the cancerous growth as benign. This prevents people from giving it up.

The bubble economy resets on the illusion that it is possible to earn 40%, 100%, or even 1000% profits on investments, while the productive economy generates only 4% profit, and this without the debt service costs factored in. In order to prevent the global disintegration of the financial system, this fundamental illusion must be addressed. The global disintegration can be avoided by an orderly return to the infinite system of economy, the American System, that was pioneered by Alexander Hamilton in the late 1700s in the U.S.A.. But who can do such a thing? The society loves to dream of easy money. "I turned $5,000 into $250,000," that is what society likes to hear, and the people are hearing it, and some (two or three) are actually doing it.

The stock-market where much of the speculation started, is not actually a rotten idea. It is a wonderful capitalist idea for generating development funds, but it is sadly abused. The stock market was invented to capitalize the physical economy on a platform of financing developing companies, and it still works great on this basis. If the focus in investing is centered on actual value and proven potential in prospective companies, rather than on the hyped up buying frenzy for illusive gains, investment can be a beneficial and relatively risk-free process for both the economy and the investor.

In order to cure the bubble economy - that is, in order to give up the bubble mentality - the society requires a refocusing onto the principles of healthy growth. It requires a phase shift in thinking from the glorification of the 'negative growth' system, to an understanding of the principles of positive growth, and this necessitates an inner reversal.

The 'positive-growth' system.

The positive growth system is based on zero usury, but not on zero profits. It is based on real profits instead of fictitious profits. The profits are earnings from enhanced productivity which benefits not only the investor, but much more so the society as a whole. The day's have not ended in which this time-honored platform pays its rewards. The problem is that this time-honored platform glitters less. In investing, most people don't seek out concrete value and productivity for society, which are a guarantee for success in investing. They seek out the spectacular, which, when it sparkles is most likely fictitious throughout.

And what about the national debt, what would repay the debt if a transition were achieved to the infinite system? The debt would be easily repaid in a zero usury environment?

What happens to it in a positive growth system? History tells us that it becomes actually repayable, whereas it would devalue itself to zero in a crash of the feudal system.

This is what had happened to the national debt that had been created under free-trade doctrine in the early years following the founding of the U.S.A., when the free-trade principle had bankrupted the nation. Once the infinite system was set up to replace the free-trade system, vast profits were generated so that the national debt suddenly became repayable without any pain to the population. And it was repaid. Under the present feudal system the national debt is absolutely unrepayable. Not even the debt service costs are payable, as they supersede the total free profit of the productive economy which can barely keep itself afloat. The debt bubble functions only because the debt service costs are rolled over into new debt, or are being monetized by printing more currency.

The same reality that makes the debt service costs unpayable, makes the debt itself unrepayable. And when the debt is unrepayable, the loan equity that is attached to it is worthless. It is worthless to the lender, because it can never be reclaimed.

This is the present global status, though everyone denies the reality of it. This is why it is still in force.

The infinite system of economy, is a simple system, fundamentally. Even a child can understand it, that is why its frightens the Empire so much which tries to cover it over, and hide it from view. The infinite system is self-developing, in that it supports no parasites, no destructive interventions, no illusions and unproductive processes, no bubble building that wastes resources, and most of all it forces a phase shift that causes people to think on a bigger scale, in terms of reality and the real human need. The only limit that exists to confine the infinite system of economy, is the scale of mankind's imagination. Physically, there are no limits.

It may be hard for a nation to give up its precious interest rate usury system that feeds its pension funds, even though, in the process of hanging on to it, the society looses its capital. But this is what is happening. Of course, in a feudal system in which money is considered an 'estate' that can be rented out, the nation has to pay (itself) sufficiently high interest rates in order to attract any money at all. The reality is, under the feudal system nobody wins. Why, then, can't society give its feudal system up for the infinite system of economy? The reason is, that it cannot think big enough. Who needs feudal looting to fuel pension funds? If the real economy expands in an a parabolic function, the fallout of wealth is more than sufficient to pay active pensions from current resources. Nothing needs to be accumulated to keep the society alive. Economic activity is a dynamic thing. The reason that the society clings to its beloved feudal system, is that the society can't recognize a bargain when it sees one. The feudal system is definitely the most expensive system in the world, and it glitters, but it has no substance.

The infinite system of economy is based on nationally owned credit for national development. There is no glitter in this, but solid growth. The society own the means for its self-development. Why should it rent it? Why should the society go for junk jewelry when it can have the crown jewels? Why should a nation not own its own money? Why should it have to rent it, and pay a king's ransom in usury? No rational reason exists for this, except that such a system affords no basis for speculative profits. All profits that are generated within this system, those from private investment included, are tied to real economic returns in the productive economy that profit the investor through dividends, and the nation as a whole through increased prosperity.

This system system is a bargain, because it blesses all involved, and it does it completely without risk and pain. Maybe the society is suspicious of it for this reason. After all, investors are used to paying ever greater prices for the same junk; having thus lost the ability to appreciate real bargains.

Indeed it may not be easy for investors who are used to promises of astronomical returns (though they can never be cashed out), to permit the governments to put the self-destructive system through a bankruptcy shutdown, and to replace it with a system that pays at the rate the economy produces wealth for society. The infinite system has no room for greed, the kind of greed that exports food out of a country while its children starve to death.

Mankind lives by its application of intelligence. By it, civilization is upheld. By it, the nations and individuals are secure. By it, man is free. But this basis becomes removed when actions and policies become separated from reality. In situations of total collapse, irrationality reigns in an environment of complete anarchy. Here, not even the feudal system remains. Here, violence and outright theft become the rule.

The requirement for positive action will never be lifted off the shoulders of mankind. Negative development systems are too destructive to human development, for mankind to be able to afford them much longer. Rational actions are needed for the self-protection of society, to save itself from its own folly. The time for such action is now, even while mankind awaits the disintegration of that on which it currently depends.

One thing can be said with certainty, that unless positive actions are taken to shut the bubbles down through which financial speculation and profiteering destroy the societies, the disintegration of the world-economic system will happen. Then, the result will be anarchy.

The oligarchy of the world has traditionally felt a need to hide the dysfunctional nature of the feudal financial system. This has two reasons. One reason is, that the oligarchy loves anarchy. In its own way, it profits from anarchy.

It should be noted that the oligarchic system exists outside the sphere of governments and stands in opposition to the institution of the nation-state. It has arrayed itself at war against it, and against society as a whole.

The second reason why the oligarchy hides the dysfunctional nature of the bubble economy, is in recognition of the oligarchy's own history that has traditionally necessitated dramatic steps by the oligarchy in order to prevent any meaningful real economic development from occurring. This underlying force that acts against any functional platform of economy is still fully active and may be hard to combat in any real effort towards avoiding a crash.

The efficiency of the **infinite economic model,** should it be implemented, would certainly put the **feudal model** that drives the bubble economies to shame and reveal its poverty. Any meaningful global economic redevelopment and reindustrialization would put an end to the bubble economy and its fictitious 1000% profits, and shut the game down, possibly for ever. A contest between these two models of economy would therefore most certainly not be allowed. That is why the bubble economy, as precarious as it is, is so intensively maintained. Most of the wars of the century have been fought specifically in order to prevent a renewed contest between the infinite system of economy, and the 'negative development' system that drives the bubble economies. The tenacity of the oligarchy in not surrendering its fundamentally self-destructive system, will likely prevent any serious efforts that are designed to put the dying world-system through a bankruptcy reorganization in order that the societies can be saved from destruction, and their economies become revitalized in the process.

No single President anywhere in the world, nor government on earth, stands the slightest chance of deactivating the 'negative development' systems without a strong grass roots support for such a move. Therefore, the responsibility for understanding the nature of both the infinite and the feudal system, on the grass roots level, and their relationship to society, is a very serious one. On it, may hang the future of mankind.

War as a means for maintaining the platform for the bubble economies, or to defeat it.

Evidence suggests that nearly all of the wars fought in the last two centuries were NOT fought for territorial gain, although this goal was put up in rhetoric to make the wars acceptable. Evidence suggests that the wars had at their root this all-pervading conflict between the infinite model of economy, and the feudal model. This war, really began with the Renaissance. The infinite model unfolded out of the Renaissance and had its highest manifest in the early decades of the USA, which operated its economy during its first century as a positive development system, standing in opposition to the self-limiting or feudal model of economy which includes most of today's 'negative-development' systems that have created the largest financial bubble in history. This war needs to be ignited and won!

One of the most blatant examples of this type of war, were war is instigated to protect the feudal economic system from being exposed to a progressive economic environment, may be the war created by England's King Edward VII. History tells us that the project was launched decades before the first bullet was fired. It started with a diplomatic effort to prevent the most far-reaching economic development project of the time, the creation of a rail line that would stretch from Paris to Japan, that would have united the entire Eurasian continent into the most far-flung economic power house the world has ever seen.

The potential for a development so huge must have been seen as a death-threat to the British Empire and its dominance of the sea. A rail link from Japan to Paris would most certainly unite the largest continent on the planet into a single economic powerhouse. On top of all that, this rail link would also provide a faster transportation channel from Europe to Japan, India, and China, which directly threatened the priority position of the British Empire. The project threatened the Empire's fictitious wealth and power to its very core. It had to be prevented. And it was. It was prevented in a manner that would make it impossible for such a project even to be contemplated again, for decades to come.

King Edward VII was an able diplomat, perhaps the greatest of his time. He served the British Empire well. Not only did he succeed in killing all the initial contracts for the Eurasian rail-link project that had been signed between the various nations as agreement in principle, he also managed to prevent any future renewal of such contracts by maneuvering the various partners into adversarial positions against each other that would cause them to destroy each other's economies in an all-out war and create a background of nationalist tensions that would prevent the reoccurrence of the project for long periods afterwards.

It has been said that Germany started World War I. Indeed, Germany was foolish to react when being provoked through the tragic assassination in Sarajevo, over which the first bullets were fired. This does not alter the fact that the war was carefully set up over the preceding decades. Nor was this fact totally unknown at the time. Even before the war began, years after the death of King Edward, the German Kaiser who was not an extraordinary brilliant man, saw through the British scheme and commented about the explosive setup that had been created, saying that Edward was still stronger, though being dead, than he himself was, who was still alive.

At this point, however, the adversarial positions were too far advanced. Only a miracle could have prevented the war. And it wasn't prevented. The Empire was saved!

Close to twenty million people lost their life in the process, and another twenty million had their lives disrupted to the very core. This was the price that humanity paid to enable the feudal empire to maintain its day in the sun.

As the nations of Europe were 'guided' by King Edward to destroy each others political, economic, and financial life-support systems that they had built up and had committed themselves to expand, so the nations of the world are 'guided' today into destroying their physical and biological life-support systems under the feudal ideology that dominates the world-financial system with its post-industrial society doctrine, free-trade policies, debt centered austerity demands, and antidevelopment policies. And again, the project is working. The whole world is playing along in the game for its own self-destruction, and the price is likely to be infinitely taller.

King Edward did succeed 'gloriously' in his goal. The feudalist model of economy and finance, and all the oligarchic structures that rested thereon, were protected and continue to make the same demands on humanity that Edward VII had made. Because of this, the world is staged to once more shoulder the cost imposed for saving the system that has fundamentally no strength in itself as it is inherently self-destructive, which cannot survive in competition with the infinite system of economy. Had the Eurasian economic development succeeded on the envisioned platform that was clearly based on the infinite model of economy, feudalism would have ended at this point for all times to come, instead of becoming a global threat for an entire century, unleashing wars and cycles of collapse and destruction, as it did.

The cost in human life by which Edward's victory was won, can never be tallied up. The actual war-costs will likely be counted as minute in comparison to the costs that the survival of the feudalist system did cause in the decades that followed, which are still mounting up. Statistics of the war-cost tell us that 10-20 million people were killed during World War I, depending on who counts what, with half a continent put to ruin in the process. Statistics never tell the full story, though, nor do they even begin to hint at the underlying story for which cause the killing and destruction had been staged. The needs of people, even their life, were counted as nothing against the priority objective of saving a dying empire and its fatally flawed economic platform that has no strength to maintain itself in the unfolding environment of productive human development, much less support this development. Today, humanity has been drawn once more to lay down its life for the empire, and this on a global scale.

The empire's story has not changed. The governments, even society itself, continues to place the maintenance of a failing system far above the needs and life of human populations. So what, the finance ministers of today tell themselves in their frustration over budget problems, and in a certain ignorance of reality,- so what if the poor and unemployed can't afford to eat?

Well, they haven't come quite as far yet, as in the olden days, saying: Are there no work-houses? Are there no slavery jobs?

But they do say: So what! So what, if the unfortunate people whose industries were destroyed by free-trade policies and deindustrialization, can no longer have access to food and health-care? "Are there no churches, or soup kitchens, or neighbors?" They don't ask the question yet: Are there no grave-yards? Are there not too many people in the world? They may think it, as they cut governmental assistance to the unfortunate, to below minimum subsistence levels, putting the blame on the unemployed themselves for being unemployed, and the poor for being poor, rather than examining the system that has made great masses of people unemployed, poor, and homeless. Oh, shallow and stupid rulers, how has society erred in electing you!

Which government, today, asks the question by whose labor the nation has been built in the first place, and for whose sake a nation is established? Who asks about such questions anymore as common wealth, common defense, common prosperity and security, even the common dignity of man? These questions are fundamental to the difference between the two competing financial and economic systems, as shown in Appendix 7 and 8. To the degree to which these questions are not asked, to that degree society has condemned itself.

The vital questions are not asked, about the horrendous human cost involved if development stagnates under the feudal model of self-defeating economy. The failure in not asking these questions makes a scientific metaphysical approach to finding solutions evermore difficult. The bankers, investors, or economists are trained in the modern economic theories based on the feudal system. They cannot see the imperative for protecting humanity as a means for solving a budget crisis. Their point of reference for recognizing value rests on an entirely different platform, the feudal platform. To the modern banker, the 'negative development' system is the only system of economy that exists. As limited as this platform may be, this platform is all that a banker is able to work with. The banker works with pre-established axioms that are considered absolute, to which everything must be subordinated, even if the process causes the death of entire segments of humanity. The banker has no control over the system chosen by society, as he is told. The banker, therefore, will always defend the feudal system, together with all the modern investors, investment advisers, and economists who are committed to the feudal platform in a near religious fashion.

Still, the society has the control to choose. The society is not bound to preestablished axioms. It is free to choose and has the responsibility to choose wisely.

In the sphere of the banker, the point of reference has been forcefully shifted by the system that the banker serves, onto an artificial reality which supersedes the actual reality. Unfortunately, this reality is all that the banker is allowed to work with. Governments, invariably, are driven by the same axioms that control the bankers, for the bankers control the economic life-blood of the nations under the feudal system. Therefore it is up to society, not its bankers, nor its government, to make the scientific choices. For this, a scientific platform needs to established in public thought in order to counter the "follow after me" demands that the world's many self-interest oriented 'negative-development' systems make on humanity. The people who operate these systems are often backed up by the immense financial resources of the feudal oligarchy, which are strategically deployed to further the various self-interests of the oligarchic empires, contrary to the common interests of humanity.

Science must look at the infinite principles, rather than the self-defeating. It must look at the operation of the infinite model of economy and its boundless development potential, instead of concede to oligarchic demands. It must look at the infinite nature of man and develop that potential. It must drive the recognition that **man is free** and has the freedom and the responsibility to establish the reality of freedom by which the nation is secure.

It has been said that metaphysics is a thing inherent in religion. This is untrue. The metaphysical capability is inherent in the nature of man. It is man's intelligence that raises the platform of physical existence to levels far above what the raw nature of the planet can provide. No other species known has even the slightest metaphysical capability, and it is none other than the metaphysical platform which provides value for the economic system, nor is there an inherent limit to this capability. The dimension of infinity and the capability of mankind in raising the physical platform are linked.

This metaphysical capability of man, however, has rarely been associated with economic policy. In fact it has not even been recognized to exist until quite late in human development. Metaphysics has become first associated with religion, because the religious context of probing the infinite, especially the Christian background, has brought about the earliest discoveries of the infinite nature of man. The first major application of this discovery to economic issues occurred during the Renaissance where religion-based discovered principles were applied to human self-government and to structures of economy based on the the recognition of man's creative potential. Out of this chain of an unfolding self-recognition, and the obvious conclusions arising from it, the nation-state was created and the world became transformed. And even this, should be seen as but a beginning.

And it was but a beginning. During mankind's second major period of Renaissance, called the American Revolution, the same processes were at work again, but on a larger scale. It is also true that both periods of renaissance were defeated in short order by monarchism, oligarchism, fascism, feudalism, colonialism, and the like, through which the oligarchy maintains its self-defeating system of feudalist economy. Great crimes have been committed against humanity for the oligarchy's self-protecting purposes.

To understand these crimes one needs to understand the position from which they were and are committed. Rather than to indict the individuals, one needs to understand the impossible position the leading oligarchs of the ages have placed themselves in, as they had to maintain a system that cannot be maintained because of the fundamentally self-destructive nature of the game that has been committed to. In the course of pursuing this impossible task, evermore exotic solutions were tried, with have invariably involved escalating brutal impositions on humanity.

Two of the more exotic ideas in the oligarchy's continuing effort to make the feudal system work, are the following.

One effort in this direction has resulted in the creation of the U.N. organization under which force the feudal system, especially financial feudalism, became globalized. It has become apparent, however, although the official commitment to feudalism has been abolished, that the actual globalization of it through the world-financial and economic system has been accomplished. Dropping the name, however, did not change the nature of the system. The present world-financial system, is a feudal system, the same feudal system by which the oligarchy of the empires had looted the world for centuries. Nor did the globalization of it change the underlying self-destructive nature of the system, but merely globalized its effect so that all nations are now affected by feudal system's near disintegration because of its inner poverty.

By the near disintegration of the world-financial system, that some people are beginning to recognize, the underlying defect of the feudal system has been, after all, revealed globally, even without it having to face the contrast of a correctly operating economic system.

Against the currently unfolding, monstrous inflation within the financial aggregates system, that is slowly beginning to be recognized, it is becoming plain to many people that the system cannot be maintained much longer by any means. The facts are so plain that they are acknowledged even by the oligarchy itself, which has shifted its base of wealth from financial aggregates to the hoarding of gold, strategic metals, minerals, energy resources, etc., even food.

The oligarchy's other major, and even more exotic attempt at saving the feudal system involves the already mentioned dramatic 'depopulation' objective, which is a policy goal to reduce the human population on the planet to such levels as existed during the 'golden' days of feudalism when 99% of humanity lived as slaves, serfs, or worse.

The strange thing is, that these extraordinary crimes that have been committed in the name of saving the feudal system, with worse still considered, and the immense dishonor they have heaped upon the face of the oligarchy and those who represent it, have not caused the oligarchy to play a better game. There is no security in a self-destructive system, not for mankind nor for the oligarchy, even without considering the effect of the mounting dishonor the oligarchy has piled up against itself. The tenacity with which the game continues to be pursued, however, though there is no hope for it ever to succeed, as it cannot succeed by its very nature, causes one to recognize a near religious fervor being reflected throughout all elements that are involved in the feudal system, including the bankers who manage the game and are totally committed to the axioms that apply, though they have no relationship to reality except that of an illusion.

Thus, a new point needs to be added to the list for solving the example of the budget balancing problem with which the book began. This point involves an in-depth exploration of the larger crimes against humanity, and the principles for dealing with them.

Here, the book comes to a close, as the subject of the world-financial disintegration is little more than but an item of concern in the much larger disintegration of civilization, as a whole.

The larger perspective is explored in the second book of Volume 1, under the title: Crimes Against Humanity. In this volume the exploration is focused on the principle of dealing with the forces that involve disintegration.

Chapter 14: An Update on the Ongoing Disintegration

The original title of this book was: "The World-Financial Crash of 1996". Well, so far (and we can be grateful for this) the Crash of the 90s has not yet occurred. What has occurred however, and this has occurred with great consistency, is the ongoing process of disintegration within which the great market crashes are but blips on a larger screen. These blips, however, are not necessary the most decisive aspects of the disintegration process. Still, they indicate to some degree the movements within.

Lyndon LaRouche compared the larger scope of the process to what happens to a flywheel that is accelerated to ever greater speeds until the centrifugal forces exceed the tensile strength of the material from which it is cast. The the flywheel flies apart! At this point the bottled up kinetic energy, which is now no longer confined, becomes a force that tears the thing apart and obliterates everything in its path until the bottled energy has played itself out. Until a similar point is reached in the financial system, the average observer will detect nothing that reveals the danger. The 'bearings' might squeal a bit louder, minute vibrations might be felt, but until that moment when the thing flies apart, everything looks normal. On the other hand, those with an understanding of the physics involved, will become concerned long before the more visible signs come apparent. They will point out the principles behind the danger and point to whatever evidence exists to support their prediction of chaos.

This chapter is designed to explore the subtle, visible signs as that have come to the surface since the beginning of 1996? The evidence speaks of processes now under way.

Tremors in Africa

Two things happened in Africa in 1996. The Ugandan dictator Yoweri Museveni, after 10 years in power, was finally able to hail himself as a duly elected president. Now, and with massive 'aid' from his masters from abroad, Museveni was finally put in a position to take his destructive war that had already devastated Uganda for a decade, into Zaire and other nations. In October 1996, acting in alliance with Laurent Kabila, the imperially appointed rebel king, Museveni joined his master's war against the nations of central Africa. The unspeakable atrocities that were unleashed in the process of this war, were by all accounts, more horrible and intense than those inflicted by Hitler, whom Museveni greatly admires.

No one knows for certain to the present day, how many people were murdered in this war. Those who have been there speak of vast numbers of bodies stacked up along the wayside, like chord wood. They speak of crematoria fires which were burning for months, which finally consumed most of them. Apart from these eye-witness reports are the 'business' facts of the war, that must be considered, because the war was directly financed by a number of big mining cartels and front organizations who 'bought' themselves mining claims to loot the wealth of Zaire that was later renamed, the Democratic Republic of the Congo.

All this is significant, because a major shift begun at this time within the oligarchic World. This shift came to light as movement within the oligarchy, to get out of financial paper assets, and into economically indispensable physical assets. In Africa, these coveted physical assets were readily accessible by means of theft through war. The war was financed for this goal. In fact, Ziare's mineral assets were sold by Kabila while the previous government was still firmly in power. Thus, the mining cartels bought themselves by war, what was otherwise not accessible to them. In the framework of this acquisition, millions of people were put to death, who stood in the way.

In other nations, like Russia and Brazil, the nation's assets were brought onto the market by other means. In most cases the theft of assets was accomplished though 'privatization' demands that resulted in auctions at which the national assets where acquired by the Empire's operatives for pennies to the dollar of real worth. This assault on the world's vital national infrastructures has steadily increased since 1996. Brazil's state mining company and all its vast assets in mineral claims, physical plants, transportation systems, shipping lines, which makes this the largest mining operation in the world, has been taken over for just a few billion dollars which covered the interest payments on its unpayable national debt for a few short months. Thus, the nation's greatest treasure was 'stolen,' without which the nation's economic redevelopment will be very difficult, if not impossible. Indeed, this is in the Empire's interest. It aims to impose this kind of impotence in order to prevent large scale economic development anywhere in the world. Imperial feudalism, financial or otherwise, cannot exist in a richly developed, advanced world.

The next phase of geopolitical, financial warfare.

This phase can best be described as the battle of the Titans. This battle is over economic development on a scale never before realized in all of human history. Something similar was attempted in the late 1800s, but was immediately squashed by the Empire's agents. Plans had been dawn up and ratified to build a railroad from Rotterdam to the ports of China, right across Asia, that would link western Europe, Russia, and Asia, into a giant economic development block. The British Empire responded with setting up the background for World War I that dashed all hopes for a hundred years, for such a project to begin again.

In 1996 a new campaign was launched by the Lyndon LaRouche organization that the world's commit itself to accomplish this vast and very necessary development project. Once completed, this transportation infrastructure will create a vast development corridor from which the development will spread into regions beyond. This will revitalize not only the entire Eurasian continent, but the world, unless the project is prevented once again.

On May 7-9, 1996, China hosted an international symposium for the implementation of this daring idea that is destined to uplift the whole world. Under the heading: "International Symposium on Economic Development of the Regions Along the Euro-Asia Continental Bridge," this daring initial meeting became a landmark conference that would soon have far reaching consequences. Already at the conference the battle lines were clearly drawn. On one side stood the Empires, represented by Sir Leon Brittain, Vice President of the European Union, whose remarks were calculated to sabotage all goals. On the other side stood the leadership of China with the enthusiastic support and proposals by Helga Zepp LaRouche, representing Lyndon LaRouche and his development concepts.

What started with this confrontation soon became open warfare on a scale that reflects the scale of the proposed development itself. The thrust of this war was financial in nature and was was directed against the four Tiger Economies of Asia: Malaysia, Indonesia, Thailand, and the Philippines. The war was fought in the form of a speculative attack against the currencies of all four of the Tiger Economy nations. It was fought single handed by the Empire's own mega-speculator George Soros. The result was the so-called Asian crisis that devastated the economies of four great nations, that put hundreds of millions of people into poverty and at risk of starvation. The effects of this war are still felt right around the world, by which hundreds of thousands of people lost their employment and the U.S. farming sector became totally devastated because of its export dependency.

At the annual meeting of the World Bank on Sept 20, 1997, in Hong Kong, Malaysia's Prime Minister, Dr. Mahathir Bin Mohamad, fought back and denounced George Soros by name in front of the vast audience of the financial elite of the world. While this fighting-back affected little, it was nevertheless a beginning of a mounting self-defense of humanity, beginning with an imposition of currency exchange controls that was once again pioneered by Mahathir Mohamad, but was later copied in principle by other nations.

This war of the Empire has most severely affected all of Asia. It even caused difficulties for China, but it didn't stop the Land Bridge Development project.

Naturally, such a crisis could never have been unleashed by a single man, had the underlying disintegration of real values, compared to the paper values, made the entire financial pyramid hollow inside. The Tigers had been hollow from the beginning. By focusing on globalized income rather than income from industrial production for their self-development, had left these nations vulnerable. They could be destroyed by simply taking away the financial interface for trade, which a national currency facilitates. With the currency devalued, this vital interface for trade becomes dysfunctional, and the nations that are not sufficiently self-developed to supply their own needs, starve.

The destruction of the Tigers, of course, momentarily propped up the big American and London financial markets with fresh capital inflows as massive amounts of private speculative capital was withdrawn from the Asian nations. Except, the speculators wanted more. As a consequence the predation was soon directed against Russia.

In the early months of 1998 Russia was being targeted in a massive way. Under the 'rules' a nation is not allowed to defend itself by imposing currency exchange controls, but must pay out whatever the market demands.

Any first grader should have been able to figure out that no nation on earth can generate the necessary resources to hold out indefinitely against such forms of attack. Once its treasury was depleted, Russia resorted to massive borrowing, but this, too, didn't work for long. Soon bonds were floated with 90% interest, and even those didn't sell. At the height of the unfolding insanity the state resorted to offering bonds with a seven DAY maturity at 250% interest. At this point a financial bail-out was attempted by the IMF. The IMF, which had already flushed all its lending capital into Asia, somehow found another 22 billion to lend to Russia. The first installment was slightly over 5 billion - 3.8 billion of that was to go for currency stabilization. It was hoped that this IMF financing of the Ruble would keep the Ruble afloat through to the rest of the year. As it was, the entire emergency fund was depleted in just a few days.

At this point Russia changed its government. The new appointees that now run the government of Russia have long been familiar with LaRouche's works on physical economy. Consequently they imposed tight exchange controls. The country reverted back to the principle of providing credits for infrastructures and reindustrialization. It defaulted on its unrepayable debt in favor of keeping the population alive. If Russia makes it through the winter without a major crisis, miracles will have been achieved which could not have been possible otherwise.

Now, with Russia becoming a partner of the Chinese driven Eurasian Land Bridge Development project, together with Japan, which became a full partner in December 1998, a new increment has been achieved in the massive commitment to this vast infrastructural work. There has also been a commitment worked out, recently, for a far reaching Soviet-Chinese scientific and technological cooperation, during the Chinese President's historic visit to the great science city of Novosibirsk. All these events came together approximately at the time of the second international symposium in support of the Eurasian Land Bridge development project. The symposium was held in November 1998. This time, however, Helga Zepp LaRouche, the Silk Road Lady of the Schiller Institute of Germany, the wife of Lyndon LaRouche, was not only most cordially welcomed at this conference, but had been asked to deliver the key-note speech.

Her husband commented recently, that with this large scale regional cooperation that is unfolding in Asia centered on infrastructure development and industrialization, coupled with the firm commitment by the major participating nations to isolate their currencies from the speculative markets, may make it possible for these nations to survive when the western system disintegrates and renders its nations irrelevant for all economic concerns.

The only situation that these nations may not survive, that is a very real possibility during the death agony of a dying civilization that sees its imagined wealth evaporate, is nuclear war. The specter of nuclear holocaust has indeed, already been brought to the foreground whenever the defunct western world-financial system was nearing a potential break down point.

The specter of nuclear war.

Let there be no delusion in anyone's mind, nuclear was is definitely on the horizon. Twice at flash points of a potential world-financial disintegration, the specter appeared on the scene. In either case, Iraq was selected as the target of convenience. This proud nation is so easily coaxed into a role that offers phony excuses to launch a massive mid east war.

The first buildup towards such a war was launched at the height of the Asian crisis which nearly caused a global financial blow-out. War has always been used as a means for drawing public attention away from critical issues in moments when great opportunities arise to overturn the dying oligarchic system that is presently ruling the world. For this reason the Yugoslav war was ignited when the breakdown of the Soviet Empire opened a window of opportunity to develop the whole of Asia to the level of prosperity that was enjoyed by most of the advanced nations of the world. But in the shadow of war, this was cleverly avoided. Instead of starting a continent wide development wave, Russia was opened up to the Empire's financial looting with brought upon it its to economic self-destruction.

The next attempt to launch a major war with Iraq as the target of convenience, occurred at the height of the Russian financial crisis. The fall-out from this crisis had again endangered the entire global system. Nuclear weapons, evidently, were at the ready, to be used at a moment's notice. Their use had already been authorized for the first planned war against Iraq. There was even talk coming out of Israel about hitting not only Iraq with nuclear strikes, but also Iran, and the Sudan in Africa which the British has long wanted to defeat. The probability is high, therefore, that the next war will turn into a nuclear war, and will spread quickly. Also, it appears that the next war cannot be so easily averted by diplomacy, than the previous attempts, since the Empire and its stooges in the U.S. have reserved themselves the right to unleash military strikes against Iraq without warning, any time they wish to do so.

The two failed attempts to ignite a war against Iraq, clearly served also a secondary purpose with a secondary target. This hidden target is President Clinton. Every single method to destroy President Clinton's political career had failed, even backfired. The Empire's campaign to have the one man impeached who could potentially stand up for humanity and defeat the Empire had turned into the largest, longest, and by far the most expensive campaign ever launched to dig up impeachable dirt against a U.S. President. Nevertheless, it brought up nothing except a flimsy sexual scandal that probably resulted from a clever entrapment. But if the Empire could drag the man into an unpopular war, it might succeeded were ever other campaign has failed. Fortunately, the intended war has been twice averted.

President Clinton may be the most attacked President in U.S. history. He came under attack almost as soon as his presidency began, starting with a string of more than a dozen assassination attempts. All this, of course, is closely tied into the breakdown of the world-financial system, including the Empire's latest attempts to get rid of him.

Contrary to popular opinion, there exist only three mayor power structures in the world. One is the British oligarchic structure that came out of the British Empire, which no longer exists by name, but which lives on in oligarchic structures which functionally operate on the long cherished model of the old British Empire. The other major power structure in the world today is the American camp that President Clinton controls. The third power structure is made up of the Indian-Russian-Asian economic block. But without the American and Asian blocks joining hands, the British power structure that is built on financial looting cannot be upstaged. The position of President Clinton is critical, here, because might just have the intelligence to forge this essential bond. He certainly has the power to do so. This makes it a priority requirement of the New British Empire to get rid of the man. They don't necessarily need to see him dead. They just need to get him out of the way, which would open up the halls of government to Al Gore.

Now Al Gore is a trusted man in the Empire. He is owned by it as has father was before him. He has been lavishly 'purchased' by Ammard Hammar of Oxidental Petroleum, like his father the Senator was whom Hammar used to refer to as "my senator". He would put his hand to his wallet as he said so.

Naturally, with Al Gore as President, the oligarchy's power would be protected. Then the world could go up in flames, and there would never be a U.S.-China economic and financial alliance forthcoming that could stop the consuming fire. This would happen even if there was no other hope to rescue humanity, because it is not in the Empire's interest to allow such a rescue to occur.

One must surmise from this, that as the financial crisis moves closer towards its final flashpoint at which the systemic rupture occurs, the chances are seriously high that the President will be assassinated in order to get the Empire's man into the President's chair. When this assassination occurs, humanity will loose the greatest opportunity in modern history, that it presently has, to rescue itself.

The murder of a princess.

One needs to realize that this point that Political assassinations are not exactly a novelty in this world. The Nov. 4, 1995 assassination of Israel's Prime Minister Yitzhak Rabin was evidently staged for the purpose of totally altering Israel's direction towards Palestine, and towards the whole region. At least, this was the outcome of it. The Empire's stooges in Israel literally had to kill Yitzhak Rabin before Israel could be moved into a totally opposite direction, as it was.

The crime of assassination, of course, is easily hidden by the factions who are escalated to power by means of the crime. The blame is easily put on terrorism, religious extremism, or even drunk driving as this was the case in the assassination of Princess Diana on Aug. 31, 1997. That the death of the Princess was not by accident, but was a political assassination is self-evident by the profusion of lies that were concocted to cover up the real cause. Even the famous blood samples that supposedly proved drunkenness turned out to have been switched. Also, why did it take more than two and a half hours after the crash has been reported, to bring the Princess to a hospital.

Lady Diana had survived the crash but suffered from internal bleeding. The first phone report of the crash was logged in at 12:26. An emergency doctor was on the scene two minutes later, at 12:28. An ambulance was called, which arrived at the scene at 12:32. From then on everything proceeded in slow motion. It took the emergency team almost an hour (48 minutes to be exact) to get the Princess into the ambulance which then crawled away at the breath taking speed of five miles per hour.

The ambulance was instructed to take the severely injured woman to the most distant hospital that could be located, neither did the ambulance crew take her right in. Less then 500 yards from the emergency entrance the ambulance pulled over and stopped for ten minutes, before taking her to where her life could be preserved. By this time, however, there was little hope that Princess Diana would pull though. By then, two and a half hours had passed since the accident. What should have taken just minutes was stretched out into an ordeal of several hours. It took an astonishing 45 minutes to cover the 3.8 mile distance by ambulance.

Now, one must realize that this didn't happen in some backward third world town at the edge of nowhere. It happened in one of the world's most advanced cities. It appears that everything possible was done to assure that Lady Diana would die before help could be provided. All the facts, as they have been perceived together since then, describe the case as a badly botched up political assassination.

Political assassinations, however, seldom have to be clean. No matter how botched they are, they are always covered up with ease. This covering up, of course, cannot be done without a high level commitment to the process, which is very much evident in the Diana assassination case.

Naturally, there exists no smoking gun evidence that links either of the above revered to assassinations to the growing vulnerability of the oligarchic system whose financial underpinning is disintegrating more and more by the day. History, however, provides this connection. Life is cheap when compared to the Empire's goals. It always has been cheap and dispensable. The only difference that one can detect about the more modern crimes of this sort, is a growing level of insanity that is reflected in these cases, which matches the growing insanity that reigns within the world-financial structures. The only reason why these assassinations were brought up, is their connection to the world-financial breakdown, where they serve as a means for protecting the imperial structure from the necessary fundamental restructuring of the system that would shift the focus from global looting to global economic development and protect humanity.

The only factor that one can count on with great confidence, regarding the Empire, is the Empire's consistency in unleashing attacks against the lightest prospects of large scale economic development, anywhere in the world. The Empire knows that this would weaken its power. Any improvement in the state of civilization has this effect, not to mention a rapidly developing spirituality. Such a development would leave no place in the world for oligarchism and its looting practice. One must congratulate the Empire's rulers, however, for having been remarkably successful in their game. The years of its environmental wars have been rather fruitful in this respect. Its war against the world's peaceful use of nuclear power, for electricity generation, has generated huge 'deficits.' The nation of Europe appear to be totally committed to shut down all of their nuclear industries that they had labored to built, that had brought them to the threshold of an energy rich future. Even the historically technological giants, like Germany and France, have fully committed themselves to this course. In normal times, or in times of war, these industries would have been protected. They would have defended with all of the nation's might. Now, the nations stand fully committed to blow up voluntarily the very energy resource on which their very future depends.

Germany was the latest to join this club of insanity. Germany caved in to the Empire's demand. The 1998 election brought in a government that is totally representative of the British devolution ideology that is promoted as an environmental necessity. Only in the area of nuclear weapons, and nuclear weapons related industries, are nuclear technologies NOT banned. The specter of nuclear war has resurfaced remarkably fast in recent years, on the world political scene.

The latest words about the commitment to use nuclear weapons has surfaced in the media in the wake of the momentous developments that occurred in support of the Eurasian Land Bridge development project. The second Eurasian Land Bridge symposium, that was held in China from Oct. 27 to Nov. 1, had barely been concluded when the Japanese partnership in the project was announced. Then, literally within days, came the historic Chinese/Russian agreement for scientific and technological cooperation that was signed in Russia's famous science city, Novosibirsk, located in Siberia. These kinds of commitments are of a quality from which higher levels of civilization are born. The Empire's apparent response came within weeks in the form of rumors that the long standing commitment by NATO against the first-use of nuclear weapons has come under review.

The collapse of the hedge

funds.

What has any of this to do with the world-financial disintegration? Well, the simple fact is, that all these trends of revenge, such as readiness for nuclear war, the destruction of nuclear power, the destruction of industries through environmental hype, and the preservation of a disintegrating world-financial systems, do all connect in the dimension of insanity. In the darkness of this dimension certain bridges are being crossed that alter the world, but no one takes notice. When Russia was driven to the brink of chaos in the summer of 1998, as financial speculators devalued the Ruble to near zero, the Government had no option left but to announce a moratorium on its debt and impose strict exchange controls. With these developments, as natural as they were for the circumstance, a whole new financial environment was created that changed the interlocked global game plan so much that the world come to the brink of a systemic collapse within a few weeks.

One aspect that links up with all the rest in the dimension of insanity comes to the surface as the sudden insolvency of one of the world's biggest hedge funds, the Long Term Capital Management fund. With a tiny amount of base capital the company had borrowed over a hundred billion dollars from the banks, then used the money to gamble on the financial derivatives market. This went quite successful for a wile, but when the ripples from the Russian collapse filtered down through the system, the financial derivatives game scored LTCM big losses, in the billions of dollars. It wasn't that the people of LTCM were lousy players. To the contrary, two of their top people received the Nobel Price in economics in 1997, for creating the formulas that were supposed to make financial derivatives gambling safe. Their system collapsed miserably because the formulas hadn't inculcated the fact that the world had become a different playing field after Russia had quit the game, which had been a formidable supplier of loot.

The volatility of the world-system can be judged by the hysteria that the LTCM collapse created. The U.S. Federal Reserve Chairman called together 16 of the top bankers the following weekend, for an emergency session at which he demanded that each of them cough up several hundred millions in new loans for the company in trouble. Greenspan needed this money to pay off the company's several billion dollar gambling debt by Monday morning. He assured the bankers, if they didn't comply, the company's huge portfolio of several trillion dollars worth of derivatives contracts would become worthless, should the company default. This could be just enough of a spark to explode the entire derivatives market. In other words, the banks were literally forced to throw good money after bad, in order to save themselves, who had become deeply exposed by this company's outstanding leveraged loans for which it had no backing.

The point is, the world-financial disintegration is on a fast pace forward. The growing insanity that the system has generated, that was itself born out of insanity, is greeting an ever greater instability in the world, even while everything seems perfectly normal on the surface. Another problem is that nobody knows how to turn the thing off, because it can't be turned of. The very attempt to do so would blow the thing up.

LaRouche's answer is, to get out of the way and let the thing blow. Translated into policy, this means that the nations must reassert sovereignty over their currency, impose exchange controls, create a system of national banking for the creation of credits for infrastructures, farming, and industries, and that in addition to all this an agreement must be attained across the world to maintain a fixed international exchange rate system, such as the old Bretton Woods system that had been destroyed by President Nixon.

Helga Zepp LaRouche's visit to Mexico

The proposal that Lyndon LaRouche has placed before mankind for some years already, is fast gaining acceptance in many parts of the world. It is talked about in Brazil, Mexico, China, Russia, Germany, Malaysia, and many other places - even in the U.S.A.. During her speaking tour across Mexico, in early December 1998, Lyndon LaRouche's wife, head of the Schiller Institute in Germany, met with a most enthusiastic response wherever she went. Her presentations were widely covered by newspapers and Television. Also the previous Prime Minister of Mexico, Jose Lopez Portillo, was on hand and supported the ideas presented with his presence and praise. Even Mexico's Prime Minister in office, Ernesto Zedillo responded publicly to the ideas presented, that soon became the topic of wide-spread discussions throughout the nation. Scathing dissensions, of course, came from the Zapatisata terrorist newspapers that unleashed its usual profusion of poisonous comments.

It appears that a movement has begun that cuts

though the insanities that still mark this ages. This movement sparks a certain resurgence of spirituality. As small as this may be, this beginning 'phase shift' represents nevertheless a phenomenon that appeared impossible just a few months previously. We may have come to a breakout point, a point of change that could uplift whole nations, even the entire world, with a superior idea that ennobles the image of man as that of a creator, explorer, discoverer, and with a spirit that inspires liberty. With this another question comes to mind.

What is the future for mankind in terms of advancing its spirituality?

The sky is the limit! There has never existed a greater opportunity for mankind to assert its rights for dominion, than exists now. We are at the threshold of a historic opportunity for mankind to liberate itself from the processes that have defaced its image, undermined its existence, bound it mentally into a tight confinement more impregnable than any prison house. The opportunity that mankind has at this hour is greater than any in history. The systems are falling apart that have devastated mankind for many ages. In the same context great infrastructures for spiritual development have been brought to light and have been implemented in many respects. This heightens the opportunity. But the opportunity must be met with spiritual resolve, or else it will become lost like many bright opportunities in the past have become lost, when in such cases the great moments of opportunity met a small people, as Schiller had put it. If this loss occurs, the tragedy is beyond contemplation, nor would anything productive be achieved by visualizing it. What needs to be visualized instead, and realized indeed, is the kind of deep reaching agitation that terminates the prevailing insanity which tolerates lies at its very core that endanger civilization today.

The real target that a society's leadership must address itself to, that it must destroy as surely as Ludwig von Wolzogen new that Napoleon had to be destroyed for any nation to be save in Europe, is not the might of an empire, the craftiness of its oligarchy, the brutality of its fascism. Not a single advanced leader who ever walked the earth succeeded in such an attempt. The target in every successful leadership campaign has always been the conscience of humanity, but not so much to 'lead' it, rather with the goal to agitate the hell out of it. When this is achieved, everything else that is needed for victory falls into place. The goal in liberating humanity must be to annihilate its homogenous insanity that keeps it tied to the ground and confined to self-destruction.

The dynamics for responding to leadership.

On the surface it appears that there exist three structures in which a society can find itself, within which it can rise up and improve itself until that moment when it prepared to take a quantum jump to the next higher level.

This perception has a fundamental flaw. It may appear that the lowest attainable level of thinking is not necessarily that which reflects the kind of homogenous thinking that is aptly described as insanity, at which state society is inherently destructive to itself, and by which it will destroys itself as it had done so in the past. We are at this stage now. This stage reflects the current state of society in many parts of the world, where people are sacrificed for profits, and the survival of nations is disregarded for a higher priority, that of saving the dying financial system, where indeed, the very continuity of life on this planet is put in doubt by the building of nuclear weapons. Insanity produces a dismal state of affairs. Still it appears that it is possible to sink still lower on the scale of spirituality. It appears that a lower state is defined by fascism and dictatorial oligarchism, both of which have murdered humanity in huge numbers for centuries. Except this appearance is deceptive, and this most deadly so.

It is deadly, because it creates a false target. The battle cry should be, don't fight the despot-kings, fight the insanity that allows the despot-kings to rule. The only valid target that one may aim at, that one must defeat, is the homogenous insanity that already includes in its sphere all the elements of destruction that are presently tolerated, such as oligarchism, fascism, globalism, etc.. There is no lower state possible than that which has been presently attained, at which society is self-destructive. It cannot sink lower than that. This state is an absolute state. It has no definable structure within which redemption could occur. It has a range of manifestations, of course. Most of these represent various types of conflict.

In an environment of conflict there is no 'movement' occurring that would give it some form of structure within which a redeeming 'movement' could be identified or implemented. This means, that within this containment to a zero state of existence, any kind of leadership becomes impossible. Movement can occur only when the confinement is removed, when the homogenous state of insanity is confronted with reality, when it is destroyed with Truth. However, for this to happen, the insanity must be confronted. It must be confronted to such a degree that it weakens or is destroyed.

When this happens, of course, the sphere of conflicting confinement no longer represents the state of humanity. Humanity has entered a new sphere that describes the confrontations. In this awakened sphere is life and movement. Therefore, the sphere has a definite structure. When the conflicting state is being addressed, the confrontational structure has been activated.

This means, there is no lower structure below the confrontational structure. Anything lower is a dimension-less zero that has no structure. The zero-dimension state has no principle or truth in support of it. It exists outside the realm of reality in which man's true image is defined. We find this state referenced at the very lowest level of Mary Baker Eddy's structure for scientific development which includes a framework for exploring the confrontational structure.

When the zero state is torn apart by confrontation and spiritual sense once again determines the course of humanity, productive leadership becomes a possible, even vital component. But not before. Until the breakout confrontation awakens humanity, the advanced guard of leadership stands and acts alone. This breakout, however, can occur quickly.

In some cases the activation of the confrontational structure occurs when the destructive processes that act upon humanity become so absurd, and the insanity so gross, that the dormant spiritual sense of humanity can no longer be confined. Often, the breakout conditions that "wake" humanity out of its slumber are incurred by the fascisms of its oligarchy that reigns in the sphere of homogenous insanity. The Golden Renaissance, for instance, was built almost directly on the ashes that humanity was reduced to, after it's world-financial system of the time disintegrated (in 1345) under the pressure of unsustainable looting. The fact that half the population of Europe perished at this time seems to have been a sufficient wake up call to start the confrontation in earnest, by which the oligarchy was dealt with as needed, to some degree and for a season.

On these fundamentals rests the hope of mankind, because these break-out conditions can be recreated. Nothing else offers any hope. Indeed, what more does humanity need beside its spirituality that it can rely on as a sure thing, that can never be extinguished, which is able to transform the world according to fundamental Principle that one cannot mock with human will nor escape for it in order to evade its effect? Thus, the survival of humanity rests with itself, and the same 'grain of Truth' that assures this survival also open's its horizon to infinity. Therefore, let us agitate the hell out of the world by introducing higher ideas that activate the confrontational structure that opens the gates of heaven on earth. This goal is always achievable. But first, we need to recognize and come to understand Mary Baker Eddy's structure for scientific and spiritual development, within which the confrontational structure is located.

THE END

Postscript Story - *The Flat Earth Society*

The opening chapter of the novel with the same title (Episode 4B of the series of novels *The Lodging for the Rose*) has been added to this book. The chapter illustrates in dialog the depth of the ongoing collapse of what is still called economics and a civilization, though the terms barely apply anymore. The dialog takes place in an airplane coming from Russia, destination London.

+ + +

Heathrow was a sea of grounded airplanes. The captain announced over the intercom that he suspected a terrorist threat had shut the airport down. For a moment it seemed to me that the world-financial system had crashed. Either way, we wouldn't be landing. No movement was discernible on the ground. The baggage carts and service vehicles were all parked in neat rows. This didn't look like a typical response to a terrorist threat. Not a soul was in sight. It seemed as if air traffic had come to a halt in the two weeks we had been away in Russia. Obviously it hadn't. A single wing of the main terminal looked like it was still in operation. It had Air Force planes parked near its gates. This part seemed to support the captain's terrorist suspicion. What a shocking return this turned out be to the Western World! If this was a terrorist threat, I found it amazing that we were allowed to come so close to the airport. Perhaps the control tower had been shut down as well. If so, perhaps it was more likely shut down for the lack of money or for a fungible currency.

Fred suggested that if the reason was economic, Russia would be in a worse mess that it had tried to hide in the usual way with propaganda and 'chewing gum' that they so often used to hold their fragile system together. We all knew that Russia's economy had been collapsing more rapidly than ours had. It merely came to light with different and less visible consequences in Russia. Like the West, Russia too had refused to take the required actions to save its economy. Perhaps it was fortunate for Russia that it had isolated itself from the West and reversed course at virtually the last moment, by which it had somehow muddled through.

We didn't land in London that day. No official reason was given as to why. The only thing that the captain was "allowed" to tell us, as he put it, was that the plane had been diverted to Frankfurt, Germany. Everything else, he said, was classified. He told us that he found it rather amusing that the West was so secretive about such a "little thing," as he called it, for which our plans had been altered, whatever the 'thing' was. I personally didn't mind the diversion, nor was I surprised by the secrecy. Secrecy, deception, and dishonesty had become the hallmark of the West. What we were experiencing was consistent with the usual games that were being played, the secret games like the Iran/Contra affair that had been kept secret for a long time, and the CIA's secret terror offensive against the Third World that had become rich in death squads and lean in humanity.

"Did I tell you that I nearly got robbed twice in a single day at Heathrow airport?" I said to Ushi as our plane climbed away and turned sharply.

"No!" Ushi answered in a serious tone.

I told Ushi that I had gone into one of the washrooms on the way to the baggage office. Travelers rarely use these out of the way washrooms unless their luggage is lost. I told her that I was barely through the door when I sensed a man standing behind me. Before the door was fully closed he had pushed me hard against the wall. "Welcome to the home office" the man had said to me in a joking manner. "Please give me everything you've got on you. Be smart! No tricks!"

I told Ushi that I heard some groaning in the background. I told her that I twisted myself right out of his lock and rammed the chap into the opposite wall.

"And," said Ushi.

"I guess he got a surprise he didn't expect, and me too, especially me. The man was in uniform," I said to Ushi. "He was one of the airport security people that had been hired to protect the public. He had nearly robbed me." I began to laugh. "Can you imagine the two of us. I just stood there in disbelief and stared at the man and shook my head. 'You're disgusting,' I said to him as I let go of his arm. 'It's even more disgusting that you want to steal from a fellow officer. I am an officer of the diplomatic service,' I said to him. 'We are struggling like hell to keep the world from blowing up, and there, you're turning against your own family as it were. With creeps like you providing security, what chance does humanity have?' With this said, I left him standing where he was and did what I came for."

I told Ushi that it really got interesting after that. I told her that he apologized profusely as I left the washroom and came running after me, pleading that I shouldn't report the incidence. I told Ushi that he started to explain the "ways of the world" to me, as he had put it. 'Stealing has become a way of life in London,' he had insisted, 'especially the stealing from your own kind.' He couldn't see why I was so annoyed with him."

Ushi laughed.

"Don't laugh yet," I replied. "It gets better, still."

"It can't get better," she said.

"Oh it can. He told me that he had been employed

earlier in one of the big investment houses, before he became a security officer at the airport. He told me what he had encountered there, to explain his actions," I said to Ushi. "He told me that everybody had been stealing from everyone else, there. He said to me that they even had the audacity to collect a commission for arranging the theft. And it was all totally legal. He said it's still going on. He said to me, 'with this considered, why should it not be legal for me to rob you in the washroom where you least expect it?' Yes Ushi that's what he said to me. He said the process is the same in both cases. It's the same game utilizing the same method with only a slight difference in the steps involved."

"You found this interesting?" Ushi interrupted. "Let me guess, you invited the man for coffee, right?" she said and grinned.

"No, no, it was lunch time," I corrected her. "I invited the man for lunch." I told Ushi that his point was that the whole market had become an organized arena for stealing. Huge profits were taken out of the market where nothing was being produced that generates the wealth that was distributed by the brokers as profit.

Ushi began to laugh as I said this. "That's really becoming comical, Peter," she interjected.

"Don't laugh," I replied. "He told me that the 'investors' brought in their money massively and cheerfully and gave it to the brokers. But did the brokers buy them any real investments for their money, of the type that builds industries that produce useful goods? No, they didn't. Nothing was bought anymore in terms of investments to finance productive processes, new industries that meet the needs of society by producing useful things, or investments that build infrastructures which are required to operate the industries, or investments that advance culture, art, science, and technologies, which enrich society? He said that they didn't buy any of these kinds of investments for their clients, because that's not being done anymore. He told me in his sarcastic kind of way that nobody can get rich honestly, especially not when the physical economy is being starved out of existence. He couldn't see why I was surprised that he was stealing."

Ushi just shook her head.

"This was my reaction too, Ushi," I said to her. "He told me that the moneys, which the investors shelled out, were immediately paid out as profit to somebody else, and of course also to the brokerage houses in the form of fees. He told me that no thought was ever given about anyone ever paying anything back to the investors. It was understood that this wouldn't happen, because the real liquidity, the real value that the investments were rated at, didn't exist for such repayment to be possible except perhaps on an extremely small scale in a few isolated cases. He pointed out to me that for as long as the investors don't want their money back this system works great. And it did work great. He said that everybody was happy in their illusion that they were rich. He told me that the people who ran the investment business knew that the investments that they solicited the public to buy, could only be paid back when something of value would be produced, which wasn't happening anymore. And so the grand illusion that something was happening was being maintained with a shiny facade of indexes, trend analysis, fancy jargons, and a lot of thick lies."

Here I began to laugh together with Ushi. "You know what he said to me," I said to her while still laughing. "He told me that he suddenly realized that he had become an honorary member of a new type of Flat Earth Society."

Ushi suggested that I was joking and getting rather silly.

"That's what I told him too," I said to her. "I told him that this was a poor analogy since the people in the financial investment society are fully aware of the truth. They just don't want to acknowledge the truth. He had just looked at me and shaken his head. 'What truth?' he had asked finally. I told him that the truth that I recognize is that we need to rebuild the world on the platform of the Principle of Universal Love. I told him that I was looking for Love-Based Economics, such as the American System of Economy exemplified by Alexander Hamilton and Franklin Delanor Roosevelt, the only kind of real economic system that can supplant the Greed-Based Fascism that had been invented by Adam Smith on behalf of the British Empire. Greed was used as a weapon against America."

Ushi laughed again.

"You are right," I said. "The man just laughed at me too. He called me a dreamer. He told me that the age of Love-Based Economics has ended long ago and that the age of Greed-Based Fascism, as I had put it, is on the way out as well, to be replaced by Rape-Based Brutality. 'We do no longer just steal anymore from one-another,' he said to me. 'We cut deeper. We almost kill to steal. What do you think the homeless are the victims of? They are the residue of economic rape? Rape is the new western song, not love,' he said in a sarcastic sounding tone of voice. 'We are entering the age of preemption. We kill, so that we can steal.'"

Ushi shook her head.

"I told him that he was wrong," I said to Ushi. "He just laughed at me. He told me that the times have changed. 'The rules have been altered.' He told me that the elite of financial Flat Earth Society is fully aware that the earth is a sphere, but that it is their goal to convince everybody else that it isn't. He told me that the financial Flat Earth Society maintains itself as a fancy facade to inspire untruthful perception. They lie to society. But mostly they want society to lie to itself and keep its thinking irrational all the way to the point that people will latch onto their Flat Earth propaganda that riches can be drawn out of nothing without any productive process being involved. He said it is their goal to convince the stupid public that the Earth isn't really a sphere, and that all their fancy notions about spherics that they might have are far too complex a concept to be real. 'Open your eyes,' they say to the people, 'see, the Earth is flat, the markets produce profits. What more do you need to concern yourself with?' That is what they said to the investors, when he was still employed in the financial world, he told me. He smiled as he said this, and added that the truth, in spite of the thickness of the lies, becomes ever harder for them to hide as the lies are wearing thin."

I looked at Fred for his reaction.

Fred simply smiled.

"The Heathrow chap told me that they had been successful for a long time in their effort to tell the public what the public wants to hear. And they were well paid for it," I said to Fred. "The man told me that they would take the people who had the slightest reservations about the brokers' Flat-Earth lies and drive them, comparatively speaking, to a sea shore and invite them to see with their own eyes that the earth is absolutely flat without a doubt. This means that they would dazzle them with graphics and profit statistics, all professionally displayed. They would even go as far as to gently ridicule the investors' 'lagging' perceptions if they didn't agree. They would always tell them to invest for the long run in the hope that the Flat-Earth illusion that they had worked so hard to 'inspire' them to accept would not be shattered, because the markets would crash should the illusions fail. 'That's how the financial Flat Earth Society works,' the Heathrow chap said to me."

I nudged Fred to get a reaction. "The man was defending his former profession that was 'good' for him while it lasted," I said. "I can't blame him far that."

Fred just kept on smiling.

"The man explained to me how it works in detail," I said to Fred. "When we had lunch he took the sugar basket that was on the lunchroom table and dumped everything out, all the sugar bags, the ketchup, the salt. He said that the empty basket is the market. He said the market is always empty. 'It never produces anything. It never pays anything back.' Then he threw four sugar bags into the basket and took them back out again, and said that somebody just made a lot of money by this process. He asked me where the money came from that makes the market such a rich place. Instead of answering he pointed to himself. 'The loot is supplied by whoever takes the stuff out,' he said to me. And he is right. He told me that the money for the profits gets sucked out of the real economy, out of everybody's pocket. He also knew that this happens silently as vast funds are being diverted away from productive investments to the point that those investments weren't happening anymore. Even he could see that all the investment funds where insanely poured into hyper-inflated stocks and bonds without backing, or into pure derivatives gambling for which no backing in equity is required, etc.. He told me that the end result is that no real investments are made anymore in the physical economy. He explained that working for a living was considered by evermore people as being much too slow in comparison with stealing. 'And so nothing of value gets build anymore or very little, he said. He said to me that it was deemed a thing of the past to build and produce things when this ordinary stuff that society needs to fulfill the requirements for its living can be imported cheaply through free trade thievery. 'We live by the proceeds of slavery,' he said. 'And that's stealing too, isn't it? That's the reason why society gets poorer and poorer. The jobs disappear. The industries disappear. Food becomes scarce. People become beggars.' He looked me into the eye and said, 'can you blame people like me for waking up and catching on to how the game is being played and thereby become thieves themselves? You may be annoyed at me for attempting to steal from you, but you are abetting the process yourself by doing nothing to correct it. You know as well as I do that the West has become a den of thieves, but you stand aside and let it happen. This tells me that you are either a pathetic hypocrite or that you have joined the Flat Earth Society like the rest of the world has, only in a slightly different way.'"

Fred laughed. "So you see, Peter, the Flat Earth Society has made converts out of almost everyone. The man is right of course. The closing of the eyelids doesn't change the reality that any nation that doesn't produce anything is poor. That's when the thieves are born in big numbers, and we all know that. When nothing is being produced, people resort to stealing, they almost have to. It's always been like that way, Peter. In fact, that's how empires maintain themselves. Empires prevent economic development in order to keep society impotent. They have to do this so that society won't challenge their power. That's how the imperials are be able to maintain their opulent living. In the poor environment that they create, they steal. They have no other options. It's a simple reality for them, Peter. Naturally, their process doesn't work. There is no wealth being produced without productive development that maintains society's existence. That's why every empire in history has failed. Financial portfolios are meaningless, Peter, when nothing is produced in terms of real wealth that the portfolios might represent. When nothing is produced, Peter, a nation is poor no matter how much money it has floating about. Money looses its value when nothing is being produced."

Fred turned to Ushi. "Tell me, would a society, like a tiny country, which has 10,000 in money and produces ten tractors per year be richer or poorer than if that same society were to have a billion in money and produced only one tractor per year?"

"It would be richer with 10,000 in money that could buy ten tractors for a 1000 each," Ushi answered. "If it produced only one tractor, that's all it could buy. It would be poorer then, whether it had ten billions or ten trillions in money. If nothing is produced money looses its value."

"You illustrated a principle," said Fred to Ushi. "The principle is that the value of a nation's money reflects the nation's productive power. Right now we are on the fast track of scrapping production in America. We have been on this track for some time already. We have become poorer and poorer. It doesn't matter how much money in financial aggregates people have stashed away in their portfolios. We have become a poorer nation by loosing our productive capability. People refuse to see that, they refuse to acknowledge that their financial portfolios are fast becoming worthless by the very process that created the portfolios in the first place. The Flat Earth Society refuses to see the reality of the universe. The people that are trapped into this society refuse to acknowledge the truth even if they can see the evidence of the truth with their own eyes. The chap that had you spoken with was right. That's what's happening economically around the world, especially in America. America was once known around the world as the greatest economic powerhouse on the planet. The dollar was worth a lot then. Its high value had been kept fungible by the productive power of our nation. In those days one would only need $2,000 to buy a car. Now one needs $40,000 to buy a lesser car, and even that car is most likely produced in foreign lands for slave-labor type wages. The whole world is becoming poorer while it's rushing down this track, Peter. Even the empire is becoming poorer. That's why the imperials are now stealing from the whole world in a desperate attempt to keep their sky-castles afloat."

"Fred turned to me. "That chap that you spoke to saw a tiny bit of the modern phenomenon that has made nearly the whole world devoted members of the Flat Earth Society. And the reason for that is, and you know that as well as I do, it's that our modern society has switched the focus of its heart from love to fascism, from producing a rich world for one another to stealing from one another."

Ushi punched me with a grin, "Isn't that what Steve told you already. He had been repeating this like a broken record, although in a slightly different context?"

"Sure, he did, Ushi. I understand the process. We all understand it. I just found it fascinating that this simple-minded fellow had figured this thing out too, all on his own, when the world's noble experts tell everybody the very opposite. 'The market is stable,' they scream. 'Invest for the long run. The market is rich. The earth is flat. Your investments have made you a millionaire. Your illusions are true.'"

"People love to be lied to if it makes them feel richer," said Fred to me. "That's how pathetic we have become as a society. People bow to these lies so deeply that they give all their living away, cheerfully. Haven't we created an amazingly convoluted world, Peter? We are destroying the foundation for our physical existence, and we are doing it cheerfully and are giving it out best efforts. I hail the little chap that he has figured this out."

"That's what made that man a rebel," said an elderly man who was sitting next to Fred. He turned to Fred. "Society isn't as lucky as that man," he said quietly. "Society has been taught to remain stupid. I know this to be true, because it had been my job to teach economics. I had taught economics for twenty years. One day a student asked me a question. This question caused me to wake up. That's when I stopped teaching economics."

"And what did the student ask?" Fred interjected. "What was the question that changed your life?"

The man laughed. "The student was a young woman. She stood up in class and asked innocently why it is that all the greatly admired economists don't know anything about economics. She had laid out to me essentially the same stuff that you just talked about with your friends. She then asked me why none of the great economists know anything about what is really happening. She told me that she found closed minds wherever she turned, especially when she dried to discuss real economics with people that make economic policies. She told me that she became most frustrated when those closed-minded people, instead of facing the truth, always resorted to asking her which school on economics she had graduated from. She said it appeared to her that unless one has gone through the meat grinder of earning a diploma in economics one is nobody to those in the club of small-minded people. She told me right in the face that this meat grinder is destroying her sense of reality. She suspected that the club people wouldn't be allowed to talk with her unless her destruction as a thinking human being was complete and she would be as stupid as they were. She said to me angrily, 'I don't want to end up being as stupid as these people are, but that's inevitable isn't it, after spending three years of submitting my thinking to lies? It seems to me that when the truth longer means anything, elitism becomes important. Whoever is too stupid or too afraid to talk about the truth is so poor that he hides behind the facade of opinion. These people then tap you on the shoulder and cry arrogantly with a smile that their opinion is better than my opinion, because they have a certificate to prove it. That's elitism. I'm sick of it. Who wants a diploma that certifies that one is an accomplished parrot of the official lie? I would never hire anyone who flashes a diploma in my face. I would answer to that person, parrots don't think. They blabber instead of discover. Parrots aren't human.' With having said all that to me the she young packed up her bag and walked out of my classroom. She didn't accuse me of inducting people into the Flat Earth Society of the economically insane. She didn't have to say this out loud. She sensed somehow that I understood this."

"Well, did you understand this? Is that why you quit teaching?" Fred asked.

"I took me a few days to understand what she had been saying. And no, I didn't quit," said the ex-teacher with a smile. "I wanted to go on teaching. I woke up that day and soon started to teach real economics. If one wakes up one is awake. I couldn't go back. I started to look into the history of our nation to discover what had made us great. Oh, I was surprised alright. What I discovered made sense. Consequently I started teaching the American System of economics. I started teaching Hamiltion. I discovered that America was founded on a credit-society principle. Out of that came the American System of Economics as it was later known. I discovered that it was the credit-society principle, which Alexander Hamilton had been building on, which had made us a rich nation. With this system Hamilton had turned the nation around from a debt-ridden bankrupt wreck that America had become under British free trade, and had turned this wreck into a rich industrial nation. I also began teaching the economics of Lincoln. I discovered that it was Lincoln's credit-society economics that had enabled the efficient industrial production that gave us the needed advantage that proved critical for winning the Civil War. The USA wouldn't exist today without that. I also began teaching the economics of Henry Carey, and so forth. By the time I had finished a year of this teaching I was as proud as a teacher as I had never been before. My students understood something. Even the young woman came back into my class again. The enrollment for the next semester had doubled."

"So why did you quit?" Fred asked again.

"I didn't quit. I was fired," said the man proudly, with a smile. "I should wear a big button on my vest that reads: I was fired by the elite! One is labeled a quack in the brain-dead world of the Flat Earth Society if one is teaching reality. I was booted out. Reality doesn't fit into this artificial world of theirs where everyone is an accomplished parrot. I was regarded a disturber of the peace. The official goal in teaching economics had been to put people to sleep in order that the imperials' greed-based fascism wouldn't be detected. It is critical for the imperials that society's young people sleep-talk, as in dreams, and not live like human beings, but like parrots that imitate the sounds they hear. I disturbed that scene. I disturbed the peace by waking people up. The school Principal had to fire me. He had no choice. I had been undermining the senility in society that the empires' looting process depends on. If the school hadn't fired me, the imperials would have forced the school to be shut down. I was a danger to their system, like Dante Alighieri had been in the 13th Century. The empire had been afraid of him. They had been afraid of a poet. That is why not a single officially recognized economist will ever tell the truth at any time; with a few exceptions. The empire owns them all. It owns their soul. They hold up their diploma of senility and parrotry, and from behind that screen of 'authority' they lie as they have been taught to do, as I once did. Some people might have started out honestly and with the best intentions, but in order to survive they gradually allowed themselves to become prostitutes for a buck, which I could never do. They had to fire me. That's what ended my career in economics after more than twenty years of teaching it. I find it amazing in comparison with my own experience that this simple chap that you had talked about had come to the same conclusion, and apparently much faster."

"Actually it isn't amazing that he did," Ushi interjected. "It is not amazing that this person had figured out some parts of that crazy game of lies and done so all on his own. Why shouldn't he have woken up? He is a human being, isn't he? It took you longer, because you had been buried in the mud far more deeply than he had been. Some never get out. Most people don't. Nevertheless, every human being has the same capacity to discover universal principles and to recognize what happens when these principles are ignored or are intentionally violated. In fact, the game has become so crude now that a blind person should be able to recognize that the facade is paper-thin. But they don't. Even the government has joined the army of thieves, and nobody objects. As our money is fast loosing its value, people have to earn vastly more in numeric terms just to keep themselves alive. Of course for those higher earnings in numeric terms, people have to pay an ever-greater portion of their earnings to the government in taxes. The government acts like an empire. That's how the government joins the parade of the thieves. The whole economic structure of our country becomes poorer by this process of universal robbery."

"The chap at Heathrow didn't say anything about that kind of thievery," I interjected."

"Of course he didn't," said Ushi and began to laugh. "He probably never considered paying taxes on the proceeds from his stealing. He must have discovered this loophole while working for the big thieves."

"I think he felt the crunch nevertheless," I said to Ushi. "He knew that the whole world is loosing its grounding in reality. He figured this out, as Steve did. He could sense that the currency speculators are in the process of destroying our world more radically than any war had in the past," I added. "The man had called the currency traders 'thieves without honor,' whatever he meant by that. I suppose he regarded himself to be an honorable thief who steals merely to stay alive. He had figured out that these currency thieves don't allow the nations to have this minimal privilege. They tell the nations that they must open themselves up to the global market in the name of globalization, or else they will be bypassed by progress. Then, as soon as the nations comply and globalize their economy, the speculators rush into these unprotected countries and loot them to the bone. The chap told me that the Flat Earth Society afterwards parades its stolen profits with big banners in the streets as proof that all their claims of prosperity are true. He told me that they parade their wealth on the streets with their big Mercedes Benz cars, their Jaguars and their Rolls Royce limousines, and almost all people stupidly treat them like royalty. He said it was absolutely pathetic to watch how small people had become."

"Oh, people have always admired the royalty that has robed them," interjected the man next to Fred. "The people have been carefully taught this stupidity."

Ushi laughed again.

I told Ushi that the man at Heathrow had laughed too, at the irony of it all, at the audacity of these financial world-robbers who were actually bragging before everyone, right in the open, about how successful they have been in stealing from society. He found it funny that people would look up to them as though these thieves had done some heroic deed. He said 'what kind of world are we living in, in which the thieves proudly display their loot in public and are honored for their crime?'

"Isn't that Rape-Based Insanity?" I said to Ushi moments later.

"Rape?" Ushi repeated.

"Oh let's be honest, we all play this game," interjected the man beside Fred. "Just go out on the streets in any North American city. How many foreign-made cars do you see that were produced in the world's poor slave-labor-wage countries? Those cars were essentially stolen. We take these people's products and pay them with our largely worthless currency. That's stealing. And even of what we pay, the workers that produce the cars get very little. The rest is stolen away for profit. That's why the poor countries remain poor and get poorer too. We won't allow them to break even, much less develop themselves. And so we fill our streets with the stolen loot that we've acquired by this 'rape' and call the result prosperity. Are we doing anything different by doing that, than the big thieves do that parade their limousines or yachts as proof that their financial system works? We coerce the poor countries to throw away the only wealth they have as a nation, their human wealth, and waste that wealth for our benefit. We give them less than what it costs them to produce the goods, and far less than what would be needed for the slaving nation to develop itself and its people. We are using their people up like an expendable commodity. That's worse than stealing. And yes, we parade the loot on our streets and are proud of our prosperity. That my friends, is what Greed-Based Fascism looks like in real life. It has become rape."

"It didn't used to be like that," said Fred. "America used to be the model of Love-Based Economics. We used to have a production-focused environment that enriched the entire society. We were so rich then that we could export from the excess that we produced and deemed this as a gift to the world. We had helped to enrich the world. Now we steal from society, even that which we export, and expect the world to follow suit. Of course there isn't much exporting going on. We have become too poor now to be able to export much anymore. We only export debt and worthless money. Of course, since we are the masters of the game, this kind of intensified thievery remains totally legal."

Ushi broke out in laughter over the sarcasm in Fred's tone of voice that appeared so artificial, so unlike Fred's normal self.

I told Ushi that the chap at Heathrow suggested that what goes on under the cloak of globalization is actually far worse than legalized theft. "It truly is rape," I said. "The chap had compared globalization to asking a storeowner to put a huge sign in the display window of his store, proclaiming to all people that the store is now an unprotected zone. The man said that families wouldn't dream off keeping their apartment unlocked when going out to work, but that is what these robbers are demanding that all the nations of the world must do, and the nations actually comply, and consequently they get robbed. Of course, when chaos erupts, the robbers pull up their noses and say, 'why, the stronger traders have every right to be successful.'"

"You mean the stronger traitors," said Ushi and laughed. "They are traitors indeed, to our innate humanity. These are the guys who used to come with sledgehammers to break down their neighbors' doors and steal their belongings. Now the traitors find this too cumbersome and advise their neighbors to keep their doors unlocked."

"No, Ushi, I protested. "The noble people of the Flat Earth Society never use such honest language," I said to her and laughed. "They never say traitor, they say trader. They never say stealing, they say profit-taking. They will never admit that the market is crashing, when it is. They call it instability."

I said to Ushi that the Heathrow chap was fully aware that this hidden language was the exact same kind of the language that had been used to create the Thirty Years War. "He told me that 400 years ago the watchword was, 'Might is right!' He said that today the watchword is the same. He told me that in the early days the watchword for was wrapped up in soft talk in order to hide the real game that kills people. He said to me, 'just read Hobbes, and remember that this kind of soft language killed half the population of Europe. We use the same kind of soft language today in the financial world. We say that the stronger investors have every right to be successful.' You are right, Ushi, that's like saying that the stronger thief that comes to rob you with a crowbar and a sledge hammer has every right to break your door down and clean out your belongings while you are away at work. Of course they don't use that kind of honest language in the Flat Earth Society. It is not in their nature to tell people how it really is. They tell the people what they like to hear. The chap said to me, 'We thieves are pleasant people. We go far out of our way to tell the investors exactly what it is that they like. Aren't we wonderful? We even hire professionals to tell people what they should like. We are helping them at every step.' He told me that the sophisticated thieves carry 'soft' crowbars and 'sledgehammers' now. And he added that this wasn't anything new, but had been invented by the ancient Greek, immortalized by the great Pericles, the god of all theives."

I said to Ushi that the chap at Heathrow had also told me that the modern criminals are now admitting some these once hidden things. When the cover wears thin the truth is right in the open. So they change the tone and call the thievery, politically correct. Tragically, society goes along with what they say. The chap told me that he himself got his flat broken in and cleaned out not too long ago. He told me that when he became enraged about it and complained to the police, the police actually told him that it was his own fault that he got robbed. The police told him that he should have had a solid steel door installed to guard against the thieves, and should have had a triple lock installed on it, and an alarm system set up inside, and bars put on his windows. That's what he was told by the police. He told me that he began to laugh when the police said this, because he remembered his own saying that the stronger traders have every right to be successful. Then he added sadly to me that when it comes to countries wanting to protect themselves against the international thieves in pinstriped suits by wanting to install tariffs and currency control measures, then the entire Flat Earth Society explodes into a rage and screams 'you cannot do that! That is against the rules! That is protectionism. Protectionism is bad. You have got to stay transparent!'"

Fred laughed as I said this. He said, "that's funny."

"The chap at Heathrow didn't think it was funny," I countered Fred. "The chap had nearly cried when he told me this. He said to me, 'our world has become such a crazy and mixed up place that stealing has become a way of life and is protected from the highest levels of governments, enforced with the power of worldwide institutions.' He said that he had never imagined that he would submit to stealing, but with so much of it going on all around it's easy to get caught up in the flow of it. After we had finished eating lunch together he apologized once more for his attempted robbery. He even paid the bill. On the way out of the restaurant he noticed another robber lurking behind us, following us. He simply told the man to go away. He told him that we were robbers ourselves, to which the other fellow replied, 'so?' But he did go away."

I suggested to Ushi that the madness that the man had become caught up in couldn't continue to escalate indefinitely. "Steve always says, something will crack."

"Don't be surprised when it does," said the retired teacher sitting next to Fred across the isle. "Also don't be surprised when the day comes when you will find that all of these things that you are so concerned about now, become insignificant and trivial, because that's what they are in comparison to what is being prepared in the background right now."

I was shocked. I said something to the effect that he must be mistaken. "How can things get worse than they already are?"

He simply shook his head. "You really don't know, do you?" he said quietly.

"What do we not know?" said Ushi to him.

"You don't know that a most powerful depopulation weapon is being deployed right now and that humanity loves it," he replied.

I told him that I had no idea what he was talking about. I told him that I was under the impression that we had prevented a nuclear war with the cancellation of the SDI.

He replied calmly that he wasn't surprised at my ignorance. He explained that he wasn't referring to nuclear war as a "depopulation weapon." He said that he was referring to the big bioengineering labs that are owned by the major food cartels. He said that these labs have begun producing super-high-yield food grains that render any farmer uncompetitive who doesn't utilize these grains.

"Isn't the increased yield hailed around the world as a breakthrough for world food-security," I interrupted the man.

He just laughed. "My dear friend," he said, "you are as blind as the rest of the world." He said that my comment would be correct if it was not for one little detail that overshadows everything. He paused and looked at me like a teacher expecting an answer from a student, then shook his head. "Those super grains produce sterile seeds," he said. "You didn't know that, did you?"

He asked us all to consider the consequences of this revelation. He said that there was a big push on by the cartels to introduce these types of super gains into every grain growing country in the world, ostensibly for humanitarian reasons, because of their higher yield. "But what will happen as the result of this globalization?" he asked and paused again.

Ushi answered for us, saying that the seed cartels would make huge profits.

He shook his head. He said that this wasn't the answer he was looking for, like he might have said to a class of students. He asked us what the result would be from the entire process as a whole, from a political standpoint. He asked me to tell him how long it would take for all of the natural seeds to become used up, which until now produce fertile harvests though they produced inferior yields.

I didn't now how to answer him.

"How long will it be until those natural grains are all eaten up," he asked again, looking at Ushi. "They will be used up as food of course, that's inevitable. They can't be used as seeds anymore as they produce inferior yields. So, how long will it be until the age of the self-sustaining harvest ends? It won't be long, I can assure you. Now imagine further what will happen when the already private high-tech seed production falls into the hands of a synarchist madman like Adolf Hitler, who hates certain societies of humanity? Until now the use of natural seed grains have been the basis for the self-sustaining grain harvests around the world. It has kept our food supply independent of the private cartels. This independence ends when the farmers' harvests can no longer be used as seeds for the following year's crops? So what happened then when a private madman or imperial master determines who will eat and who won't?"

The man looked at Ushi with a questioning look, like a teacher preparing a student for an exam. "How long will it be until mankind becomes totally dependent on the cartel's seed company for its very existence? We will most certainly get to this stage when the farmer's harvests don't produce fertile seeds anymore. That's unavoidable the way we go. So, won't the cartels then be in a position to choke off the world food supply at will, or large portions of it, and starve major segments of humanity to death at their whim? That's already on the political agenda, folks. It's part of the imperial New World Order. Food has become a weapon to break targeted nations. You should realize that the cartels are a part of the Synarchist World Empire that Hitler had once represented for a brief span, and that most of the leaders of America now represent like him. Since synarchism already dictates the world's food policy via private cartels, believe me you don't want to be vulnerable to that policy any further than you already are. They've set up a trap. Unfortunately that trap is precisely what the whole world is now rushing into."

There was no answer forthcoming, either from Ushi or from me. We knew exactly what he meant. We knew all too well that the food cartels are 'owned' by the synarchist fondi, the same fondi that had been demanding depopulation for over half a century already as a means for assuring the survival of the fondi's feudal imperial system that feeds on poverty and starvation.

It appeared that the man understood that we understood. He called this tragic new development in the world the new economics of the future. He called it Depopulation Economics.

I told him that it shouldn't be called economics at all, but fascism, because that's what it adds up to.

He nodded. "This new reality makes society's financial stealing from one-another a trivial affair, doesn't it?" he added with a stern expression. "Of course the scourge of stealing is welcomed by the rulers of the world. They use it as a smoke screen to hide their real game," he added. "And how do you suppose all of this became possible?" he asked.

"That's obvious," I answered him. "For what other reason would society have been de-educated in the schools and been drawn into mindless games, trivial pursuits, and have been brainwashed with destructive ideals? The goal must have been in place already for a long time. Their goal has always been to isolate the people from the real world so that they won't interfere with the teachings of the Flat Earth Society and their controllers. People have become all too easily manipulated with lies, all the way to the point that they love those lies and protect them, even while those very lies are destroying their world."

"Don't get me wrong," said the man. "This is not just the wave of the future." He emphasized, future. "This is happening now and is happening in every arena that affects human existence, from the monumental all the way down to the trivial stuff like that which causes the word's financial and economic systems to disintegrate."

He addressed himself to Fred. "This should gives you a sense of what is happening on the still larger scale," said the man to Fred. "The trivial stuff of the financial scene is still relatively easy to deal with. What doesn't work financially can always be shut down and be replaced, almost overnight. One can always find solutions for that in times of a great crisis, but when society is suddenly faced with the fact that the foundation for its food supply has been destroyed, and food is cut off selectively to certain countries, no easy solutions can be created, certainly not over night. Now you must think of this in terms of a weapon. What will people eat then when their natural harvests are used up and no food can be grown, because their harvests don't produce fertile seeds anymore for growing the next crops. What happens then when the cartels refuse to sell or refuse to produce? Oops! Yes, without food people will starve and die. You can't change the physical reality. It takes years to recreate a fertile grain culture in which the harvests will supply the seeds for the next year's crop."

I protested. I played the class rebel. I interrupted the man. "Not all the grains are so affected," I said. "And if worse comes to worse people can always eat beans."

The man just laughed. "You will soon find that you loose this flexibility too. The entire farming system is about to be wrecked in a more deep-reaching manner than you can yet imagine. There are movements afoot to take gigantic sections of farmland out of food production and devote it to the production of ethanol as an alcohol-type motor fuel to augment gasoline."

"That will never work," Fred interjected immediately. "It takes more energy input to produce the ethanol than the ethanol gives back as a fuel. The economics involved are prohibitive. Producing ethanol doesn't add to our energy supplies, it uses it up more rapidly. It will never fly, I tell you."

"It will fly," countered the man calmly. "Believe me, it will fly. "Producing ethanol isn't about creating a new energy resource. You are right it would never fly as an energy source as it consumes more energy than it gives back. Ethanol will fly, because it is put on the agenda to wreck the global food supply infrastructure in a big way. America, for example, won't be exporting corn anymore. America's corn it will be distilled into ethanol. Vast tracts of sugar cane, almost all of the Brazilian production, will become devoted to ethanol distillation. In addition, vast amounts of oil seeds will soon be grown, not for food, but for the production of bio-diesel fuel. An enormous increase in fertilizer use and the use of already scarce water resources will be required to make this go. Most of these resources will be diverted from other and often more-essential uses. So you are right. It won't fly in the standard sense. The process is too expensive. Ah, but when it's paid for by the taxpayers and by the poor farmers that have to work longer hours for less, it will become profitable for the cartels. And so it will fly as a wrecking ball and the public will be taught to love it. Just as people can be taught to hate and got to war in a rage, so can they be taught to love the bio-fuel insanity that is destroying their food supply. They will call ethanol, the green gasoline, and they will hail the politician that demand that 20% of the motor fuels burned in the USA come from the new corn liquor, ethanol. Millions of barrels of that stuff will have to flow from the stills every day. That takes a lot of corn, as you can imagine."

"Wow," I said in amazement, interrupting the man.

"Wow is right," said the man. "The destructive potential of this wrecking process goes deep. It leaves almost no part of the food supply system untouched. What is planned here goes far beyond those little things that are associated with a collapsing world-financial system that the man at the Heathrow had been talking about. The imperials' biological food weapon has the potential to make everything trivial that you've been talking about so far."

"We are already experiencing some of that to some degree," I said, looking at Ushi. "We have given tons of money to charities that feed the hungry in the world. The imperials take their food away, and we donate a few scraps to keep the victims from starving to death. This cycle never ends. Nothing is solved by it. We should have given our money to the people that put themselves at the front line to change this insane system. At least we would have been fighting for a solution then. But we didn't do this, did we. How much did we donate to LaRouche? Peanuts, really. How stupid we've been.

The man next to Fred nodded his approval and added that this tragedy isn't about food, really. It's about depopulation. It should be called Depopulation Economics, which is really fascism in a new and grosser form. Then he paused and added after a minute that this horrible fascism was actually not the worst yet, in comparison with what's on the horizon. He said that that a worse form was already in the works to be unleashed as required by the synarchist maters of the world. He called this new and worse fascism 'the still hidden phenomenon of Hysteria-Based Economics,' a kind of hysteric fascism that has never been seen before on our planet.

He told us that we were already seeing the beginning of this fascist slide to hell in the sphere of animal husbandry. He promised that we would soon see the emergence of new pandemic diseases in animals. Some of these are expected to become transmitted to people and become fatal. He told us that the plan is to create a pattern all over the world, of government-imposed mass-killings of animals, supposedly to protect the human population from the spreading infections, and to protect the stocks. He told us that his contacts informed him that once this kind of pattern of mass-killings of animal has been established all over the world as a new form of biological response to diseases, certain conditions would be created under which the same process would then be applied against people. The killing would be said to be regrettable, but necessary in order to protect the rest of mankind from a deadly outbreak of something incurable that spreads like the flu. He told us that these processes of "emergency mandated genocide" are planned to begin small with the sacrifice of small and highly localized populations that would be collectively killed under a nice sounding code name. A phrase would be invented to fit the crime, in with the term "emergency" would be given a prominent place. They might call it, patriotic emergency sacrifice so that others can live."

This time I was shaking my head. "That's insane," I muttered.

The man cautioned us that this still unimaginable process was not designed to remain small, but was designed to be expanded under emergency management to encompass ever-larger targeted populations. He said that in this manner mankind would be culled back like a herd of cattle to the low population levels that the imperial regards as ideal for maintaining a primitive form of feudalism for a very long time to come. The man pointed out that Bertrand Russell had lamented many years ago already that no effective methods exist to make depopulation a viable process. Russell had advocated more intense forms of fascism than had already blacked the face of mankind during World War II. The man reminded us that Russell had complained bitterly that wars don't kill enough people, even the big wars, so that Russell suggested that biological warfare would be more effective. The man told us that Russell's dream is about to come true.

Fred laughed. "Russell would rejoice if he could see how far mankind has 'progressed' beyond his wildest dreams, seeing the 'wonderful' new depopulation tools that are new being developed under the secret mantle of Hysteria-Based Fascism. Vast mass-detention facilities are already being build," he added. "Sprawling concentration camps will soon be a standard part of the American landscape, popping up in almost every state. The inner details of their construction, of course, remain a state secret. There may be gas ovens installed to incinerate the infected. The facilities are being build quietly by a trusted enterprise that is awarded all the no-bid contracts. It's a political thing."

"That too won't fly!" I interjected.

The man next to Fred promised that it will fly. He said that once the planned biological 'emergency management' is put under the usual synarchist UN mandate, and is supported by UN research, meaning lies, and UN enforcement agencies that will be fully equipped with special powers and specialized equipment to do the killing, no nation on earth will have the power to stop the process in order protect its people.

"This project will never fly," I protested again. "Killing livestock to prevent a pandemic is one thing, but killing people? That will never happen."

The man just laughed. "Who will prevent it?"

"No one will carry out this kind of mass killing of people!" I countered him.

He just kept on laughing. "What do you mean by mass killing? The worst has already been done. Remember Hiroshima!"

"This won't happen again," I countered.

"It did happen again three days later, in Nagasaki, remember? A quarter million people were killed in these two cities."

"Those were exceptions," I countered again. "The people who did this genocide were chosen for the job. They were probably profiled for absolute, unreserved obedience."

"Oh was it that?" said the man. "What about Dresden? Half a million people were sacrificed in the biggest massacre ever. A thousand bombers dropped three-quarter of a million firebombs onto that city in 14 hours. It was an orgy of killing that renders the term, genocide, too weak an expression to describe it. It was worse than genocide, and it was done. That's history. Probably 5000 airmen, all of them run-of-the-mill folks, had a hand in this massacre, and they all did their duty, every one of them. Yes, and it was a massacre. You can't call it anything else when you deliberately burn a large city to the ground that had no military value and was choking with refugees fleeing the war. They burned them alive with firestorms hotter than a steel furnace. The smoke plume could be seen hundreds of miles away, as far away as London. Roasting out entire cities became almost a routine thing in those days when the concept of humanity lost its meaning. Japan was devastated by these massacres. Millions were killed in the firestorms our airmen set off in Japan. So don't tell me that the mass-killing of human beings is not possible. It has already been done. We've crossed this line so many times."

"But it has been done in war," I interjected. "The airmen were killing an enemy."

"No, they were killing human beings, people like themselves," the man replied, and he wasn't laughing anymore. "The enemy label is artificial. You should know that. But let me ask you, if a bunch of honored elite of the biological experts would define a whole city as a global biological threat, by being infected with a deadly virus that could spread across the world, wouldn't that qualify the people in that city for the label of enemy? Those people would be roasted out of existence so fast, I tell you, that it would be over before society knew about it. The details would never be made known to the public. They would be covered up for a long time."

"It wouldn't happen," I countered him again. "No society will kill their own people. Society won't stand idly by and allow itself to be slaughtered," I said to him strongly. "Our love will prevent it."

The man just laughed and laughed again. "Society itself will carry out the crime, my friend, it always has in the past. You can reach back into history as far as you like. This has always worked. Just look at where Christianity came from. Look at the self-proclaimed champions of love. Take a look at how easily this love-bound society has been induced to perpetrate the most horrible civil killing, murdering their own kind. You can read the mandate for it in the Bible. As I recall it was degreed by the law of the ancient priests that whenever a man was found with a woman while being married to somebody else, both were guilty of an offence against God and were executed under the priestly laws, so as not to offend God further. It was even demanded that the execution be carried out by the members of the community among which the victims had lived. The villagers were individually required to stone the victims and watch them die from their injuries. This meant picking up stones and throwing them at the very people that had lived in their own midst, people that they knew, people that they had to now face in pain until they were dead from injuries caused by them. If a society could do this to its own people that they knew; who had lived in their midst; that they all had lived with, and worked with, and struggled with; how much more would they do this to strangers if commanded to do so by a higher authority? This kind of utter insanity was probably carried out for thousands of years and may still be on the agenda in some places. This kind of genocide is not new. The Ku Klux Clan is another example of this type."

I raised my hand to stop him.

The man raised his hand too. "You speak about love?" he said to me. "Don't make me laugh. Just look at the Spanish Inquisition that had burned 38000 people alive at the stake because they didn't sing the right words. Look at Hitler's holocaust. Large-scale depopulation was already been on the agenda whether you like it or not, and it will be carried out again on command whenever the natural humanity of society is overruled by some kind of synarchist dictator who controls the thinking of society. And that control is real. We already had three UN sponsored worldwide conferences on depopulation. Did you know that? Almost the whole world has already been made to believe that the earth is dramatically overpopulated, while in physical terms the opposite is the case. Just ask anyone, and people will tell you that there are too many people in the world. The entire western world now stands behind this depopulation ideology and supports it religiously. And it is all totally based on nothing but lies. I am merely saying that today's synarchists have already plans in place to expand the historically proven processes for the mass killing of human beings. They plan to apply them again."

"Only if we fail to create a new renaissance on an ever-wider humanist platform can this insanity happen," I said quietly. "But we won't fail this time."

"Now that's what I want to hear," said the man. "And I want to hear it in stronger words still. No ifs. I want commitment. I want to hear you say that a renaissance is possible and will be done, and nothing can prevent that. But can you say this honestly. Sure, the world has become too dangerous for as long a people agree with the imperials that the earth is too full, that there is a need for depopulation. I am tell you; time is running out for your commitment to begin. The imperial's depopulation project is already near the implementation phase. Nothing less than a budding total commitment to achieve the most profound renaissance of all times will be sufficient to turn this sinking ship around and bail it out. Fighting the ethanol hoax is nothing in comparison with that. This greater challenge demands a ten-times-greater response, especially now that the depopulation goals are wrapped up in secrecy and silence until the thing is under way."

I shook my head again.

"What else would you expect?" said Fred to me. "Would you expect to read newspaper articles on how the fondi intends to murder two thirds of humanity, one person at the time? It wouldn't be in good taste, would it? So the project has been moved underground. But it remains on the agenda. It will happen in some form. One day you will read in the papers that a new and deadly virus has emerged that spreads faster than the 1918 flu did. Then you will read that the hosting population has been identified. You will read that the 1918 flu had spread across the entire Northern Hemisphere in a few months and killed fifty million people. You will read that this time a swift response is needed before it will be too late. The stories will of course be vastly exaggerated, but in real history the 1918 tragedy has happened. Then the next day you will read that mankind has only two days to prevent a much greater tragedy from happening again. Nobody, I tell you, will stand in the way of this 'preventive program' that assures that that mankind will survive. In this case nobody would be given the time, much less the resources, to determine whether the emergency is actually real or is just an imperial political project to kill a segment of society. The unfolding hysteria in society, which the media would stir up, would lead to demands coming from society itself, for swift decisive actions."

"My hope would be," Ushi protested now, "that the truth would spread so fast that someone would pull the pluck on this project before the genocide begins."

Fred laughed, but then stopped himself. "This is getting funny," he said. "Where were you in 1979 when the so-called nuclear accident was perpetrated on Three Mile Island that had injured no one. Instant hysteria had been created in the population that shut down almost all nuclear energy development projects in our country and around the world. The Three Mile Island event was a coldly calculated 'Pearl Harbor' event. It was designed to destroy the nuclear power industry. It was designed to darken the world. We would have had already several thousand nuclear power plants operating in the world by now if it hadn't been for the Three Mile Island Pearl Harbor type hysteria. The so-called accident was arranged by sabotage according to back-door information. Apparently a wrench had been jammed into a valve actuator so that it couldn't be operated. This fact became known almost right away. It exonerated nuclear power. But revealing the truth didn't change anything. The truth was out in the open, but few heard it and none of those had listened. A vast mass hysteria had been unleashed at the instant that the 'accident' happened. The hysteria covered up the truth before it could have become known. The massive hysteria was build up on carefully orchestrated lies following a carefully managed schedule. Did you know that FEMA, the Federal Emergency Management Agency, was implemented just one day before the so-called accident happened? Consequently, the truth didn't interfere. That is how the fondi destroy civilization and get away with it, and get society to actively support the process of its self-destruction."

Fred paused. "Tell me what you remember about President Kennedy being killed?" he said to me. "The Vice President's mistress of several decades had revealed in public that on the day before the President was shot, the VP had said to her, referring to the President, that 'after tomorrow that son of a bitch will never embarrass me again.' She declared in public that her lover, the VP, had told her that this wasn't just a threat. It was a promise. And to her great surprise, true to the promise, on the very next day the President was shot dead with three different bullets. That's how her lover, the VP, took over the office of the President. It was a replay of Shakespeare's Hamlet. Now tell me, Ushi, can you remember ever hearing even a word about that? Of course you haven't, though her story was out in the open. Very few people have heard her story, and those few were evidently too scared to act on it. The Vietnam War was immediately cranked up, which Kennedy had tried to shut down. That truth too wasn't heard for some time. That's how it has always been in history, Ushi. The critical truth isn't heard. The critical truth never spreads like wildfire. The cover-up artists put up such a huge array of barricades that the truth simply can't be seen. And so it will ever be unless we change the setup, and that appears to be still a long way off. The task to uphold the truth is enormous. And so, the depopulation project will like unfold quietly with society still supporting it as the killing goes on. Society will be blabbering like a trained parrot, crying that the earth is too full of people, we have to depopulate."

Ushi interrupted Fred again. "It's not that the earth has become too small for the present population. It is society, which has become too small in its thinking to support itself on the earth. Society has become too 'small' a people, in its love for its own humanity. By this smallness society is actively engaged in shutting down the very infrastructures it requires for its living. We've all seen the evidence of this, haven't we? Under those circumstances the biggest world would be too small."

"That has become today's policy, not our policy, but the imperial policy than has been imposed on us," said Fred. "The policy is called, deceptively, the postindustrial-society doctrine. It's officially hailed as the new and final utopia. Deindustrialization, of course, is sheer insanity in real terms. As we all know, the policy is orchestrated by the fondi to prevent another renaissance from unfolding in the world that would create the kind of humanist power and love for the truth that the fondi wouldn't survive. We all know that the nuclear industry was shut down to keep society poor and to keep the fondi's empire in existence and dominant around the world. Today's fondi, as we all have already found out the hard way in Venice, continue to have their roots in the synarchist ideology that ran the Jacobin terror operations for the British. The British central bankers and the imperial financier oligarchy dictated the wiping out of the elite of France, during the French Revolution. The simply killed all those that had supported the American Revolution. The Martinists may have started the synarchist movement in France, but the control came from Britain. Shelburne and his crowd were directing the barbaric advocates for the use of terror, and they used the terror for political objectives. We know this too. So, when it comes to the killing an entire city in the name of a biological emergency, it won't be a big feat in this sense. It would be 'business as usual' in comparison with what has already been done in the past."

"But while there is time there is hope," said Ushi. "Hope remains until the last moment before the sword falls. While there is time there is space for repentance and for society's growing up. The Principle of Universal Love can be a powerful motivator."

I shook my head. "That kind thinking puts us still too close to the edge," I replied.

"Yes, but it puts us one step away from it," Ushi countered.

"Before the sword falls we have hope," the man next the Fred repeated Ushi's words. "But after it falls all hope might be lost. We all know that unspeakably monstrous atrocities have been committed throughout history. They have been committed again and again, and mankind survived in the long run. But another, still worse atrocity, is also in the planning stage right now. Killing every person in a city is nothing in comparison with those larger goals that are also being pursued."

"What could be worse than killing an entire city of human beings for a political objective, as we have seen too many times already?" interjected Ushi.

"How about making an entire country or region uninhabitable for all times to come?" said the man. "Would you agree that this would definitely be worse?"

Ushi simply shook her head.

"You think I am joking," said the man. "The modern synarchist crowd has a new weapon under development that dispenses radioactive uranium in powdered form with particles smaller than the wavelengths of light. These radioactive particles are so small that they are invisible. They behave like a gas and become dispersed through the air. They pass right through the filters of the best gas mask. They also pass through the lungs, into the blood, and penetrate the walls of the tiniest cells in our body. The radiation that comes from these uranium particles fires off nucleonic bullets that knock out links in the DNA chains. What happens then is unpredictable. Ninety different diseases have so far been identified that can be linked to this kind of damage. It's like living with tiny atom bombs lodged in one's body. The current plan calls for spreading hundreds of millions of pounds of this deadly stuff onto a country, or even just near a targeted country. Once these bombs are dropped, their radioactive particles will poison the land for all times to come. Nor will people be able to see them, or feel them, or smell them. They simply won't know that they have become infected until they get sick, which may take up to five years. By then it's too late. And that scenario will never end. It takes 4.5 billion years for radioactive uranium to loose just half of its presence. For all practical considerations the thereby poisoned environment remains radioactive forever. It is believed that at first only a few people would die from the planned massive poisoning of an entire country. Then, slowly, within the space of a decade millions are expected to become ill from it. In the long run the genetic defects are expected to become evermore accumulative. The increasing defects invariably become transmitted through the offspring, destroying the genetic structure of mankind with no end in sight since the radioactive poison becomes a part of the environment. And that means the global environment becomes poisoned."

Fred nodded. "The days are over when the killing stops on the day the war ends and guns fall silent," said Fred quietly. "The killing goes on forever. The days are also over when you have to attack a country directly, in order to destroy it. It is enough that you drop your bombs nearby. This means that a new geometry in warfare has begun. A country now has to defend itself without being directly attacked. If millions of uranium bombs are dropped on North Korea, China would cease to exist as a function nation in a relatively short period. They Chinese know this, and they would respond to stop the bombing, or else they would perish. They might respond with a nuclear counter-strike and destroy the entire USA. Likewise if Iran is pummeled with millions of uranium bombs has I hear is being planned, then Russia will likewise cease to exist. That's the new reality. Russia knows this too. I cannot imagine that Russia would not respond to such a reality with all they've got to stop the American bombing. If this would mean that they had to launch all their missiles to obliterate the American home base to stop the bombing, meaning the entire USA in a single strike, they would do this without hesitation. They would have to. That would be their only chance for survival, as slim as that chance might be."

"The uranium bombing campaign would likely kill us all," the man continued. "It only takes a few weeks for the airborne uranium particles to become spread around the world. Of course the point will be reached at a certain stage when the most effected countries may need to be evacuated. At the very least, the most effected cities were the uranium weapons would be dropped into heavily would have to be abandoned, and that would include many big cities. Entire new cities would have to be built to replace the polluted ones. And even after that is done, it would be doubtful whether the gene pool would ever rebuild itself. The current plans seem to be focused on depopulating all of the oil countries and the resource-rich regions of Africa and Asia as a first step, whose natural resources the synarchists say, belong to them. The real purpose behind this plan, of course, is more likely in part the imperials' long standing goal to put the hopes of mankind for a new renaissance far out of sight, if not totally. They have been pursuing this goal for centuries in order to protect the synarchist way of empire from ever being in danger again. And that my friends is what has been prepared for our future and the future of mankind, or should I say the future of our planet since mankind will likely become extinct under this plan."

"That's insane!" I protested.

"I didn't say it wasn't," said the man. "Unfortunately, this insanity is almost impossible to stop."

"That's worse than nuclear war," said Ushi.

"We have 65,000 nuclear bombs built," said Fred. "The new plan is to put the radioactive equivalent of 10 to 100 million nuclear bombs into the air. The plan is a;so not so secret as our friend suggests. The new weapon has a name. It is broadly referred to as Depleted Uranium Ordnance. The propaganda is already being prepared that will tell everyone that this stuff is harmless, that the earth is flat, that the moon is made of cheese, that everything is roses."

"I get the drift," I interrupted Fred. "I heard about this stuff too. My first reaction was that this is insane. I still think it is."

"My friend, you will soon be taught to think otherwise," said the man next to Fred. "As a retired teacher I can promise you that you'll be amazed at what can be accomplished with politically correct education - oops, I mean cultural warfare. The new warriors have learned from the mistakes of the past. Nuclear war had been painted with such black colors, and rightfully so, that the whole world is now scared of it. It has become politically impossible for any government to pull it off. This won't happen with the planned uranium war. That's why they call it Depleted Uranium ordnance instead of Dirty Uranium bombs. But there is nothing depleted about it. Uranium is uranium. It emits alpha radiation that can't be depleted. But the millions of uranium bombs that are planned to be built will deplete the human gene pool. And that's on the agenda. It will only take a week to drop the 10 million DU bombs. We've got plenty of bombers. But once this is done, it will seal the fate of mankind forever. Most likely you won't even hear about it until after the deed is done, or it will become so deeply hidden behind terrorist hype and war propaganda that the average person will miss it. Besides, it wouldn't matter then. The time for action is now. When World War II ended, the killing stopped. That era has ended. Now, when the war stops the killing goes on and can never be stopped by any means that we presently possess. It can only be prevented."

"Can you imagine the potential compensation claims that might be made against America through international courts, if that ever happens and the real dimension becomes known? It would tear the world apart before society begins to die and fade into oblivion," said Ushi. Can you imagine the cost involved in the short run, in building brand new cities for a nation of tens of millions of people, or even just the cost to relocate so many people out of the polluted areas that will become uninhabitable, and to create new industries and new food resources for these people?"

"This kind of compensation is impossible," said Fred. "The very best that we can do is that society develop the new technologies and industrial processes that enables a people to build brand new cities with ease. It is possible to do this, to build twenty million new houses with ease if we utilize nuclear energy as a driver and molten basalt as building material. Unfortunately, this kind of development will take a couple of decades to complete. Until then the USA will probably have to host those many of the tens of millions of refugees whose country would have then been made uninhabitable by us. Compensation payments wouldn't cut it. Real physical help would be required, and it would be required on a gargantuan scale from the entire nation and the whole world. That's what we are setting ourselves up for when we hatch out plans to cause irreparable damage in the world."

"That's insanity. It must be stopped before it starts!" I interjected.

The man laughed. "Have you ever been in the army?" he said.

I said that I hadn't.

"Let me fill you in," said the man. "The entire army runs as a vertical operation. Everybody is dominated by somebody. The whole thing is run by a long chain of little dictators. The higher you go the more sweeping do the powers become that the little dictators wield. The man on the top, the Supreme Commander, would naturally assume absolute power if he were not held back by the laws of the land and the Constitution that prevent dictatorial power. That's the American way and always has been. The American President, even in the role of the Supreme Commander, does not have the right to become a dictator. This does not mean that it won't be tempting for a President to assume such absolute dictatorial powers, especially when a vast synarchist apparatus stands behind his back urging him to do so and supplies the legal and political means. That's when the insanity begins that you have to fear. That's when the tragic and the grim becomes the routine of the day by which entire countries will fall by the wayside as they are becoming uninhabitable. It has been said for decades that no ruler or President or Prime Minister would ever be as insane as to start a nuclear war. My experience has been that such people can be found and be put into high places. It has already been done several times. Look at Hitler. Look as Stalin. Look at Mao. I tell you that even more insane people than those can be found and be given the key to the world. Then put such a man onto the top of the vertical heap that projects his insanity down to the last man in slavish obedience. Grim would be too soft a term."

"This has to stop before it gets to that," I cut him off.

"There is only one way," said Ushi. "We all know what this is. It is the one way that has been avoided for millennia. But it always comes down to this one way, the implementation of the Principle of Universal Love. All our hopes converge there. As the options to rescue ourselves become fewer, this one hope remains. It might be possible to solve the financial breakdown crisis by financial technical means, but that kind of option doesn't seem to exist to address the insane imperial attacks on the world food supply. Now with DU weaponry on the horizon we hit a brick wall. There are no technical options available. There exists only that one option that remains, the Principle of Universal Love. No matter how difficult those steps seem that are required to implement this one option that we have with which to prevent this final doom that is hanging on the horizon, those steps must be taken. We have no choice bu to take this one option that reflects the principle of our humanity and reflect its power. If we cannot find a way to do this, then all hope is lost; then the human future is lost and the human journey may end."

"I don't think that this kind of extreme solution is possible," the man interjected.

"I don't know about that," said Fred. "I can remember when a few extreme things were happing. I remember a senator by the name of, Church, who in the mid-1970s dug into the secret empire of our National Security Agency, and the CIA, and into the whole secret government apparatus, and its covert operations. I can remember that he dug up such a stench, coming especially from the CIA, that the whole thing was nearly shut down. The CIA was saved by the thinnest strand of a hair. A compromise was reached that gave Congress oversight over it. Of course, in real terms nothing was changed by the concession. The whole secret government survived and was built up even bigger under the mythical heading of national security that meant secrecy. Nevertheless the fact remains that the whole mess had nearly been shut down out of people's love for their country and there humanity. It was a beginning."

"The secrecy was used to hide the synarchist atrocities that became worse every year," said the man. "However, nothing was ever accomplished with this secret use of fascist force. It hadn't increased America's security one bit, or protected the reputation of the nation. To the contrary, it made America more vulnerable as the nation lost its humanity in the process. Consequently the stench continued unabated with corpses piling up by the millions now, which America created throughout the Third World. All of it was illegal, of course. Obviously, somebody had played Supreme Dictator already then, in the service of imperial insanity. Obviously too, this trek to hell hasn't stopped yet and is constantly getting worse. That's the historic pattern and the future that comes out of it. It looks grim. If this patterns isn't reversed, we're lost."

"In this case we have no hope at all," I said to the man. "I see no one standing in the hustings fighting for a brighter sense of humanity, or any humanity at all."

"Wrong again, there is always hope," said the man. "But you won't like the answer that justifies this hope."

"The answer is simple," said Ushi. "The answer has to be to take down every vertical structure and replace it with a lateral structure. That's the only possible answer."

The man smiled. "You are right. That is the only possible answer. This answer was put on the table 100 years before anyone even asked the question, and it was put on the table by a woman from a small town in New England, named Mary Baker Eddy. The woman created a worldwide church in the late 1800s and placed its government entirely on a complex lateral array of constitutional law. With this pioneering example she closed the door to the vertical process entirely, to the synarchist process. She even closed the door to the democratic process that is vulnerable to be abused in a vertical world. It is impossible for anyone to become a dictator under an absolute constitution that functions laterally. I am not saying that the woman's process is functioning yet. But I am saying that it is on the table as a model for all mankind and for all times to come. Without the growing focus around the world on absolute constitutional principles that become a platform for forging a worldwide community of principles, the kind that invariably create a universal renaissance, the escalation of synarchism will continue unabated as is has for centuries. If this escalation isn't halted and totally reversed it will eventually extinguish all hope. Nothing short of the self-government of society on a platform of profound universal principles will stop the march of synarchism. Things will get worse and worse, even to the point that nuclear war itself becomes obsolete when its horror is being superceded with worse horrors. In order to overturn the entire process and to rescue ourselves from the horrors already created, we have no choice but to re-stage the self-government of society onto a platform of higher-level principles that leave no room in the world for synarchist force and fascist insanity."

"So why do you say it won't happen?" Ushi interrupted him. "You said earlier that the Principle of Universal Love is impossible to implement. You were adamant that it won't happen."

"I didn't say it's impossible," the man replied. "I just don't see it happening. It is one thing to understand what is necessary and quite another thing to do it. I understand the problem that dooms us all. I also understand what needs to be done to create a New World, the kind in which we can live and survive. I even know that whatever needs to be done to get us there is possible to do. But do you see me fighting for it? Do you see me putting my money down, making speeches, educating student's the right way, demanding the governments of the world to regard the truth? No, you don't see this happening. As I said to you earlier, I am retired. The whole world is retired with me. Nothing is happening. We've come to the most crucial moment in history and no one is lifting one finger. The new renaissance that we desperately need is possible, but I see nothing moving towards it. I see no one fighting and rushing to uphold the truth. We live in a pathetic world my friends. And so, my friends, what needs to happen won't happen."

"That makes you a pathetic creature too," Ushi interjected.

"I never said that I wasn't pathetic," he replied and laughed. "Of all the pathetic people in the world I am their saint. How much more pathetic can a person get than I? I understand the crisis; I understand the solution; I understand that the solution is possible; but when it comes to acting I'm pathetic. I find my hands and feet shackled with apathy. Nobody can be more pathetic than that. And as I said, I'm not alone. The whole world is with me. I am their saint."

The man paused momentarily as our plane was touching down on the runway. The Frankfurt International Airport was still open. "All that I wanted to say to him while we taxied to the gate was that he might be mistaken about himself. I wanted to say that he knew this too, that he knew that if we don't accomplish what needs to be accomplished to save our world, we would loose it, and that I didn't believe that anyone, him included, could be so pathetic as to sit back and to let it all happen. But I didn't say this. I kept my peace. Ushi said it instead.

"I urge you to consider how precious the birth of a normal human child really is," she said to the man. "It is precious beyond comprehension, and until now the integrity of this marvel of our humanity has endured all changes and all challenges. But that's precisely what is set up right now to end. The humanity that we cherish has become fragile beyond anything we have ever dreamed of in the past. With the coming dark world of uranium weapons the genetic continuity of mankind is being targeted for a massive assault. No human being can sit idle in the shadow and let this happen. In the shadow of this doom, when it comes to pass, which lasts for all times to come, nobody will talk about such small stuff as a nuclear holocaust anymore. Even as we speak the nuclear terror treat is being maintained primarily for its psychological-potential as a smoke screen. The uranium bombs and munitions have become the real front, haven't they? We all know that they have. As you said they will be put quietly and secretly into the arsenals to give the synarchists a more effective and less visible weapon for annihilating the selected populations that the fondi fear because of the development potential of any humanist population. If that's what you want to see happening, then by all means remain pathetic like a fool. If not, then shed your apathy. Wake up, man! The coming Uranium War, the Last World War, has the most efficient depopulation effect ever imagined, because the effect is so long delayed in coming to the surface that no enemies will retaliate, because once the damage is done, it cannot be undone. There is no point in retaliating then. The radioactive uranium poison will remain in the global environment practically forever. That's the horrid face of today's synarchists depopulation objective. And this horrid face of that objective is your face too, because you won't stand up and stop being pathetic, you won't being a coward in this essential fight for the future of mankind. If we as society won't begin to love one another as human beings, and do this honestly with an intensity that prevents the synarchist objective from being realized, then we have already lost."

Fred agreed with the man's self-assessment that he is a pathetic fool, but Fred said his folly was more in the nature of a coward. "If we don't wake up soon and change the way we regard one-another, and begin to relate to one-another as human beings with love, which is an intensely active thing, then all the hell of horrors that is being planed today will be implemented. And that is scary, because universal love demands action of a kind that you haven't contemplated for years. You are afraid, and that's why you are pathetic."

Fred said to him that mankind has gone along with the synarchist process at every step along the way, from the murdering of millions to the imposition of infertile seeds and the wrecking of the food supply system. "That's history! It's water that passed under the bridge though it is still happening. Only now we face something worse that is yet to come that can flush the whole bridge away. We face the eternal poisoning of entire countries and potentially the entire planet with the fallout of many millions of uranium bombs. We stand on the gallows already, with the final trap doors ready to be sprung beneath us. When do you plan to shed your apathy and replace it with agape? You can't call yourself a human being and remain in apathy in those moments. And those moments are now. Only a coward would remain pathetic in those critically decisive moments. If I hear you correctly by what you said to us, you are not that kind of coward at heart," added Fred. "It's something that makes you a coward. I suspect that you are a coward because you are a liar. You speak the truth to us, but you are lying to yourself."

The man stood up silently and shook Fred's hand without saying a word and disappeared down the isle into the forward cabin. Our plane hadn't fully come to a halt at the gate.

"Is the age of the Flat Earth Society coming to a close; or has it not yet fully dawned?" I said to Fred. I pointed out of the window. "As you can see, the trivial things that by themselves aren't much in the global sense are not as trivial really when they add up into a mountain. But what does this tell us about the big things that remain still hidden, that we can't yet see with our eyes? It's because of so many of those trivial things coming together that our flight has been diverted to Frankfurt. Our deeply mixed up world has already become dysfunctional so that we couldn't land in London anymore and no one was allowed to tell us why. The truth, obviously, has no meaning anymore. How much harder will it yet be to fight for the truth that is kept intentionally hidden, that can't be seen at all by society, even by us?"

Fred didn't answer this time.

I suggested to Ushi as we stood up to leave, that Steve might be interested to hear about what we had discussed on the plane.

"Why don't you tell Steve yourself?" Ushi said moments later while we were standing in line. "Come with me to Leipzig for a few days, Peter. I am certain that Steve will be there. He came back from Italy a couple of days ago."

I hesitated, looking at Fred.

"Oh, I'm sure Fred doesn't mind giving this top agent a couple of days off," said Ushi to Fred in a loud tone of voice.

Fred began to laugh.

"You owe us!" Ushi added.

Fred simply nodded.

Postscript - Part 2: The (real) Principle of Economics

The research element of this prolog is designed to accomplish the following objectives:.

(1) To illustrate the fundamental principle of economics;

(2) To illustrate that there exists only one such principle, not two or three;

(3) To illustrate the financial aspects of this principle;

(3) To illustrate that the present world-financial and economic system is doomed beyond repair;

(4) To illustrate how the breakdown of civilization can be prevented by preempting the disintegration of the doomed world-financial and economic system.

Actually, the real goal lies beyond this. The goal is not just to illustrate a principle, but to do this in such a way that the reader comes to the conclusion, based on an understanding of this principle, that our present economic system is hopelessly doomed. Then, perhaps, the reader will be motivated to take action towards rescuing society and protecting human civilization. If this goal is not achieved, then please forgive the author of this article for having failed, for then your life is in danger, and the danger continues to be hidden from you.

So, how does a person go about achieving the goal that must be achieved? I suppose, the first set of questions that should be answered is probably the most natural set of questions a person might have about the principle of economics:

How can I know what this principle is?

How can the principle be distinguished from what is mere opinion?

The world abounds with people who have strong opinions about economics. How can one 'measure' this principle to determine what is truth? Can we judge truth by its effect?

In order to answer the first question, we need to go to the laboratory. I propose that we take a knife and go together to a grocery store. I will select one of the yellow fruits there, peel off its skin part of the way, and then hand the fruit to you with the statement that this is a banana. I will invite you at this point to take a big byte of the fruit to test its flavor. Finally I will ask you to tell me if my statement, that this yellow fruit is a banana, is a statement of truth.

You may laugh here. The answer is obvious, isn't it? Virtually everybody knows what a banana looks like, what it feels like, and what it tastes like. But what about economics? How does an economic process relate to truth? What is the criterion for judging its truth?

The American economist and statesman, Lyndon LaRouche, has defined precisely such a criterion by which truth in economics can not only be determined, but can be measured. He states that in this specific realm truth is located in the" increase of the potential population density" of a region, a country, or a world. This statement defines what one should reasonably expect from an economic system as its accomplishment. Evidently the success of civilization is not measured by how many millions or billions a few individuals have been able to leach out of the economy of a society's labor. Rather, it is measured by how well a society as a whole is able to support its existence. Here, the LaRouche measurement comes into play.

Truth in economics, located in the increase of the potential population density.

In order to test the principle of economics for truth, let us go back to the beginning of civilization, to the time when humanity was made up of hunters and gatherers. For the sake of this exploration, let us assume that a certain valley was biologically rich enough to support a group of thirty people. They would hunt throughout the valley. They would gather up its fruits and grain. They would do this year after year. Naturally, there would always be enough food available to sustain a group of thirty people. However, when additional people would come into the valley to settle there, an equal number of people would die.

It may be shocking to you, to hear that this tragedy reflects the principle of economics. Indeed, it does. In this case the experiences of humanity reflects the physical limitation of the natural world without any kind of economic system. It should be noted that this tragedy has actually happened for hundreds of thousands of years. The result has been, that on such a starvation limited basis of existence the population density of the early civilizations had remained at the same level for several hundred-thousand years, without any appreciable increase. It should also be recognized that the near complete constancy in population levels was not the result of deficiencies in human procreation, nor was it the result of any magical voluntary restraint in procreation. Rather, it reflected the limits imposed upon humanity by the natural environment that it had to rely on in the absence of any kind of economic system.

Now, suppose someone discovered that the various grains or fruit, which they all ate, can be gathered up throughout the valley and put into the ground as seeds closer to home so that more food can be created for them by this process, and this at a much shorter distance from where they lived. This innovation meant that the people didn't need to forage quite so far anymore. This, in turn, meant that other tribes could now settle in the valley, in areas that were no longer needed to sustain the original group of thirty people. In other words, the potential population density of the valley was increased by the improvements of the economic process. This does not necessarily mean that more people moved into the valley to take possession of it. It merely means that the potential was there for this to happen, which probably did happen over a span of time.

The single (or only) principle of economics

The interesting aspect is that there exists a direct interrelationship between the quality of the economic process and the increase in the potential population density of an area. It is furthermore interesting to note that this interrelationship can be observed universally. The principle involved is the same whether we deal with a stone age society, or our modern society. One can also observe that there has been a continuing increase in the potential population density on this planet over the last few thousand years, which reflects a continuing increase in humanity's scientific understanding (for better farming methods) and technological development (for more efficient tools.) Thus we have come to a point at which 5000 times as many people now exist on our planet than existed during the stone age era, while the potential population density is still greater than what we presently utilize.

The beginning of an economic system.

This economic success story also tells us something else. It tells us that the greater efficiency of the food creating process now left the people in the valley more time for other pursuits. It gave them more time to think. Guess what happened because of this. I would say that the people came up with further innovations, which, once again increased the potential population density in the valley.

It might have been, that by having more time to think, the people of the valley concluded some day that they wouldn't loose quite as many seeds to the birds if they poked holes into the ground with a stick, planted the seeds into these holes, and covered them up again. They may have reasoned also, that even more efficient farming can be achieved if they would first loosen the soil up by tilling it, before sowing the seeds.

The end result of this kind of thinking was, that every time the economic process was improved by a more intelligent perception, the potential population density of the valley increased some more. Eventually, the people's farming efficiency became increased still further when more refined tools were created, such as advanced tools for tilling, or tools for harvesting, or transporting the products, and so forth, which altogether made it is possible for thousands of people to live in the same valley which previously supported no more than thirty individuals.

Obviously, our modern scientific, technological, industrial, and cultural infrastructures are vastly more advanced than those in the early ages. Education plays a large role, today, in increasing the efficiency of our economy. Educational development, which is one of the foundations for society's scientific development, which in turn is the foundation for technological progress and industrial efficiency. We have a vast economy operating today, that delivers food to our table, that provides our clothing, transportation, housing, health care, even relaxation. Nevertheless, the fundamental truth that is found in the modern economic system, is measured the same it was measured in the early ages, in the increase of the potential population density of an area, a region, or a world. The proof of the pudding is in the eating.

Defining the elements of the principle of economics.

With the proof of the principle of economics now understood, we can begin to think about defining the elements of the principle of economics. What are the natural principles that we can utilize for economic action? We have found that zero economic action had rendered the early societies stagnant and always existing at the edge of starvation. But as soon as the economic activity increased, humanity suddenly moved away from the edge of starvation. This happened because the potential population density increased in general more rapidly than the society's need to utilize the increased potential.

It can be said that the trend shown in the above graphics reflects the natural tendency as related to the human economy. If one plot this interrelationship graphically, one comes up with two curves shown that follow a hyperbolic progression. Please note that the blue curve, which represents the normal increase in the potential population density, is leading the brown curve, the actual population increase, by an ever widening margin. These two curves reflect the nature of humanity's actual increase in population density, and its potential increase in population density. The brown curve should therefore match closely the actually observed increase in population density throughout World over the last 3000 years as previously presented.

The factor of money.

When we talk about the principle of economics in modern terms, we must also consider other movements behind the scene, most of which are shaped by a complex array of forces. One of these is money. Money facilitates the interchange of physical values in an economy. The increase of this value, of course, must correspond to the natural increase in the physical economy which corresponds with the increase of the potential population density that the principle of economics brings about.

If we plot the interrelationship between a society's needed money supply, in the for of credit for industrialization and development, then the economic product of the physical economy would be increasing. But What would be the interrelationship between the two?

In this graphic presentation two hyperbolic progressions are shown, one of which (the green one) is increasing slightly faster than the other. It represents the economic product of society. The other curve, the brown one, represents the increase in the money supply of society. One would assume that the money supply should be larger at first, during the initial stages of development, but then should be overtaken once the infrastructural development is complete. It is tempting to believe this, except this concept will never work in practice. It would be entopic in nature. Development would slow down, then stop, and finally reverse itself. This is contrary to the principle of economics where development is an unending and literally infinite process. Which means, that society must always provide itself with a rich measure of development credits, without any limits being imposed.

These credits must be forever leading the process.

There can never be a point when human development is totally satisfied. Development continues without end. For this reason the two curves can never be seen as isolated from each other. The credits must always be focused on increasing humanity's potential for a greater population density with an increased quality of life. It is essential that society provides these credits to itself freely, with no financial profit demands attached. Development credits are designed to increase the society's self-development, rather than financial consideration becoming a burden that hinders its self-development.

Our modern monetarism is build on a different, and therefore defective, platform. On this platform, which is essentially a feudal platform, financial credits are issued with a debt burden attached that effectively hinders human development while it creates financial empires that are drawing society's investment resources away from its physical economy, thereby starving it, and society as a consequence.

Today's IMF supported world-financial system, is such a counteracting system that isolates financial resources into speculative bubbles which strangle not only any ongoing development, but also strangle the economic process itself. By its fundamental platform the IMF system operates totally contrary to the real principle of economics.

The machine-tool element of the principle of economics.

It must be understood that there is more to the principle of economics, however, than can be described in terms of financing in order to create physical output. Money, itself, doesn't produce anything. The modern economy is build upon layers and layers of infrastructures. The modern economy requires transportation infrastructures, such as highways, bridges, railways, canals, and so forth. A modern economy also requires an industrial infrastructure which produces the economic machine, like tractors, tillers, elevators, water pipes, automobiles, ships, refrigerators, clothing, shoes, and a whole range of other products. Except, who produces the machines that lie at the heart of the industrial infrastructure of a nation? The requirements of a modern economy cannot be met with hand-powered equipment. It is impossible, for instance, to built railway locomotives, grain cars, ships, or even consumer appliances, without a vast array of machinery, which are technically speaking, powered tools, that we call machine-tools. Of course, in order to create the required machine tools, a modern economy must absolutely have a strong and highly developed machine-tool industry. Without the machine-tool industry an industrial infrastructure cannot exist, and without an industrial infrastructure, modern civilization cannot exist. A society needs industrially produced goods to support its transportation system, its farming, its housing, its production of clothing, medicine, books, etc, and its food distribution system. In other words, without a strong machine-tool industry at the very foundation of a modern economy, there exists no economy. It is as simple as that.

Human civilization is build on the use of tools, and on the building of these tools. In the modern world the tools of the economy are undeniably machine-tools. Strategically directed financial credits must assure that the machine- tool industry, on which so much depends, is prosperous and viable. Few people realize that this industry is actually more vital to a nation than its farming industry, because the farming industry depends on industrial products, which in turn, the nation depends on for its existence. The machine tool industry is without a doubt the main driver that has enabled the large increases in the potential population density that has been achieved during this century.

The energy element, of the principle of economics.

One must consider this element as major element, which will in the near future become the most important element of the principle of economics. The production of energy, not human muscle, powers the economic machine of a modern economy. Even in ancient times people have found it expedient to utilize animal power for economic processes, such a oxen to pull a plow, or a cart, or horses to provide transportation. We still measure our modern industrial engines in terms of "horsepower" produced, like the engines of cars, for instance. The expediency of applying produced energy to the economic processes, has been established quite early in human development. Nor has this process been abandoned. If fact it has been evermore intensively implemented throughout the whole of human development. Today's economy requires a truly huge amount of energy input to power the economic engines. Every facet of modern life is linked to energy intensive processes, and this for good reason. The use of energy has given us vast freedoms, the freedom to move, the freedom to create comfort in our home, the freedom to build things which can never be built with human hands. It has been discovered by Lyndon LaRouche that there exists a direct correlation between the energy utilization within a given area, and the potential population density that is being created.

Increasing the produced energy flux density as an element of the principle of economics.

In exploring the principle of economics another factor of the principle can be recognized, which has a strong influence on the increase of the potential population density of an area. This factor is called energy flux density. This factor is related to the intensity of the energy being produced in an economy. For example, in earlier ages artificial light was produced with candles. It is certainly possible to light a large cathedral with 10,000 candles, in order to make it nice and bright for a service. It is also possible to achieve the same result with ten modern lamps of a 1000 candle-powers each. The end result is identical in the tow cases, but there is a huge difference in the effort that is required to achieve the identical results. The same applies to energy production. It is certainly possible to blanket a country with windmills and solar collectors, and then combine all of their output to create a 200 MW power source. But can you image what enormous effort would be required to create this country wide monstrosity, not to mention the fact that a a larger amount of energy input is required to create the solar cells, than the solar cells give back in their lifetime. Now compare this enormously costly monstrosity to a modern nuclear power plant which requires very little space and can even operate with most of its components put under ground. A modern nuclear power plant provides the highest energy flux density in the world, and even this is only the beginning of a developing trend that is focused on the discovery and the utilization of new physical principles. Through the development of nuclear fusion, for instance, a much higher energy flux density can be achieved than is presently possible with an atomic fission reactor. The point is, the continuing increase of the potential population density on this planet requires a corresponding increase in energy production that can only be achieved with opting for ever higher energy flux densities.

Higher operating temperatures as an element of the principle of economics.

Let me explain what this means. This means that

our future energy must be produced by recreating the process that powers the sun, which is a process of hydrogen fusion. The higher temperatures of this process will open doors which are vital for humanity's future development, but which are presently closed. For example, the super-high temperatures of nuclear fusion will allow the molecular separation of rocks, all of which are rich in metallic silicates, into their constituent elements. This means that the new energy resources that are under scientific development right now, provide us access to the virtually unlimited mineral and metallic resources that will be required by humanity to enrich the earth. With these advanced unlimited material resources, food production can be shifted into automated large scale indoor facilities, so that the fields of the world can be redeployed for better uses than growing food.

The infinite potential of man - a vital foundation for the principle of economics.

The point that comes to light, here, which is deeply rooted in the principle of economics, reflects a characteristic that places no limits on human development whatsoever. Everything else that one finds being paraded before the public in the name of sustainable development is utter nonsense, as it is all totally focused on limits. The only sustainable development is that which is anchored in infinity, itself. Any other conservative option is NOT sustainable. It prevents the development of new fields of resources before the old resources become exhausted or outgrown. It is inherent in the principle of economics that no artificial limits are placed on human population density, and that mankind's actual population density increases to some degree with the realized increase in the potential population density on the planet. To meet this requirement is an essential factor of the principle of economics, because the larger the resources are that modern technologies make available to mankind, the more people will be required to create the advanced technologies and the required facilities, and to operate the processes that enrich the whole earth and human life by the same process.

The general welfare focus a vital element of the principle of economics.

This element of the principle of economics was first put onto the map during the early stages of the development of the USA as a nation. In those days the general welfare focus had nothing to do with creating the required scientific, technological, and infrastructural foundation on the scale that new physical principles require. It had nothing to do with efforts for creating vast new resources which humanity will soon become dependent on. It had nothing to do with international cooperation for meeting those needs. Still, it was recognized as a vital factor even in the late 1700s. It was recognized that society as a whole must cooperate for its general welfare, and that the purpose of an economy is to provide for its welfare. This focus includes advancing ALL processes that make human living richer, more efficient in what needs to be done to meet the physical needs, in order to raise the platform of society to higher levels, especially culturally. Poor housing, for example is destructive to the realization of human potential, including far too small spaces for living. The human being requires enriched environments for mental development and the development of the human genius. Sufficiently well-developed housing should not be regarded as a luxury, but a necessity for society's self-development. Homelessness, the imposition of poverty and slum-type living, should be regarded as a crime against society. By gouging on people's living, society is shooting itself into the foot before the race for its future beings. The same needs to be said about education. It is stupidity that causes society to shift the burden for advanced education onto the shoulders of its children, because its education is the foundation for society's future welfare. Society is gouging on its future, by gouging on its education. Inadequacies in transportation fall into this category too. Society has become strangled by defective housing planning and transportation that make long commuting to and from work an unavoidable burden for countless people. Those many hours of commuting time that are spend each day consume a large portion of countless people's life, not to mention the economic waste in physical resources that is thereby imposed by society on itself.

The same must be said about health care. Politicians say we cannot afford adequate health care. The reality is that we cannot afford not to have it. Neither is health care expensive in terms of consumed resources. Very little in physical resources goes into caring for people's health needs. What makes health care unaffordable is the increasingly ravishing price gouging that has become built into the health care systems that is designed to generate financial wealth for a few who have created for themselves positions to demand this wealth along the whole chain associated with the healthcare system, from doctors to insurance companies, to pharmapseudical companies, to hospital services. Healthcare has become privatized for profit creating rather than maintaining society for its essential well being. From an economic standpoint, the well-being of society is one of society's indispensable assets, but in modern times its becoming increasingly a luxury. That is how society is gradually destroying itself.

It is ironic that many people regard the general

welfare principle today as an outdated relic of soft-headed socialism. Nothing could be further from the truth. The general welfare focus has nothing to do with socialism. It is a fundamental element of the principle of economics. The human being is the most precious resource that society has. Everything that is of value to society has been created by human beings. To throw this potential away with stupid neglect is criminal insanity. The human being is an essential element for increasing the potential population density of a nation, and thereby for the upgrading of the human condition. The truth of this statement is amply illustrated by the results that are experienced when this element is removed from the economic process, as we have it today all over the world.

The General Welfare Principle that is fundamental to the principle of economics is violated in also another area that will one day be considered a crime against society, but which is celebrated today. The fast diversion of economic resources from the general welfare into wasteful living for the pleasures of a few is strangely hailed by society. People love to see the multi-million dollar mansions being built on the hilltops and the ocean going yachts of the super wealthy, or airplanes, or racing cars, or whatever their fancy may entail. However, in economic terms, all of those opulent excesses add up to a huge waste of resources that add nothing to the general upgrading of the human conditions of society, but represent a drain of resources at every level. The craftsman who builds the mansions, or whatever, may realize that his labor is wasted as it accomplishes nothing for uplifting civilization. However, no even he may realize that the labor of the woodsman is likewise wasted, who cuts the trees to furnish the lumber for the mansion. In the same manner is the labor of the farmer wasted who feeds the various laborers of these lost causes that afford nothing for the advance of society.

One may argue that this is how the world has always been run. The rich provide employment to fulfill their pleasure. But in doing so they steal from the living of society at ever stage along the way. One day the growing understanding of the principle of economics in society will change the world to prevent those wasteful processes. Indeed, this day, as distant as it may seem at the present, may arrive sooner as one might think. The enormous demands that the universe is imposing on mankind with the near return of the next 90,000-year Ice Age, will force society to become highly efficient in creating the technological and economic infrastructures for worldwide indoor agriculture and industrial food creation when the coming Ice Age conditions decimate our agriculture that presently provides our food. Almost our entire food chain is based on agriculture and biotic processes that are keyed to our present warm climate of the interglacial period that we are now in, which may end in a hundred years time. To replace all of this soon-to-be-lost potential will require economic processes of an intensity and efficiency that has not even been dreamed of today. If we fail ourselves in creating these resources the human journey may end in horrendous food wars and in huge waves of dying from as yet unimagined diseases that erupt from the biological breakdown and starvation of a multibillion-strong world population.

What happens when the principle of economics is being ignored?

In today's world the principle of economics is being ignored on a grand scale. The general welfare focus no longer exists. It has been replaced with a feudal ideology by which people steal from each other to create financial wealth rather than develop the world with the aim to make the world more efficient in meeting the human need. People rather steal from each other, and they do this in many ways. They do it whenever profits are demanded from processes that inherently do not produce anything, such as the trading of imaginary assets on the world financial markets that do not increase the potential population density, but have a negative effect on it by absorbing into its idle speculative pursuits ever increasing amounts of the global society's financial resources. This negative effect is best illustrated by the triple curve that the American economist Lyndon LaRouche has developed some years ago, originally for a presentation to the Vatican.

The triple curve shows in principle the then prevailing economic situation around the world. It shows the collapsing physical economy in response to financial resources being drained from it into purely speculative ventures for the so-called wealth creating. The resulting financial aggregates have gone sky-high in notional values, such as stocks, bonds, etc., are in real terms not wealth at all, but represent a debt-claim against the physical economy that is rapidly collapse. The wealth, therefore, that the rich of society image themselves to own, has thereby become increasingly meaningless as the so-called wealth has lost its relationship in equivalent terms with the physical economy that it stands as claim against. The shaded area is the boundary where the collapse process takes on catastrophic proportions. The following graph shows that the ongoing collapse is not fictitious, but is directly represented in massive increases in purely financial gambling that is sealing evermore intensely the vital financial resources from the physical economy.

The graph shows the world increase in financial gambling to the year 2000. Since then, the situation has become dramatically worse. Since the financial looting of the physical economy becomes evermore difficult since there is less available to be looted, a new process has been initiated in order to prevent the collapse of the entire. The process that has been chosen, is to print evermore money with which to saturate the speculative financial world. The result has been an increasing collapse of the world-financial system. As the following graph, presented by Lyndon LaRouche, shows.

This advanced triple curve is made up of two hyperbolic progressions, one represents society's money supply, which now increases more intensely and already supercedes in notional amounts the debt it supports, which the physical collapse accelerates. Indeed, why would any person build a factory and bother with producing physical things, when money can be collected from gambling processes that require no effort at all? That's in essence the "Wall of money" policy that holds the present world financial system in place as an essentially empty shell. Naturally, the new money is immediately absorbed into the speculative monetarist system where it fuels the growth of useless financial aggregates. This growth in finical aggregates (or debt) is a cancer, which increases in size at the expense of the physical economy and welfare of society. The third curve, the red curve, represents this decay of the physical economy. This curve, is a mirrored image of the financial debt curves. This physical-economy curve is going negative, and it is going negative hyperbolically.

You may say "this doesn't effect me, I am not engaged in financial gambling." Don't delude yourself. Everyone of society is effected by this growing insanity, and this not only in term of increasing unemployment and so forth. Everyone's entire future is at stake. If you think that your life-savings are safe, think again. For every dollar that you entrust into the hands of the banks, their financial gambling fever has a hundred-fold gabling exposure that your assets may be required to pay for when the game goes sour. The following graph shows shown the size of the exposure as it was in the past. In today's world the exposure is many times larger. The red dot represents the bank's equity, its buildings and whatever it owns. The little white square is your deposit, the assets that the bank is managing for you and society, and the big square, which is small in today's terms, is the exposure the banks have taken of in your behalf for their profit in gambling. In 2005 the combined outstanding gambling exposure of the U.S. commercial banks are just short of the 100 trillion mark, as the following graphic, released by the LaRouche organization illustrates.

Your exposure isn't just in the potential loss of your deposits. Your prime exposure is that the civilization will collapse that supports your existence when the commercial financial system, which is essentially already bankrupt disintegrated totally, by the which the physical economy is bound to disintegrate as well. The collapse has gone so far already that the system cannot be saved in its present form. Nothing short of a global bankruptcy reorganization before the disintegration begins, can protect society from the effects of a catastrophic collapse that has no precedent in history.

The negative curve, of the triple curve, represents the physical economy in a world in which the principle of economics is being ignored or has been intentionally reversed. This curve presents a negative progression, because when the principle of economics is being ignored, the physical economy is collapsing at an ever increasing rate of decline. Nobody can forecast at what day and month the total collapse will happen. One can only recognize the trend and the inevitable consequences. The negative element of the triple curve represents our present world-economy which has been collapsing hyperbolically over the last thirty-five years. The collapse, itself, coincides with a corresponding change in focus away from the general welfare focus, which is a vital element of the principle of economics. Today's focus on "my money," a fictitious personal welfare mania , involves totally different objectives than the general welfare focus. This self-centered mania exhibits all the features of the feudal ideology that empires where built on, which existed by looting humanity. In today's world the ancient feudal looting has been modernized and become endemic.

Two trends can be recognized when the general welfare focus becomes supplanted by the "my money" personal welfare focus. One trend is manifest in the collapse of the physical economy, which is represented by the lower curve of LaRouche's triple curve. The other trend manifests itself as an increase in the financial aggregates, such as stocks, bonds, and financial derivatives, in such a manner that they no longer represent the physical economy, which alone creates the profits that benefit society. This separation of the financial world from the physical reality also follows the pattern of a hyperbolic progression that increases evermore steeply, by which the total collapse of the system is assured. Nothing can prevent this total collapse without shutting the defective system down before it destroys society, and replacing it with with a financial system that is focused on the (real) principle of economics.

The way in which the upper and lower curves of the triple curve are mirrored, is interesting. It suggests that the increases in the financial aggregates are robbed out of the physical economy, that is society's living and society's future, which thereby collapses at the same rate by which the financial (debt-claim) aggregates increase. This mathematical relationship does indeed reflect what has been happening throughout the world. Now the end result of this progressing theft from the physical economy, which has inflated the world-financial system so severely, and collapsed the physical economy so dramatically, is a catastrophic disintegration of both the financial system and the world economy in a single sweep. Most people do not recognize the interconnected nature of the physical and financial collapse. Those who have a faint awareness that the world-financial bubble is about to pop, see it as an event that happens in isolation of the physical economy. This is an error that my cost them their life. The spiraling financial inflation and the physical collapse of the world economy are not separate processes than can have a life of their own. They are nothing more than multifaceted aspects of the same process, the process of ignoring the principle of economics. If humanity allows this process to play itself out to its bitter end, it will disintegrate its civilization. This outcome cannot be avoided unless the process that drives it is terminated. This, of course requires that humanity rededicate itself to the principle of economics.

Also, there is a great urgency connected with this. The processes of financial inflation and physical collapse have been so deeply reaching that both, the world's physical economy, and the world's financial system, are standing right now at the very brink of a collapse that promises to be so severe that it threatens to disintegrate the world's financial system and the physical economy in a simultaneous catastrophe that humanity may not recover from for a very long time, if ever.

Economic collapse invariably lowers the potential population density.

It should be recognized that the world-financial inflation and the collapse of the physical economy have unfolded with the characteristic of a hyperbolic progression. Such a progression begins slowly but then increases steeply like the flaring of a horn. It should also be noted that it is the physical economy, which provides for all our human needs, and that this structure is poised to disintegrate together with the world-financial system. This means that the presently ongoing collapse of the world economy should already be reflected in terms of a corresponding collapse of the potential population density of the nations and the world. Has this been happening? One could answer, both, Yes, and No.

It should be recognized that every aspect of collapse in the physical economy reflects itself in an equally collapsing potential population density. This interrelationship hardly noticeable at first, because the potential population density of a nation is seldom fully utilized in a growing economy. This means that it generally exceeds the real population density by a substantial margin. However, as the economy continues to collapse, the line will be crossed one day beyond which the potential population density drops below the real population density. At this point the people start starving and dying, while the rich who have stolen their living will end up with a bag of financial aggregates that are essentially useless, since financial aggregates by themselves have no intrinsic value, but have value only in relationship to a productive economy. This is happening right now in many places throughout the world, most notably Russia. If an economy dies, so dies the wealth that killed it, and with it dies humanity whose needs are no longer met.

At the present time, quite a number of nations are caught up in this collapse processes, most of them so deeply that they are experiencing a population collapse. Russia, for instance is loosing in excess of a million people a year, with all the new births factored in.

The cheapening of the world-economy.

Another element of the collapse process is the credit starvation of the nations' most vital economic infrastructures, especially the machine-tool industry and the education system that supports scientific development that is a vital infrastructure for the machine-tool industry. The "my money" ideology has cheapened the economy. In this cheapened economy only the simplest processes are being kept alive. Usually these processes are those from which short term profits can be gauged. The cheapening of the economy also tends to create slave labor conditions by which people become physically used up, to be discarded later. In this environment education decays to the point that people can no longer rationally think. The fundamental reality drifts thereby further and further out of sight. Nevertheless, the reality remains that there exists only one single principle of economics, that which develops towards infinity. Any other pursuit, no matter what direction it is in, shuts down the principled economic process, and collapses humanity with it. In a very real way we have reached the paradox that humanity is finding it presently too expensive to support its existence.

The needed reversal - getting back to the principle of economics.

I real terms, today's world-financial and economic system is finished. It has run its course. It has regressed to a state beyond repair. It is dead for all practical purposes. The separation between the world-financial inflation and the physical collapse of the world economy has become infinite or nearly so. The dream world of financial aggregates, and the real economy which can no longer meet the human need, have become paradoxical to one another. This paradox can only be resolved by recognizing the neither state is legitimate, and by acting upon this recognition. But how is one to do this?

How to start a new economy based on the principle of economics?

The answer is really quite simple. You go back to the basics. You create a financial system that reflects the physical reality, and create a national banking system which provides the financial credits for development needs. This accords with the principle of economics. What does this mean for the USA, as an example?

It means, that since the separation between financial dream-world and the physical reality has become so great that the gap can never be bridged, you end the dream and let it go. This means shutting down everything connected with the speculative system. For this the nation must impose currency exchange controls, in order to keep the hot money out of the country. It must also nationalize the Federal Reserve, which is the chief corner stone of the speculative system. It must also put the entire private banking, mutual fund, and brokerage system, into a state of bankruptcy receivership, which has been the hot money casino industry that destroyed the nation's financial equilibrium. The government in control must even close the USA to the vast dollar pools that float around in international markets for purposes of speculation. They fulfill no legitimate purpose in terms of increasing the potential population density, so let them become devalued to zero, which they will be if they exist outside the national economy. Then the nations of the world also need to get together and create a new Bretton Woods type international agreement for stable currency interchange rates as a means for facilitating international trade on a equitable basis with long term stability.

All these measures may appear harsh and unreasonable, however one needs to judge them in the light of the alternative which is a total disintegration of the financial and physical world. It must be understood that without these kind of controls it will never be possible to bring the nation's monetary system, which is presently hyperinflated, into line with the physical reality and the needs of the nation. The principle of economics does not allow for financial inflation, which, as we have seen, destroys the economies of the world.

The principle of economics is one that enhances human development and productivity. This means that the IMF must be scrapped, which is debt oriented, which puts humanity into chains. The entire world debt structure is illegitimate by design, so it must go, too. The IMF system operates totally contrary to the principle of economics. It literally denies a nation the right to create its own currency for its self-development. The IMF insists that a nation has NO right to do this, but must borrow its financial credit from speculative lenders at sky high rates of interest. In ancient times this was called usury, and was forbidden by law. The same applies to the EU (European Union) which operates on an identical platform as the IMF, applied in a more localized sphere, but with a much greater scope and depth of penetration. It is a type of world-government that has the power to tell a nation to shut down viable industries and create unemployment.

The sovereignty of nations is one of the most crucial elements of the principle of economics, which cannot be ignored without the most horrendous consequences, such as the world is presently experiencing.

The point is, the nations of the world have little choice in the realm of economic policy. The principle of economics is imperative. It cannot be mocked with human will or imperial dictates. So the choice is plain. Humanity faces an economy that doesn't function anymore, and the financial wealth that has been squeezed out of it, isn't worth anything anymore, either. The only positive thing that humanity has going for itself, with which to assure its survival and protect its civilization, is the option it has to rededicate itself as fast as possible to the real principle of economics. It must therefore heroically shut down this misfit, which is erroneously called an economy, and everything that is connected with it, which has begun to murder its citizens world-wide by the millions. Humanity must take this step and utilize the principle of economics so rescue whatever elements of the present economy are still functioning and then go forward on the basis of this principle. Even as it shuts the speculative system down, world-wide, humanity must extend itself new financial credits through nationally owned institutions, and devote those credits to the financing of crash programs in education, infrastructure building, reindustrialization, and above all extend the fullest possible support to farming and to the machine tool industry. If this happens, and only then, humanity has a chance to save its civilization. Unfortunately, there is no indication that anyone in a position of power is thinking along these lines.

Lyndon LaRouche's forecasts were based on the principle of economics.

For many years the American economist and statesman, Lyndon LaRouche, has forewarned about the collapse that is presently upon us, and about the impending total disintegration of the presently still somewhat functioning economic processes that are fast being destroyed. he didn't predict the doom of the present system by looking into a crystal ball. He didn't have to. By understanding the principle of economics, a child could have made the same prediction. And here lies the problem. The principle of economics is well understood by the leading circles of the imperial oligarchy, which does everything in its power to prevent this principle from being recognized and applied. The global imperial oligarchy is committed to this deception, because its feudal ideology and related processes for looting, by which it derives its power, run contrary to the principle of economics. Thus, it parades its looting system in front of the eyes of humanity, which is centered on usurious banking, speculative insanities, and IMF world indebtedness, and calls this travesty the principle of economy. And it calls everyone a lunatic who doesn't agree, including Lyndon LaRouche. The fact is, Lyndon LaRouche is neither a lunatic nor a genius. He is merely a man with a keen scientific mind who has his eye open wide to reality. He is isn't fooled by the oligarchy's parade, nor should anyone else be.

So far, humanity has shown no willingness to open its eye to reality, and to rescue itself. This is largely because it is unable to recognize the grave danger it is in. Humanity is unable to recognize the danger, because of its inability to recognize the principle of economics, especially the fundamental inter-tie of the principle of economics with the potential population density. This inter-tie threatens to become a deadly factor when the entire economic process grinds to a halt in times of anarchy and disintegration. This means that humanity has to draw the line, absolutely, before the disintegration occurs. It must not allow the point of disintegration to be reached at which its very existence is threatened. The process of collapse must be stopped before this happens. If the collapse is not stopped, and disintegration occurs, the principle of economics has absolutely no meaning anymore, since there exists no economy in which it would be reflected, nor anything resembling a civilization in which an economy would play a role.

Now we must explore the question: What must be done by humanity to rededicate itself to the principle of economics?

Once the emergency measures have been taken which shut down the speculative and feudal processes, the nations must extend to themselves national credits, not credits borrowed from a looting and bankrupt world-financial system. They must utilize these credits wisely in such a manner that they enrich the economic process and society by creating economic infrastructures that produce a larger return in physical development than the financial credits are worth. This prohibits inflation and enriches humanity. In other words, this process provides for increasing the potential population density on the planet. The development infrastructures of this type are education, science, the machine-tool industry, large scale industrialization, farming, and so forth.

The general welfare focus.

Still, this giant step forward does not fully utilize the principle of economics. It gives humanity a good start, perhaps, but a start is not enough. Society must get back to the general welfare focus, which is an element of the principle of economics, and it must do this this in a big way. It must do this not because it is written in the Preamble of the Constitution of the USA, but because the general welfare focus it is a part of the principle of economics. It is in fact fundamental to the process of economy that increases the potential population density of a nation or the world. It is essential to this process. In today's world of nuclear power and vast economic needs, society must cooperate on a very large scale to create and apply the needed technologies. In today's world of nuclear power and the need for continent wide development processes, global cooperation becomes essential. This cooperation must be based on a community of principle of sovereign nation states. In other words, the general welfare focus must be on the whole world.

The Eurasian Land-Bridge development as a reflection of the general welfare focus.

By its very definition, the general welfare focus must of necessity be global. It must bring about the kind of international development that enriches the whole world, like LaRouche's Eurasian Land Bridge proposal is intended to do, which has finally been adopted by the governments of China and Japan. This land bridge development consists of three development layers. Its backbone is a railway link that spans from China to Western Europe on three routes across Asia, on a northern route, a southern route, and a central route. This is the main layer of the project. Along these trunk lines new cities are to be built that serve as economic centers for secondary development lines reaching out from them into the anterior. That's the second layer. And again, along these lines smaller development centers are to be build, with more lines reaching out from them. On this basis, huge economic development corridors are to be created by which many still isolated nations become connected to the world, to its commerce, to its ideas, to its culture, by which everyone benefits and the potential population density of the planet becomes dramatically increased.

Global economic development is a part of the general welfare focus, which is a fundamental element of the principle of economics.

Some people may be tempted to believe that the Eurasian Land Bridge development project is an optional project. Whoever believes this is gravely mistaken. Far from being optional, it is one of the fundamental aspects of the general welfare focus that is a fundamental element of the principle of economics. This means that the Eurasian Land-Bridge development project can no more be omitted than the principle of economics, itself, can be omitted. One has not much of a choice in this matter. Either the principle of economics is thrown out of the widow and humanity dies, or it is applied in all its essential aspects and humanity prospers and develops itself. It is in the nature of a fundamental principle that it cannot be half applied. This also means that the Eurasian Land-Bridge development is only one example of the kinds of processes that must be set into motion around the world. Africa needs the same kind of economic development uplift that Asia requires. It needs great projects in water development. It needs highway and railway networks, nuclear power, and industrialization. Right now, Africa is starving to death, dying of AIDS, and is being destroyed by the ravishing of imperially organized wars. And all this is happening while the economic potential of Africa is so huge that it could feed the entire world all by itself, and this with food to spare. Nor can the general welfare focus be limited to Asia and Africa, alone. It must embrace also India, Russia, China, Iran, Indonesia, Malaysia, the Middle East, and all of Europe. Yes, Europe is in desperate need for economic redevelopment. In 1990, Lyndon LaRouche developed the Paris-Berlin-Vienna Productive Triangle concept, which was intended to mobilize the industrial capacity within this defined triangle as an engine to redevelop the European continent from Norway down to Africa, and from Portugal to the Ukraine, and the world as a whole. But this was then. Today, this industrial capacity no longer exits, and in those few places where a substantial capacity still exists, like in Poland, the pressure is on from the EU to shut most of it down.

China as an example of the general welfare focus as an element of the principle of economics.

General economic development and industrialization is written in capital letters in China. The nation that was once known for ox carts and and an insane political dictatorship has freed itself of this past and become one of the fastest advancing nations on the planet. While Europe is shutting itself down, this nation has committed itself to more than 10,000 major infrastructure projects, 3,500 of which are scheduled to be located along the Eurasian Land Bridge corridor. China also has plans to build 200 brand new cities over the next 25 years, and upgrade its older cities. It also has planes for large scale water development projects designed to bring its dry regions into agricultural production, which will add an area to its agricultural base of the size of all of Germany. Over the next decade, China has also plans to double its already extensive railway network, which by then may be the largest in the world. It is also committed to such engineering marvels as building a 57 Km bridge across the Bohai Straight, or building a 1241 Km canal from the Three Gorges Dam to the dry north that will cross over and under 219 rivers on its path, including the mighty Yellow River, the Yuang He, and 44 railway lines.

The discovery, development, and application of new physical principles as an element of the principle of economics.

The commitment to the principle of economics is not satisfied, however, with the building of great projects alone. The principle of economics requires constant advances in the application of new physical principles in order to satisfy the basic requirement made on an economy, to increase the potential population density of a nation or the world. These developments are especially needed for creating new energy resources. Historically the energy flux density of power generating machines has been increased by one or two orders of magnitude for each new type of technology. Steam powered machines, for instance, generate a hundred times the power output of water powered machines of comparable size. The internal combustion engine raised this factor to a thousand. Nuclear fission engines have raised it to ten-thousand. When nuclear fusion becomes a practical power source, this factor will likely be raised to a million or more. Humanity must dedicate itself to develop this advanced energy resource of nuclear fusion, not because it is achievable, but because its development needs require it. This energy resource is required for the utilization of new materials, new resources for food, new transportation systems, and new methods for space flight propulsion.

The principle of economics requires still more than this. It requires that development never stops. The interludes of regression, like those which have occurred during the dark ages, and the collapse into a new dark age that we are facing today, cheat humanity at a staggering cost in human lives and lost development. If the Roman Empire had not ushered in the dark ages, humanity would likely have stood on the moon in 600 A.D., so great had the scientific advances been at the time of the Greek Classical Period. Then, where would we stand today?

The principle of economics cannot coexist with imperial objectives.

Still, we have a similar hurdle to cross in this age, which the highly advanced people of the Greek civilization had failed to cross. In a Sept. 12, 1999 interview in Wiesbaden, Germany, one of the highest ranking advisors of Prince Phillip of the British monarchy, by the name of Martin Palmer, has made it clear that his empire harbors plans for humanity that run contrary to the principle of economics. He pointed out that his empire is committed to "break up" the great nations of the world into tiny impotent states, to be ruled by his empire. He made it clear that it is futile to resist his empire's plans which have been pursued unaltered for 200 years, which have resulted in two world wars and a cold war that brought humanity to the threshold of its self-extinction. "Perfidious Albion is alive and kicking," were his final arrogant remarks.

Indeed, the man is historically correct. When the first proposals were put forward for a Eurasian Land Bridge development project, Perfidious Albion created the conditions for World War I in order to stop the project, and empire succeeded. The world became so devastated that the project was not pursued again for a hundred years, and even now, Perfidious Albion, the British Empire, is determined to prevent it from becoming reality. Whether humanity will be able to rescue itself from the abyss that this empire has pushed it towards, especially so over the last thirty five years, depends on its wisdom in defending itself against Perfidious Albion. Perfidious means treacherous and devious, as in turning one against the other, while Albion is an ancient name for the British islands. The empire that has ruled from these islands has been at the center of the darkest periods of modern history, in areas all around the world. It's axiomatic viruses have pervaded the minds of humanity more deeply than ever before, and made them stupid. The great irony of history is that humanity faces this empire at its most critical period with a near total disregard for its very existence, much less its commitment against humanity, and with an insanity that has rarely been equaled in history.

Nevertheless, the fight is not over. In fact it has barely begun, because the world-financial and economic disintegration that threatens humanity also threatens the base of power of Perfidious Albion himself.

About the research series:

Discovering Infinity

The series is made up of nine books , created by Rolf A. F. Witzsche, in North Vancouver, Canada, over a span of more than 15 years.

Work on the series began in the early 1980s, but its central element is rooted in a new form of science that had been created a hundred years earlier by a New England woman named Mary Baker Eddy (1821-1910). The woman was probably the most accomplished scientists in the field of exploring the power of intelligent perception for elevating human existence. The science became widely known for its application for the healing of disease on a scientific metaphysical basis. While the series presented here focuses on the leading-edge aspects of her science that are still largely unknown in today's world, the series takes us still farther back in time, to the work of another great pioneer of humanity, to Dante Alighieri (1265-1321) who is regarded by some as the first stepping stone towards the Golden Renaissance, a period of scientific and spiritual development that uplifted mankind probably more profoundly than any other period in history. A new self-perception of mankind dawned that ended the Dark Ages and uplifted the world. Both developments stand tall among the great turning points in the history of mankind.

It is sadly obvious that we need such a renaissance-turning-point again in our modern dark world. Our world has become a world of unspeakable fascism, greed, war, terror, torture, inhumanity, nuclear bombs, slavery, poverty, and financial disintegration. I addition to that we face the return of the Ice Age that's looming darkly on the not so distant horizon. With these shadows fast falling around us we find that our civilization hangs in the balance once again, and more precariously so than it did in the time of Dante who foresaw society's doom and worked to prevent it. As in Dante's time the strength of our civilization is failing; our defences are wearing thin; our riches are crumbling; and the light of our hope for getting out of this trap is getting small, matching the smallness in thinking that has become the hallmark of modern society.

Dante found himself in a similar kind of world. His home city had been the center of the greatest financial world empire up to this time, which was rotten to the core. Dante became a rebel bearing warnings and presenting critical choices that could have avoided the doom that later happened. But instead of being heeded Dante was banished from the city.

As a rebel in 'exile' Dante poured the principles that he understood into his writings. The best known of these works is his epic poetic trilogy the **Commedia,** or translated, the **Divine Comedy.** The **Commedia** is a serious work designed to lift society out of its 'smallness' by raising its perception of truth and its self-perception to higher levels of thinking. The **Commedia** presents three such levels, presented in a progressive sequence. Dante's three levels are incorporated into the makeup of the research series presented here, which is focused on our modern world.

In order to be able to do accomplish the complex task that Dante had laid out for himself, he had to first create a high-level language, a new kind of language with a depth and quality that can convey the complex ideas that he wanted to express. On this track he gathered together the most beautiful aspects of all the Italian dialects that he could find from the numerous sources across the country. It is being said that he literally created the Italian language for this purpose. Of course there was nothing more worthy of that language than his own poetic works.The language that he created became the central language of the Golden Renaissance, the Italian Renaissance, the renaissance typified by the Council of Florence of the mid 1400s. Dante would have been proud of this development, but he died long before the Renaissance became a reality. Nevertheless he understood the principles that the Golden Renaissance represented, and he expressed these principles in the **Commedia.**

The **Commedia** tells us the story of a pilgrim and his guide. The two journey together through the three stages that Dante called: **Hell; Purgatory; and Paradise.** The research series presented here is designed to follow this three-step pattern. In fact, it is designed to take us through the journey twice, once in the perspective of the pilgrim, and once in the perspective of the guide. For this reason the series is made up of six sets of books, Volume 1 through 6.

Volume 1 through 3 are written from the standpoint of the pilgrim.

Volume 1 corresponds with Dante's concept of **Hell**, but seen in modern terms. Actually Dante's personal hell has been two-fold. He was a rebel against the financial empire of his time. He saw doom spelled in big letters in the corrupting decadence that stank with arrogance but was in real terms a hollow, empty shell. He must have spoken out powerfully with calls for sanity for which he was banished from his beloved home city.

While he didn't live long enough to see the collapse of the financial system that he had warned about, he understood that the system would collapse by the sheer weight of its gravity if it continued its course, and by the weakness of its emptiness. The collapse occurred 24 years after Dante's death, with consequences far worse that he might have imagined. The collapse had weakened the population across Europe so severely that it opened the door to the Black Plaque that swept like wildfire across the land and destroyed nearly half the European population.

Since we are now poised for a replay with a possibly deeper and wider financial collapse, the first book of the series, Volume 1 (Volume 1A) focuses on the hell that Dante had fought against. The tile for this volume is, **The Disintegration of the World's Financial System.** Indeed, when the mighty giant that is deemed as solid as the Rock of Gibraltar becomes an empty shell the inevitable happens.

But Dante's personal hell had a second feature, that of injustice, inhumanity, death threats; he was banished under the threat of death. The modern face of this feature becomes the focus for the second part of Volume 1 (Volume 1B). It focuses on the crimes committed by those who would uphold today's dying private empire in order to hold back its built-in demise. The tile for this volume is, **Crimes Against Humanity.**

In the Greek legend in which Saturn is devouring his sons, the god-giant perpetrates this crime not in a rage of 'greed' so that he may nourish himself, but out of fear. Dante the poet had been banished by the mightiest financial empire of his time, out of fear. The empire had been scared of the humanity of the poet.

Volume 2 mirrors Dante's concept of **Purgatory**, a stage of healing. The title for this volume is **Science and Spiritual Healing.** The healing here is a kind of self-discovery, the discovery of a spiritual dimension in our humanity that takes us beyond the crude limits that we have placed on ourselves in the 'smallness' of today's prevailing closed-minded thinking.

Volume 3 takes us to still higher ground. It presents the scientific platform of Christ Science, Dante's **Paradise,** but advanced in great measures to a true science. At this stage the pilgrim finds that the guide inevitably leaves him standing alone in order that he may be guided by his own human resources. America's spiritual pioneer, Mary Baker Eddy, the founder of Christian Science, the discoverer of "the divine Principle of scientific mental healing," has done exactly the same. In the late 1800s she developed a vast pedagogical structure for scientific and spiritual development, evidently in support of her science, but she left humanity alone with it. She only outlined its design, even though the structure is so enormous in scope that it encompasses all of her major words, with some strikingly advanced concepts added. She never imposed it as a dogma as to how it must unfold in the mind of the student. Just as the guide stepped aside at this point in Dante's poem, Mary Baker Eddy had posed a lot of questions in the way her pedagogical structure is outlined, but she never really provides any answers for them. It is as if she is saying, like Dante had, that the answers must emerge through the process of discovery as one individually begins to search for the truth.

Volume 3 presents the details of the discovery of Mary Baker Eddy's pedagogical structure and the subsequent exploration of it. What is presented in this volume resulted from a process in which one is always alone, supported only by the substance of science and the spiritual riches of our humanity. The title of this volume is: **Universal Divine Science - Spiritual Pedagogicals.**

At this point the second cycle begins. The next three volumes, Volume 4 through 6 take us through the same journey once more, from Dante's **Hell**, to **Purgatory**, and to **Paradise**, but from the standpoint of the guide instead of the pilgrim.

Volume 4 takes us through **Hell** as seen by the guide who must plot a safe path through the jungle. Here the great concepts demand clarity: Is evil a power, or is it a negation without power? Is darkness substantial, or is there substance only in light against which darkness cannot stand? The title of this volume is, **Light Piercing the Heart of Darkness.**

Volume 5 explores the dimension of **Purgatory** with the eyes of a guide who must turn the spiritual potential, by means of science, into a profound renaissance that uplifts the whole world. In this case the guide understands the advanced pedagogical structures that the pioneer of the past has provided, who then finds himself challenged to apply them to create a portal to a new world. The title of this volume is, **Scientific Government and Self-Government.**

Perhaps the profoundest realization that we have learned in the historic periods of renaissance is the now evident fact that our 'bread' does not come from the sky, from heaven, nor does it come from the Earth, but is created as the product of the human mind, drawn from the discovery and application of universal principles in which our infinite dimension comes to light.

Volume 6 is once more split into two parts, both representing Dante's **Paradise** from the standpoint of the guide. The first part, Volume 6a, has the title, **The**

Infinite Nature of Man. Mary Baker Eddy made a statement in 1884 that must have shaken the starched motions of that time. She wrote, "Woman is the highest term for man." In the context of her science this statement bears not a sexual reference, but a spiritual one. It reflects the highest concept of humanity that we find described in the biblical Apocalypse as "a woman clothed with the sun and the moon under her feet and on her head a crown of twelve stars."

This non-sexual reference to woman as a metaphor for the spiritual identity of mankind, the highest idea of our humanity, comes with no small challenges attached for one to live up to. It is no small challenge to discover what worlds upon worlds it encompasses. In this realm even the guide is alone, and infinity itself becomes the frontier where there are no inherent limits.

The second part of Volume 6, (Volume 6b), is focused on the spiritual dimension of leadership. The title for this final book in the series is simply called, **Leadership.**

So what is it that we are after to provide leadership for? What kind of leadership makes any sense in the infinite domain? Is the goal to achieve victory? Or does a new type of leadership unfold that raises the standard of achievement?

The research series presented here contains still one more volume, the **Introduction Volume** that opens the series. Its title is, **Roots in Universal History**.

This introductory volume sets the stage for the series by exploring who and what we are as human beings in the vast scope of universal history. In this sphere of the real world the roles of the pilgrim and the guide are blurred and intermingle. In this sphere we are all but children growing up, or children that refuse to grow out of their infancy as it is so often the case. In this sphere history sometimes offers itself as a guide, but to what end? And who listens anyway what history tells us? Dante must have felt that society needs more than just history, because history by itself comes with an empty promise all too often. Dante must have felt that something more is needed, like timeless principles and a humanity with built-in riches that we have barely begun to explore, much less to utilize. Evidently Dante wrote the **Commedia** to open the door to this universe of principles and the wide dimension of our profound humanity.

I have written the nine volume research series in an attempt to bring back the spirit of Dante's 'devotion' to looking more deeply into what shapes us and our world. His achievements became a stepping stone to the greatest renaissance of all times that began the greatest period of humanist development in the entire history of civilization. It is my hope that this still existing potential that Dante had one tapped into may be realized anew in our time. The principles that Dante had glimpsed so long ago are valid for all times according to the nature of principles. Consequently they are valid today. For this reason the great renaissance that we desperately need in our time has the potential of becoming realized. We are not looking for utopian dreams coming true, but for the truth of our humanity coming to light with a light "brighter than the sun" that had already been discovered several times before. We may yet realize that the potential for getting back to this light still exists.

Maybe Dante's greatest legacy is the cradle that holds the potential for our awakening towards an infinite future that remains forever within our reach to be claimed if we care to take the steps involved. Those steps comprise the critical choices that Dante had dealt with, which are now before us. But how will we choose? Will we explore the depth of our humanity and experience its freedom? Nobody can really answer that question. Nobody can see into the future. We can only look at our world as it is and explore the dimensions of the present civilization. What one sees in today's world is far from encouraging. In comparison with Dante's world we are in a far-more precarious state. Our economies are collapsing, choking with unemployment and poverty. Our world-financial system is disintegrating on the globalized platforms of imperial looting and slavery. And in the shadow we have war wrecking the world, now endless war, with atomic bombs evermore on the horizon that can eradicate civilization. And then we face the darkest and latest invention for the mass killing of human beings, the little-known dirty-uranium bomb that has already been pre-positioned by the millions, if not tens of millions, which could end human existence altogether.

During the years when the research series, **Discovering Infinity** was written to a large extend, the world was much brighter than it is today. Nevertheless it became evident at this time that a profound impetus was needed to power the transition of society out of its ever-deepening hell. It was seen as obviously impossible to eradicate terror with more terror, and war with more war, and the looting of society with evermore powerful looting by globalizing the process. It was recognized that we can only solve these problems asymmetrically by proceeding from a higher-level standpoint. Since the asymmetric countering of force, violence, and terror is to love, even to love universally, I began the huge task of writing a series of novels that is designed to explore the Principle of Universal Love. Over the years the work unfolded into the now 12-part series of novels, **The Lodging for the Rose.**

About the research series: Discovering Infinity

The series of novels, **The Lodging for the Rose** was preceded by two novels that serve somewhat like a preface for the series. The first of these novels, **Flight without Limits,** explores the hypothetical potential of being able to move instantly to wherever one wants to be in physical space. While we don't have that potential and probably never will, no such inherent limitation appears to exist in the mental realm. What inertia would hold us back in the mental realm, to prevent us from being where we want to be, or need to be? It appears that no real limit exists in the mental sphere where our humanity comes to light. Herein lies our future.

The second novel that preceded the series is the novel, **Brighter than the Sun.** It deals with the hell of a staged nuclear-war accident and the power of love that draws three families together by their individual struggles in countering this hell. In the unfolding story the Principle of Universal Love is gradually coming to light.

The reason why the platform of the novel was chosen to explore the Principle of Universal Love in parallel with the research series **Discovering Infinity,** reflects the nature of the response that is needed in our nuclear world to protect our existence and save our civilization that is rapidly collapsing into the shadow of terror, poverty, fascism, and imperial slavery and looting of the world. The Principle of Universal Love cannot be explored in a cold theoretical fashion to counter the darkness of these shadows. We would loose love farther on the theoretical platform, instead of facing its imperative in the world of our daily living where it should be our light.

The very concept of the Principle of Universal Love needs to be uplifted in life by giving it a shape that is found in its practical development at the grassroots level of our social existence. Surely, Dante would have agreed that love needs to become an active universal impetus.

The 19th Century spiritual pioneers, Mary Baker Eddy, wrote the following about love as a principle that can only be understood in its universal manifestation rather than as a 'privatized thing.' She wrote: "LOVE - What a word! I am in awe before it. Over what worlds on worlds it hath range and is sovereign! the underived, the incomparable, the infinite All of good, the **alone** God, is Love... No word is more misconstrued; no sentiment less understood. The divine significance of Love is distorted into human qualities, which in their human abandon become jealousy and hate. Love is not something put upon a shelf, to be taken down on rare occasions with sugar-tongs and laid on a rose-leaf. I make strong demands on love, call for active witnesses to prove it, and noble sacrifices and grand achievements as its results. Unless these appear, I cast aside the word as a sham and counterfeit, having no ring of the true metal. Love cannot be a mere abstraction, or goodness without activity and power." (Miscellaneous Writings, p.250)

Indeed love shouldn't be deemed something as small and rare like a gem that one picks up with "sugar tongues and puts on a rose leaf" for special occasions. It needs be the universal impetus, and it will be that when we can find it in the true face of the humanity of mankind that we all share and bring to light as human beings. It needs to unfold as an all-embracing, active expression, a light that enriches individual living. Only then can we expect to see our civilization unfolding on that higher level where fascism, slavery, war, looting, and poverty cannot exist, and the world is secure. Right now we are so far from this state that seems like but a dream, while the loss of civilization and the extinction of mankind loom in the foreground as a growing threat.

The series of novels, **The Lodging for the Rose** was written in parallel with the research series **Discovering Infinity** in order that it may enable us increasingly to see ourselves primarily as human beings - not divided by sex, marriage, wealth, power, but as a single humanity of human beings, individual in our living, but sharing a common universal human soul. In a sense, this is what Dante tried to convey in the **Commedia**. My series of novels is designed to take the Principle of Universal Love out of the theoretical sphere into the down-to-earth practical sphere towards a profound new renaissance in civilization. On this line the research series **Discovering Infinity** and the series of novels **The Lodging for the Rose** are designed to unfold in parallel.

Rolf A. F. Witzsche

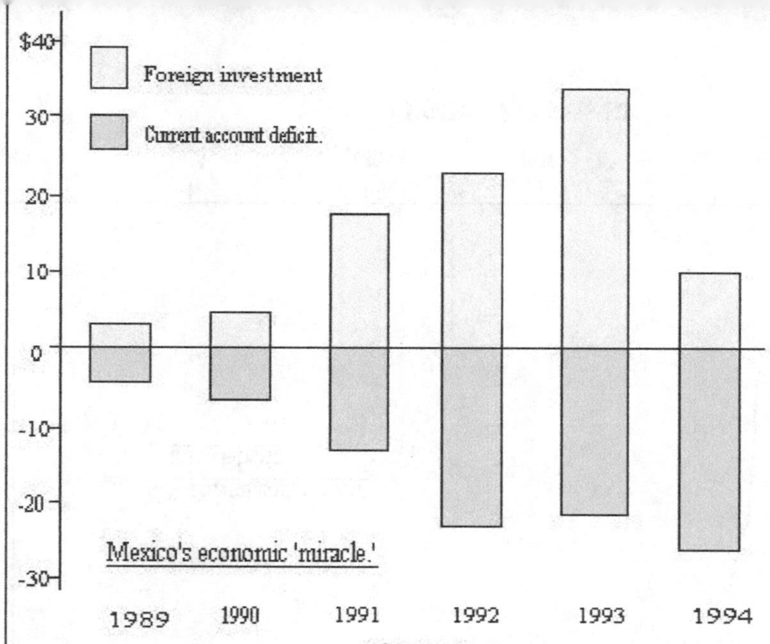

Figure 3 Source EIR

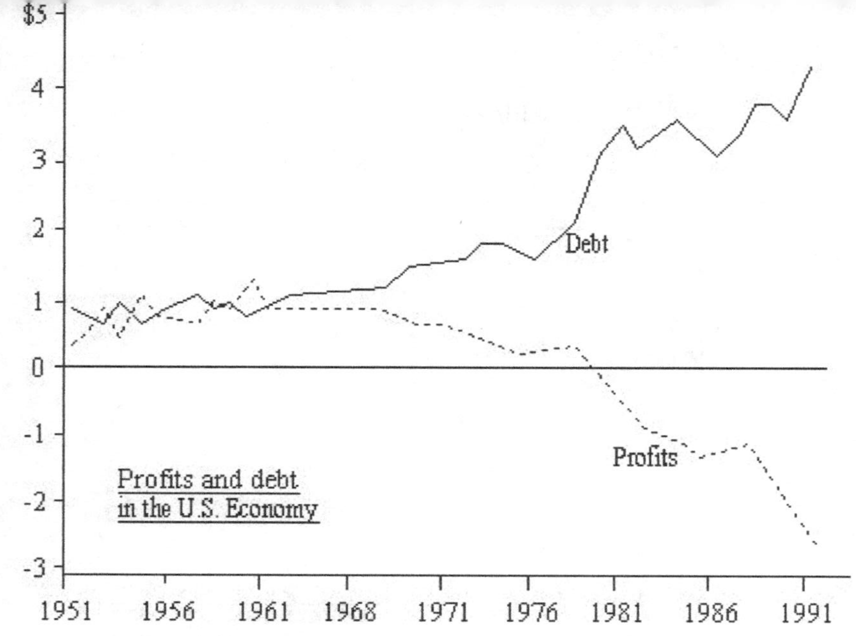

Figure 4 Source EIR

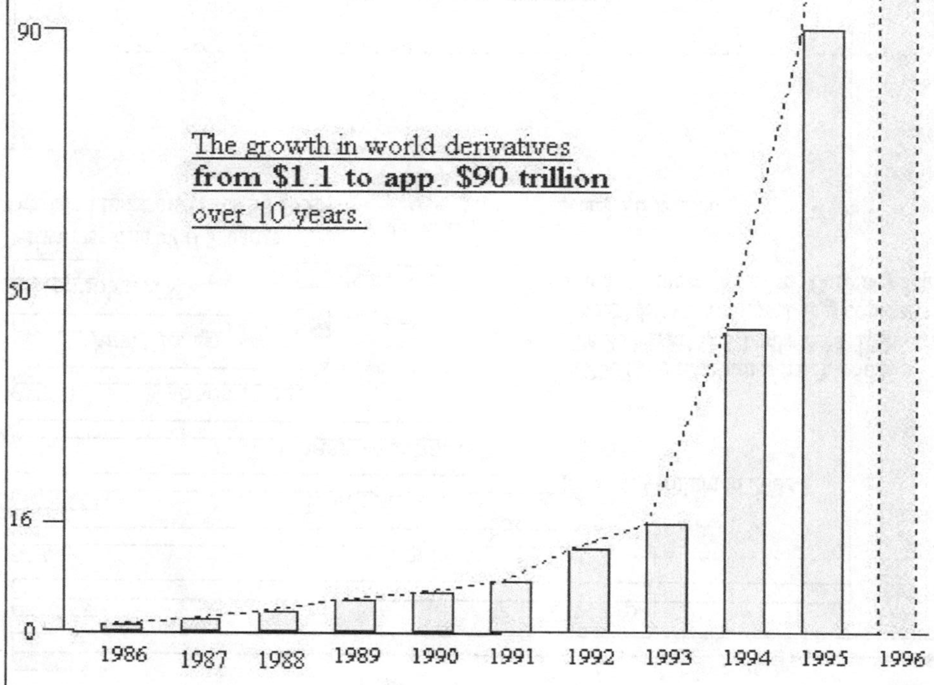

Figure 1

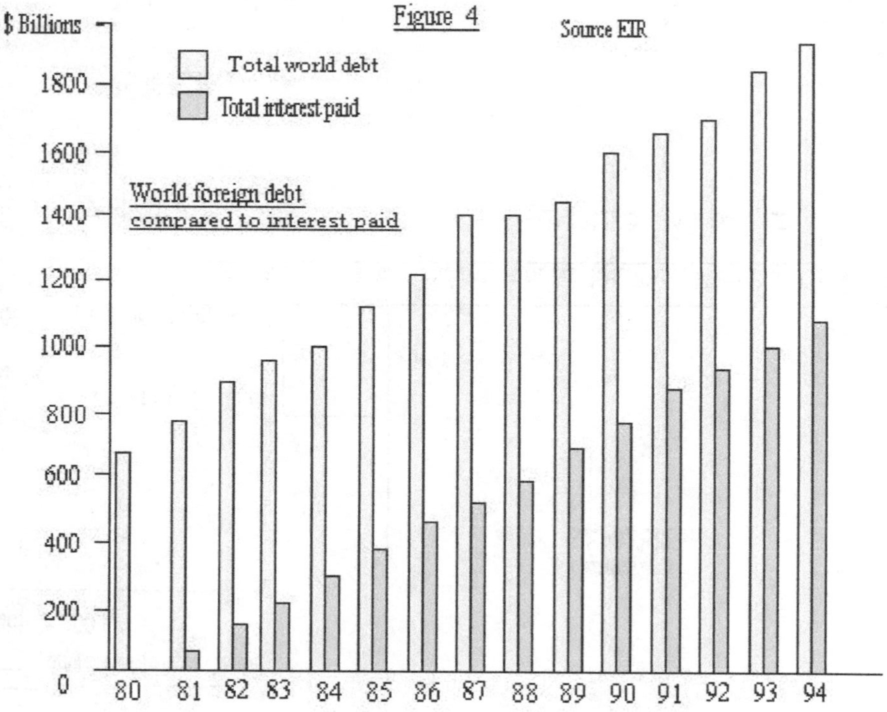

Figure 2 Source EIR

Appendix 1

Appendix 1

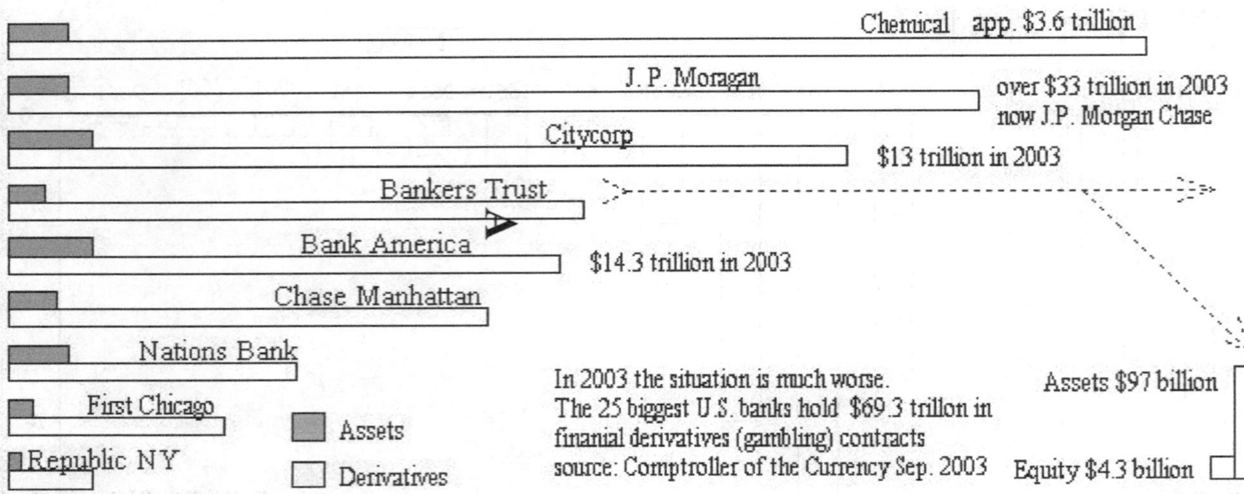

Derivatives held by U.S. banks compared to assets (June 30 1995)

Figure 2 Source: EIR Jan.1/96

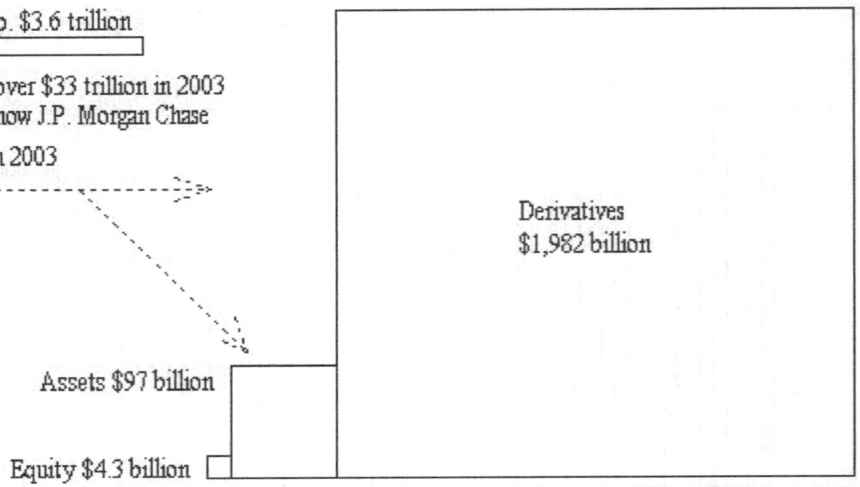

Derivatives vs equity and assets of Bankers Trust New York Corp., 1994

Figure 3 Source EIR

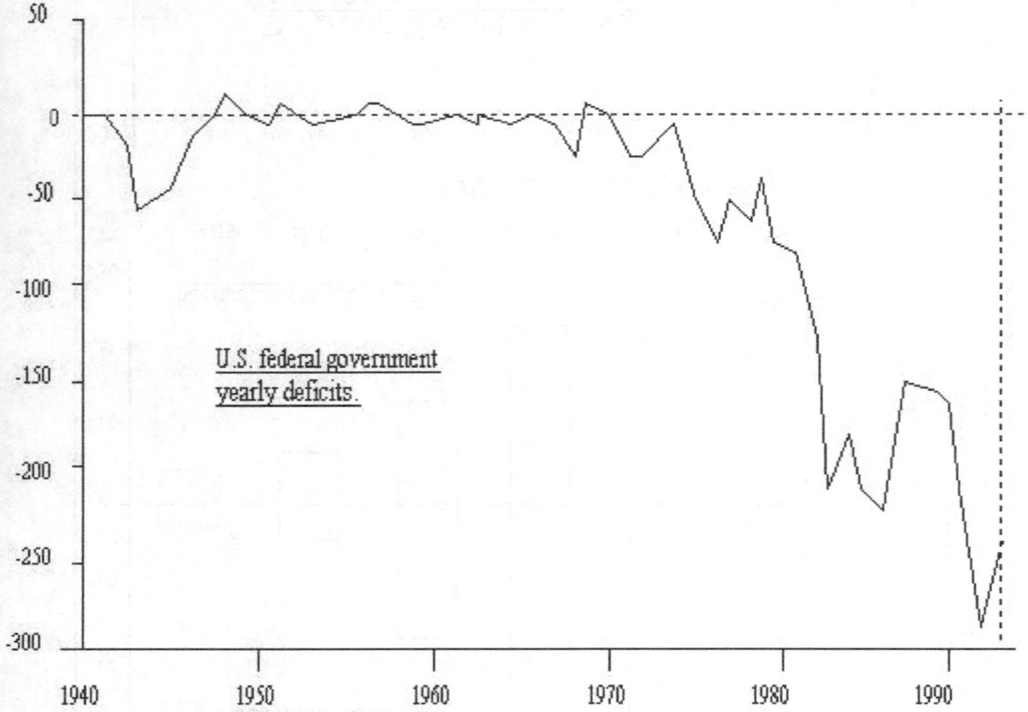

Figure 1 Source EIR

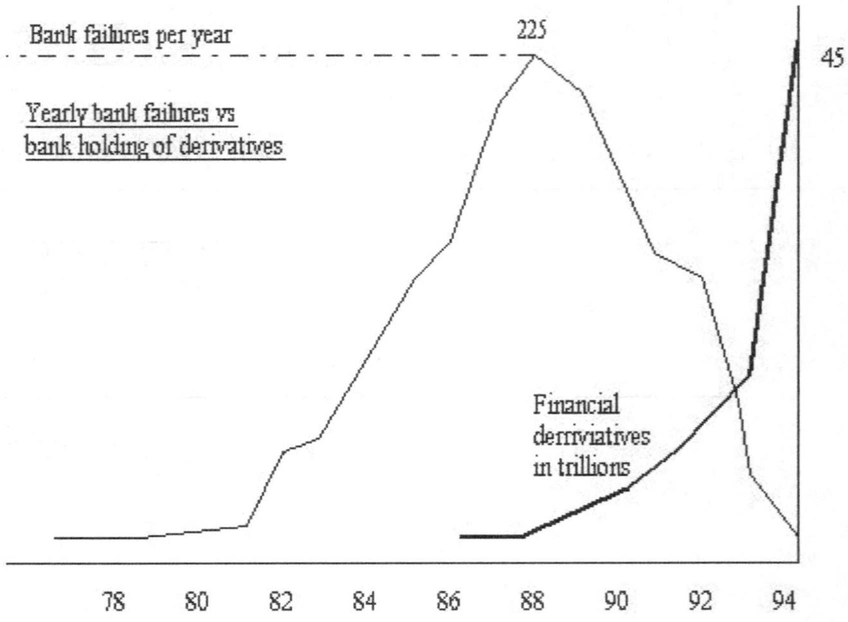

Figure 4 Source EIR

Appendix 2

Appendix 2

Appendix 3

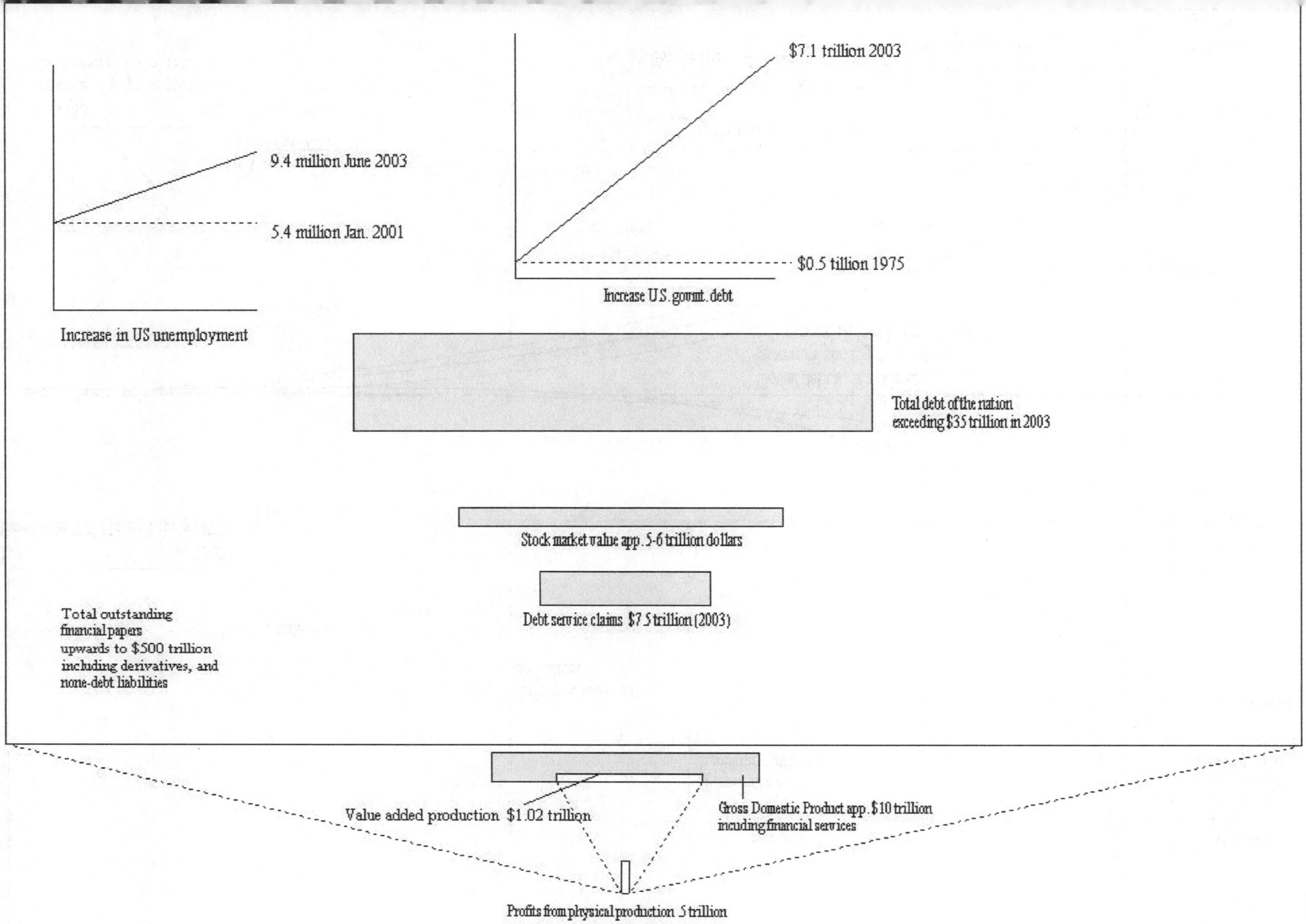

9.4 million June 2003
5.4 million Jan. 2001
Increase in US unemployment
$7.1 trillion 2003
$0.5 tillion 1975
Increase U.S. govmt. debt
Total debt of the nation exceeding $35 trillion in 2003
Stock market value app. 5-6 trillion dollars
Debt service claims $7.5 trillion (2003)
Total outstanding financial papers upwards to $500 trillion including derivatives, and none-debt liabilities
Value added production $1.02 trillion
Gross Domestic Product app. $10 trillion incuding financial services
Profits from physical production .5 trillion

Appendix 3

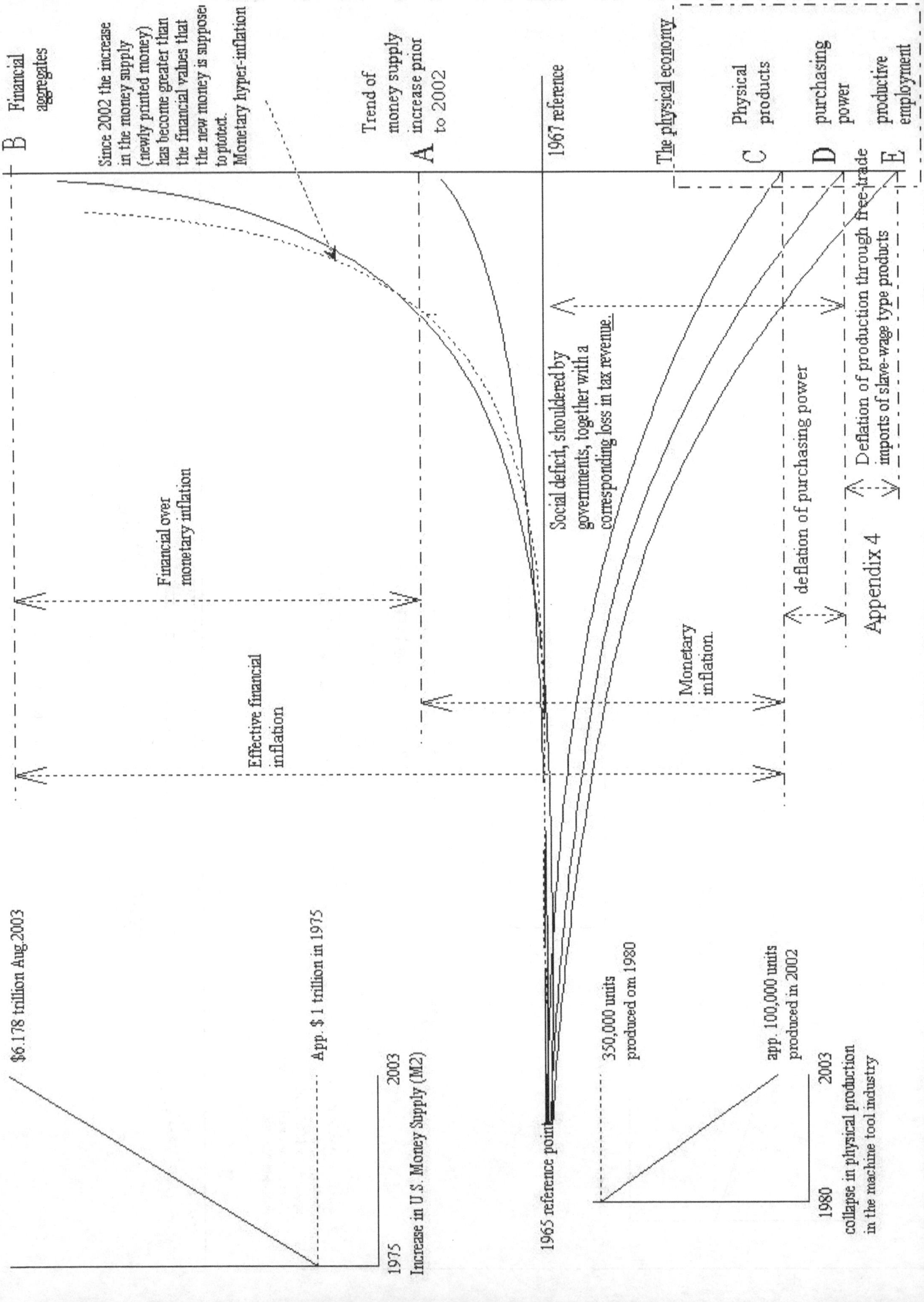
B Financial aggregates
Since 2002 the increase in the money supply (newly printed money) has become greater than the financial values that the new money is suppose to protect. Monetary hyper-inflation
Trend of money supply increase prior to 2002
A
1967 reference
The physical economy
C Physical products
D purchasing power
E productive employment
Deflation of production through free-trade imports of slave-wage type products
Appendix 4
deflation of purchasing power
Social deficit, shouldered by governments, together with a corresponding loss in tax revenue.
Financial over monetary inflation
Monetary inflation.
Effective financial inflation
$6.178 trillion Aug.2003
App. $ 1 trillion in 1975
1975
2003
Increase in U.S. Money Supply (M2)
1965 reference point
350,000 units produced om 1980
app. 100,000 units produced in 2002
1980
2003
collapse in physical production in the machine tool industry

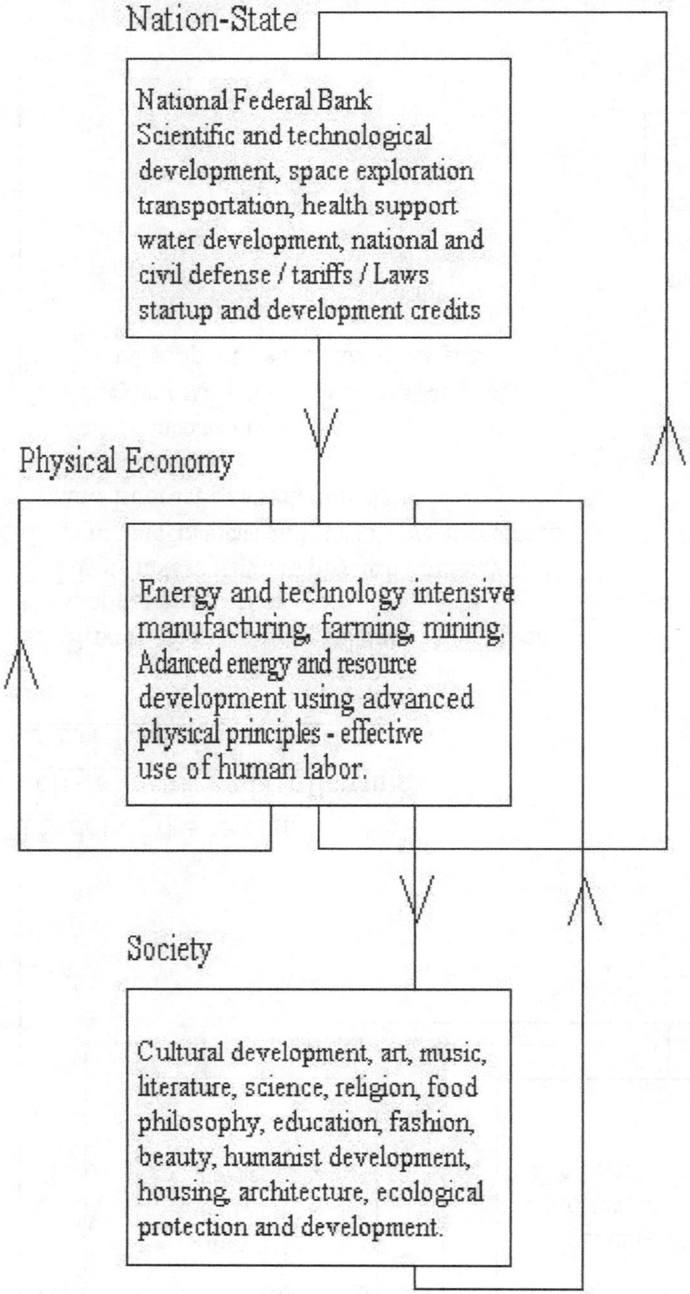

Nation-State
National Federal Bank
Scientific and technological development, space exploration transportation, health support water development, national and civil defense / tariffs / Laws startup and development credits
Physical Economy
Energy and technology intensive manufacturing, farming, mining. Adanced energy and resource development using advanced physical principles - effective use of human labor.
Society
Cultural development, art, music, literature, science, religion, food philosophy, education, fashion, beauty, humanist development, housing, architecture, ecological protection and development.

Figure 1

Infinity oriented model of economy.

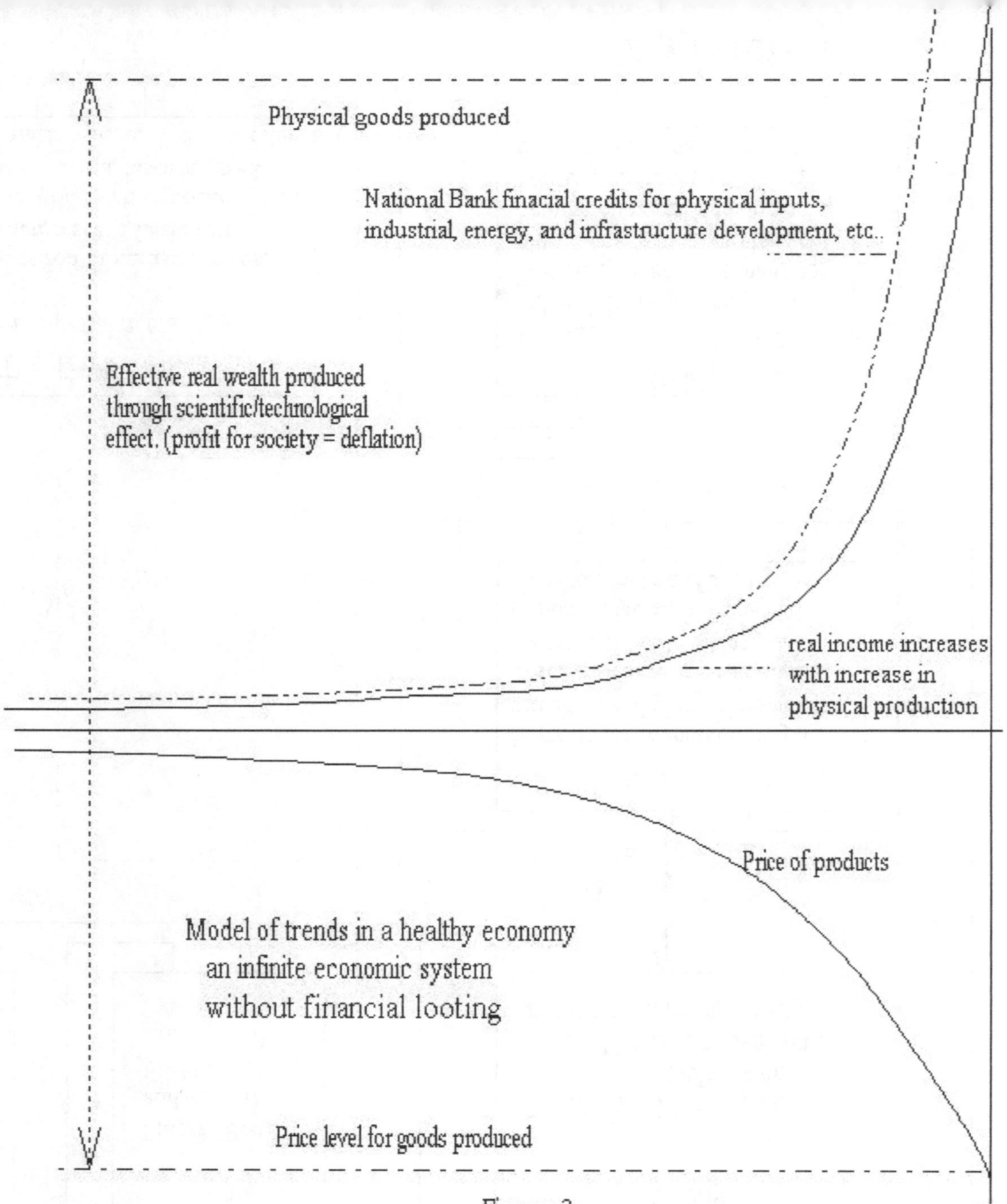

Physical goods produced
National Bank finacial credits for physical inputs, industrial, energy, and infrastructure development, etc..
Effective real wealth produced through scientific/technological effect. (profit for society = deflation)
real income increases with increase in physical production
Price of products
Model of trends in a healthy economy an infinite economic system without financial looting
Price level for goods produced

Figure 2

Appendix 5

Appendix 5

Appendix 6

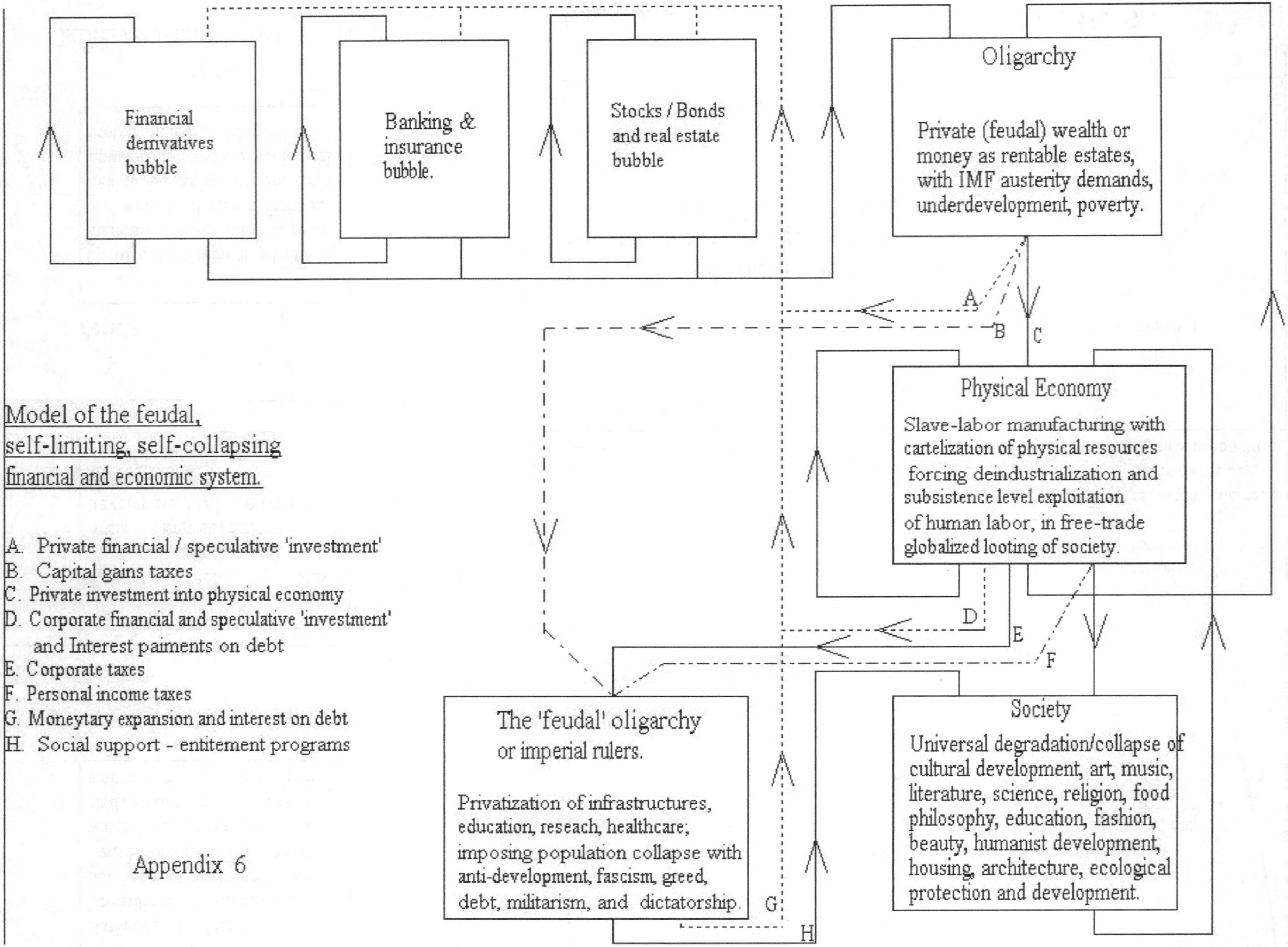
Financial derivatives bubble
Banking & insurance bubble.
Stocks / Bonds and real estate bubble
Oligarchy
Private (feudal) wealth or money as rentable estates, with IMF austerity demands, underdevelopment, poverty.
Physical Economy
Slave-labor manufacturing with cartelization of physical resources forcing deindustrialization and subsistence level exploitation of human labor, in free-trade globalized looting of society.
Society
Universal degradation/collapse of cultural development, art, music, literature, science, religion, food philosophy, education, fashion, beauty, humanist development, housing, architecture, ecological protection and development.
The 'feudal' oligarchy or imperial rulers.
Privatization of infrastructures, education, reseach, healthcare; imposing population collapse with anti-development, fascism, greed, debt, militarism, and dictatorship.
A
B
C
D
E
F
G
H

Model of the feudal, self-limiting, self-collapsing financial and economic system.

A. Private financial / speculative 'investment'
B. Capital gains taxes
C. Private investment into physical economy
D. Corporate financial and speculative 'investment' and Interest paiments on debt
E. Corporate taxes
F. Personal income taxes
G. Moneytary expansion and interest on debt
H. Social support - entitement programs

Appendix 6

Appendix 7

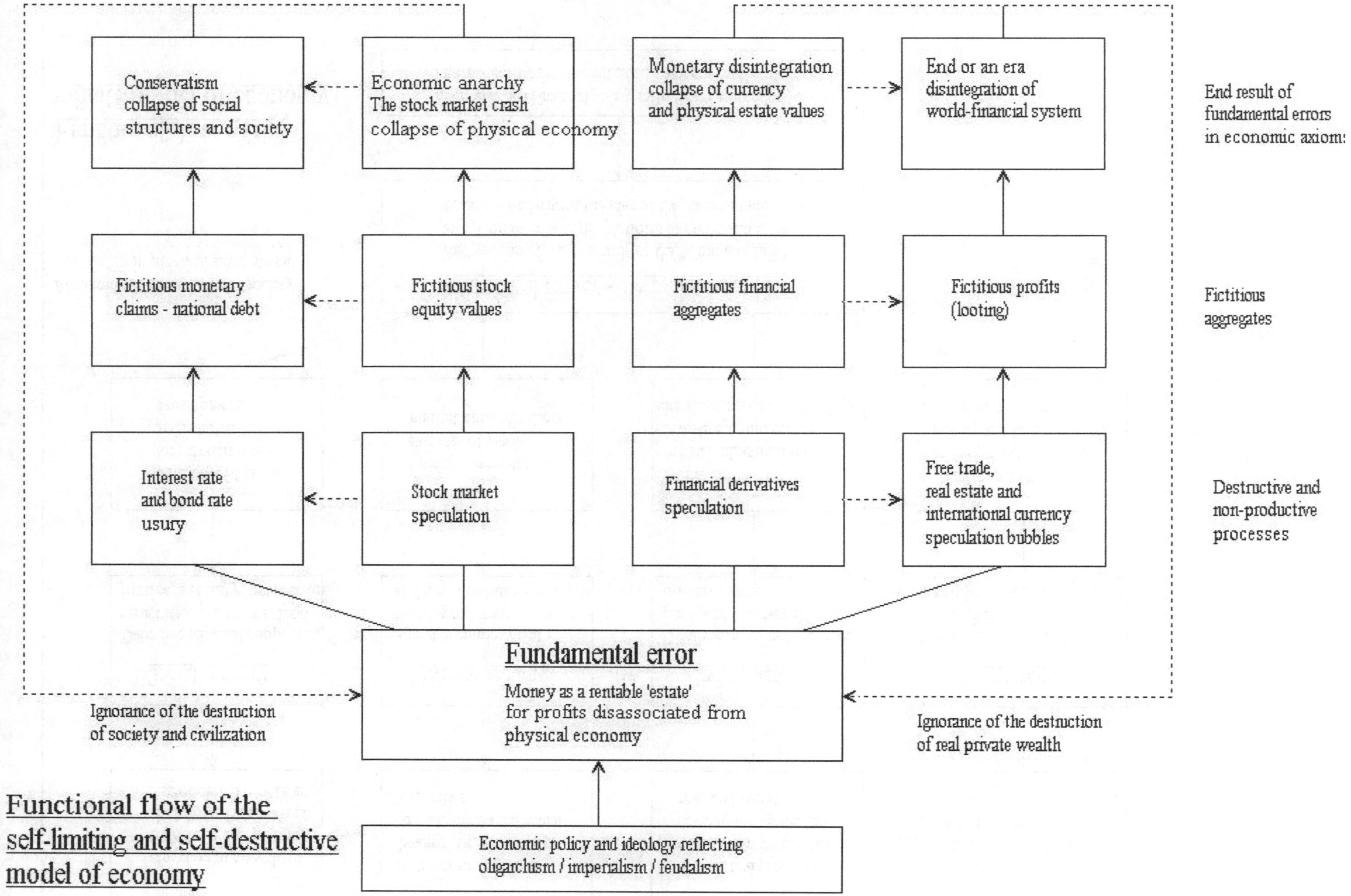
Conservatism
collapse of social
structures and society
Economic anarchy
The stock market crash
collapse of physical economy
Monetary disintegration
collapse of currency
and physical estate values
End or an era
disintegration of
world-financial system
End result of
fundamental errors
in economic axiom:
Fictitious monetary
claims - national debt
Fictitious stock
equity values
Fictitious financial
aggregates
Fictitious profits
(looting)
Fictitious
aggregates
Interest rate
and bond rate
usury
Stock market
speculation
Financial derivatives
speculation
Free trade,
real estate and
international currency
speculation bubbles
Destructive and
non-productive
processes
Fundamental error
Money as a rentable 'estate'
for profits disassociated from
physical economy
Ignorance of the destruction
of society and civilization
Ignorance of the destruction
of real private wealth
Economic policy and ideology reflecting
oligarchism / imperialism / feudalism
Functional flow of the
self-limiting and self-destructive
model of economy

Appendix 7

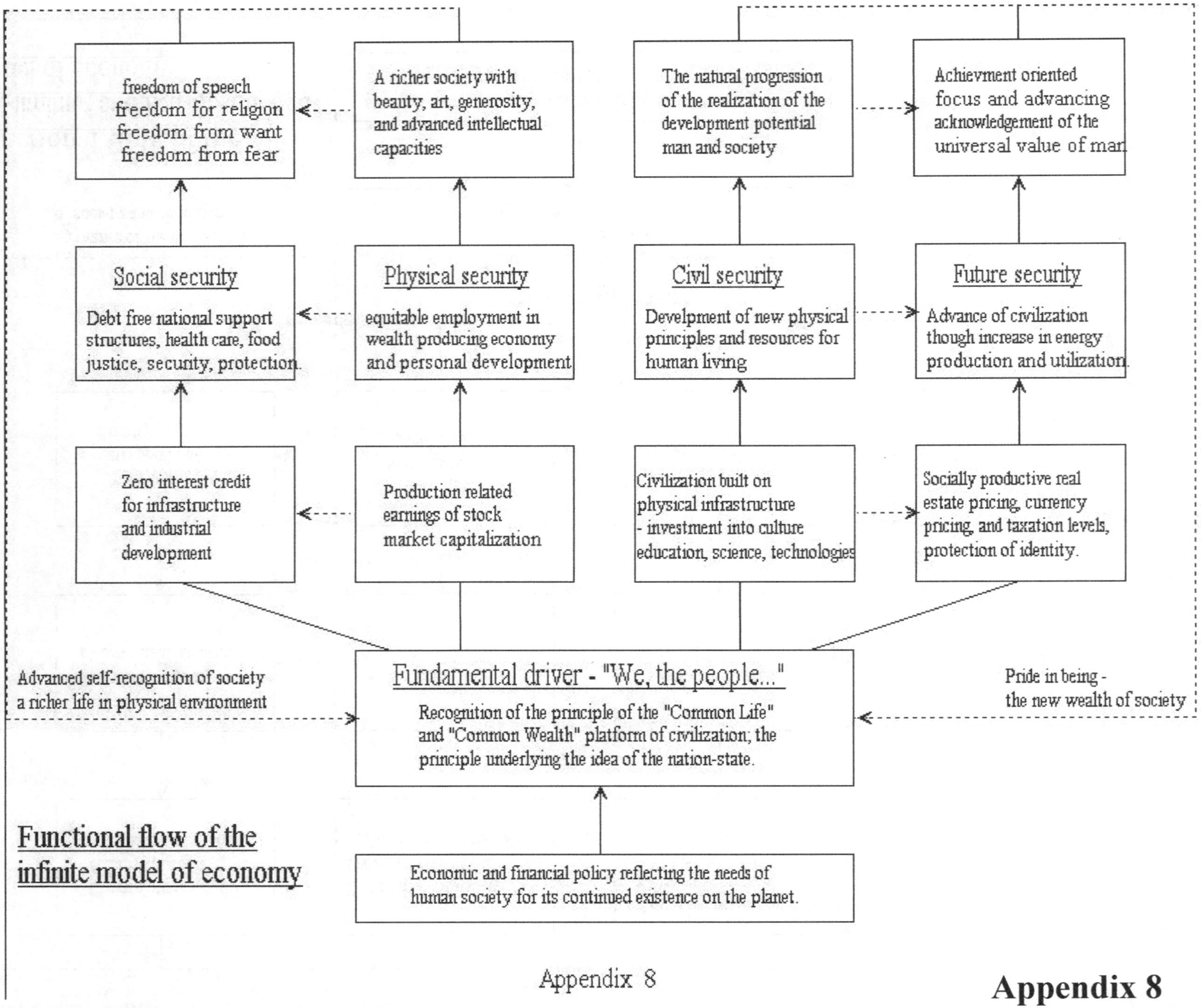
freedom of speech
freedom for religion
freedom from want
freedom from fear
A richer society with beauty, art, generosity, and advanced intellectual capacities
The natural progression of the realization of the development potential man and society
Achievment oriented focus and advancing acknowledgement of the universal value of man
Social security
Debt free national support structures, health care, food justice, security, protection.
Physical security
equitable employment in wealth producing economy and personal development
Civil security
Develpment of new physical principles and resources for human living
Future security
Advance of civilization though increase in energy production and utilization.
Profits for society
Zero interest credit for infrastructure and industrial development
Production related earnings of stock market capitalization
Civilization built on physical infrastructure - investment into culture education, science, technologies
Socially productive real estate pricing, currency pricing, and taxation levels, protection of identity.
Constructive processes
Advanced self-recognition of society a richer life in physical environment
Fundamental driver - "We, the people..."
Recognition of the principle of the "Common Life" and "Common Wealth" platform of civilization; the principle underlying the idea of the nation-state.
Pride in being - the new wealth of society
Functional flow of the infinite model of economy
Economic and financial policy reflecting the needs of human society for its continued existence on the planet.

Appendix 8

Appendix 8

Appendix 9

Fictitious and inflationary financial (so-called) earnings

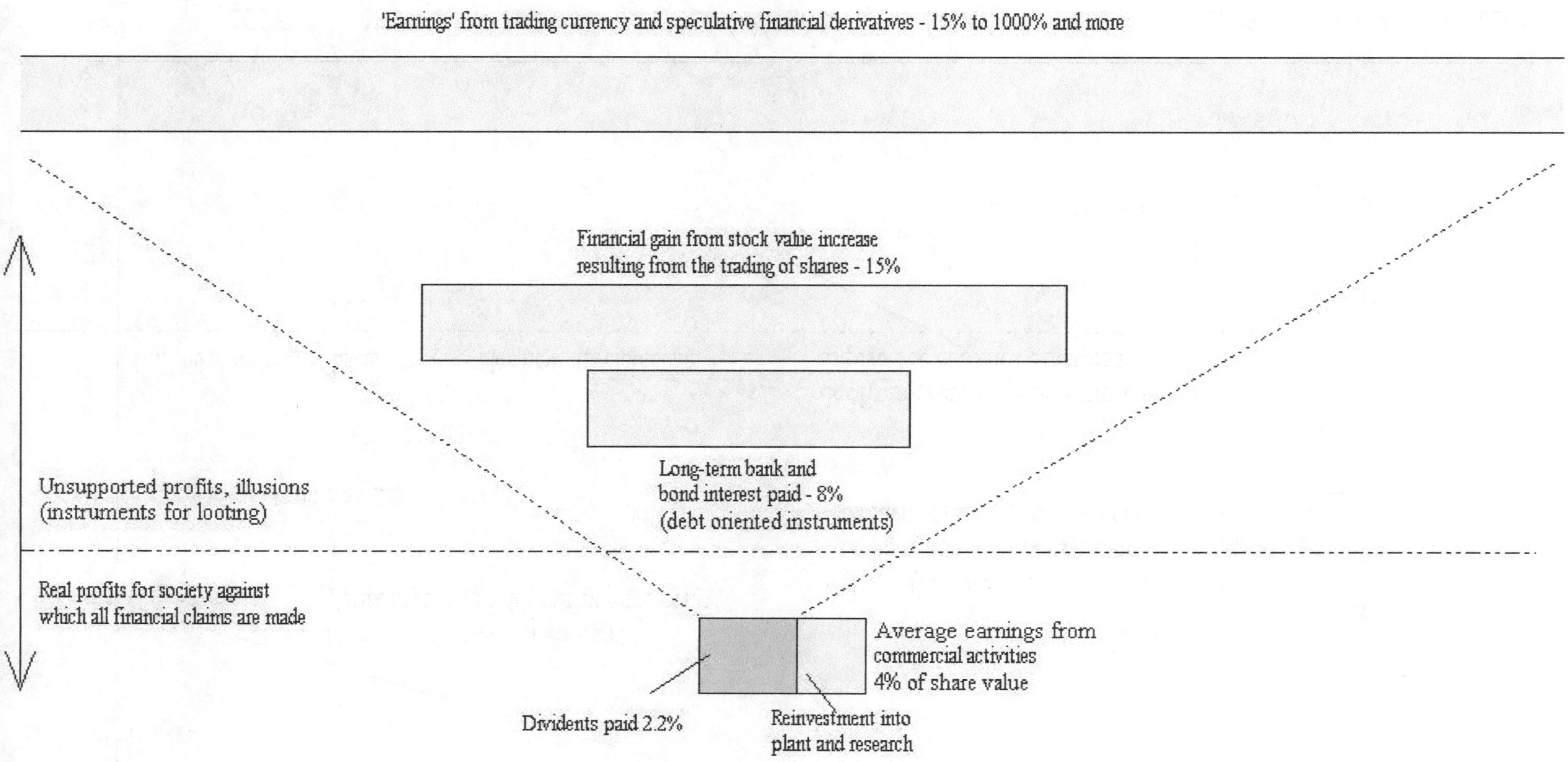

Fictitious or inflationary profits
compared to real wealth generated
from production or economic activity

Appendix 9

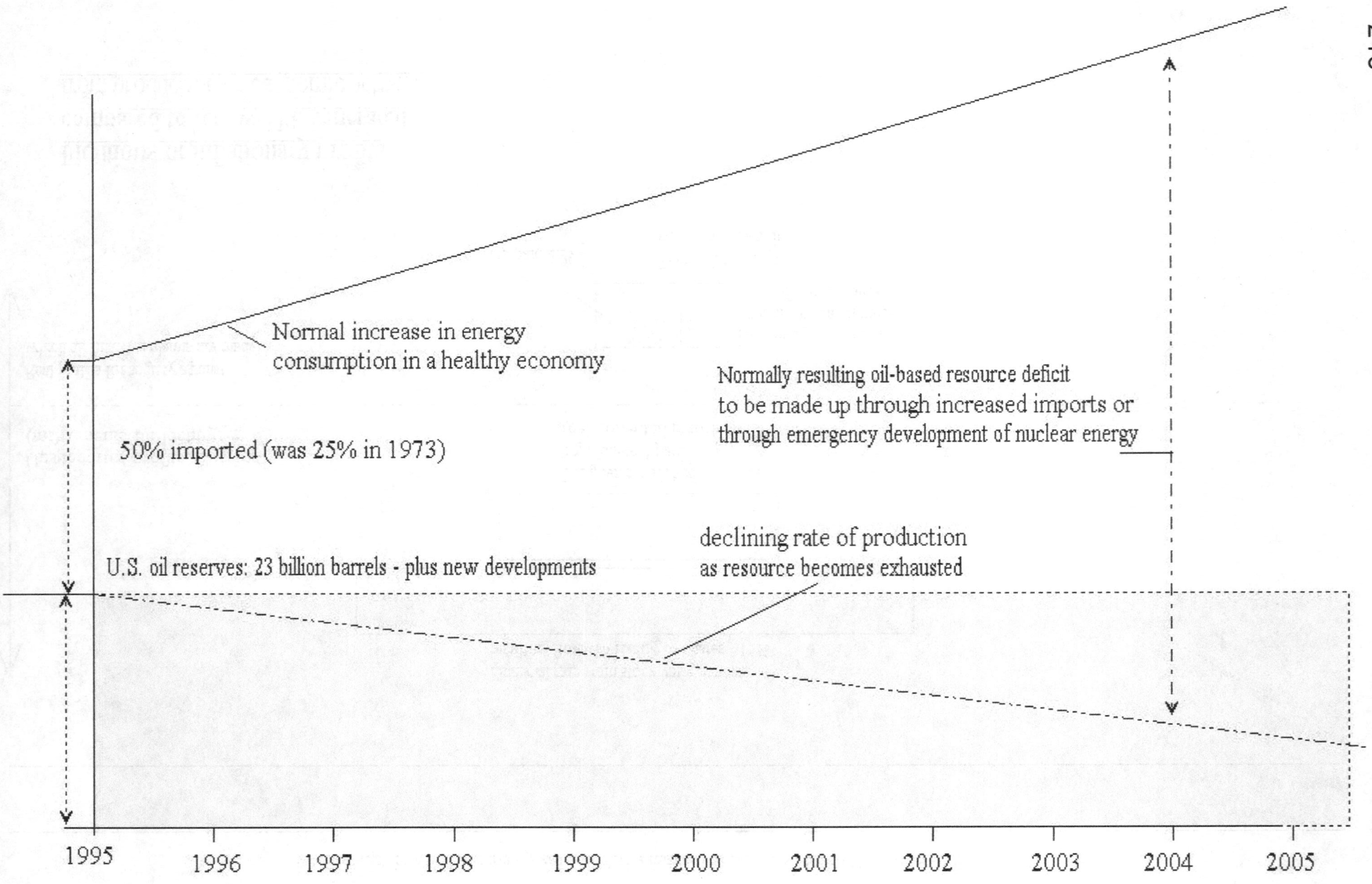

The widening gap between U.S. engergy supplies and the society's needs.

Appendix 10

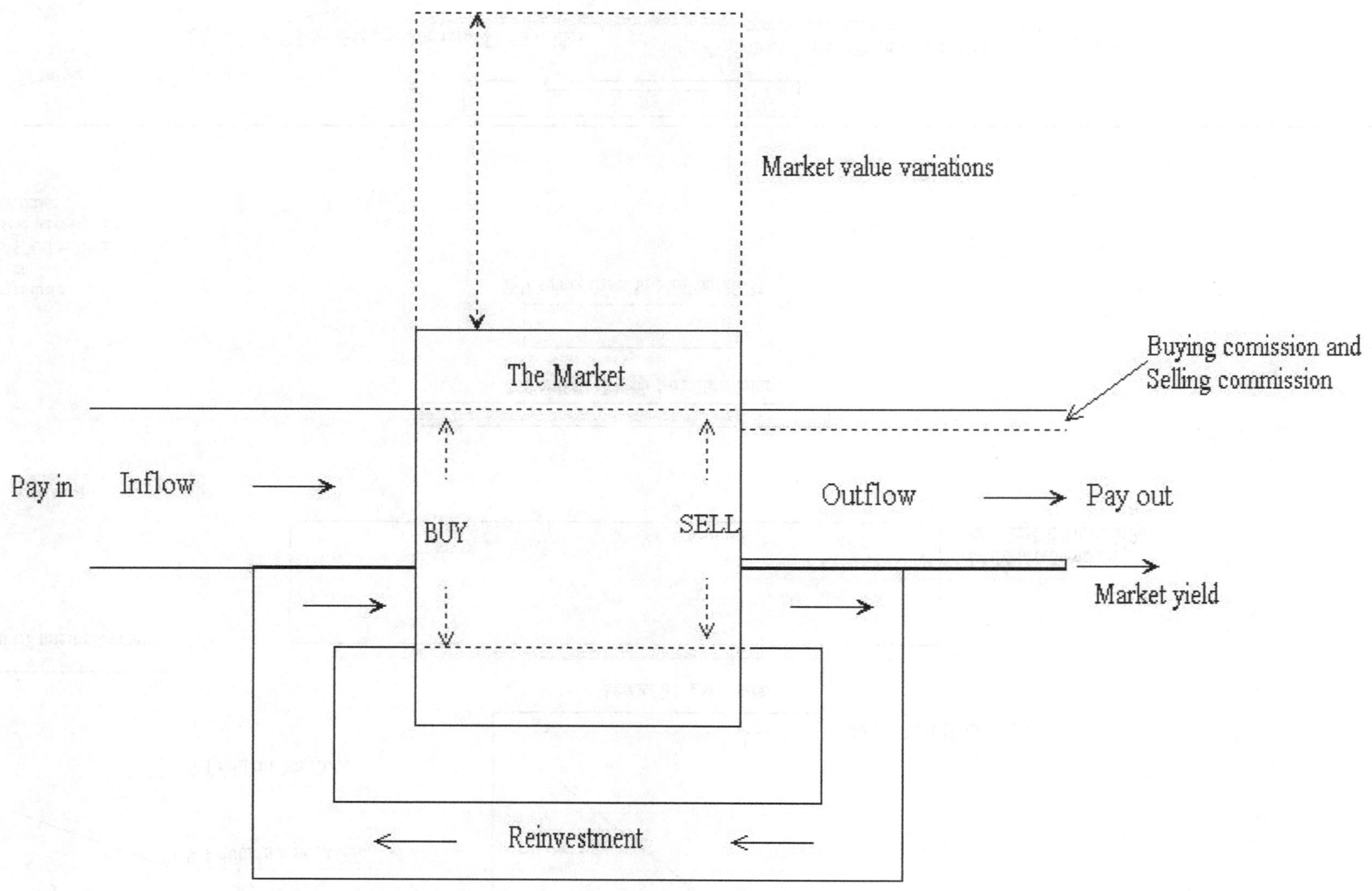

The Stockmarket model

Appendix 11

Appendix 11

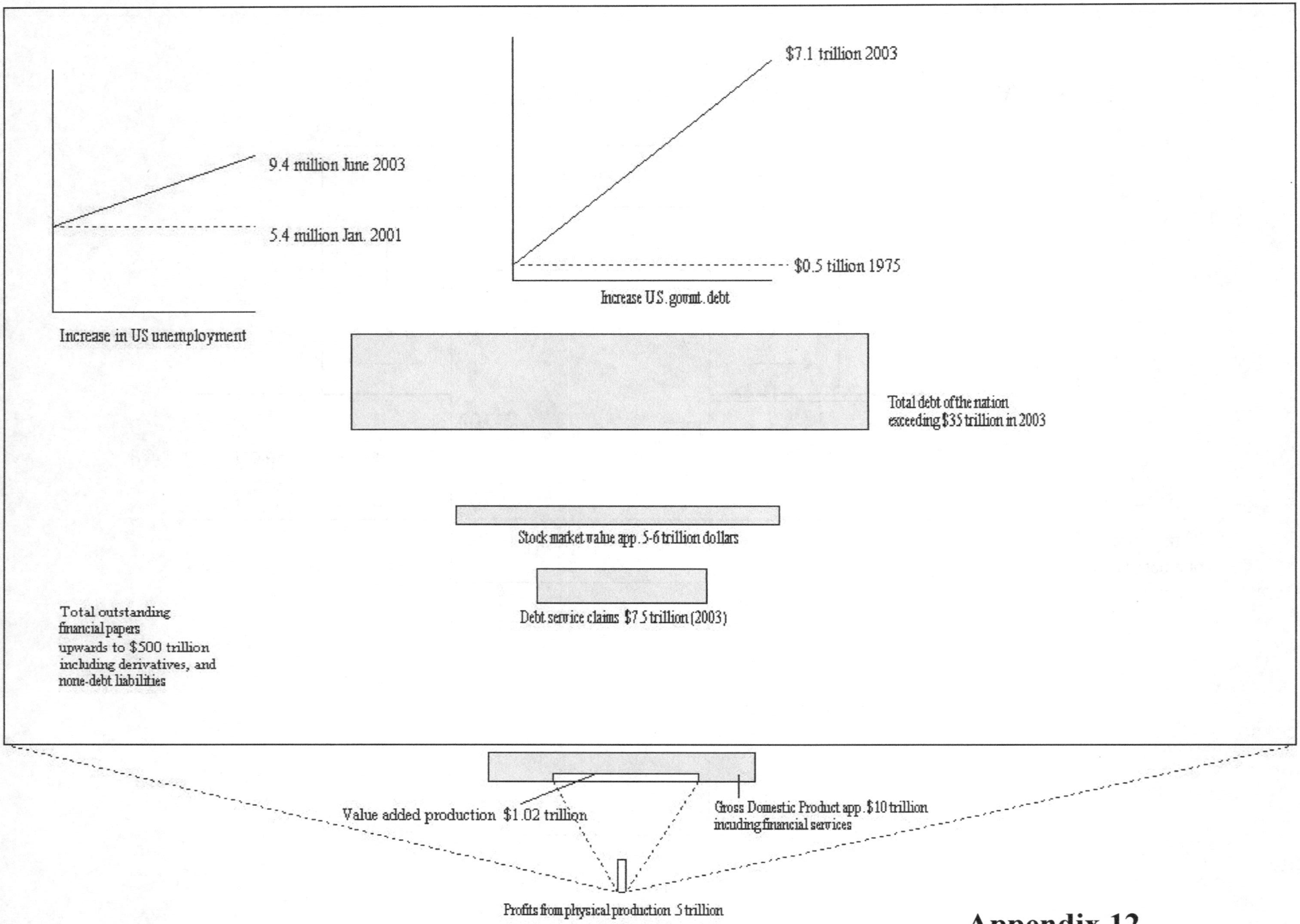
9.4 million June 2003
5.4 million Jan. 2001
Increase in US unemployment
$7.1 trillion 2003
$0.5 tillion 1975
Increase U.S. govmt. debt
Total debt of the nation
exceeding $35 trillion in 2003
Stock market value app. 5-6 trillion dollars
Debt service claims $7.5 trillion (2003)
Total outstanding
financial papers
upwards to $500 trillion
including derivatives, and
none-debt liabilities
Value added production $1.02 trillion
Gross Domestic Product app. $10 trillion
incuding financial services
Profits from physical production .5 trillion

Appendix 12

References Index

1 Version 2, 2003
2 According to an engineering study by Hal B. H. Cooper, Jr., Phd, P.E. - Planning Coordinator, Washington Association of Rail Passengers, Seattle, Washington
3 See Leviticus 19
4 Executive Intelligence Review March 21, 1997, p.27 - Washington, USA.
5 see Fidelio magazine, Winter 1996, p.24, table I.
6 Doug Casey's International Speculator, January 1997, p.4 - Agora Inc., Baltimore MD
7 Bruce Steward of Vancouver, Canada
8 The New Federalist April 26, 1999 p.3
9 Encyclopedia Britannica
10 reported in The New Federalist Aug. 25,1997, p.4
11 See The New Federalist newspaper, Aug. 25, 1997, p.3
12 See EIR May 23, 1997 p.4 - Personal bankruptcies devastate U.S. households
13 Financial newsletter by Doug Casey, Feb.1997
14 Encyclopedia Britannica
15 The Wall Street Underground, Feb., 1966
16 WSU Feb./96
17 The New Federalist, January 8, 1996 p.8
18 1966 age distribution - Britanica Atlas 1970 p.294
19 Fleur Cowles, People as Animals - UK Robin Clark Ltd. 1986
20 Bertrand Russell, ^The Impact of Science Upon Society^ - NY. Simon and Schuster, 1953, pp.102-104
21 Adrian Day's Investment Analyst, Sept. 1996
22 EIR Jan. 1 1996, p.A27
23 Source: Bank for International Settlements, see Executive Intelligence Report, p.29 July 28 1995, EIR News Service Inc, P.O. Box 17390, Washington, D.C. 20041-0390

More works by the Author

Rolf A. F. Witzsche
http://www.rolf-witzsche.com

List of novels - focused on universal love

http://books.rolf-witzsche.com

Flight Without Limits
(space travel science fiction)

Brighter than the Sun
(the nuclear fire)

The Lodging for the Rose
(spiritual science fiction - a series of novels)

Episode 1 - **Discovering Love**
Episode 2a - **The Ice Age Challenge**
Episode 2b - **Roses at Dawn in an Ice Age World**
Episode 3 - **Winning Without Victory**
Episode 4a - **Seascapes and Sand**
Episode 4b - **The Flat Earth Society**
Episode 5a - **Glass Barriers**
Episode 5b - **Coffee Sex and Biscuits**
Episode 6a - **Endless Horizons**
Episode 6b - **Angels of Sex in Queensland**
Episode 7 - **Sword of Aquarius**
Episode 8 - **Lu Mountain**

Books of single stories from the novles

low cost books, for details see:
http://books.rolf-witzsche.com/stories/index.html

Exploration books

http://books.rolf-witzsche.com

The Lord of the Rings's Metaphors
An exploration of the metphors in J.R.R. Tolkien's epic saga, The Lord of the Rings

Small Research Books
http://books.rolf-witzsche.com/stories/research/index.html

Discovering Infinity

A research book series focused on scientific and spiritual development.
for details see:
http://science.rolf-witzsche.com

Volume ii (Introduction) - **Roots in Universal History**
Focus on Reality

Volume 1A - **The Disintegration of the World's Financial System**
Focus on Truth

Volume 1B - **Crimes Against Humanity**
Life Denied

Volume 2A - **Science and Spiritual Healing**
History as Truth

Volume 2B - **The Lord of the Rings' Metaphors**
The Future Determining the Present

Volume 3A
Universal Divine Science: Spiritual Pedagogicals
Structure for Discovery and Scientific Development

Volume 3B - **Science and Health with Key to the Scriptures in Divine Science** - The divine Principle of scientific mental healing

Volume 3C - **Bible Lessons in Divine Science - 1898**
The Scientific Process to Know the Truth

Volume 4 - **Light Piercing the Heart of Darkness**
The Demands of Truth

Volume 5 - **Scientific Government and Self-Government**
Platform for Freedom

Volume 6A - **The Infinite Nature of Man**
The Fourth Dimension of Spirit

Volume 6B - **Leadership**
The Dimension of Leadership

and other titles

Made in United States
Cleveland, OH
13 August 2025

19379884R00122